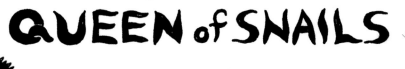

QUEEN of SNAILS

A Graphic Memoir

MAUREEN BURDOCK

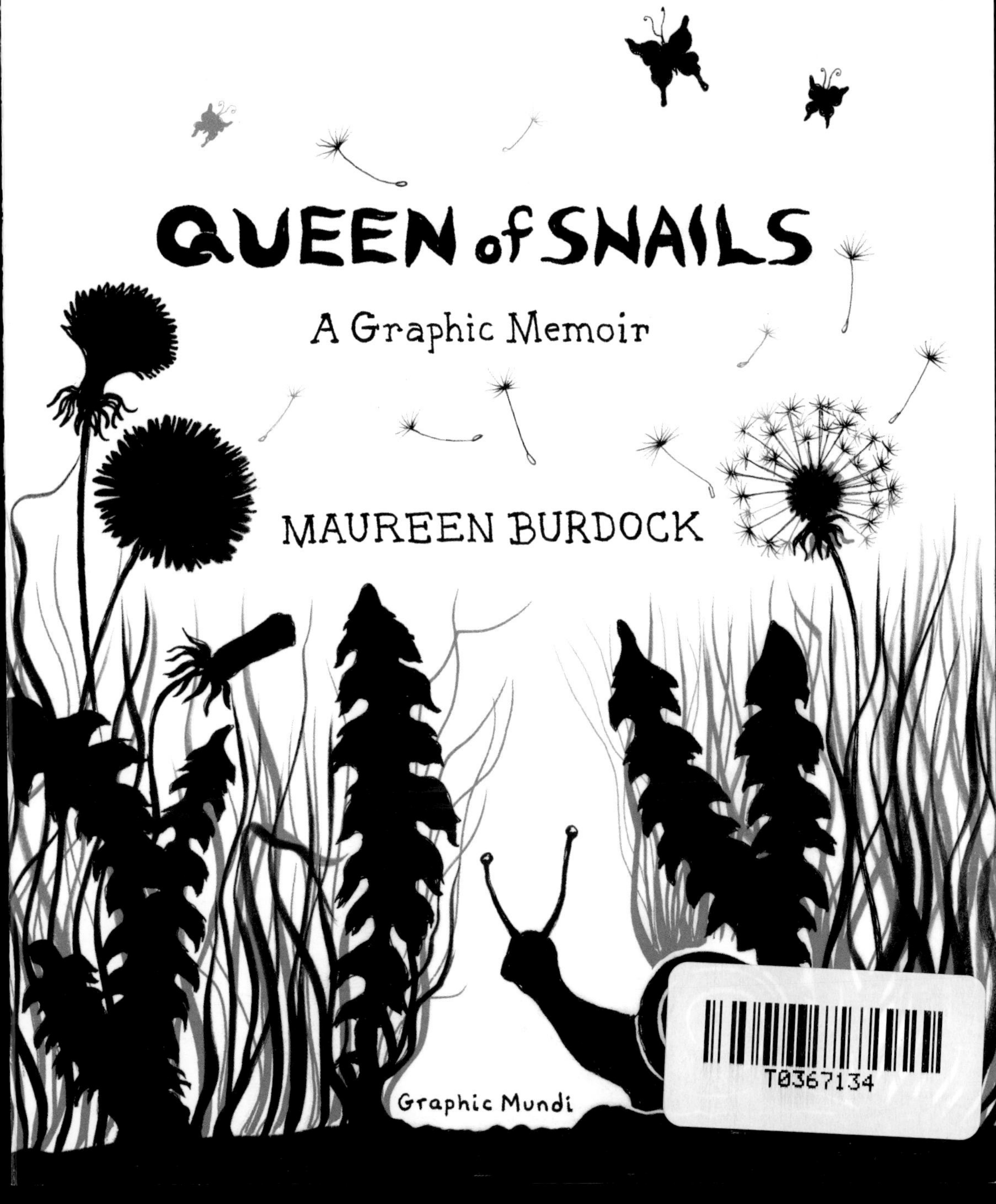

Graphic Mundi

Library of Congress Cataloging-in-Publication Data

Names: Burdock, Maureen, 1970– author.
Title: Queen of snails : a graphic memoir / Maureen Burdock.
Description: University Park, Pennsylvania : Graphic Mundi, [2022]
Summary: "Explores the author's family history in graphic
    novel format, examining the emotional baggage of violence,
    abandonment, and displacement"—Provided by publisher.
Identifiers: LCCN 2022019080 | ISBN 9781637790366 (paperback)
Subjects: LCSH: Burdock, Maureen, 1970–Childhood and
    youth—Comic books, strips, etc. | Burdock, Maureen, 1970–
    Family—Comic books, strips, etc. | Women artists—United
    States—Biography—Comic books, strips, etc. | Mothers and
    daughters—Comic books, strips, etc. | Children of divorced
    parents—Comic books, strips, etc. | Displacement (Psychology)—
    Comic books, strips, etc.
Classification: LCC PN6727.B853 Z46 2022
LC record available at https://lccn.loc.gov/2022019080

Published by The Pennsylvania State University Press,
University Park, PA 16802–1003

10 9 8 7 6 5 4 3 2 1

graphic mundi
drawing our worlds together

Graphic Mundi is an imprint of The Pennsylvania State
University Press.

The Pennsylvania State University Press is a member of the
Association of University Presses.

It is the policy of The Pennsylvania State University Press to
use acid-free paper. Publications on uncoated stock satisfy the
minimum requirements of American National Standard for
Information Sciences—Permanence of Paper for Printed Library
Material, ANSI z39.48–1992.

For my children,
Onawa Aquene
& Seth Nagarjuna

Prologue
UNMOORED

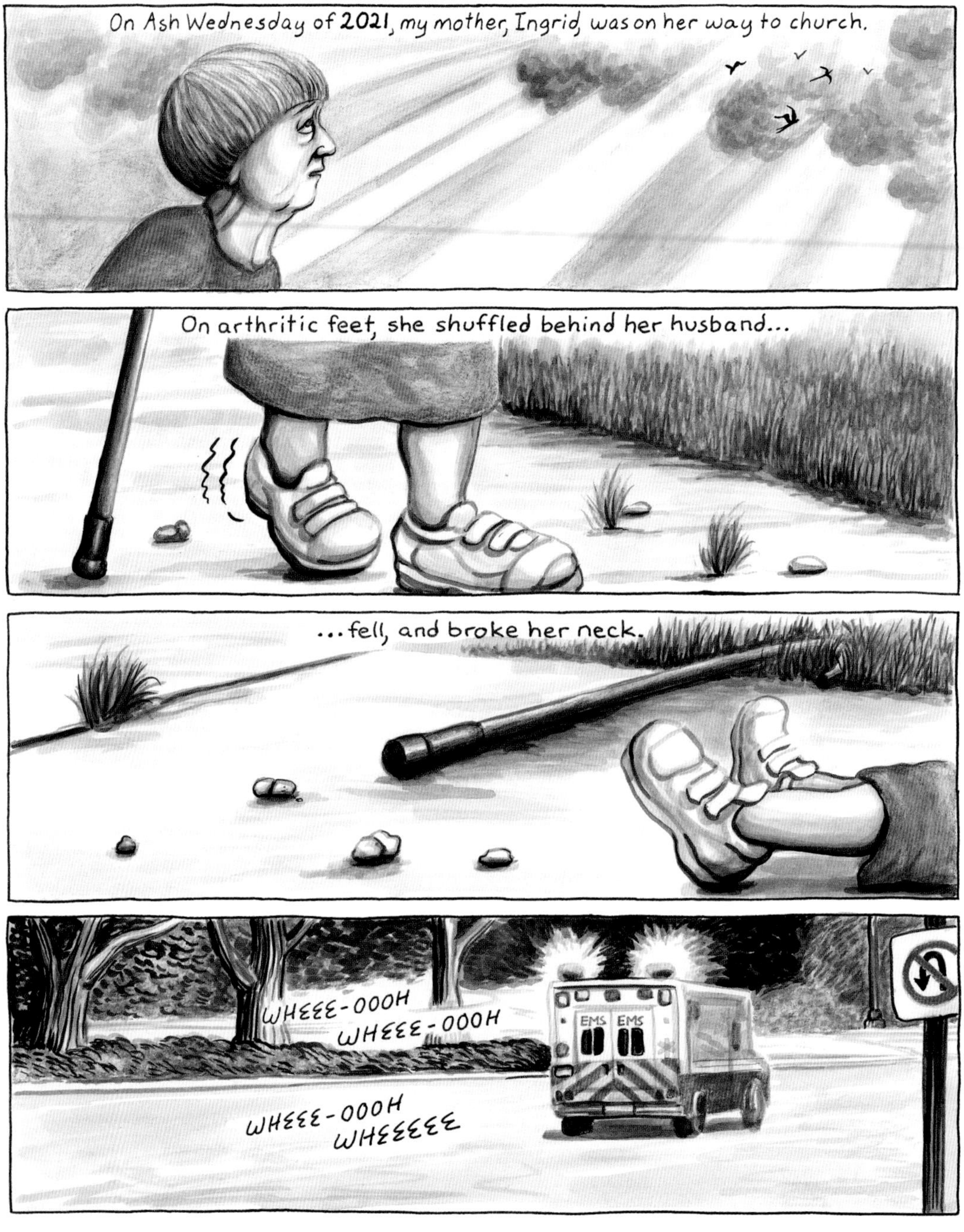
On Ash Wednesday of 2021, my mother, Ingrid, was on her way to church.
On arthritic feet, she shuffled behind her husband...
...fell, and broke her neck.
WHEEE-OOOH
WHEEE-OOOH
EMS EMS
WHEEE-OOOH
WHEEEEE

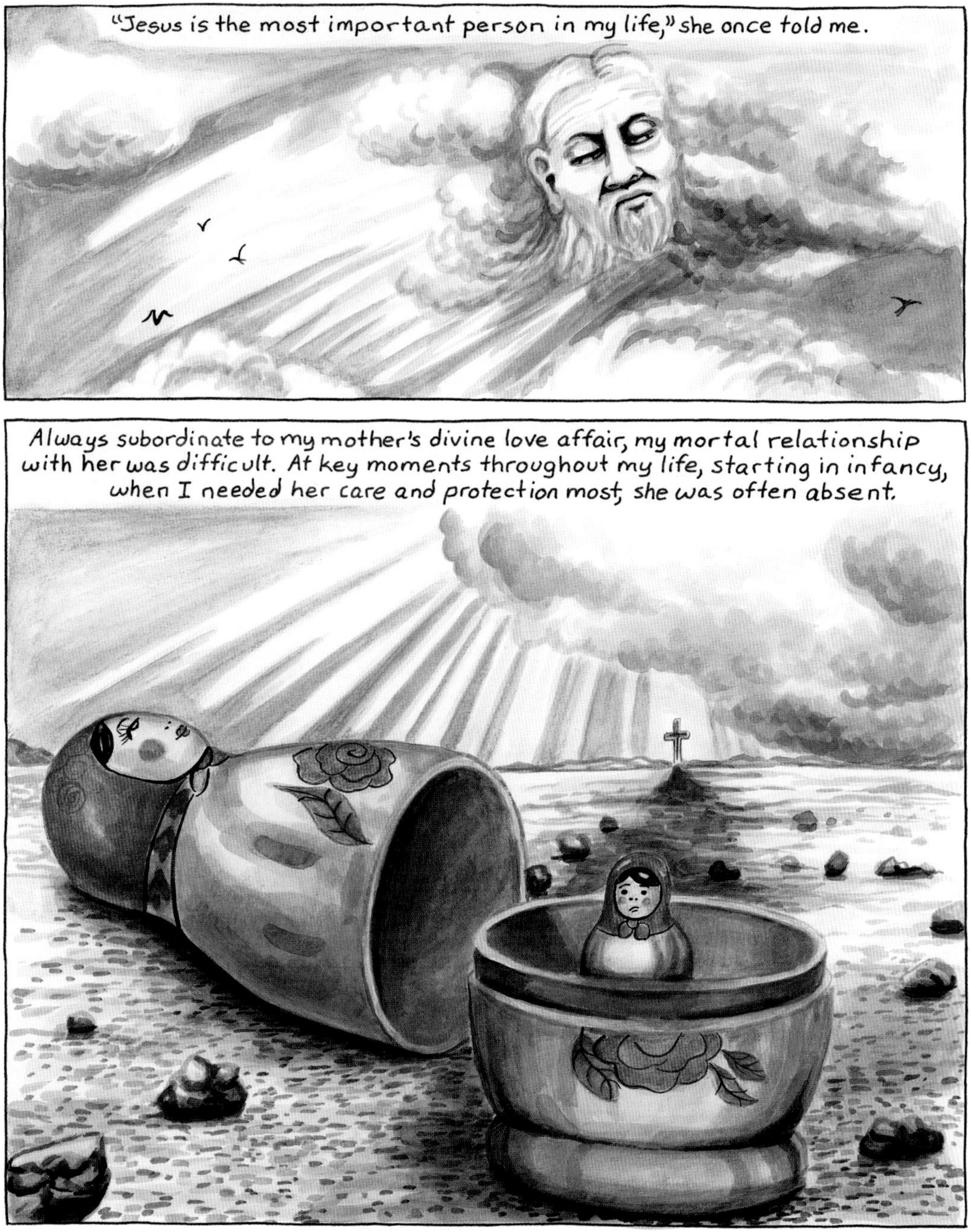
"Jesus is the most important person in my life," she once told me.
Always subordinate to my mother's divine love affair, my mortal relationship with her was difficult. At key moments throughout my life, starting in infancy, when I needed her care and protection most, she was often absent.

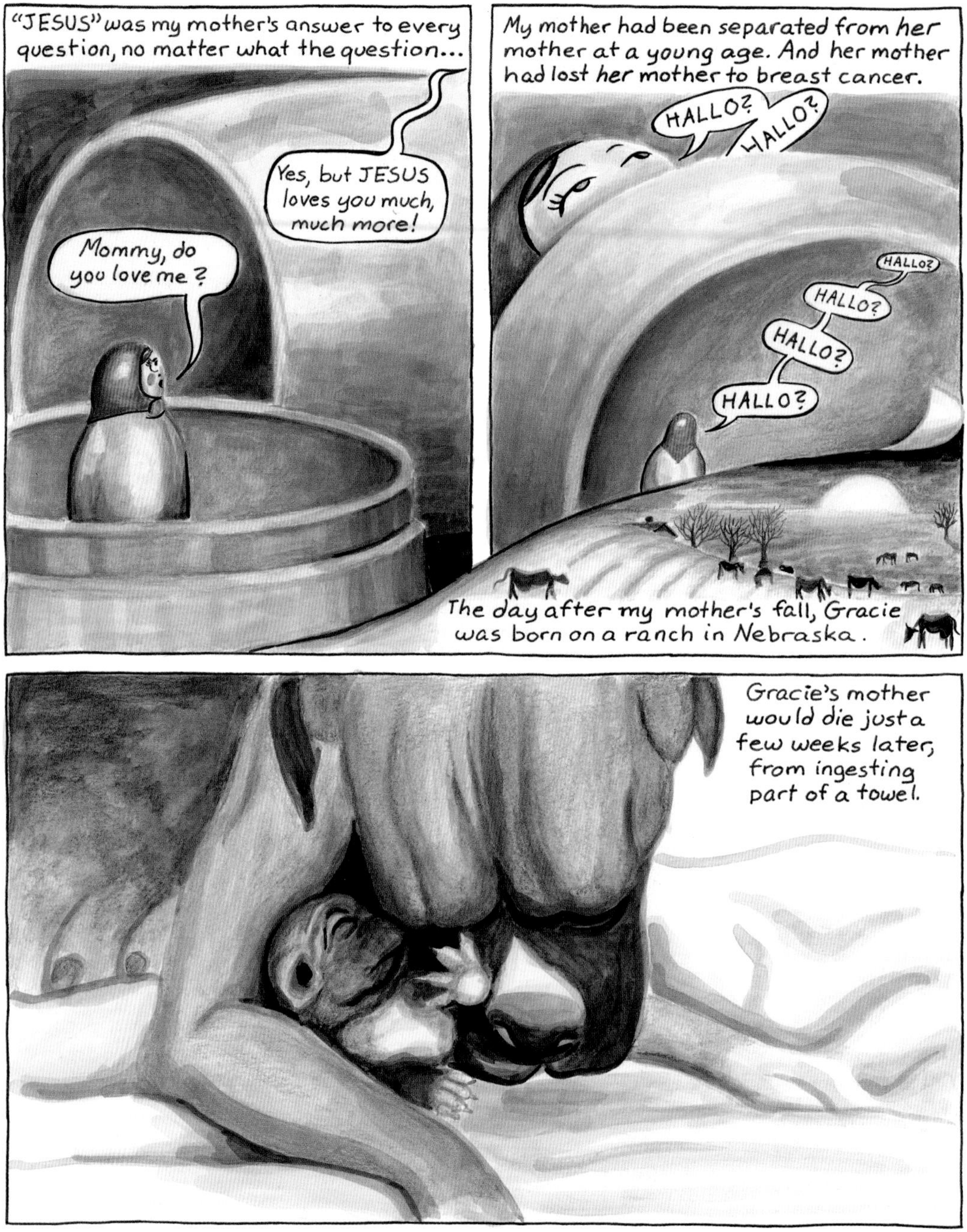
"JESUS" was my mother's answer to every question, no matter what the question...
Mommy, do you love me?
Yes, but JESUS loves you much, much more!
My mother had been separated from her mother at a young age. And her mother had lost her mother to breast cancer.
HALLO?
HALLO?
HALLO?
HALLO?
HALLO?
HALLO?
The day after my mother's fall, Gracie was born on a ranch in Nebraska.
Gracie's mother would die just a few weeks later, from ingesting part of a towel.

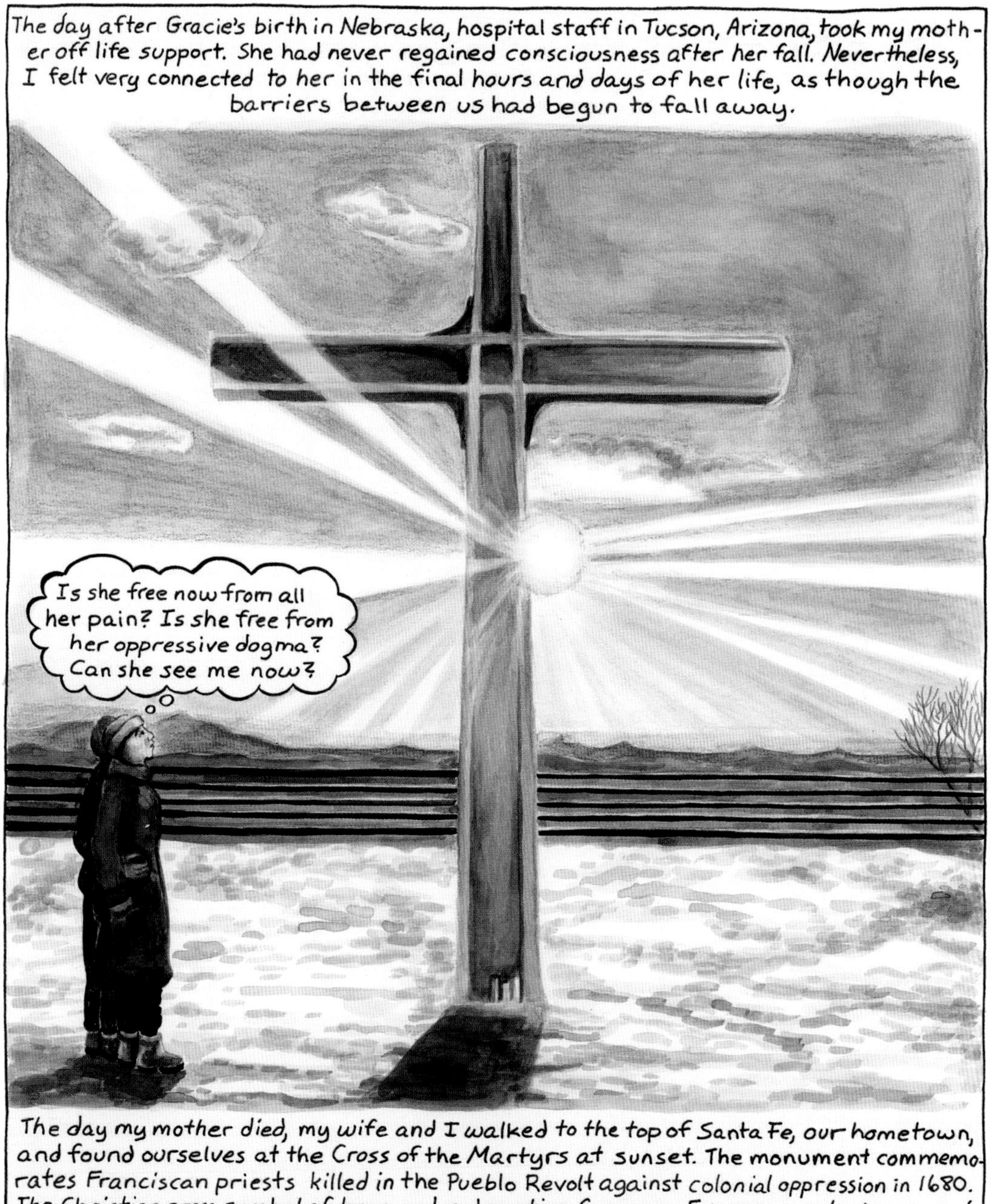
The day after Gracie's birth in Nebraska, hospital staff in Tucson, Arizona, took my mother off life support. She had never regained consciousness after her fall. Nevertheless, I felt very connected to her in the final hours and days of her life, as though the barriers between us had begun to fall away.
Is she free now from all her pain? Is she free from her oppressive dogma? Can she see me now?
The day my mother died, my wife and I walked to the top of Santa Fe, our hometown, and found ourselves at the Cross of the Martyrs at sunset. The monument commemorates Franciscan priests killed in the Pueblo Revolt against colonial oppression in 1680. The Christian cross, symbol of hope and redemption for many European colonizers and immigrants, is a dark symbol of brutality and genocide for many Native peoples.

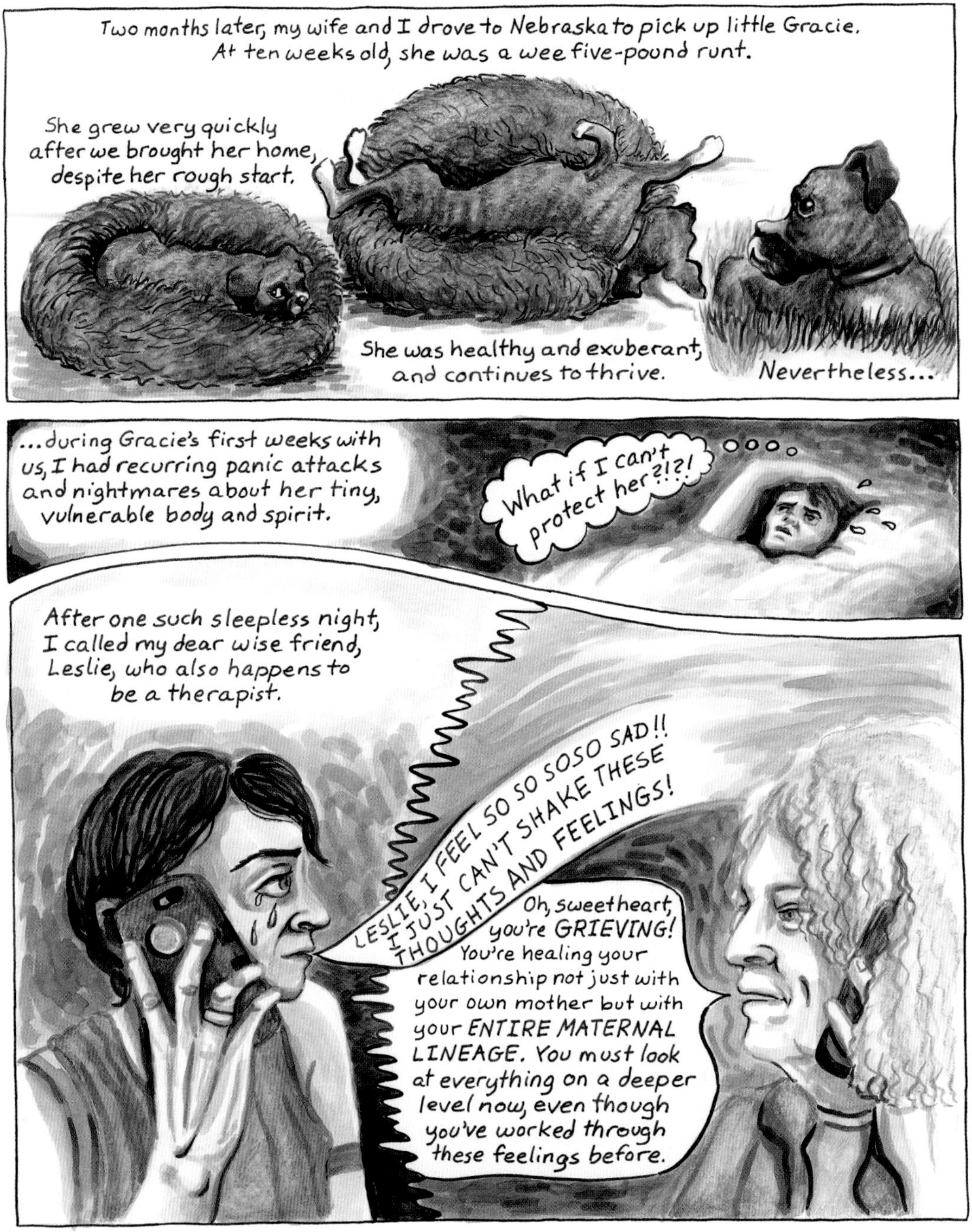
Two months later, my wife and I drove to Nebraska to pick up little Gracie. At ten weeks old, she was a wee five-pound runt.
She grew very quickly after we brought her home, despite her rough start.
She was healthy and exuberant, and continues to thrive.
Nevertheless...
...during Gracie's first weeks with us, I had recurring panic attacks and nightmares about her tiny, vulnerable body and spirit.
What if I can't protect her?!?!
After one such sleepless night, I called my dear wise friend, Leslie, who also happens to be a therapist.
LESLIE, I FEEL SO SO SOSO SAD!! I JUST CAN'T SHAKE THESE THOUGHTS AND FEELINGS!
Oh, sweetheart, you're GRIEVING! You're healing your relationship not just with your own mother but with your ENTIRE MATERNAL LINEAGE. You must look at everything on a deeper level now, even though you've worked through these feelings before.

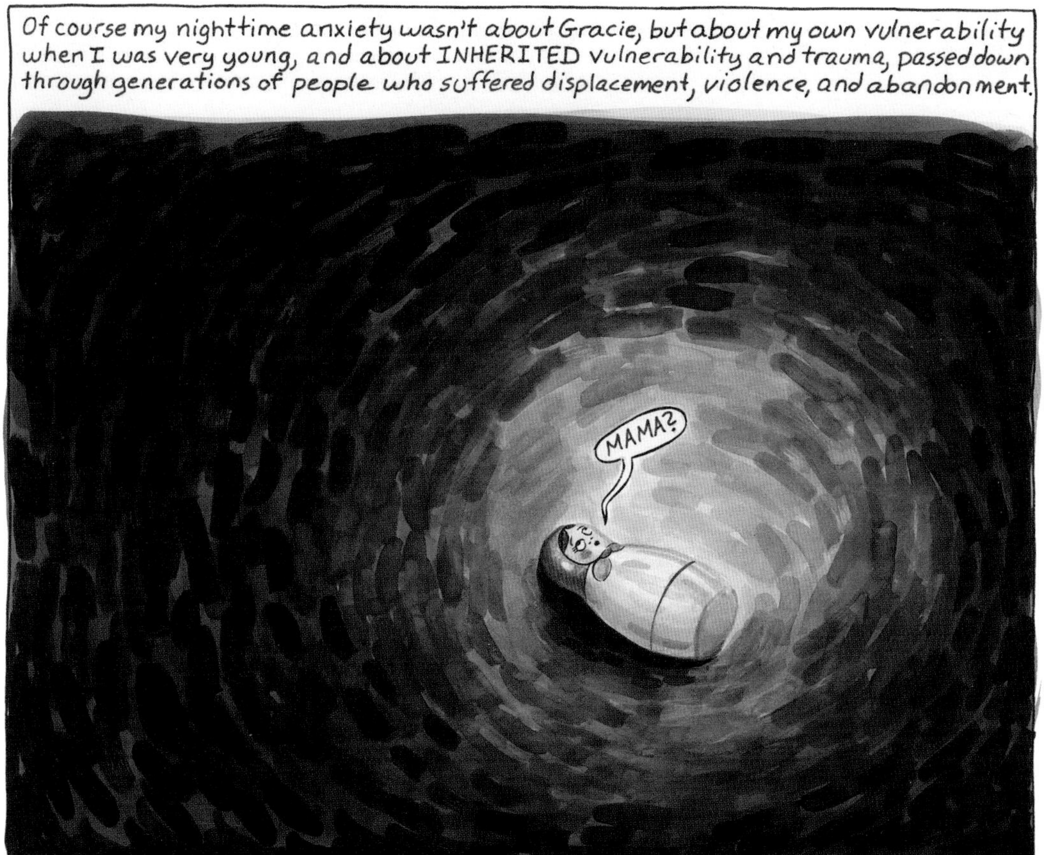
Of course my nighttime anxiety wasn't about Gracie, but about my own vulnerability when I was very young, and about INHERITED vulnerability and trauma, passed down through generations of people who suffered displacement, violence, and abandonment.
MAMA?

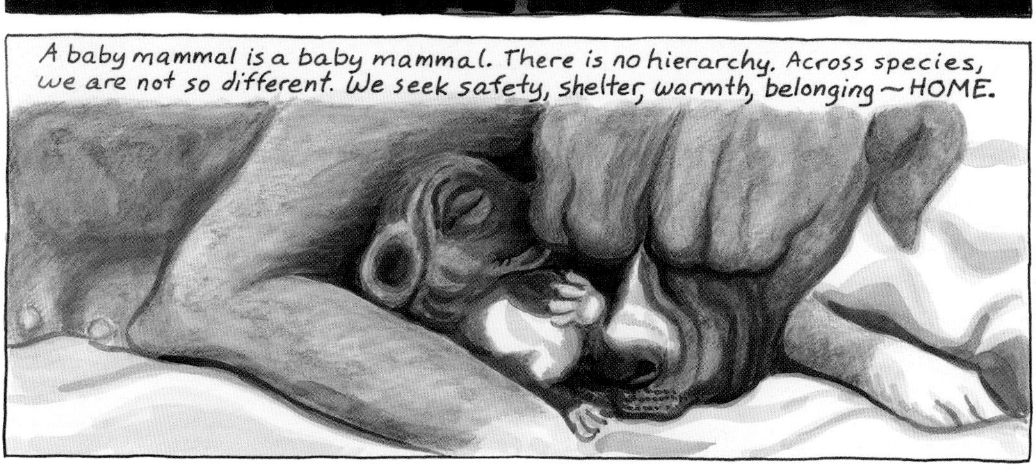
A baby mammal is a baby mammal. There is no hierarchy. Across species, we are not so different. We seek safety, shelter, warmth, belonging ~ HOME.

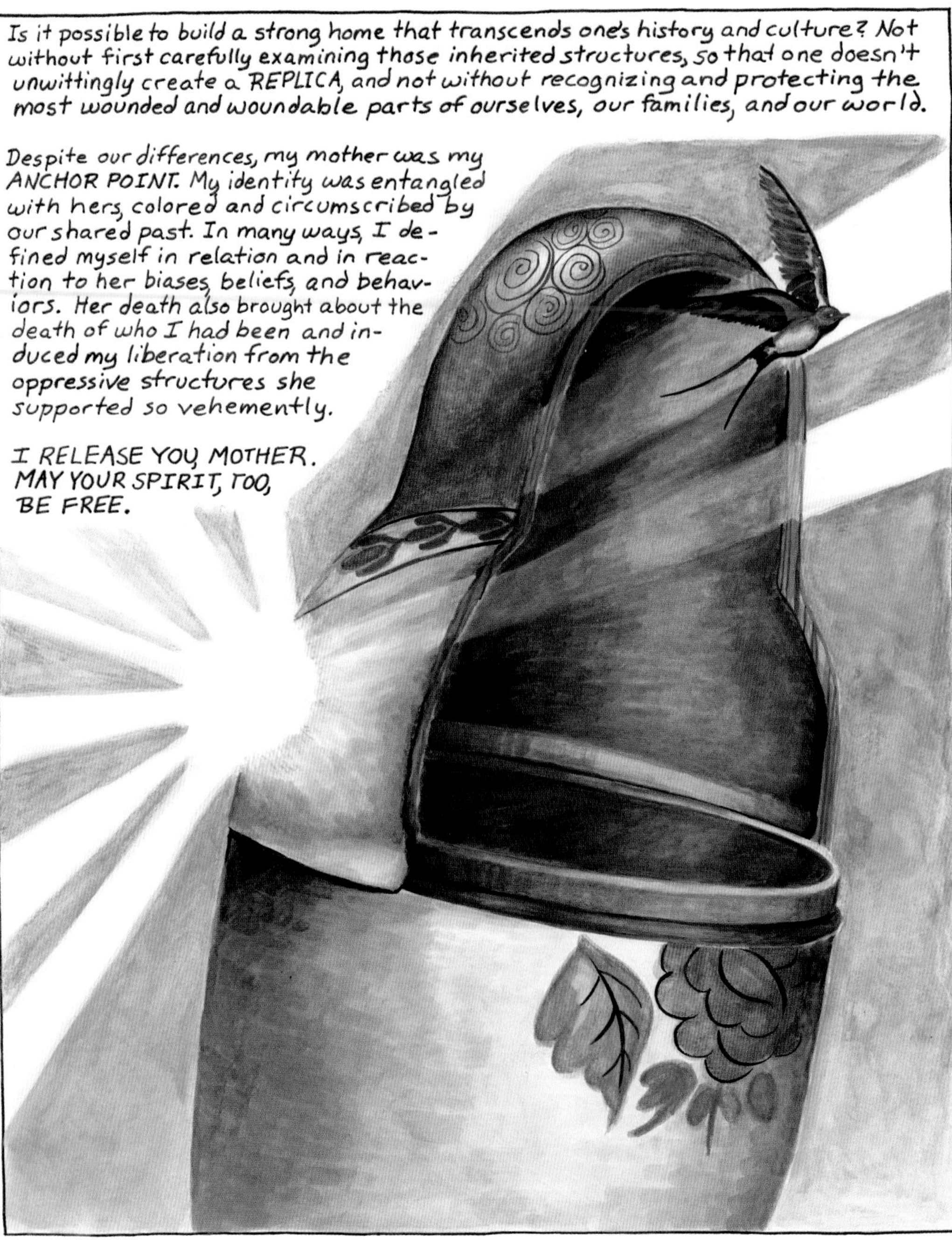
Is it possible to build a strong home that transcends one's history and culture? Not without first carefully examining those inherited structures, so that one doesn't unwittingly create a REPLICA, and not without recognizing and protecting the most wounded and woundable parts of ourselves, our families, and our world.
Despite our differences, my mother was my ANCHOR POINT. My identity was entangled with hers, colored and circumscribed by our shared past. In many ways, I defined myself in relation and in reaction to her biases, beliefs, and behaviors. Her death also brought about the death of who I had been and induced my liberation from the oppressive structures she supported so vehemently.
I RELEASE YOU, MOTHER. MAY YOUR SPIRIT, TOO, BE FREE.

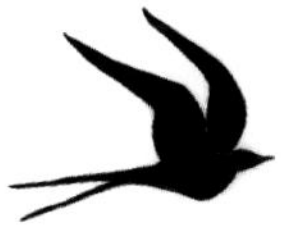

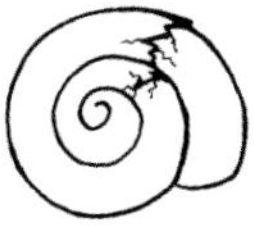

There is a crack, a crack in everything
That's how the light gets in.

~Leonard Cohen

Part One

QUEEN of SNAILS

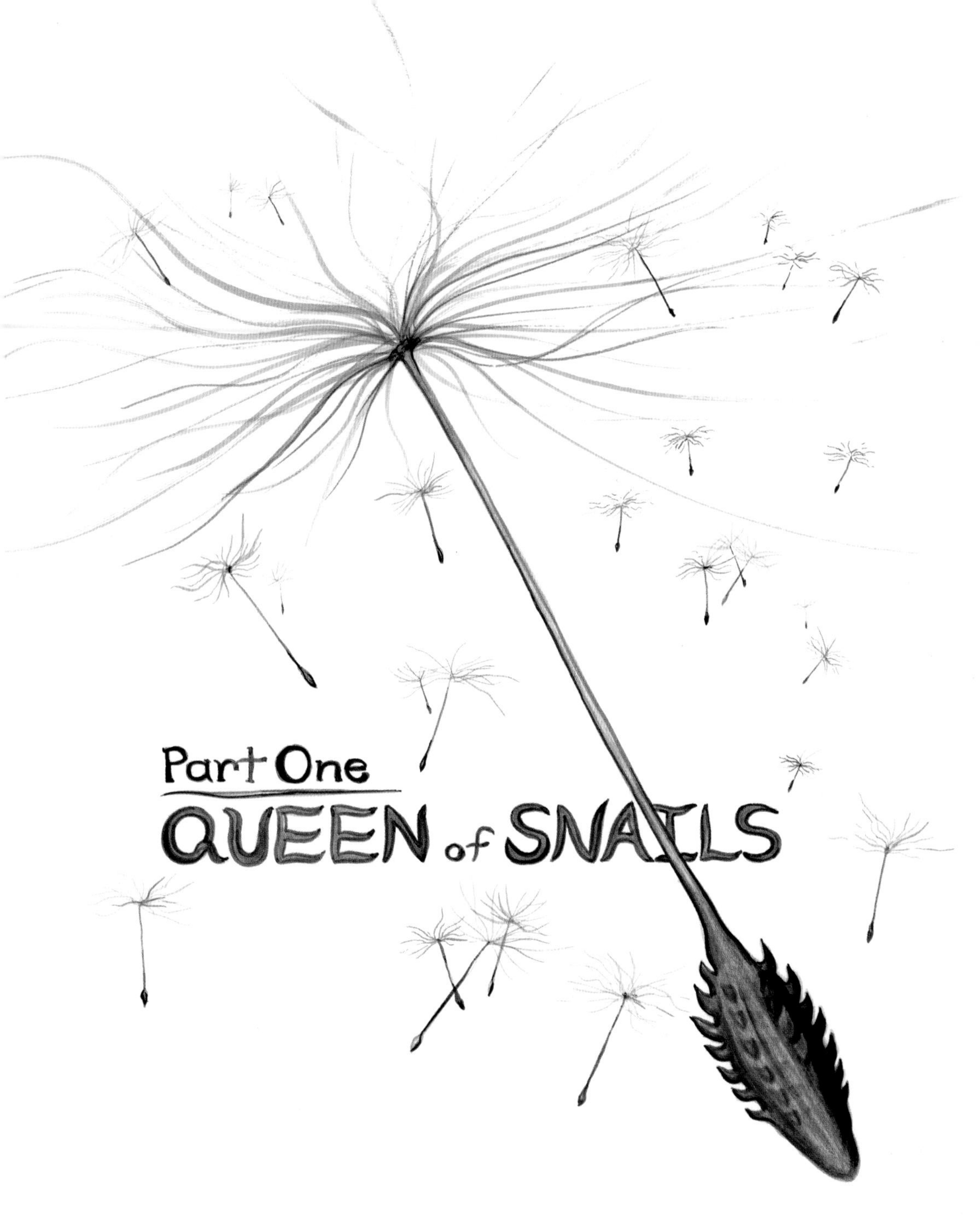

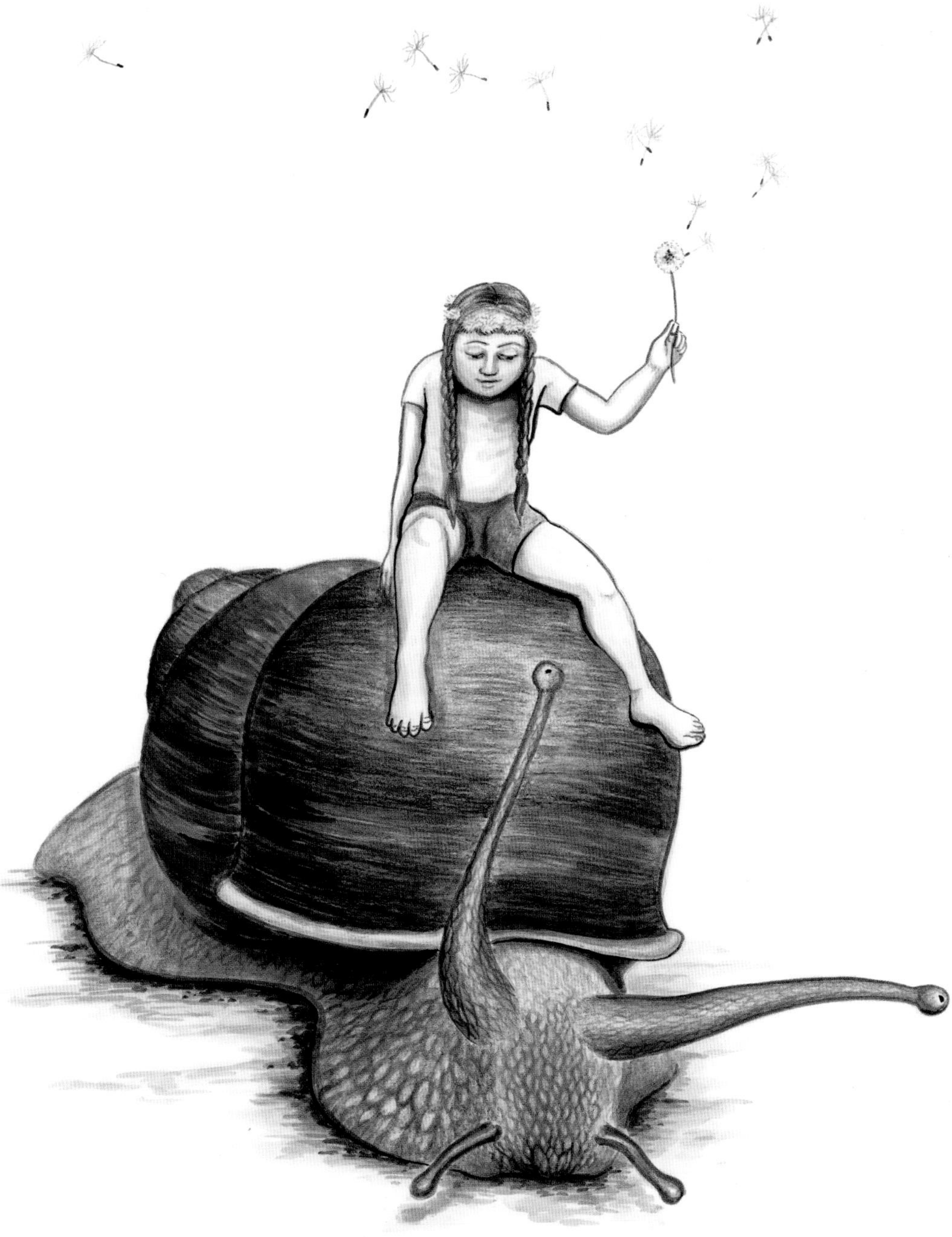

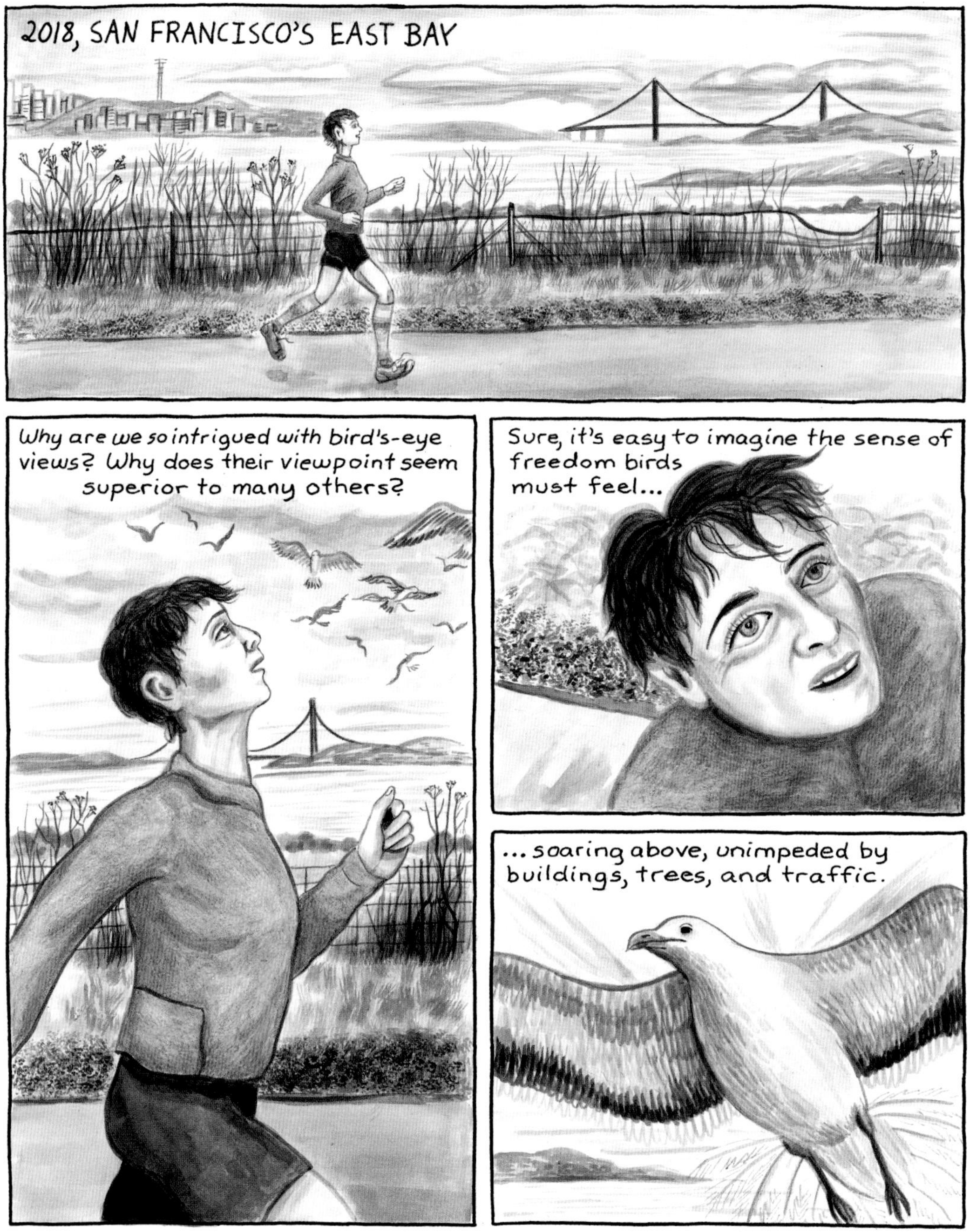
2018, SAN FRANCISCO'S EAST BAY
Why are we so intrigued with bird's-eye views? Why does their viewpoint seem superior to many others?
Sure, it's easy to imagine the sense of freedom birds must feel...
...soaring above, unimpeded by buildings, trees, and traffic.

But, breathing deeply and easily, in sync with the rhythm of my footfalls, I enjoy a sense of freedom, too.

It's probably not the soaring sensation gulls might feel, but my own love of terrestrial movement.

My eyes refocus on the damp pavement before me, and on the countless snails the recent rain has conjured. I don't want to crush anyone!

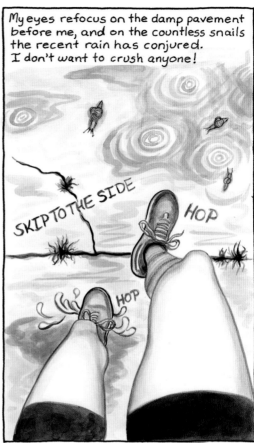

SKIP TO THE SIDE

HOP

HOP

What about the snail's-eye view? Why should the gods be in the heavens? The sensuous sliding, the feeling of it all with every open pore, the be-here-now consciousness required by the snail's pace ~ surely these attributes are also worth revering!

Here, let's move you off this bike path, out of harm's way!

15

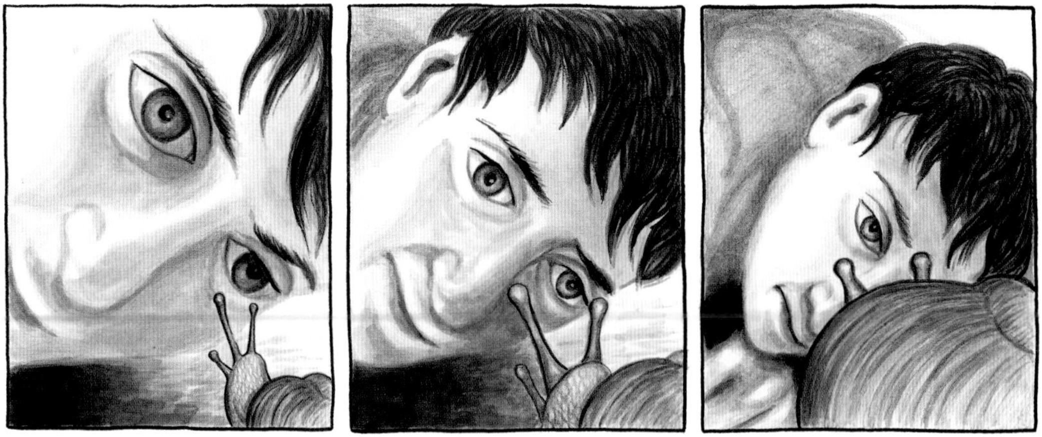

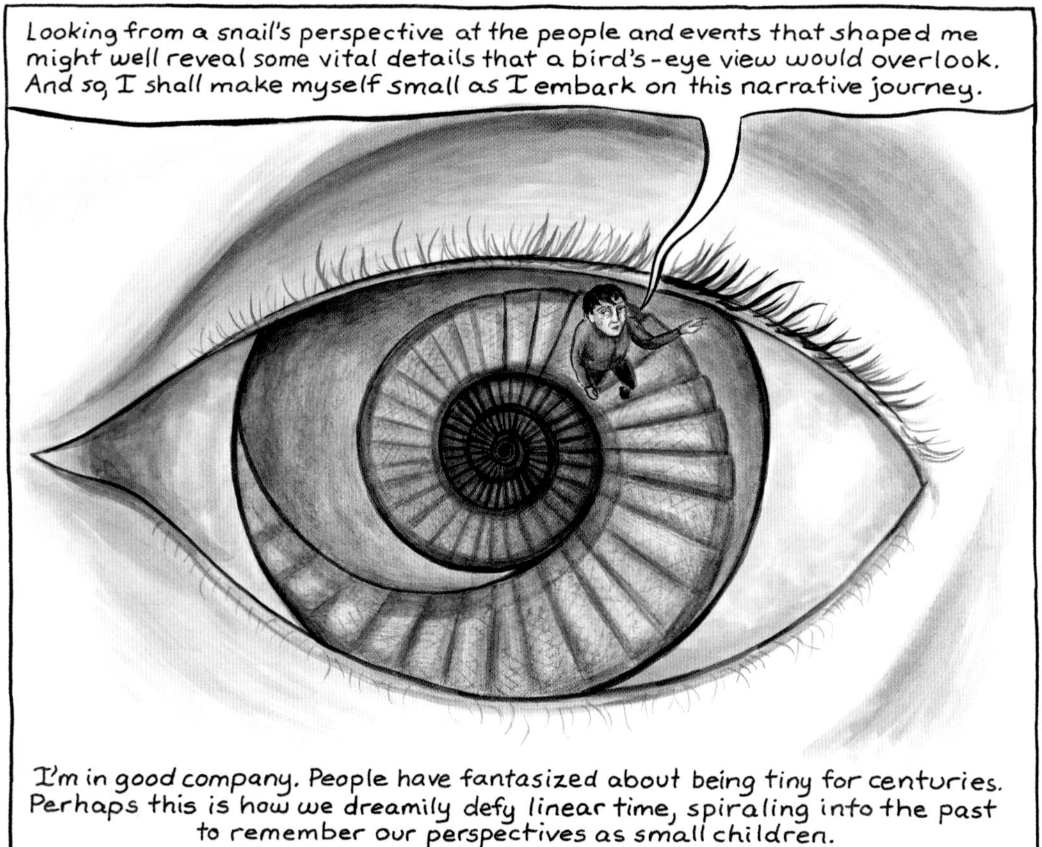
Looking from a snail's perspective at the people and events that shaped me might well reveal some vital details that a bird's-eye view would overlook. And so, I shall make myself small as I embark on this narrative journey.
I'm in good company. People have fantasized about being tiny for centuries. Perhaps this is how we dreamily defy linear time, spiraling into the past to remember our perspectives as small children.

English tales of wee Tom Thumb appeared in print in the early 1600s.

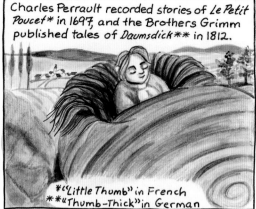

Charles Perrault recorded stories of *Le Petit Poucet** in 1697, and the Brothers Grimm published tales of *Daumsdick*** in 1812.

"Little Thumb" in French
***"Thumb-Thick"** in German

Perhaps these stories were inspired by earlier Japanese yarns about *Issun-bōshi.**

A childless old couple prayed to the gods to give them a child.

They were blessed with a tiny son, but he never grew taller than an inch.

* "Little One-Inch" appears in the *Otogizōshi*, a series of illustrated stories written between 1392 and 1573.

When Issun-bōshi was old enough, he set off with a bowl as a boat, a needle as a sword, and a piece of straw as a scabbard. Like Tom Thumb, *Petit Poucet*, and *Daumsdick*, he was a plucky fellow. Here he is, fighting an *ushi oni*, a terrible sea monster.

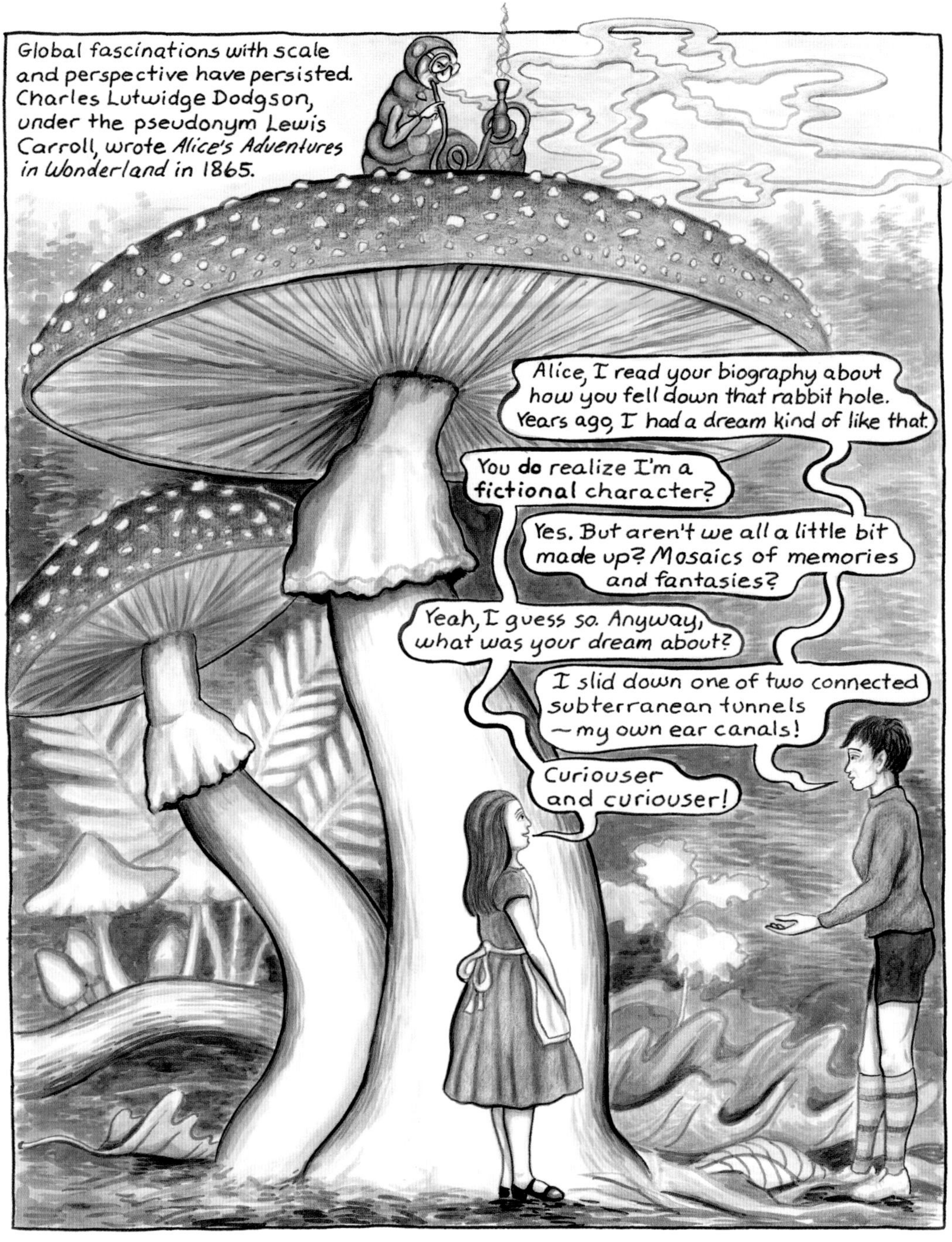
Global fascinations with scale and perspective have persisted. Charles Lutwidge Dodgson, under the pseudonym Lewis Carroll, wrote *Alice's Adventures in Wonderland* in 1865.
Alice, I read your biography about how you fell down that rabbit hole. Years ago, I had a dream kind of like that.
You **do** realize I'm a **fictional** character?
Yes. But aren't we all a little bit made up? Mosaics of memories and fantasies?
Yeah, I guess so. Anyway, what was your dream about?
I slid down one of two connected subterranean tunnels —my own ear canals!
Curiouser and curiouser!

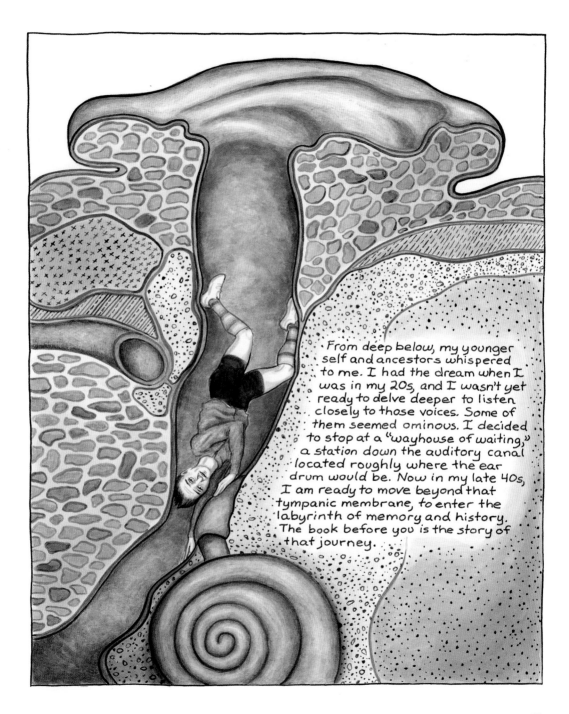

From deep below, my younger self and ancestors whispered to me. I had the dream when I was in my 20s, and I wasn't yet ready to delve deeper to listen closely to those voices. Some of them seemed ominous. I decided to stop at a "wayhouse of waiting," a station down the auditory canal located roughly where the ear drum would be. Now in my late 40s, I am ready to move beyond that tympanic membrane, to enter the labyrinth of memory and history. The book before you is the story of that journey.

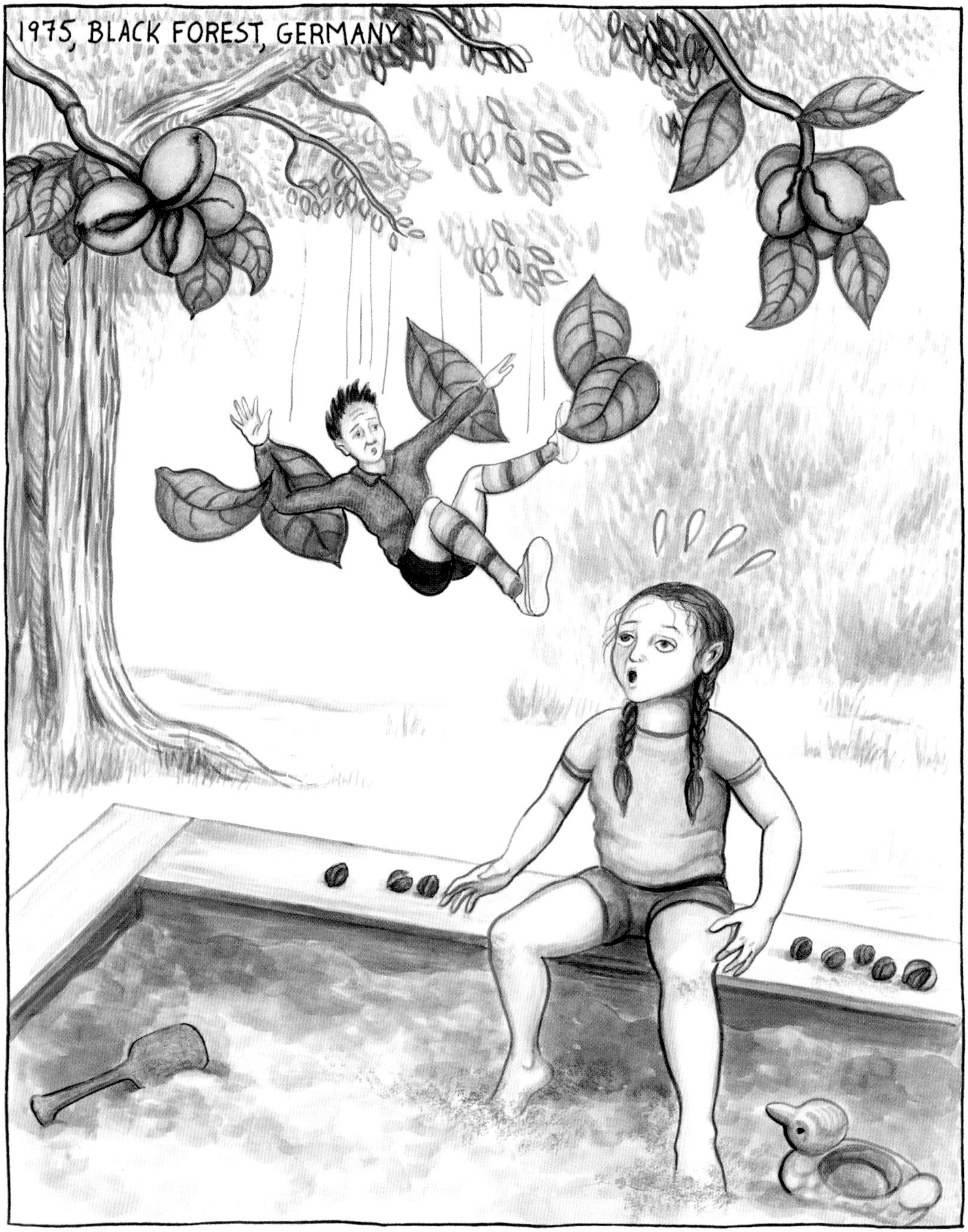
1975, BLACK FOREST, GERMANY

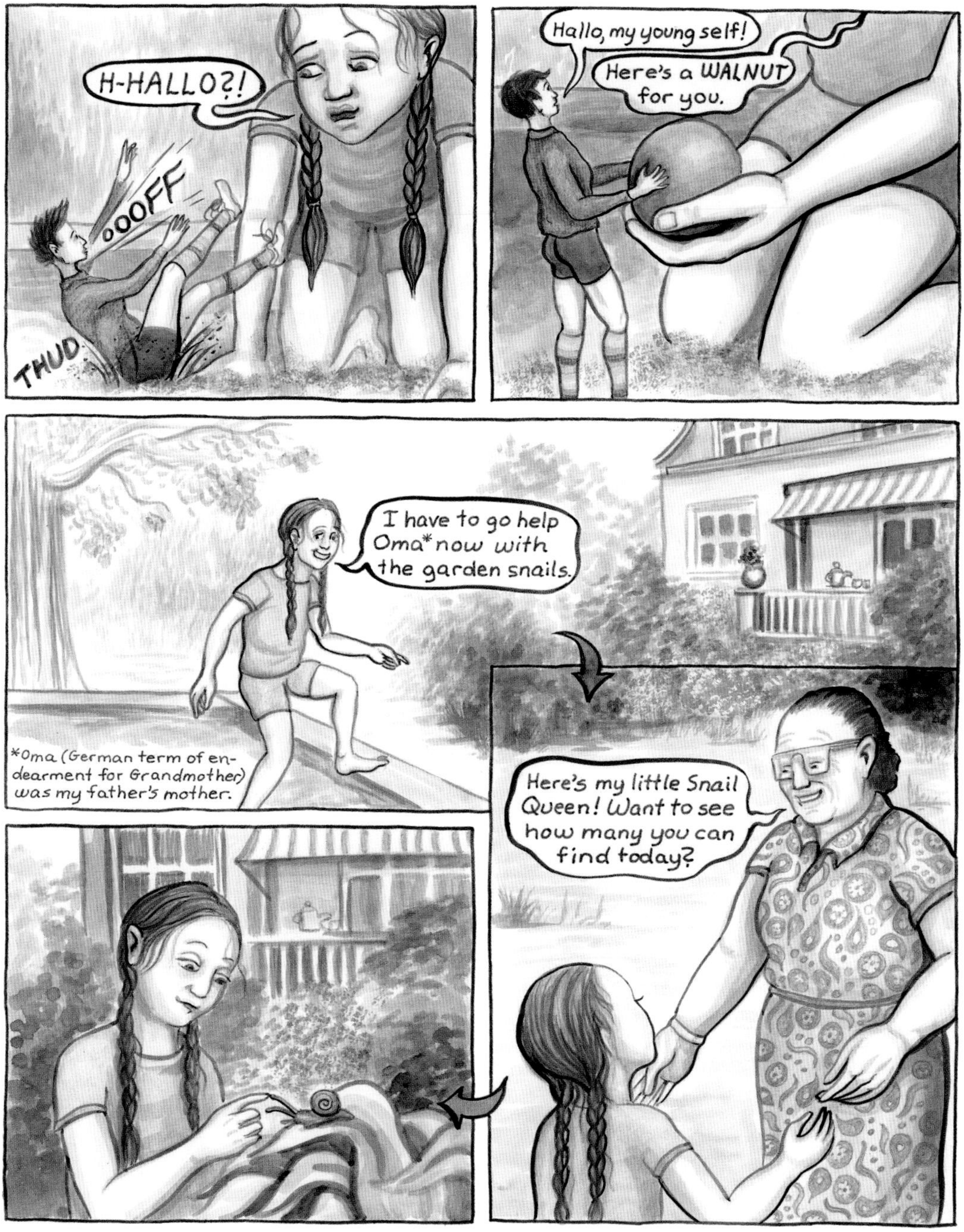

H-HALLO?!
oooFF
THUD
Hallo, my young self!
Here's a WALNUT for you.
I have to go help Oma* now with the garden snails.
*Oma (German term of endearment for Grandmother) was my father's mother.
Here's my little Snail Queen! Want to see how many you can find today?

I admired the snails' beautiful shells, and I was fascinated by their cool, slimy little bodies and by the snot-like tracks they left behind. I liked touching their sensitive feelers with my fingertip, watching them contract in response.

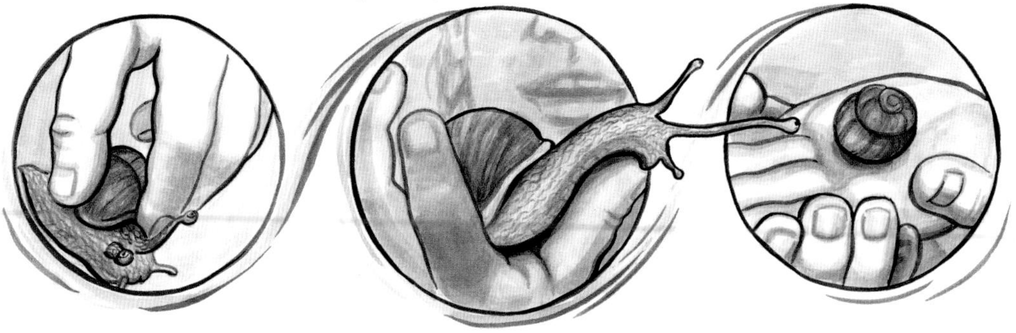

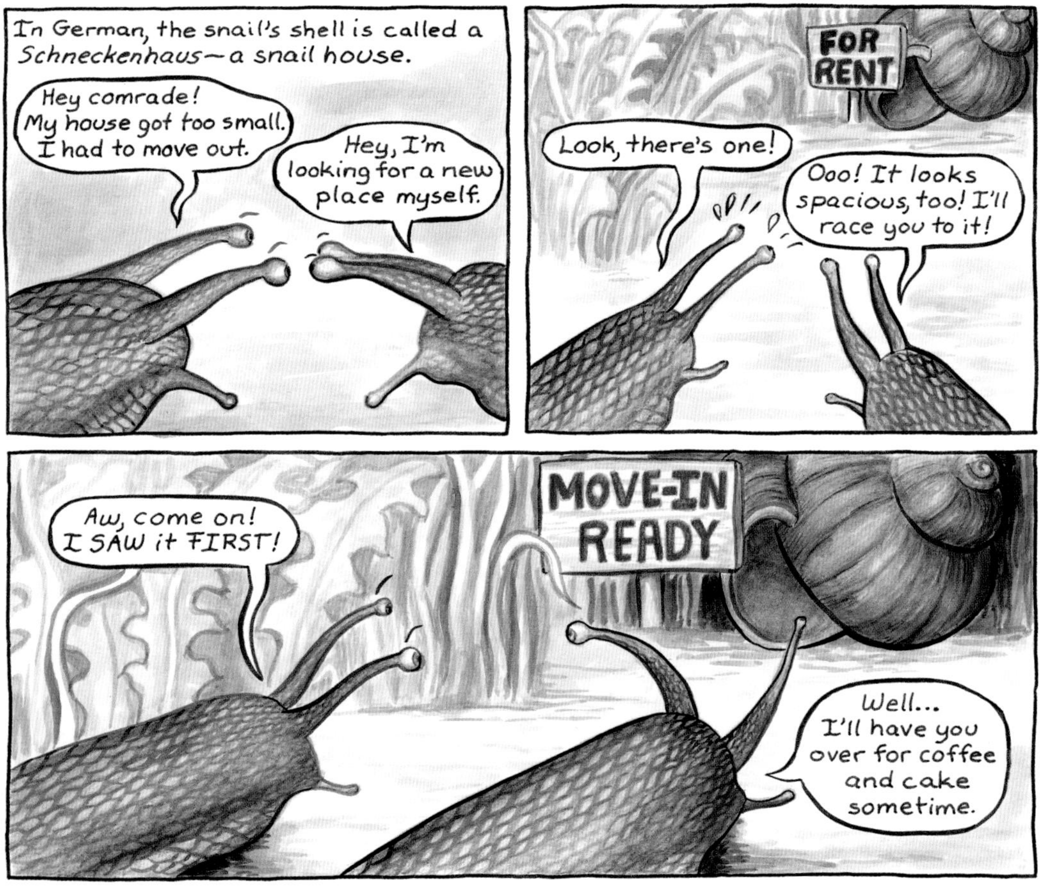
In German, the snail's shell is called a *Schneckenhaus*—a snail house.
Hey comrade! My house got too small. I had to move out.
Hey, I'm looking for a new place myself.
FOR RENT
Look, there's one!
Ooo! It looks spacious, too! I'll race you to it!
MOVE-IN READY
Aw, come on! I SAW it FIRST!
Well... I'll have you over for coffee and cake sometime.

I thought snails could move from home to home, the way my parents and I were often moving from one apartment and city to the next.

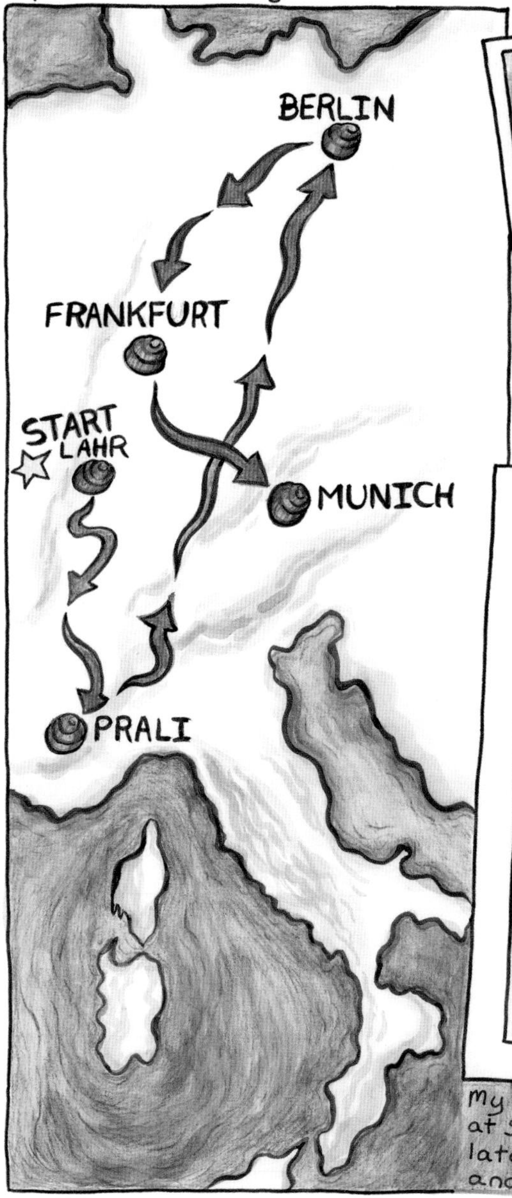
BERLIN
FRANKFURT
START
LAHR
MUNICH
PRALI

Both of my parents had travelled quite a bit before my time. In fact, they had met in South Korea in the mid-1960s.

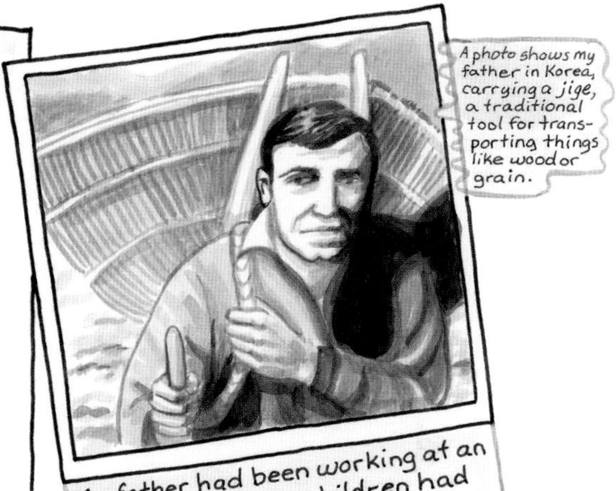
A photo shows my father in Korea, carrying a jige, a traditional tool for transporting things like wood or grain.
My father had been working at an orphanage (many children had been orphaned during the Korean War). He would later become a translator of English, French, Spanish, Italian, and Russian.

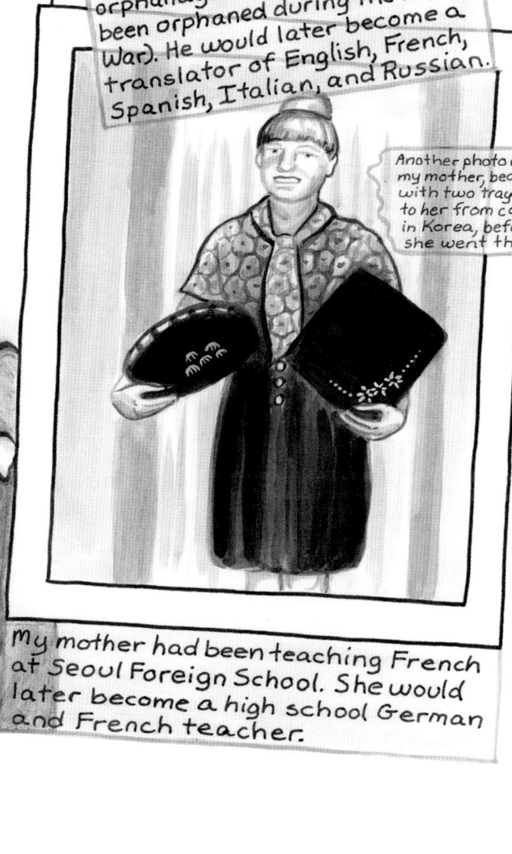
Another photo reveals my mother, beaming, with two trays gifted to her from contacts in Korea, before she went there.
My mother had been teaching French at Seoul Foreign School. She would later become a high school German and French teacher.

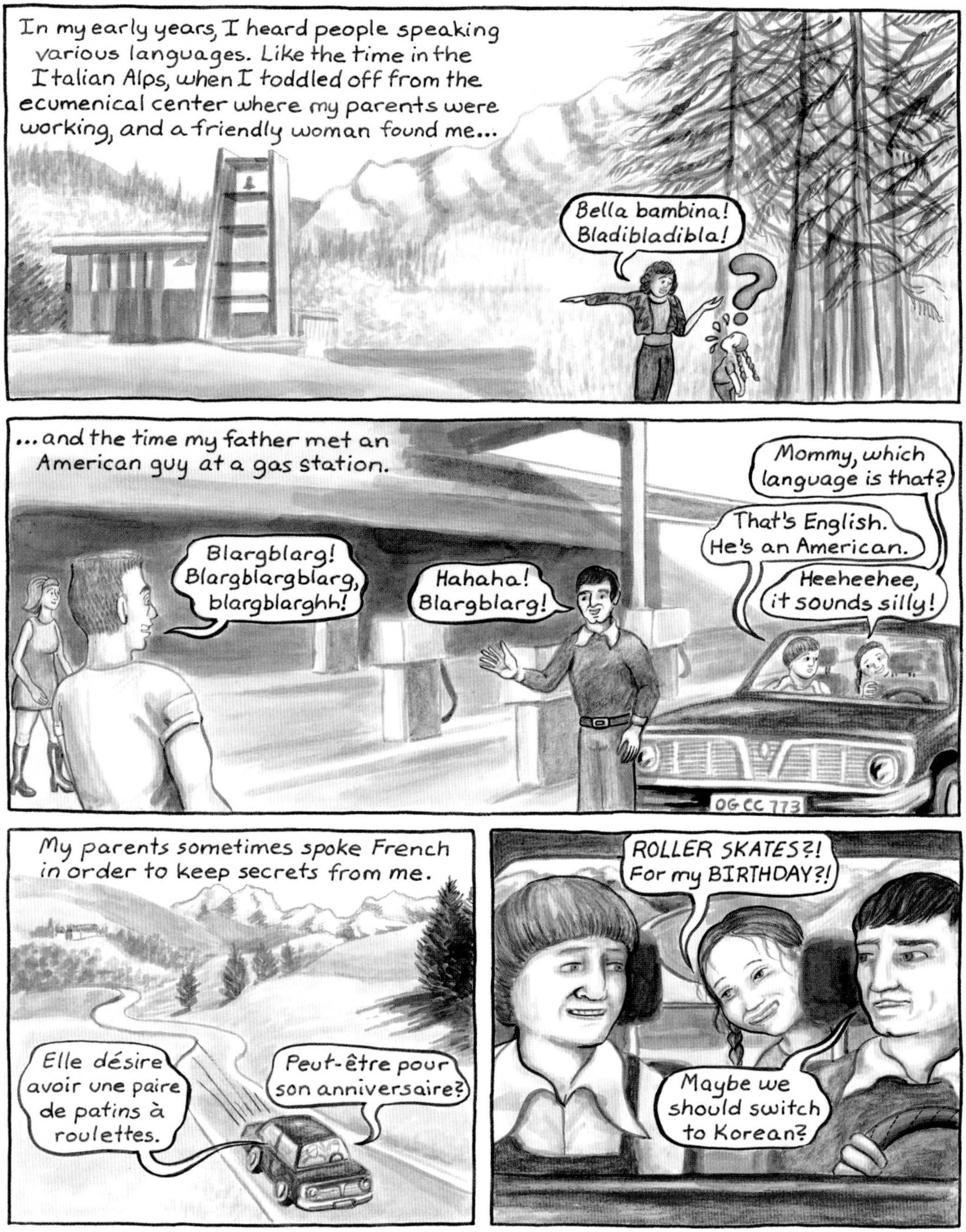
In my early years, I heard people speaking various languages. Like the time in the Italian Alps, when I toddled off from the ecumenical center where my parents were working, and a friendly woman found me...
Bella bambina! Bladibladibla!
?
...and the time my father met an American guy at a gas station.
Blargblarg! Blargblargblarg, blargblarghh!
Hahaha! Blargblarg!
Mommy, which language is that?
That's English. He's an American.
Heeheehee, it sounds silly!
OGCC 773
My parents sometimes spoke French in order to keep secrets from me.
Elle désire avoir une paire de patins à roulettes.
Peut-être pour son anniversaire?
ROLLER SKATES?! For my BIRTHDAY?!
Maybe we should switch to Korean?

There were wonderful objects in my parents' bedroom—treasures from their travels.

Maureen, what are you doing in here? You have your own room!

Daddy, I'm just playing with your carving from Russia. How do you say "BEAR" again, in Russian?

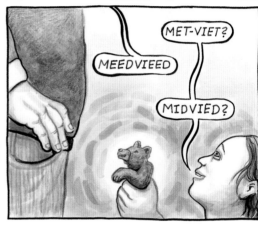

MET-VIET?

MEEDVIEED

MIDVIED?

If you cleaned your OWN room, then you wouldn't need to play in ours!

But it's much nicer in here.

Those were a special gift from a friend in Korea. Please be extra careful!

May I take them to the park?

NO!

Okay...I'll take my boat.

As an only child, I was independent early. When I was six, one of my favorite haunts was the park near our apartment in Munich. The Würm River flowed through it. I can still recall its sweet green musty smell. Becoming familiar with varied landscapes and people was normal and exciting. My feeling of "HOME" was expansive in that sense and always with me.

Snails, too, carry their homes with them.

They hatch with their shells, tiny and intact, and are one with them till they die. Snails' homes go with them and grow with them.

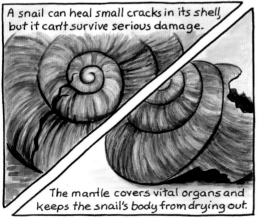

A snail can heal small cracks in its shell, but it can't survive serious damage.

The mantle covers vital organs and keeps the snail's body from drying out.

They are as aware of their mortality as any other living creatures.

26

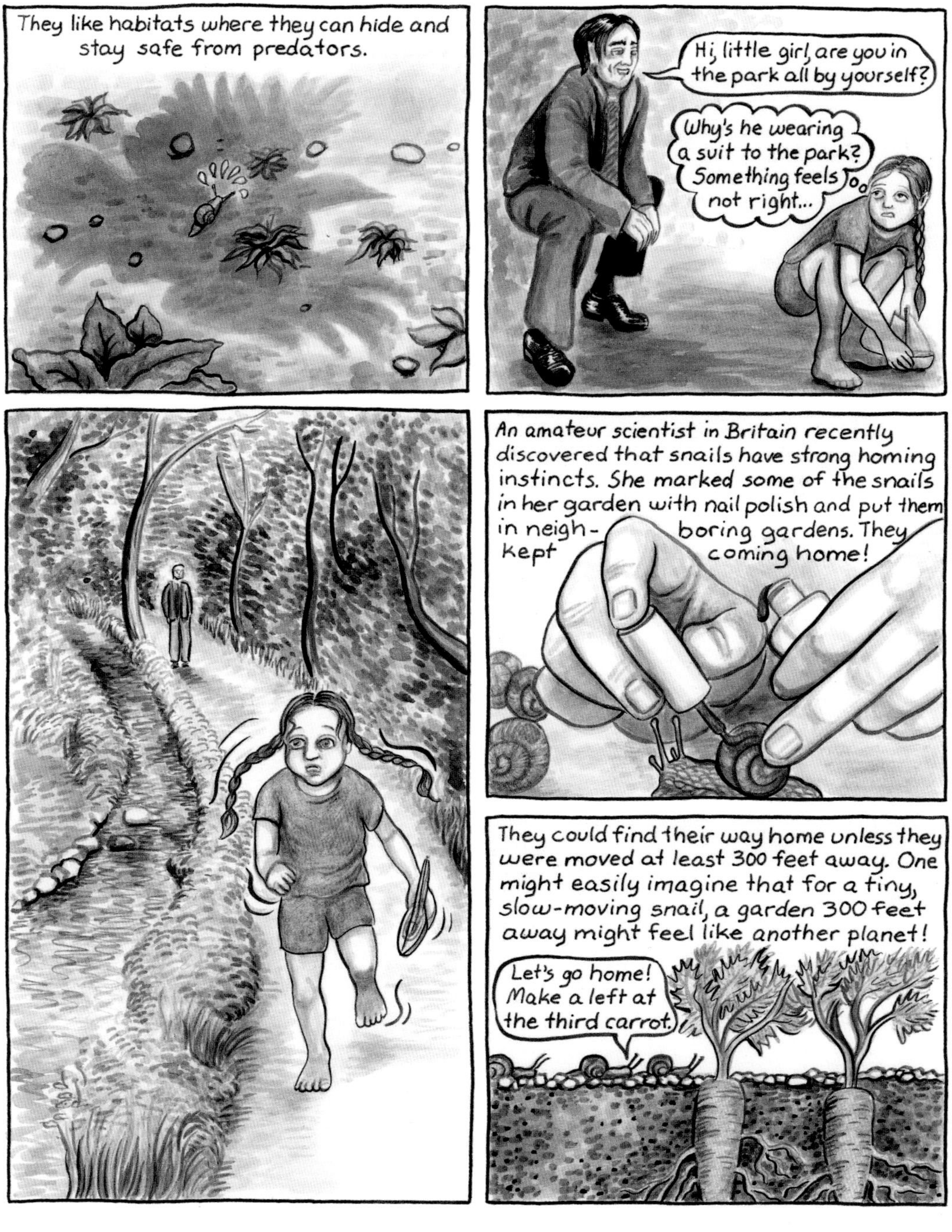

They like habitats where they can hide and stay safe from predators.
Hi, little girl, are you in the park all by yourself?
Why's he wearing a suit to the park? Something feels not right...
An amateur scientist in Britain recently discovered that snails have strong homing instincts. She marked some of the snails in her garden with nail polish and put them in neigh- boring gardens. They kept coming home!
They could find their way home unless they were moved at least 300 feet away. One might easily imagine that for a tiny, slow-moving snail, a garden 300 feet away might feel like another planet!
Let's go home! Make a left at the third carrot.

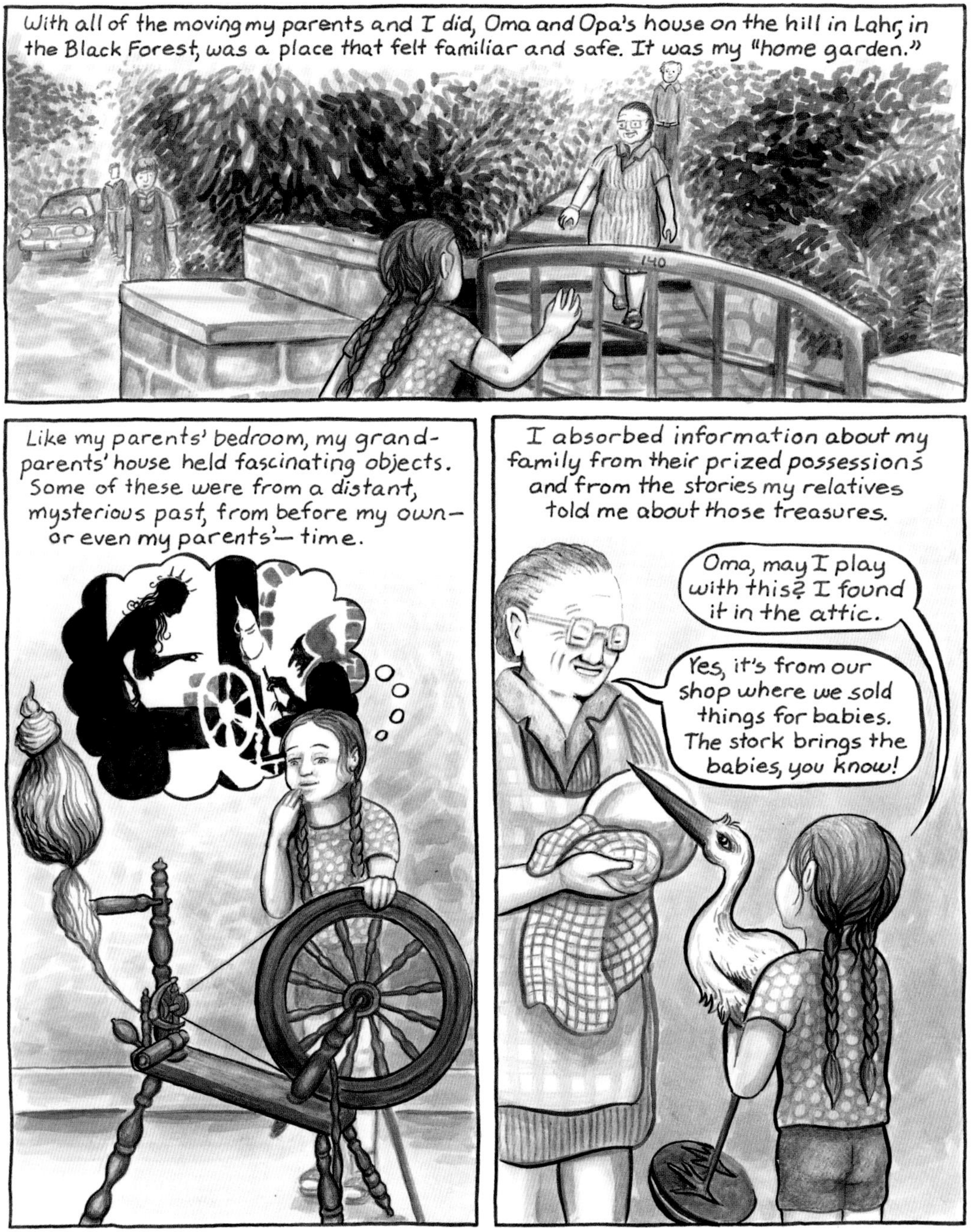
With all of the moving my parents and I did, Oma and Opa's house on the hill in Lahr, in the Black Forest, was a place that felt familiar and safe. It was my "home garden."
140
Like my parents' bedroom, my grand-parents' house held fascinating objects. Some of these were from a distant, mysterious past, from before my own—or even my parents'—time.
I absorbed information about my family from their prized possessions and from the stories my relatives told me about those treasures.
Oma, may I play with this? I found it in the attic.
Yes, it's from our shop where we sold things for babies. The stork brings the babies, you know!

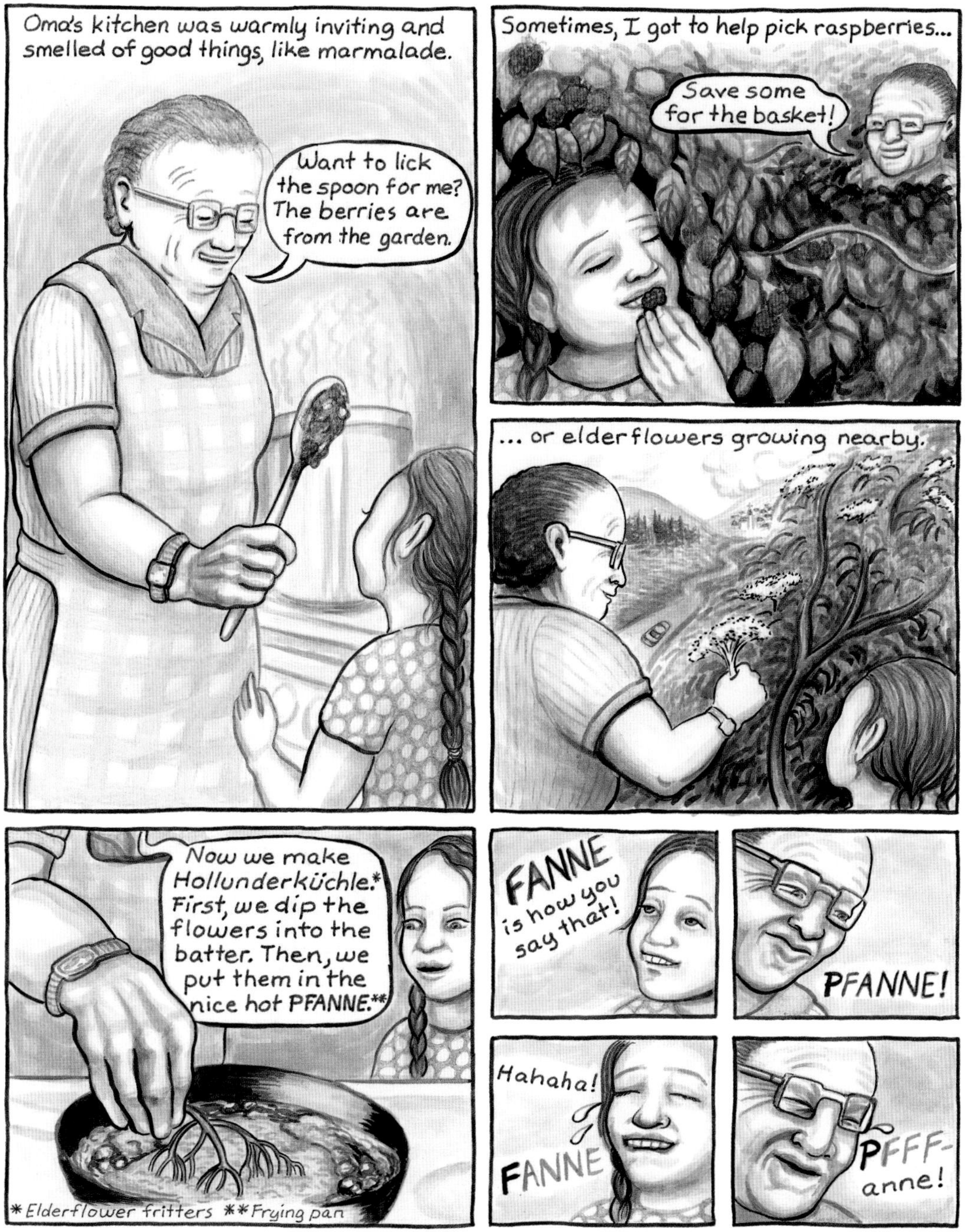
Oma's kitchen was warmly inviting and smelled of good things, like marmalade.
Want to lick the spoon for me? The berries are from the garden.
Sometimes, I got to help pick raspberries...
Save some for the basket!
... or elderflowers growing nearby.
Now we make Hollunderküchle.* First, we dip the flowers into the batter. Then, we put them in the nice hot PFANNE.**
*Elderflower fritters **Frying pan
FANNE is how you say that!
PFANNE!
Hahaha!
FANNE
PFFF-anne!

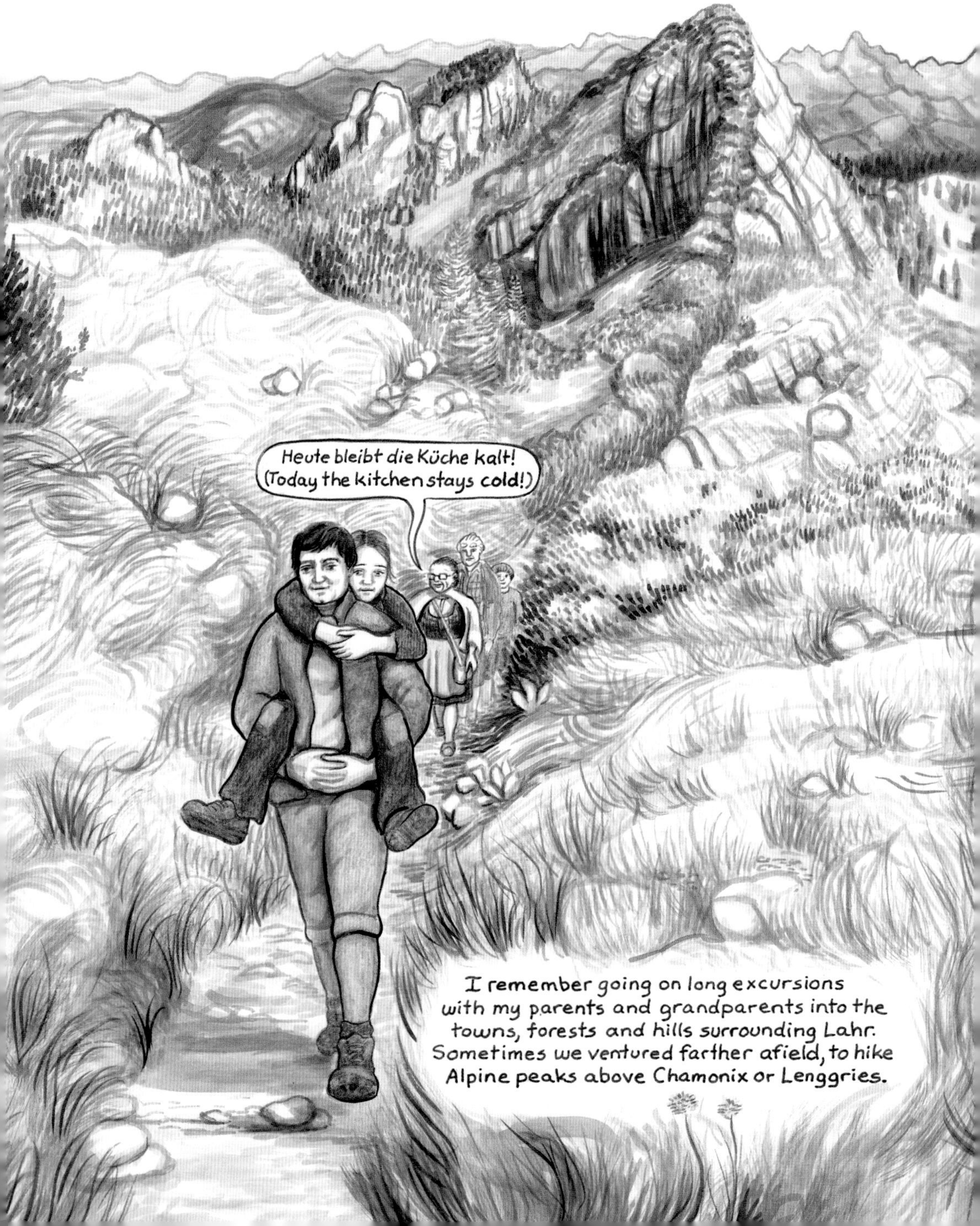
Heute bleibt die Küche kalt! (Today the kitchen stays cold!)
I remember going on long excursions with my parents and grandparents into the towns, forests and hills surrounding Lahr. Sometimes we ventured farther afield, to hike Alpine peaks above Chamonix or Lenggries.

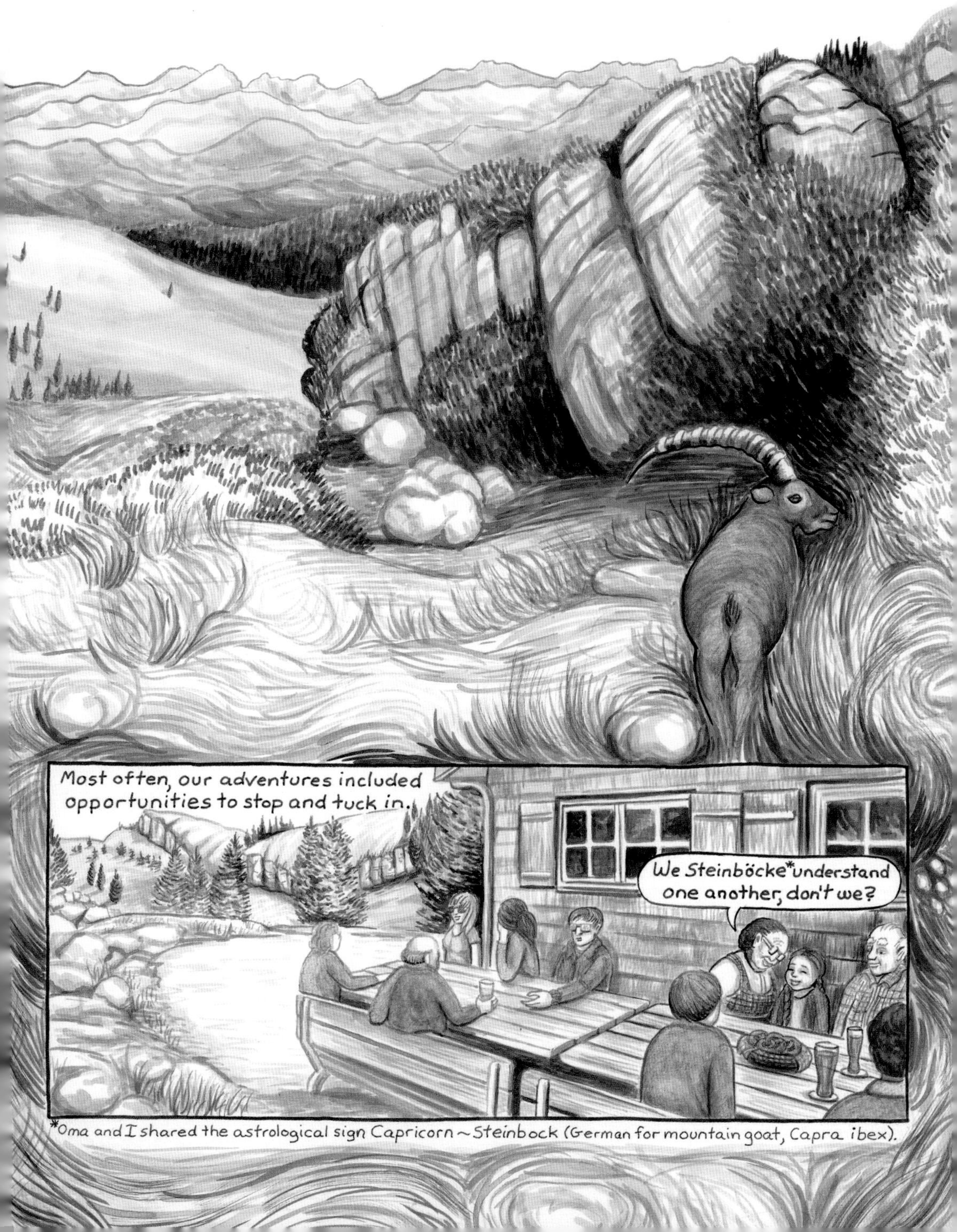
Most often, our adventures included opportunities to stop and tuck in.
We Steinböcke* understand one another, don't we?

*Oma and I shared the astrological sign Capricorn ~ Steinbock (German for mountain goat, Capra ibex).

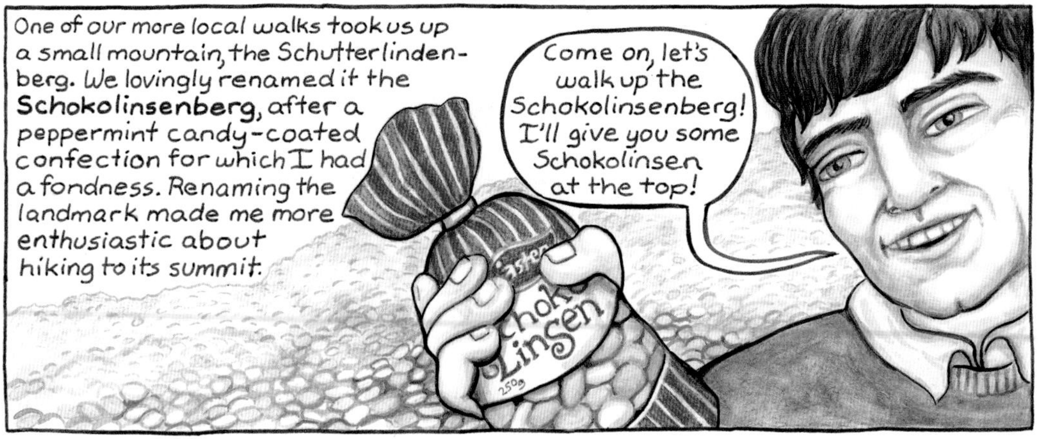
One of our more local walks took us up a small mountain, the Schutterlindenberg. We lovingly renamed it the **Schokolinsenberg**, after a peppermint candy-coated confection for which I had a fondness. Renaming the landmark made me more enthusiastic about hiking to its summit.
Come on, let's walk up the Schokolinsenberg! I'll give you some Schokolinsen at the top!
Schoko Linsen
250g

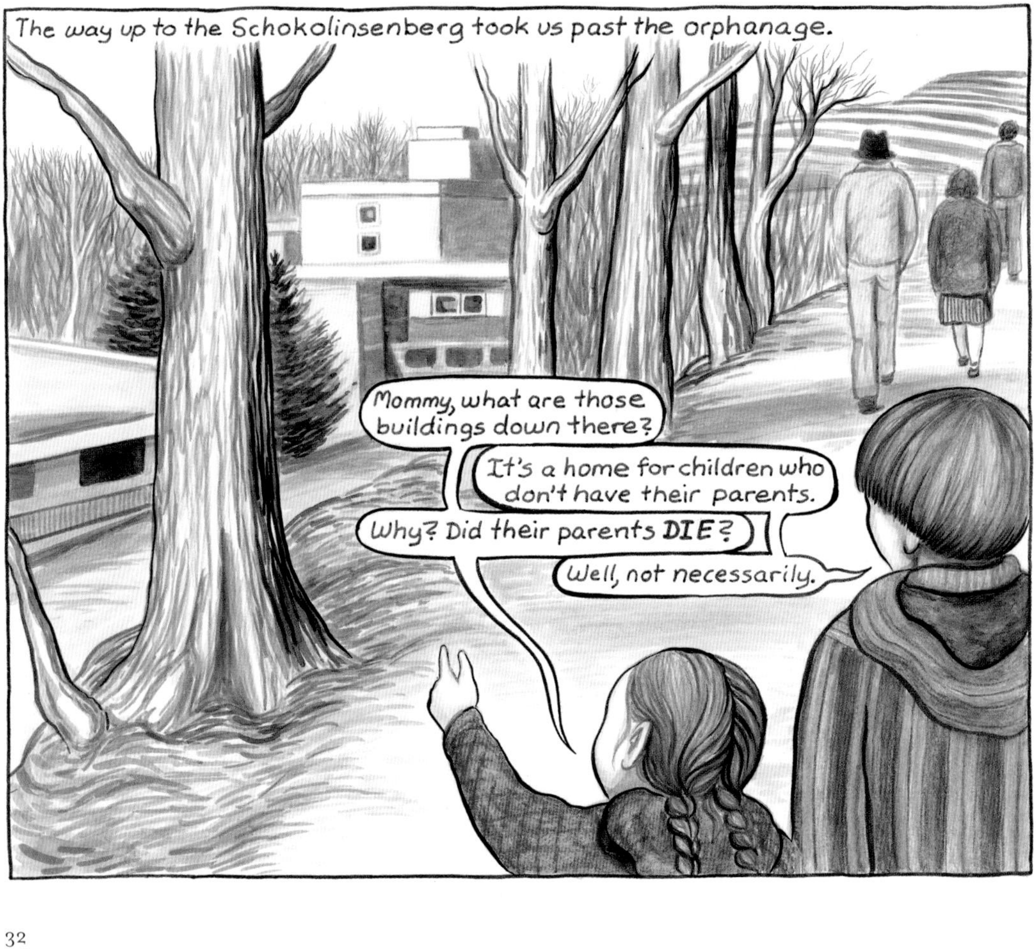
The way up to the Schokolinsenberg took us past the orphanage.
Mommy, what are those buildings down there?
It's a home for children who don't have their parents.
Why? Did their parents **DIE**?
Well, not necessarily.

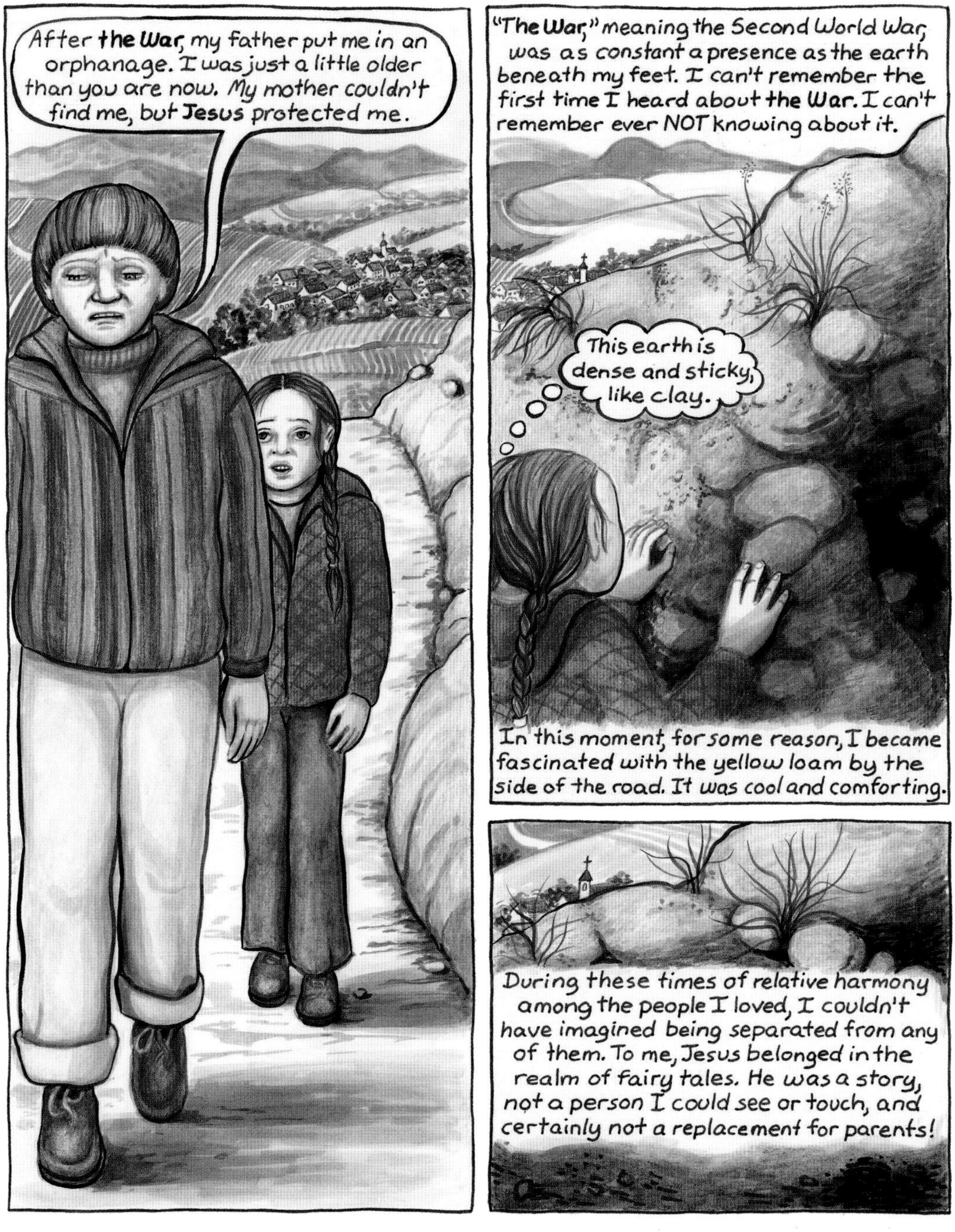
After **the War**, my father put me in an orphanage. I was just a little older than you are now. My mother couldn't find me, but **Jesus** protected me.
"**The War**," meaning the Second World War, was as constant a presence as the earth beneath my feet. I can't remember the first time I heard about **the War**. I can't remember ever NOT knowing about it.
This earth is dense and sticky, like clay.
In this moment, for some reason, I became fascinated with the yellow loam by the side of the road. It was cool and comforting.
During these times of relative harmony among the people I loved, I couldn't have imagined being separated from any of them. To me, Jesus belonged in the realm of fairy tales. He was a story, not a person I could see or touch, and certainly not a replacement for parents!

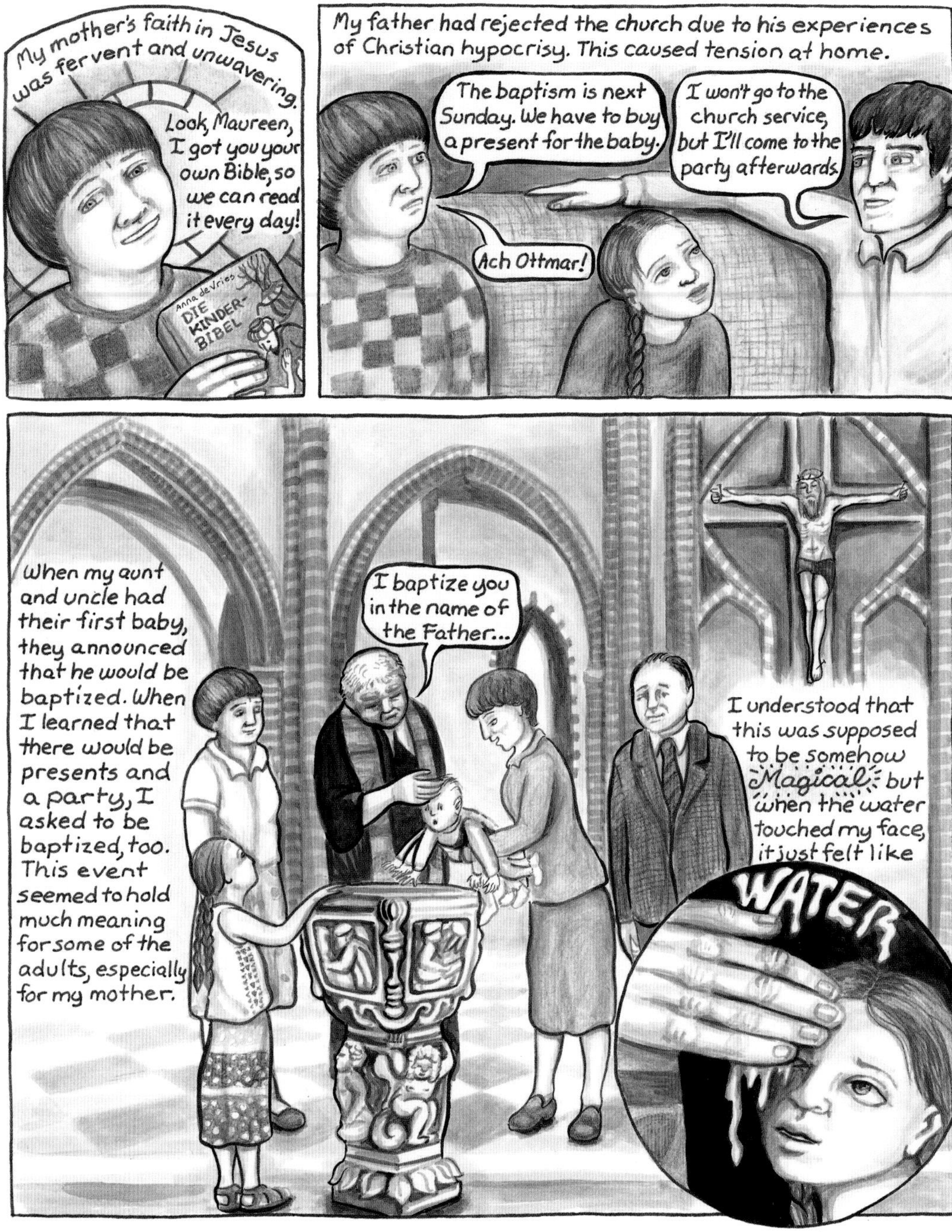
My mother's faith in Jesus was fervent and unwavering.
Look, Maureen, I got you your own Bible, so we can read it every day!
Anna de Vries
DIE KINDER-BIBEL
My father had rejected the church due to his experiences of Christian hypocrisy. This caused tension at home.
The baptism is next Sunday. We have to buy a present for the baby.
I won't go to the church service, but I'll come to the party afterwards.
Ach Ottmar!
When my aunt and uncle had their first baby, they announced that he would be baptized. When I learned that there would be presents and a party, I asked to be baptized, too. This event seemed to hold much meaning for some of the adults, especially for my mother.
I baptize you in the name of the Father...
I understood that this was supposed to be somehow Magical but when the water touched my face, it just felt like
WATER

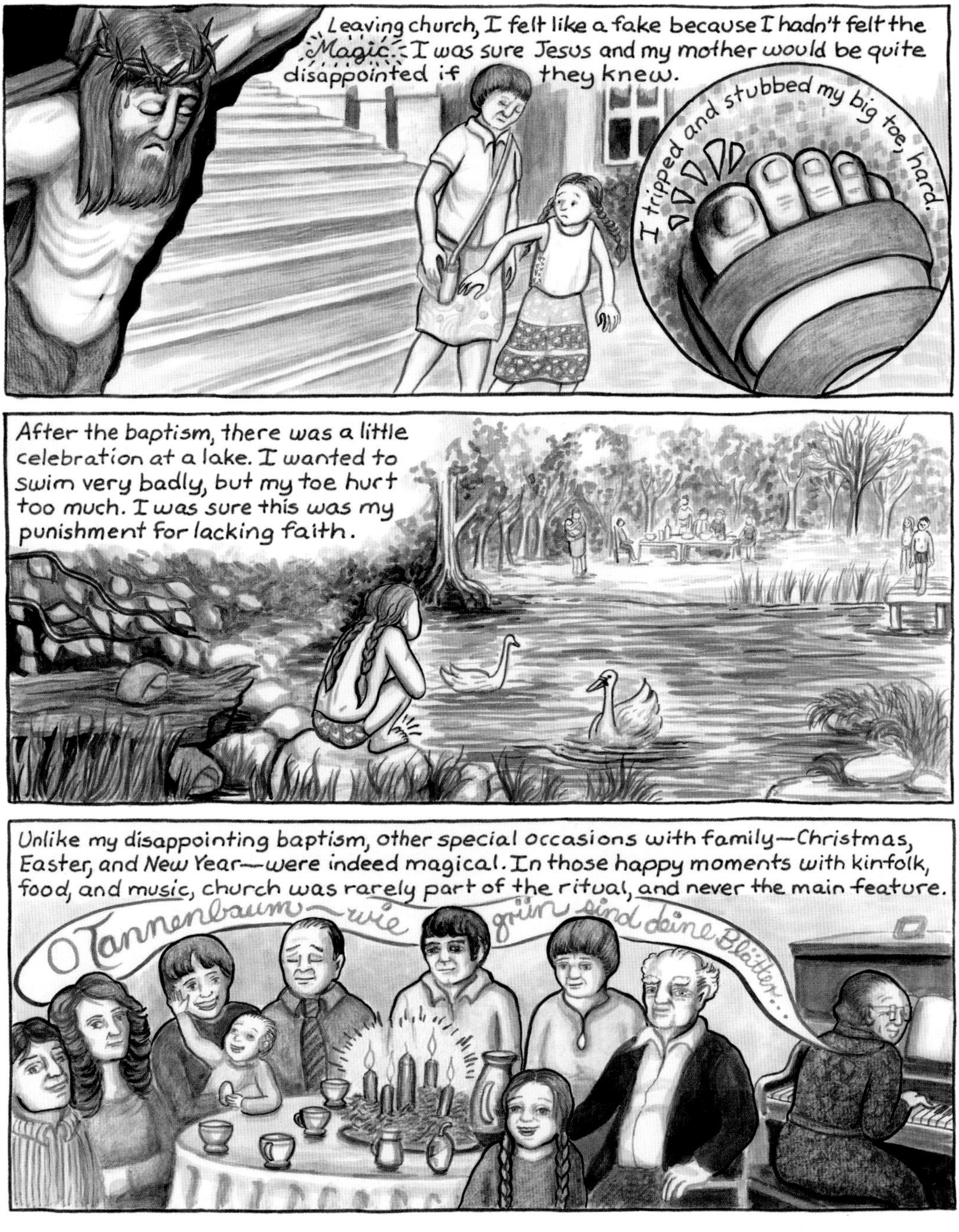
Leaving church, I felt like a fake because I hadn't felt the Magic. I was sure Jesus and my mother would be quite disappointed if they knew.
I tripped and stubbed my big toe, hard.
After the baptism, there was a little celebration at a lake. I wanted to swim very badly, but my toe hurt too much. I was sure this was my punishment for lacking faith.
Unlike my disappointing baptism, other special occasions with family—Christmas, Easter, and New Year—were indeed magical. In those happy moments with kinfolk, food, and music, church was rarely part of the ritual, and never the main feature.
O Tannenbaum— wie grün sind deine Blätter…

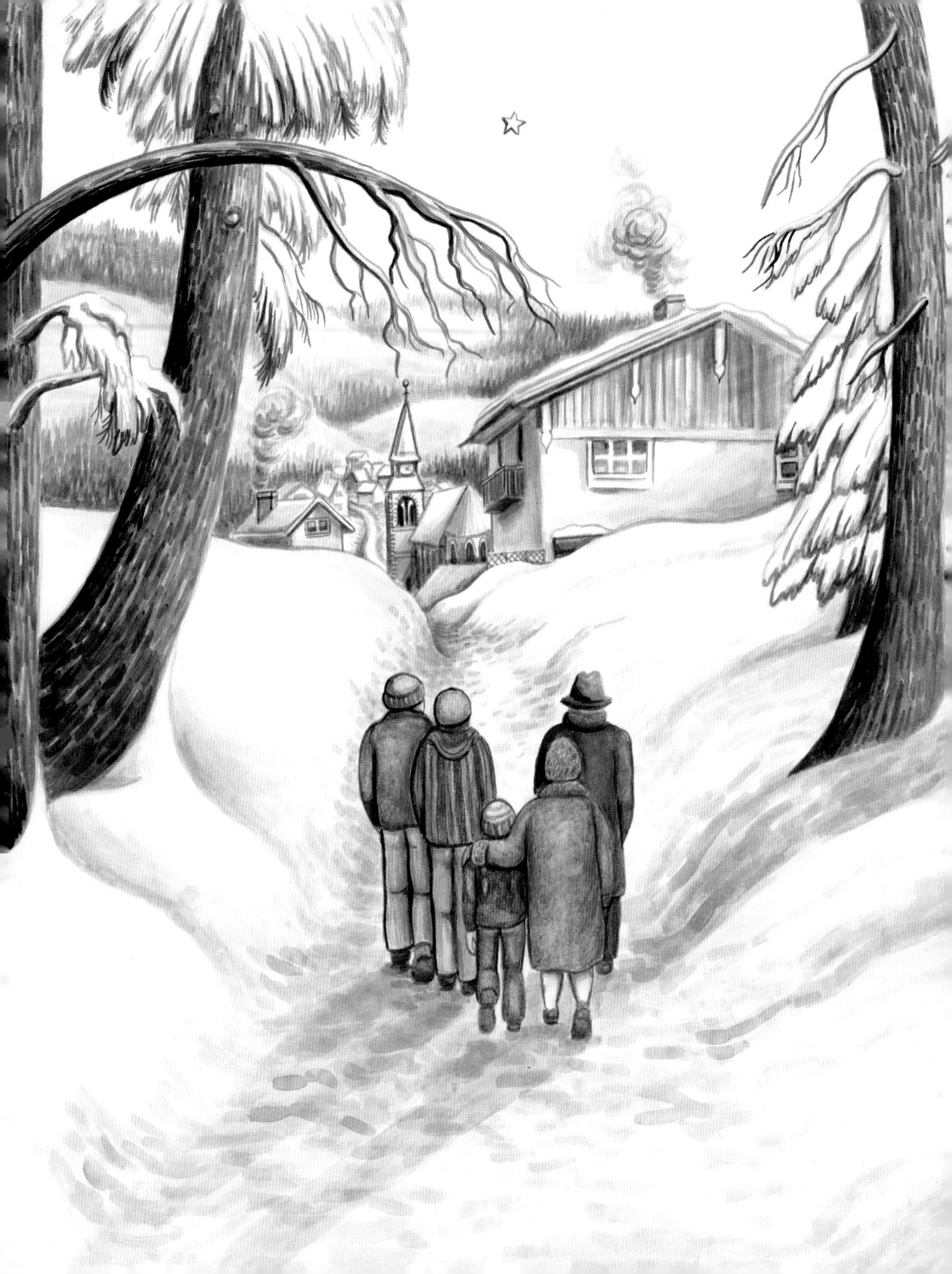

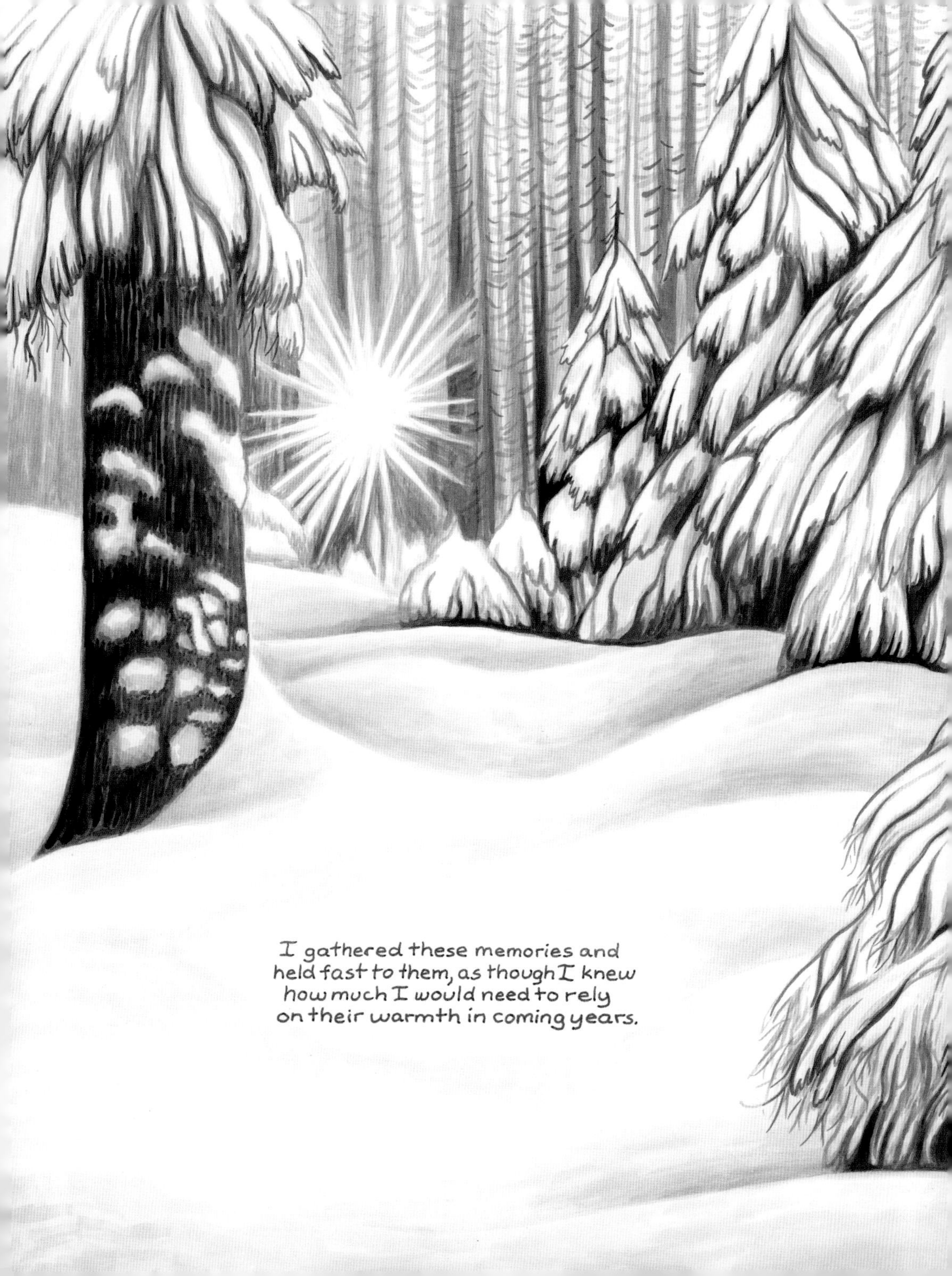
I gathered these memories and held fast to them, as though I knew how much I would need to rely on their warmth in coming years.

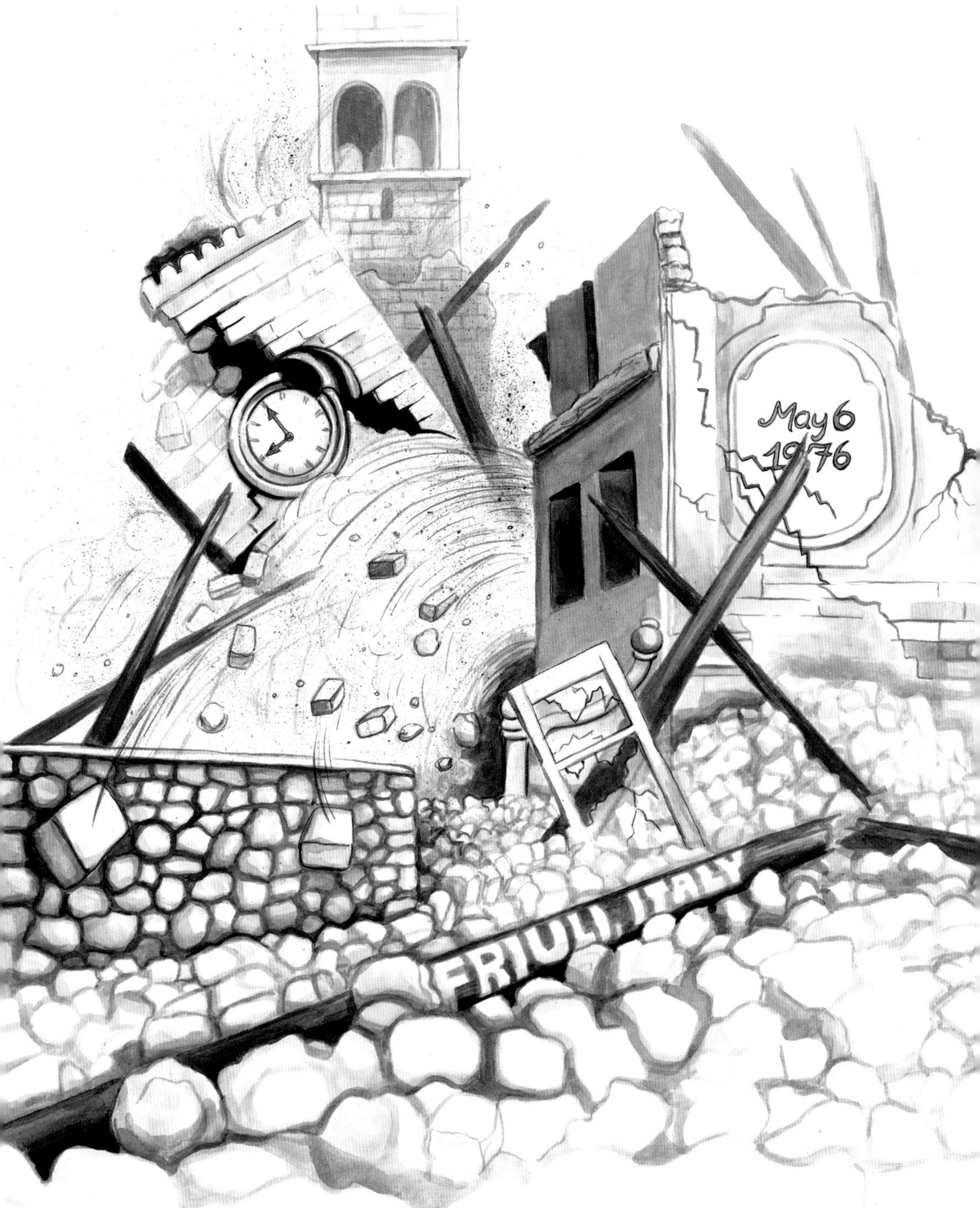
May 6
1976
FRIULI, ITALY

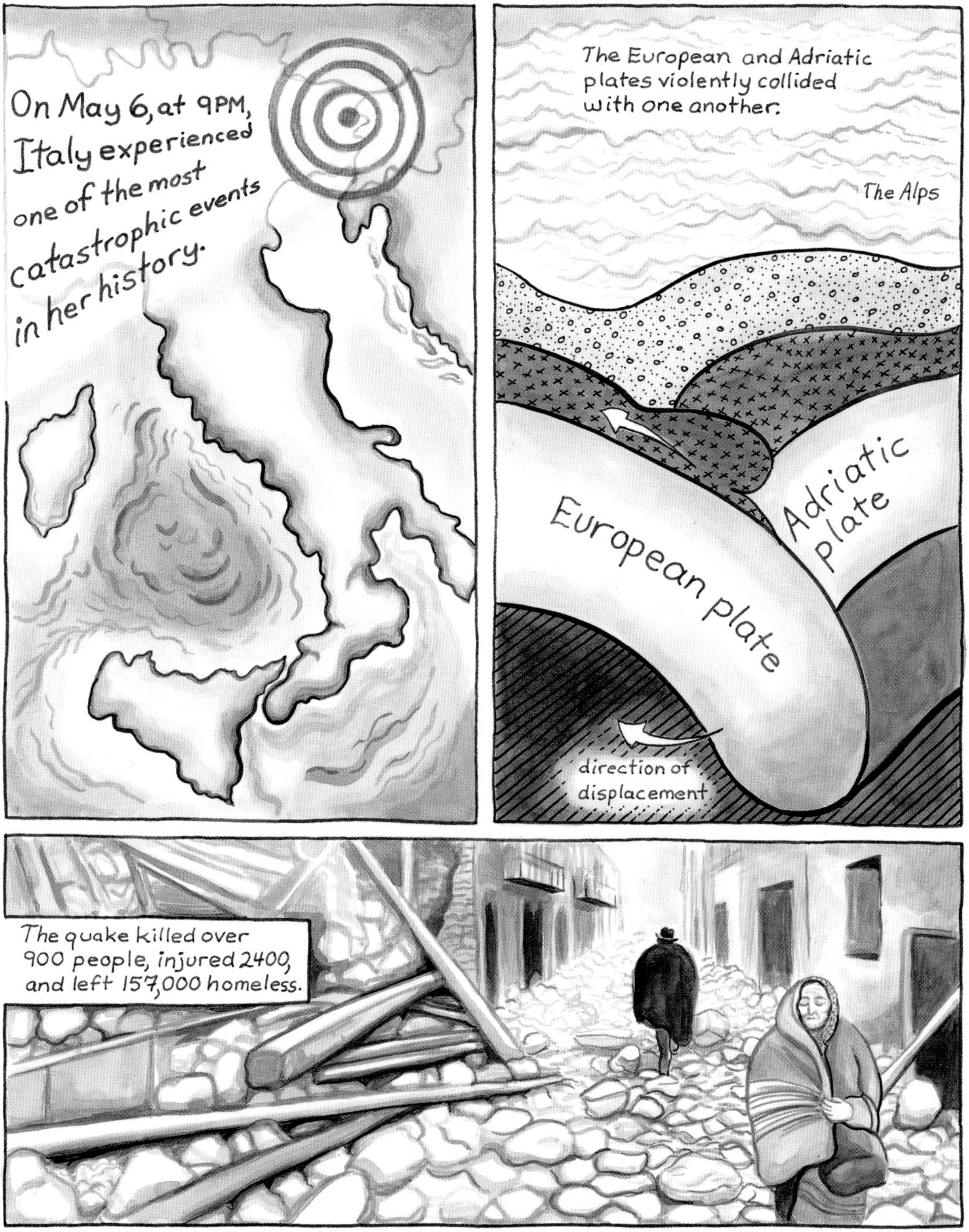
On May 6, at 9PM, Italy experienced one of the most catastrophic events in her history.
The European and Adriatic plates violently collided with one another.
The Alps
Adriatic plate
European plate
direction of displacement
The quake killed over 900 people, injured 2400, and left 157,000 homeless.

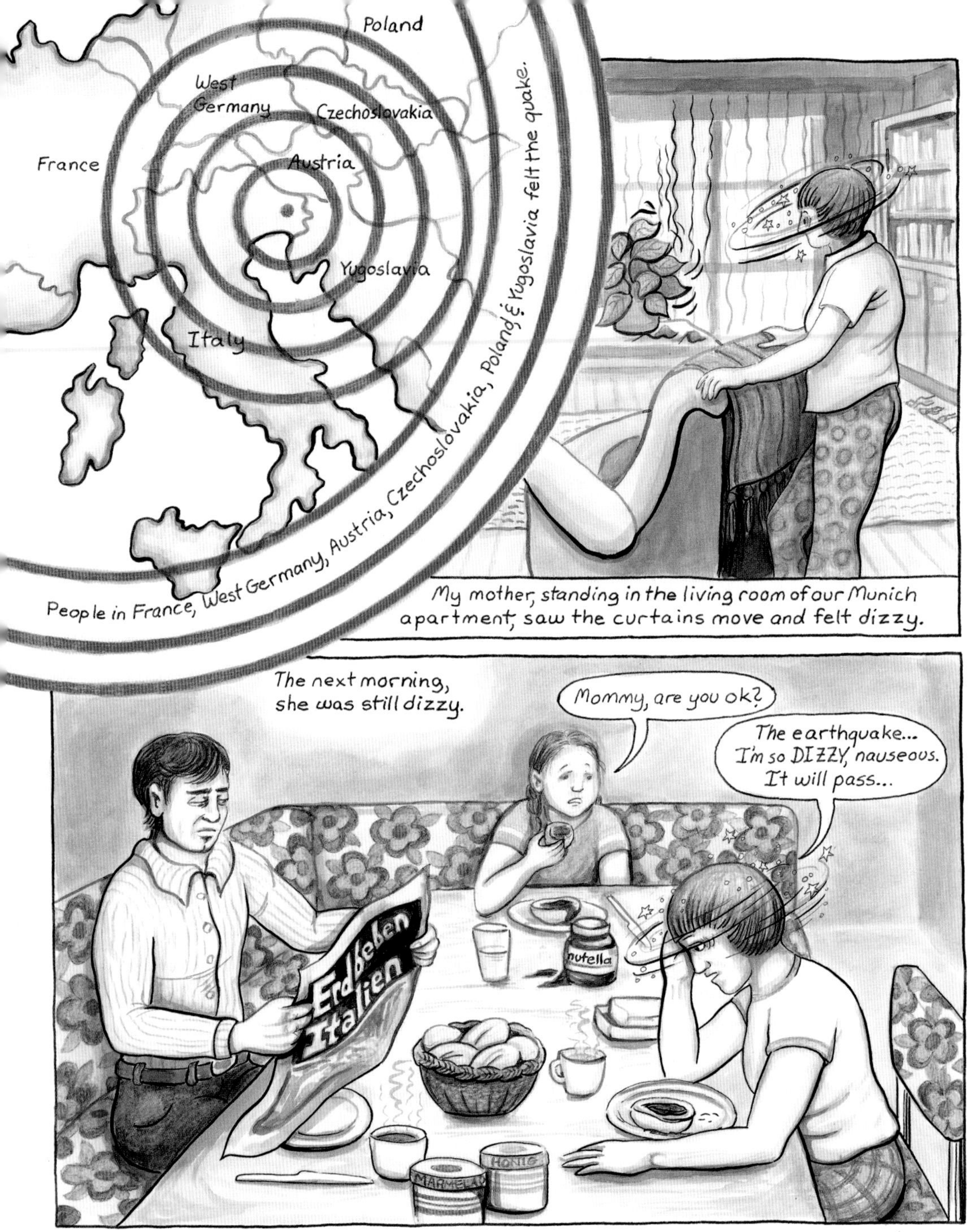
Poland
West Germany
Czechoslovakia
France
Austria
Yugoslavia
Italy
People in France, West Germany, Austria, Czechoslovakia, Poland & Yugoslavia felt the quake.
My mother, standing in the living room of our Munich apartment, saw the curtains move and felt dizzy.
The next morning, she was still dizzy.
Mommy, are you ok?
The earthquake... I'm so DIZZY, nauseous. It will pass...
Erdbeben Italien
nutella
MARMELA
HONIG

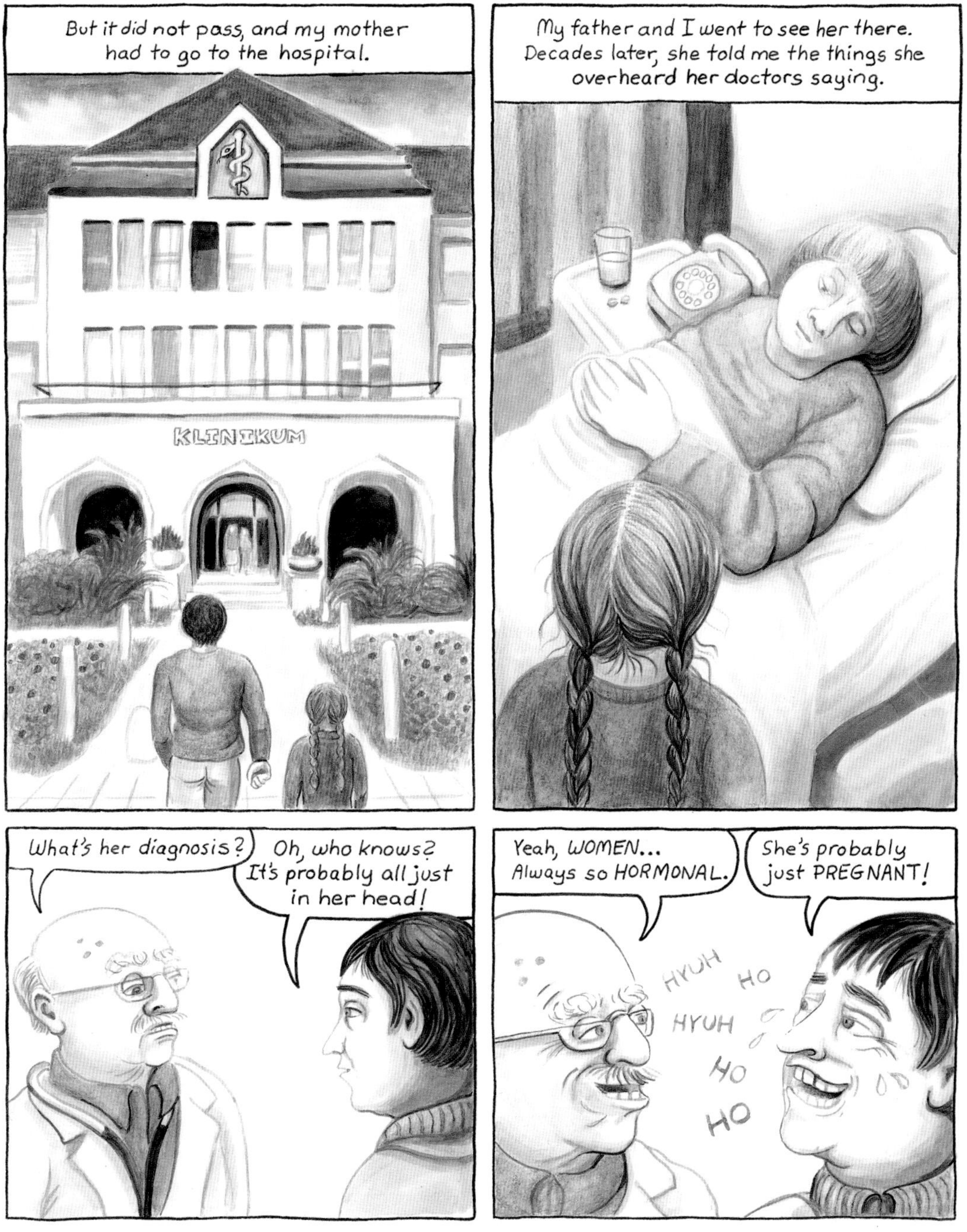
But it did not pass, and my mother had to go to the hospital.
KLINIKUM
My father and I went to see her there. Decades later, she told me the things she overheard her doctors saying.
What's her diagnosis?
Oh, who knows? It's probably all just in her head!
Yeah, WOMEN... Always so HORMONAL.
She's probably just PREGNANT!
HYUH HO HYUH HO HO

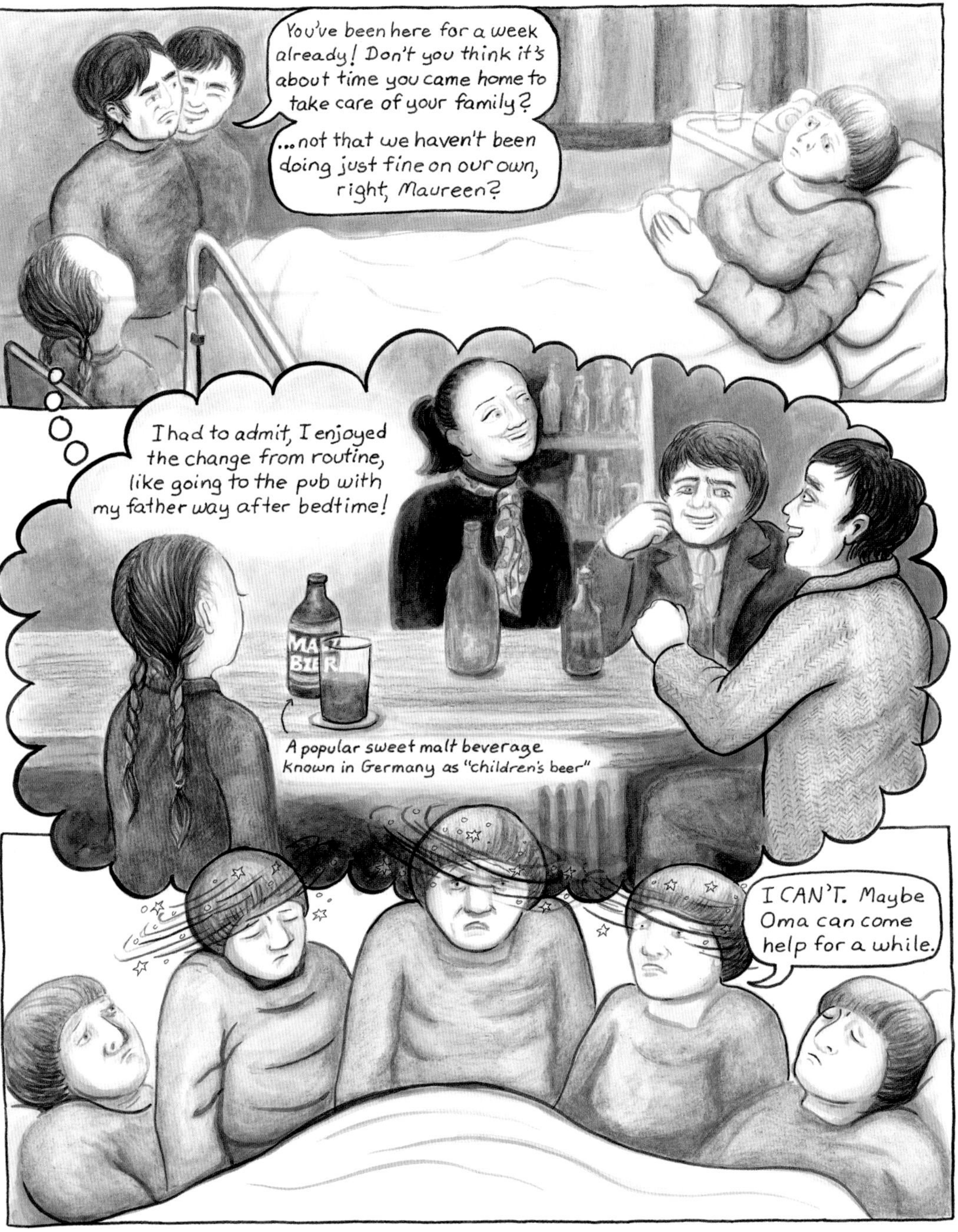
You've been here for a week already! Don't you think it's about time you came home to take care of your family?
...not that we haven't been doing just fine on our own, right, Maureen?
I had to admit, I enjoyed the change from routine, like going to the pub with my father way after bedtime!
MALZ BIER
A popular sweet malt beverage known in Germany as "children's beer"
I CAN'T. Maybe Oma can come help for a while.

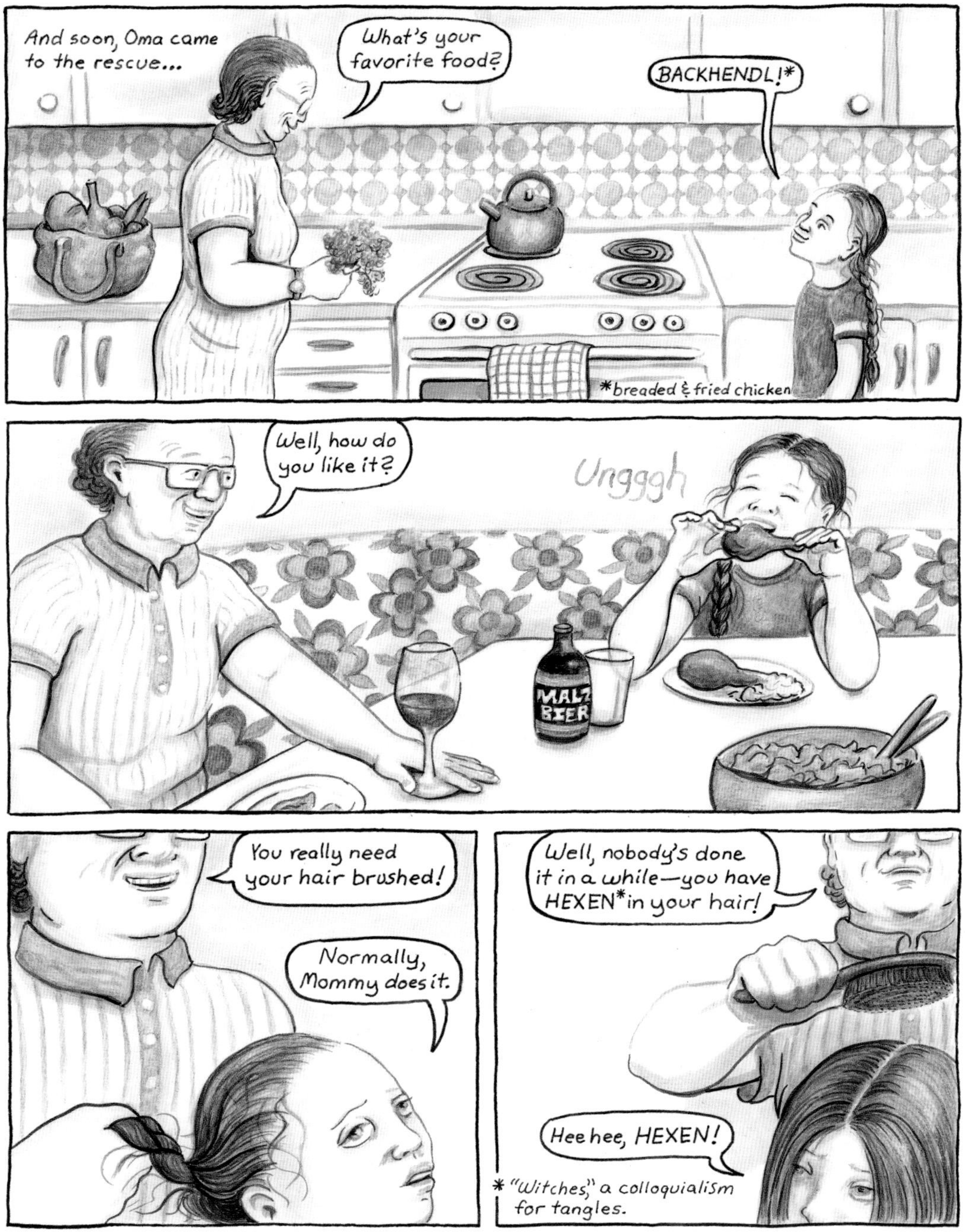
And soon, Oma came to the rescue...
What's your favorite food?
BACKHENDL!*
*breaded & fried chicken
Well, how do you like it?
Ungggh
MALZ BIER
You really need your hair brushed!
Normally, Mommy does it.
Well, nobody's done it in a while—you have HEXEN* in your hair!
Hee hee, HEXEN!
* "Witches," a colloquialism for tangles.

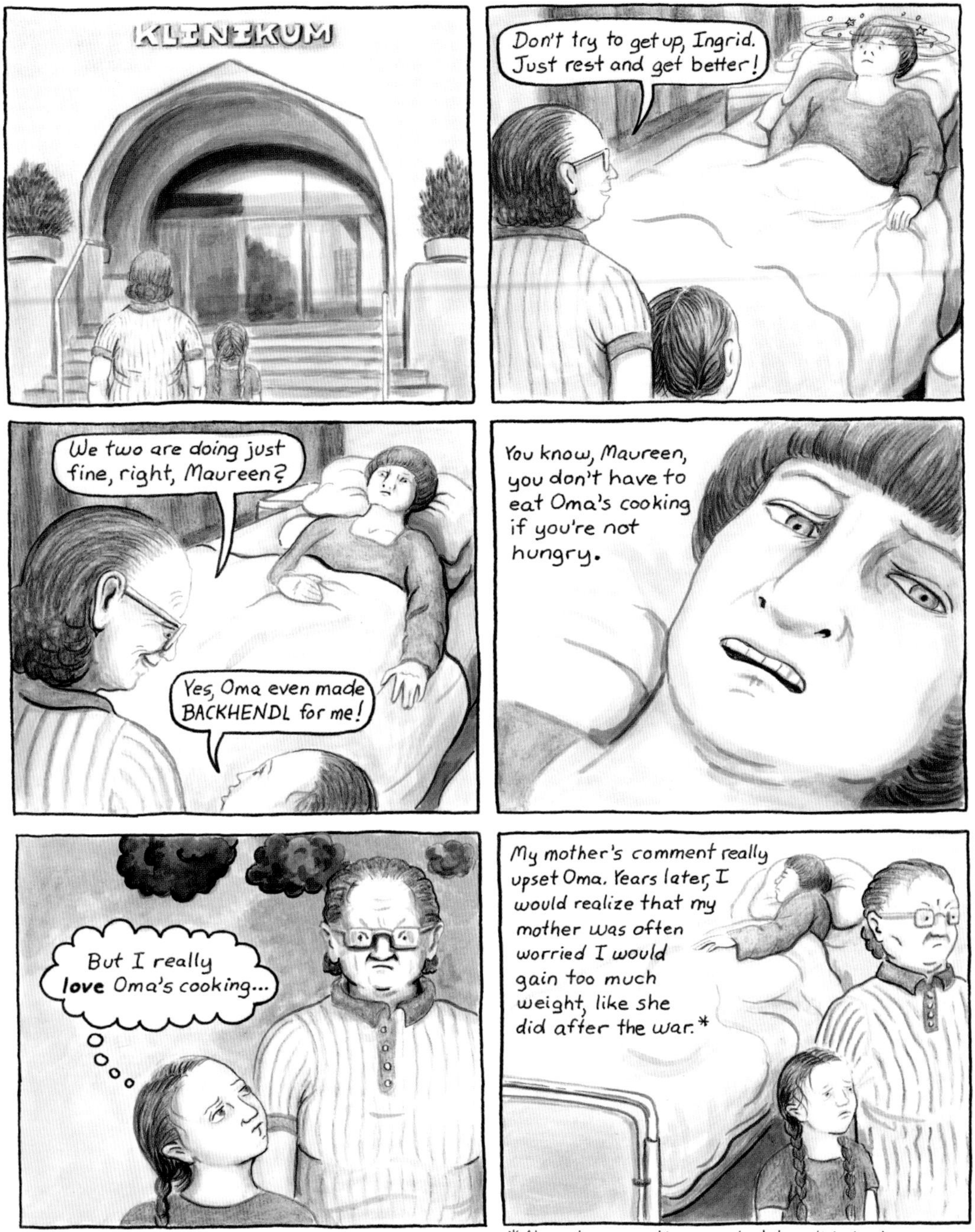
KLINIKUM
Don't try to get up, Ingrid. Just rest and get better!
We two are doing just fine, right, Maureen?
Yes, Oma even made BACKHENDL for me!
You know, Maureen, you don't have to eat Oma's cooking if you're not hungry.
But I really **love** Oma's cooking...
My mother's comment really upset Oma. Years later, I would realize that my mother was often worried I would gain too much weight, like she did after the war.*

*Also, she sometimes acted terribly jealous.

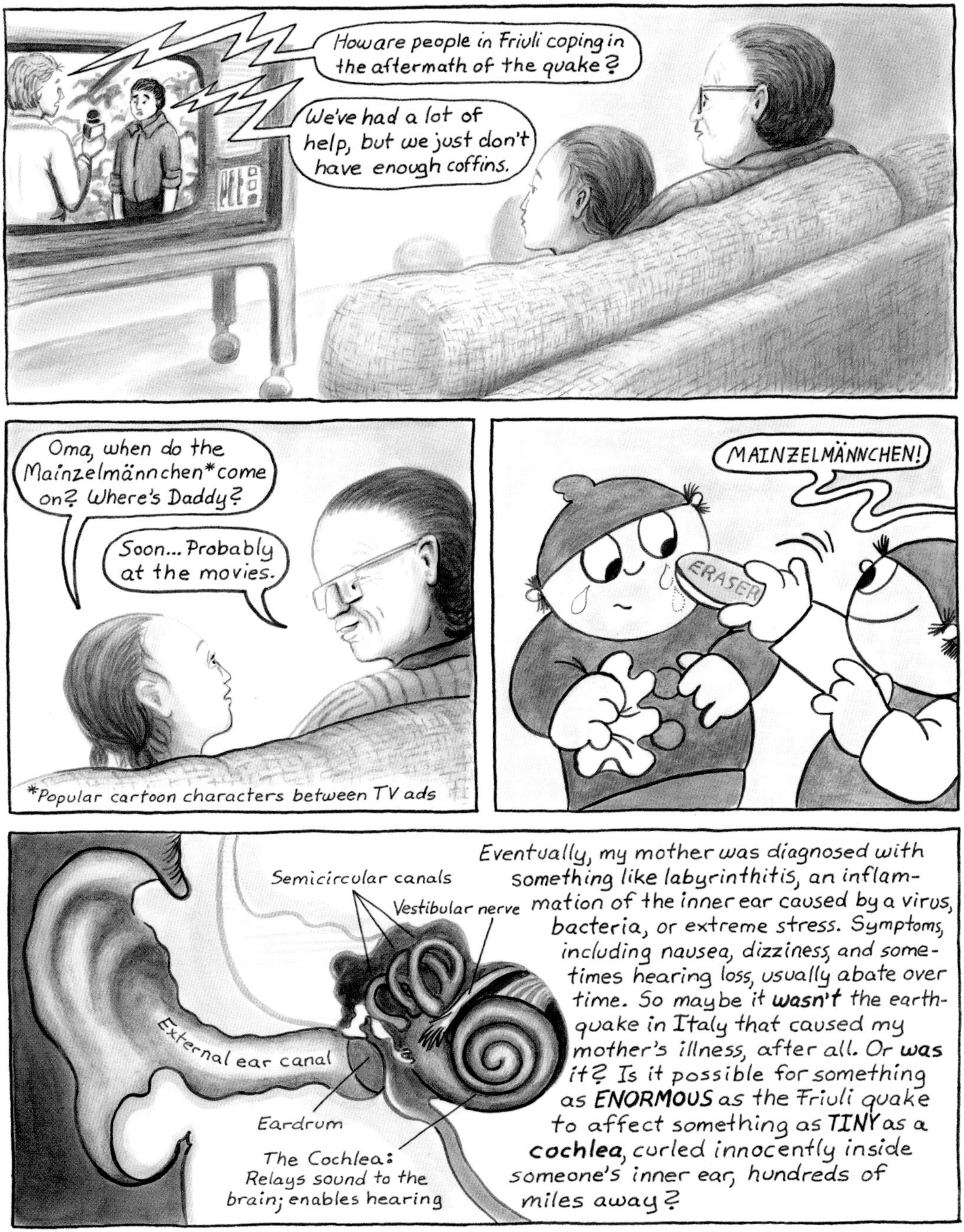
How are people in Friuli coping in the aftermath of the quake?
We've had a lot of help, but we just don't have enough coffins.
Oma, when do the Mainzelmännchen* come on? Where's Daddy?
Soon... Probably at the movies.
*Popular cartoon characters between TV ads
MAINZELMÄNNCHEN!
ERASER
Semicircular canals
Vestibular nerve
External ear canal
Eardrum
The Cochlea: Relays sound to the brain; enables hearing
Eventually, my mother was diagnosed with something like labyrinthitis, an inflammation of the inner ear caused by a virus, bacteria, or extreme stress. Symptoms, including nausea, dizziness, and sometimes hearing loss, usually abate over time. So maybe it **wasn't** the earthquake in Italy that caused my mother's illness, after all. Or **was** it? Is it possible for something as **ENORMOUS** as the Friuli quake to affect something as **TINY** as a **cochlea**, curled innocently inside someone's inner ear, hundreds of miles away?

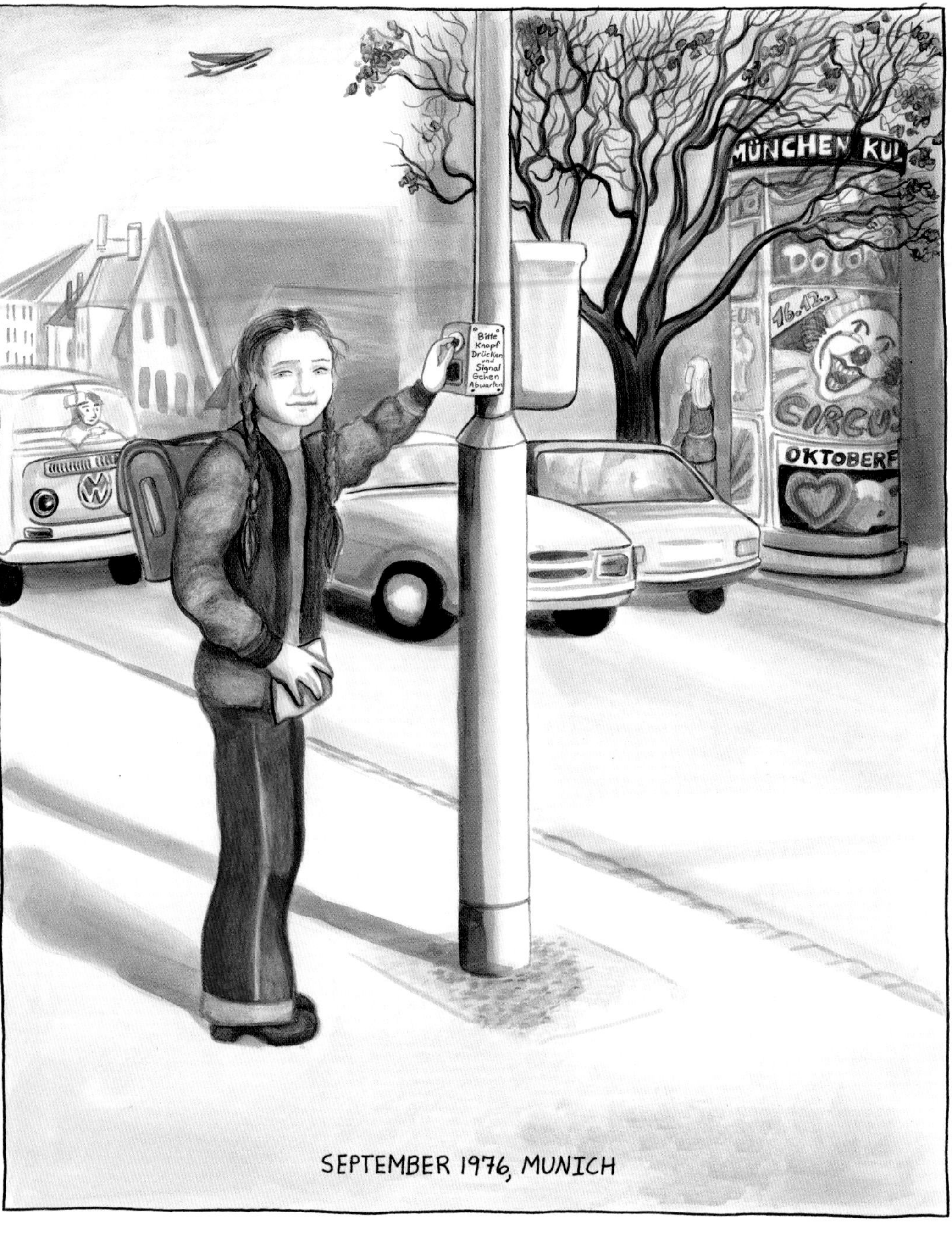
Bitte Knopf Drücken und Signal Gehen Abwarten
MÜNCHEN KUL
16.12.
CIRCUS
OKTOBERF
SEPTEMBER 1976, MUNICH

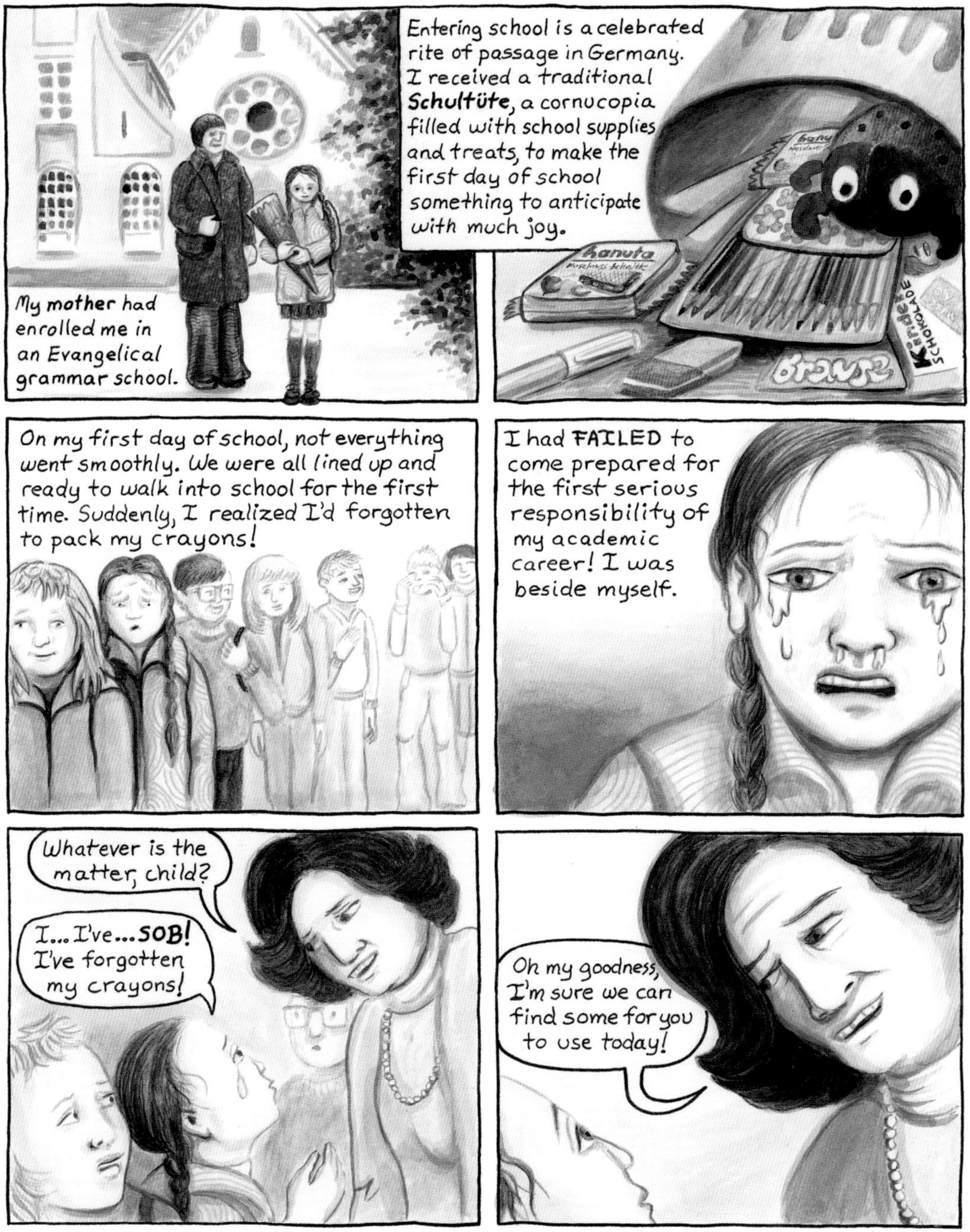
Entering school is a celebrated rite of passage in Germany. I received a traditional **Schultüte**, a cornucopia filled with school supplies and treats, to make the first day of school something to anticipate with much joy.
My **mother** had enrolled me in an Evangelical grammar school.
hanuta
Kinder SCHOKOLADE
brause
On my first day of school, not everything went smoothly. We were all lined up and ready to walk into school for the first time. Suddenly, I realized I'd forgotten to pack my crayons!
I had **FAILED** to come prepared for the first serious responsibility of my academic career! I was beside myself.
Whatever is the matter, child?
I... I've... **SOB**! I've forgotten my crayons!
Oh my goodness, I'm sure we can find some for you to use today!

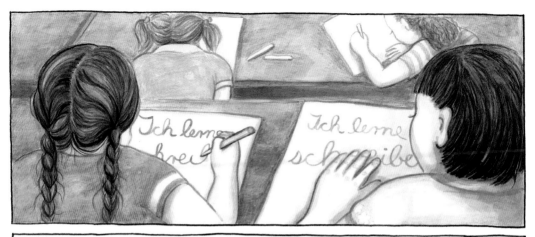

Ich lerne
Ich lerne
Despite the rough start, I was soon able to write, and to follow Heiner and Hanni and their dog Waldi on their happy adventures in our first-grade reading book.
Heiner und Hanni lernen lesen
By Christmas, I could read just about anything.

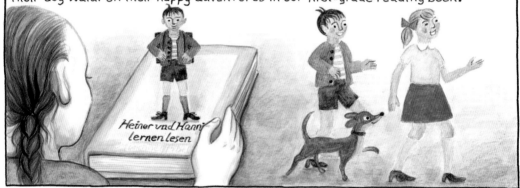

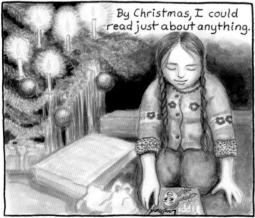

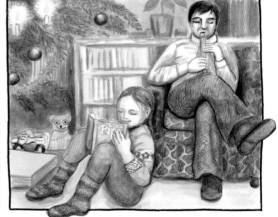

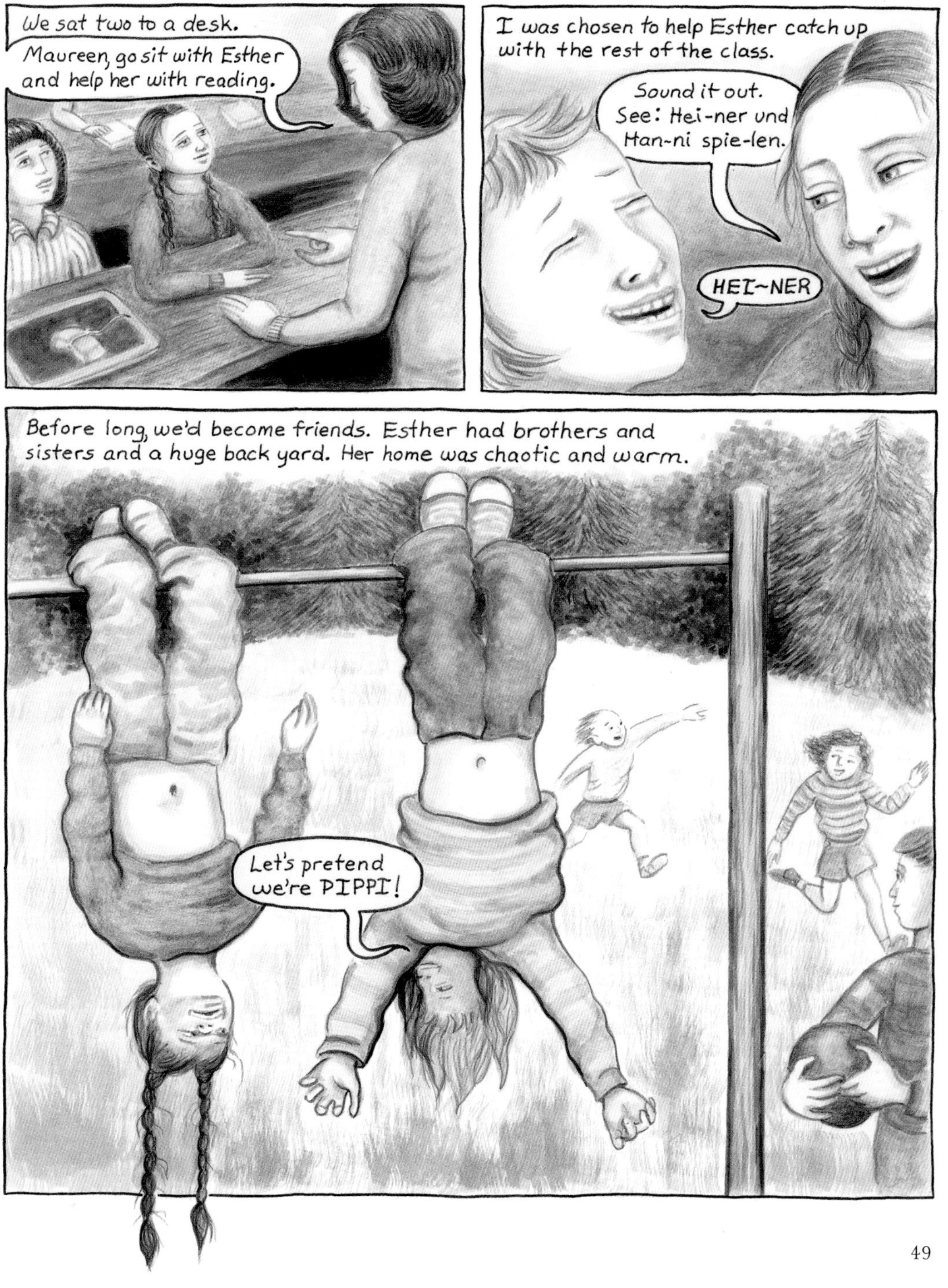
We sat two to a desk.
Maureen, go sit with Esther and help her with reading.
I was chosen to help Esther catch up with the rest of the class.
Sound it out. See: Hei-ner und Han-ni spie-len.
HEI~NER
Before long, we'd become friends. Esther had brothers and sisters and a huge back yard. Her home was chaotic and warm.
Let's pretend we're PIPPI!

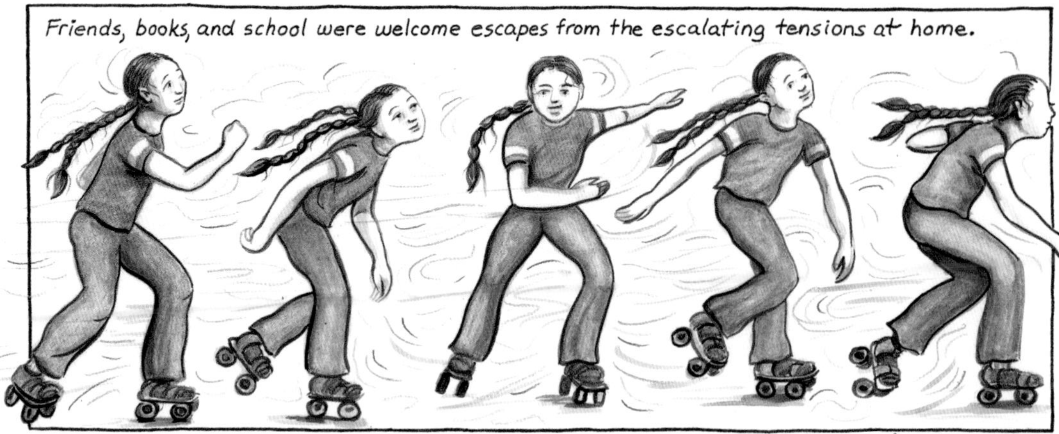
Friends, books, and school were welcome escapes from the escalating tensions at home.

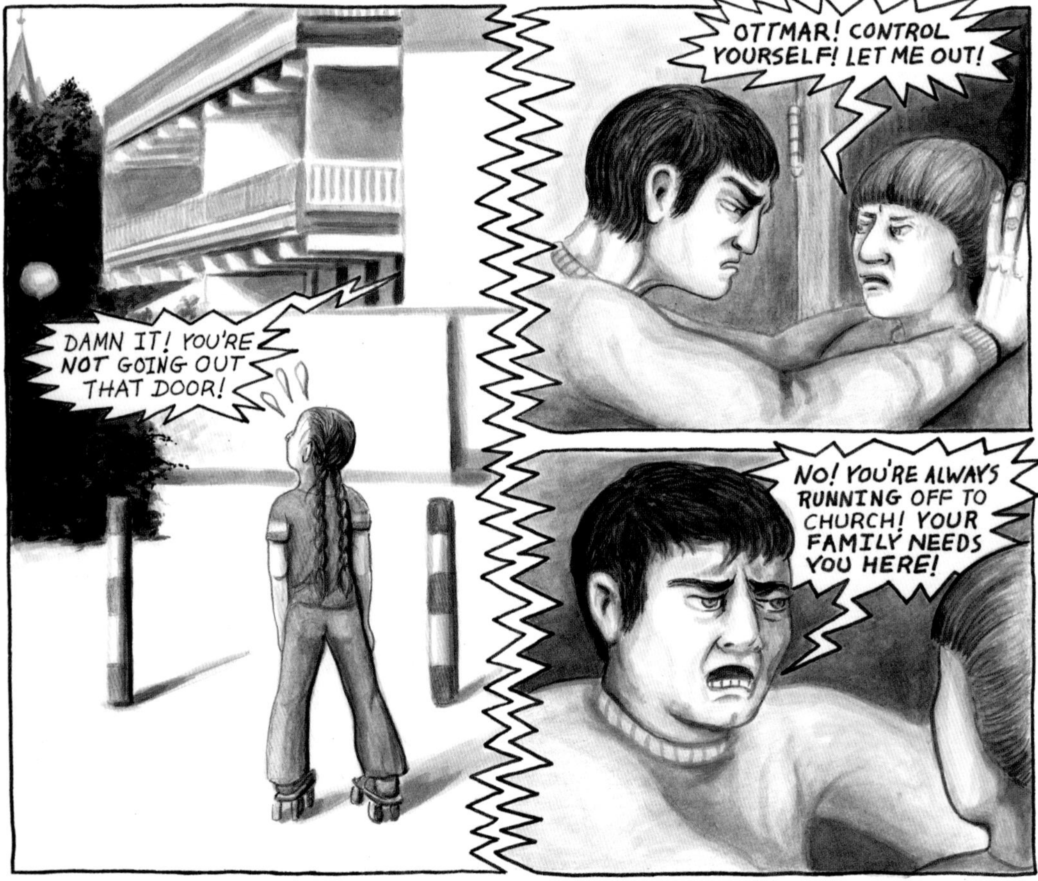
DAMN IT! YOU'RE NOT GOING OUT THAT DOOR!
OTTMAR! CONTROL YOURSELF! LET ME OUT!
NO! YOU'RE ALWAYS RUNNING OFF TO CHURCH! YOUR FAMILY NEEDS YOU HERE!

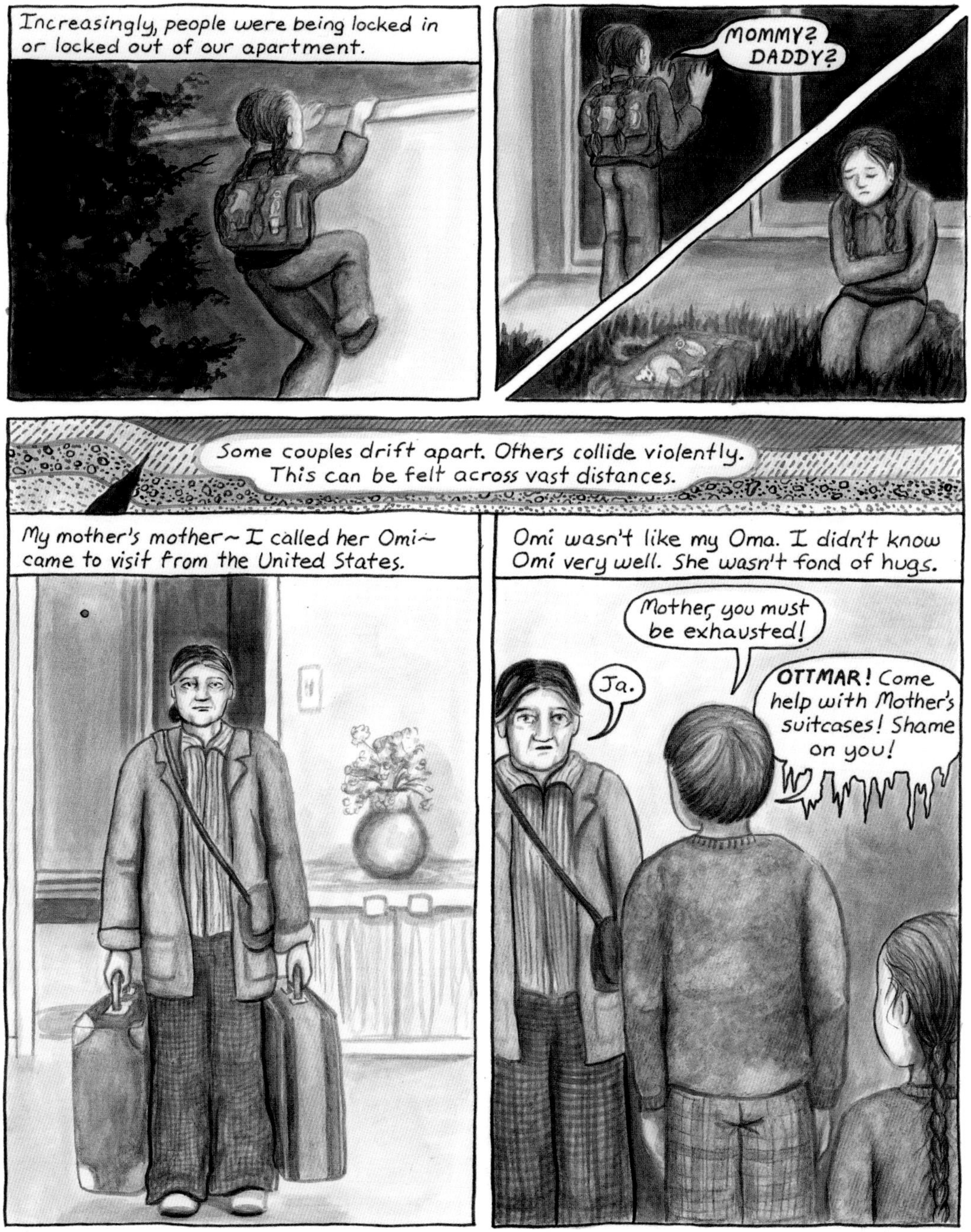
Increasingly, people were being locked in or locked out of our apartment.
MOMMY?
DADDY?
Some couples drift apart. Others collide violently. This can be felt across vast distances.
My mother's mother~ I called her Omi~ came to visit from the United States.
Omi wasn't like my Oma. I didn't know Omi very well. She wasn't fond of hugs.
Mother, you must be exhausted!
Ja.
OTTMAR! Come help with Mother's suitcases! Shame on you!

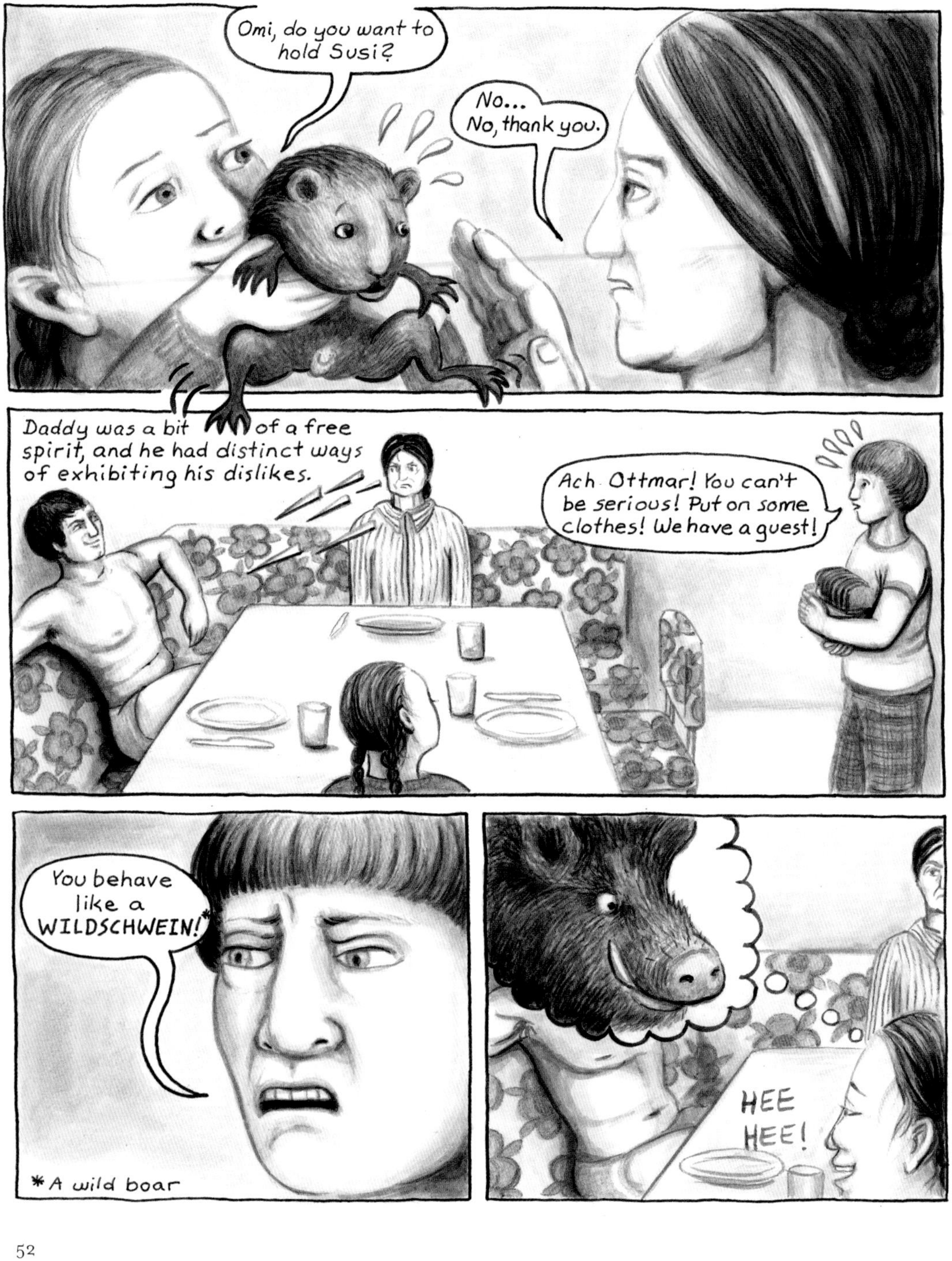
Omi, do you want to hold Susi?
No... No, thank you.
Daddy was a bit of a free spirit, and he had distinct ways of exhibiting his dislikes.
Ach Ottmar! You can't be serious! Put on some clothes! We have a guest!
You behave like a WILDSCHWEIN!*
*A wild boar
HEE HEE!

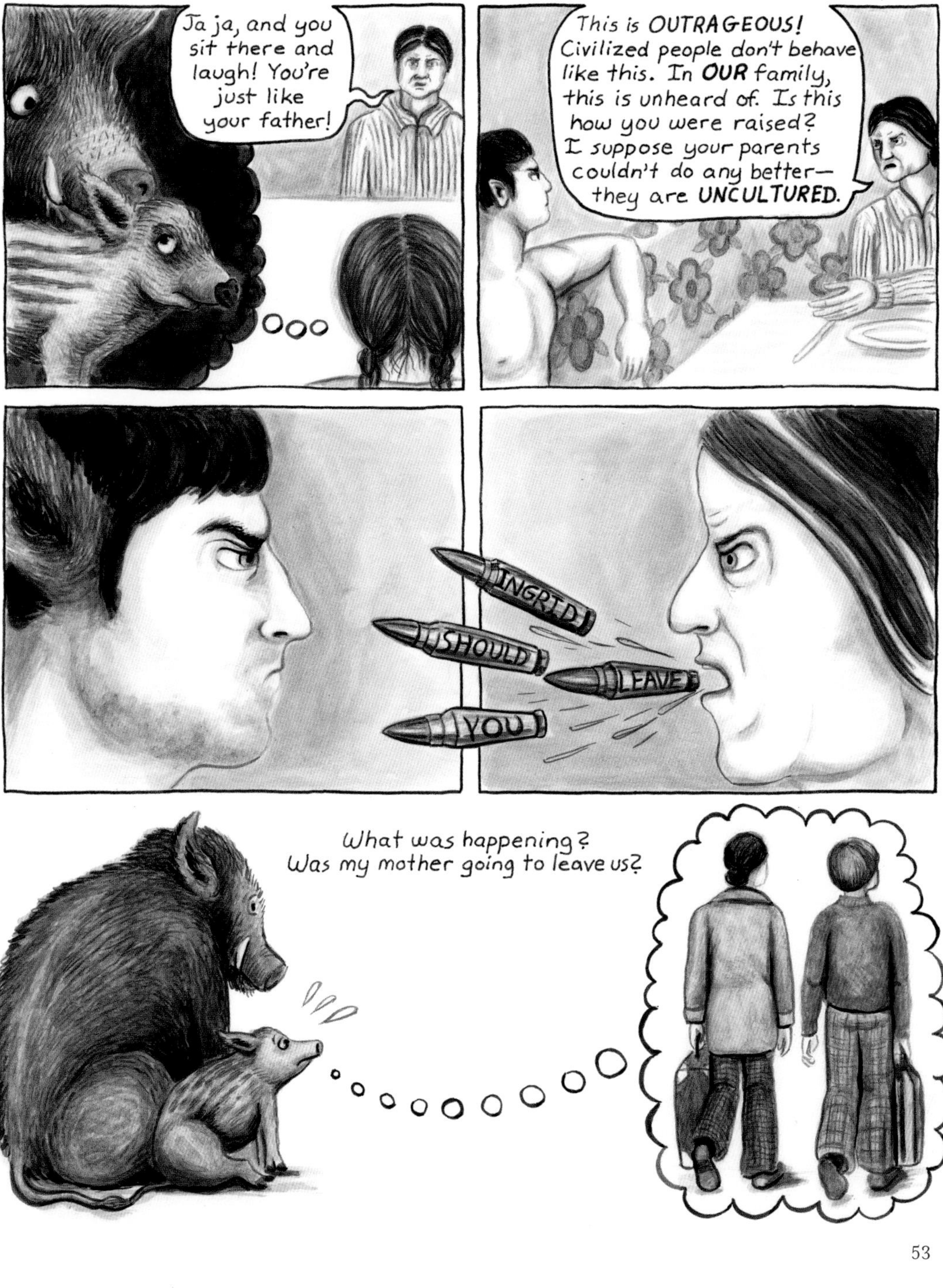
Ja ja, and you sit there and laugh! You're just like your father!
This is OUTRAGEOUS! Civilized people don't behave like this. In OUR family, this is unheard of. Is this how you were raised? I suppose your parents couldn't do any better— they are UNCULTURED.
INGRID
SHOULD
LEAVE
YOU
What was happening? Was my mother going to leave us?

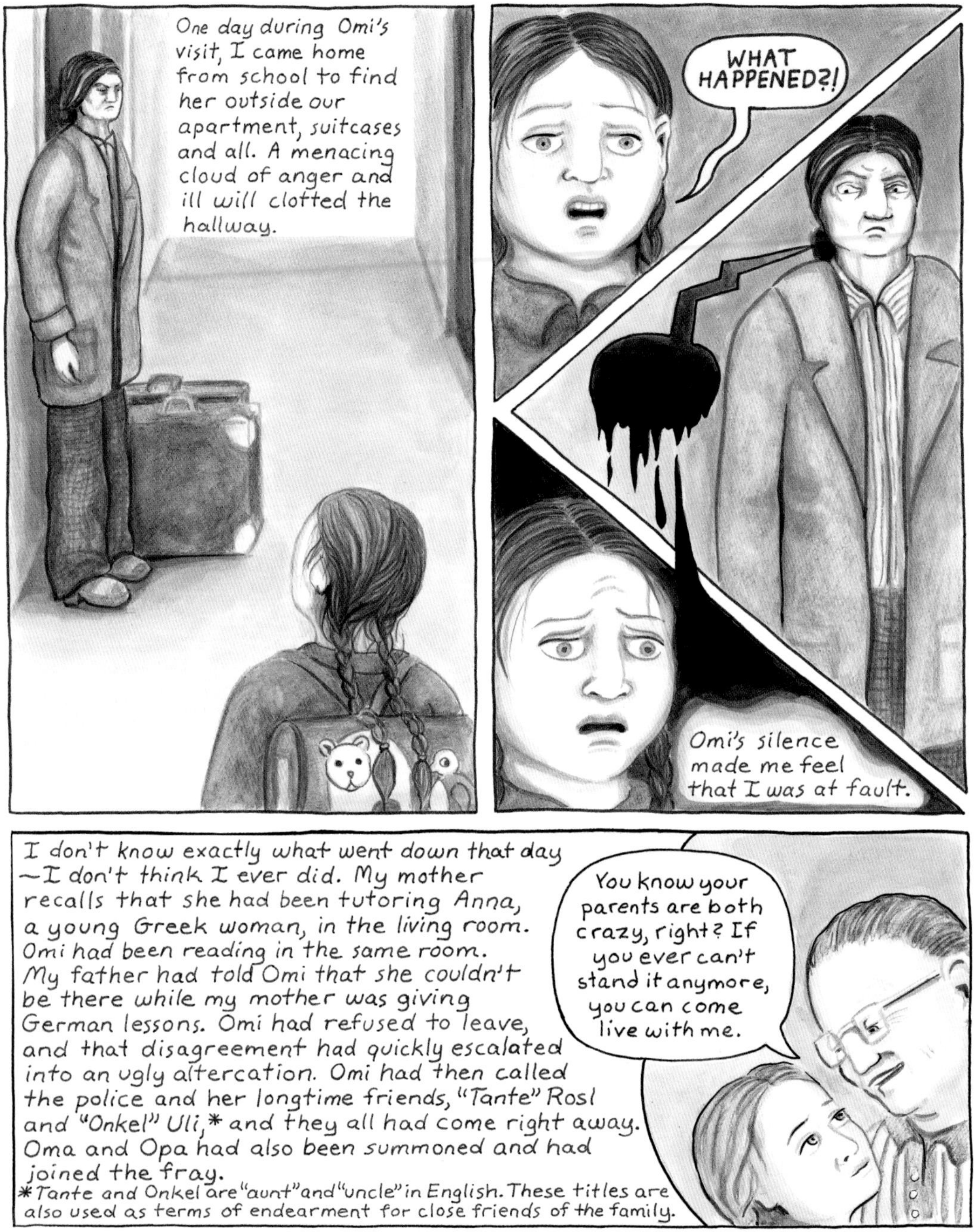
One day during Omi's visit, I came home from school to find her outside our apartment, suitcases and all. A menacing cloud of anger and ill will clotted the hallway.
WHAT HAPPENED?!
Omi's silence made me feel that I was at fault.
I don't know exactly what went down that day —I don't think I ever did. My mother recalls that she had been tutoring Anna, a young Greek woman, in the living room. Omi had been reading in the same room. My father had told Omi that she couldn't be there while my mother was giving German lessons. Omi had refused to leave, and that disagreement had quickly escalated into an ugly altercation. Omi had then called the police and her longtime friends, "Tante" Rosl and "Onkel" Uli,* and they all had come right away. Oma and Opa had also been summoned and had joined the fray.
*Tante and Onkel are "aunt" and "uncle" in English. These titles are also used as terms of endearment for close friends of the family.
You know your parents are both crazy, right? If you ever can't stand it anymore, you can come live with me.

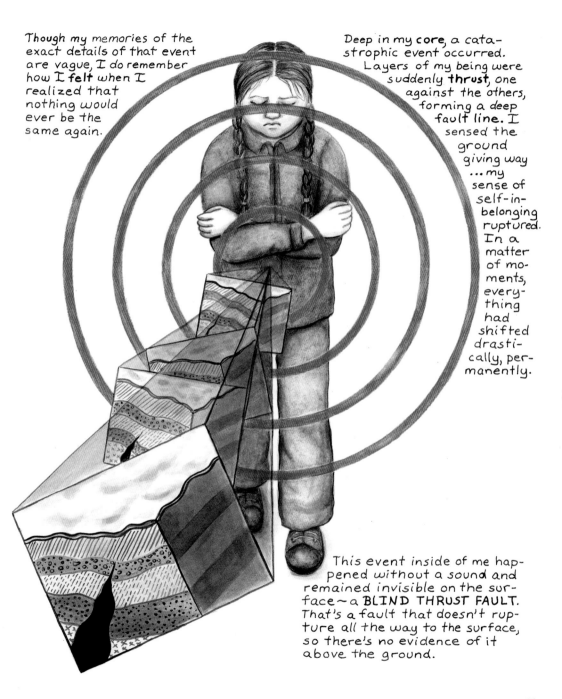

Though my memories of the exact details of that event are vague, I do remember how **I felt** when I realized that nothing would ever be the same again.

Deep in my **core**, a catastrophic event occurred. Layers of my being were suddenly **thrust**, one against the others, forming a deep fault line. I sensed the ground giving way ...my sense of self-in-belonging ruptured. In a matter of moments, everything had shifted drastically, permanently.

This event inside of me happened without a sound and remained invisible on the surface~a **BLIND THRUST FAULT.** That's a fault that doesn't rupture all the way to the surface, so there's no evidence of it above the ground.

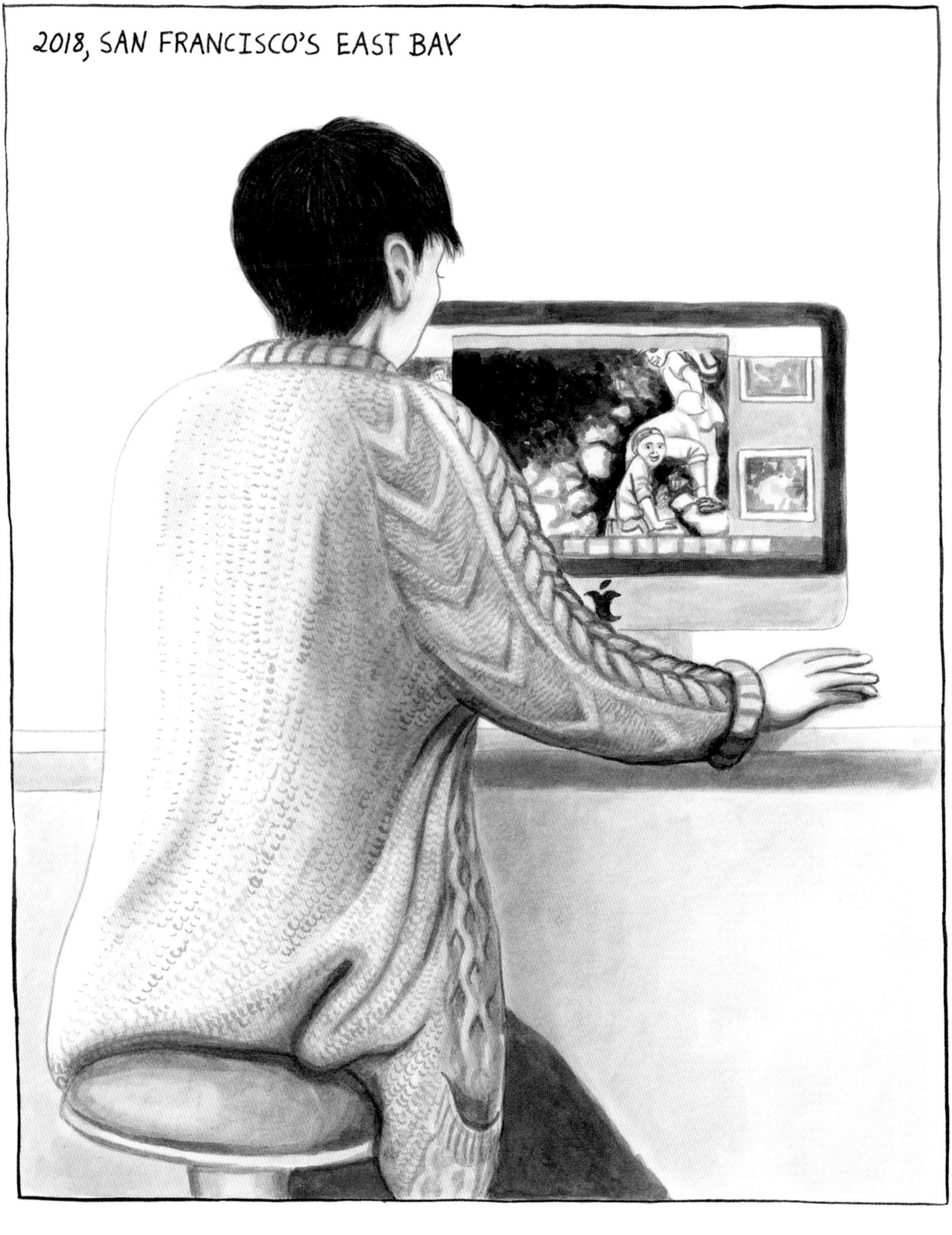
2018, SAN FRANCISCO'S EAST BAY

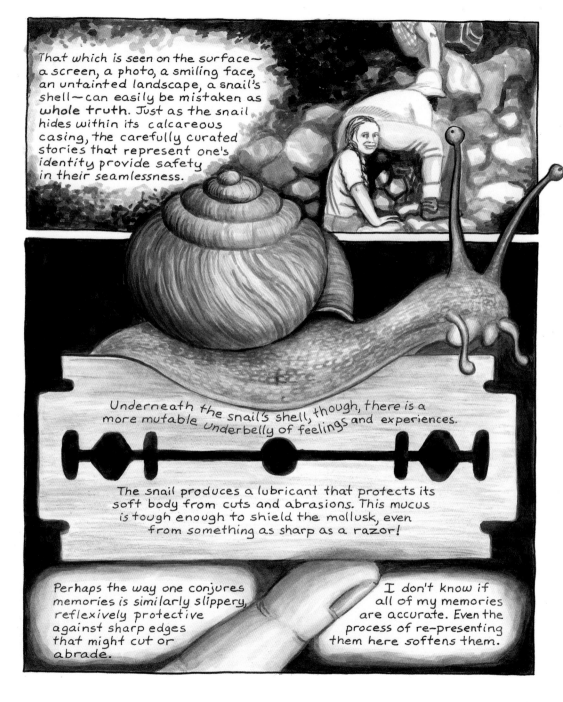

That which is seen on the surface—a screen, a photo, a smiling face, an untainted landscape, a snail's shell—can easily be mistaken as **whole truth**. Just as the snail hides within its calcareous casing, the carefully curated stories that represent one's identity provide safety in their seamlessness.

Underneath the snail's shell, though, there is a more mutable underbelly of feelings and experiences.

The snail produces a lubricant that protects its soft body from cuts and abrasions. This mucus is tough enough to shield the mollusk, even from something as sharp as a razor!

Perhaps the way one conjures memories is similarly slippery, reflexively protective against sharp edges that might cut or abrade.

I don't know if all of my memories are accurate. Even the process of re-presenting them here softens them.

Snails engage in an extensive and intricate mating dance that can last up to 12 hours.

A snail appeared to me recently in a dream with a message:

After giving me this information, my snail went into a state of **ABJECT SHOCK**, as she suddenly realized that she had a genetic condition which would cause her to become

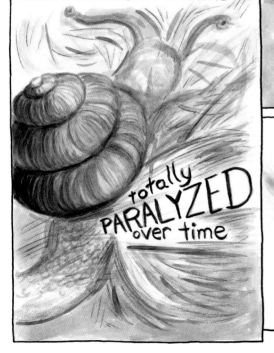

totally PARALYZED over time

We hold distinct sensations and memories in different areas of our soft bodies. When we mate, we transmit those memories by rubbing against one another. That's how we pass our stories on to the next generations of snails.

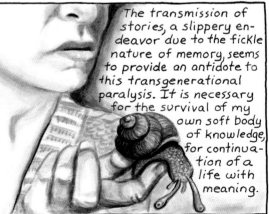

The transmission of stories, a slippery endeavor due to the fickle nature of memory, seems to provide an antidote to this transgenerational paralysis. It is necessary for the survival of my own soft body of knowledge, for continuation of a life with meaning.

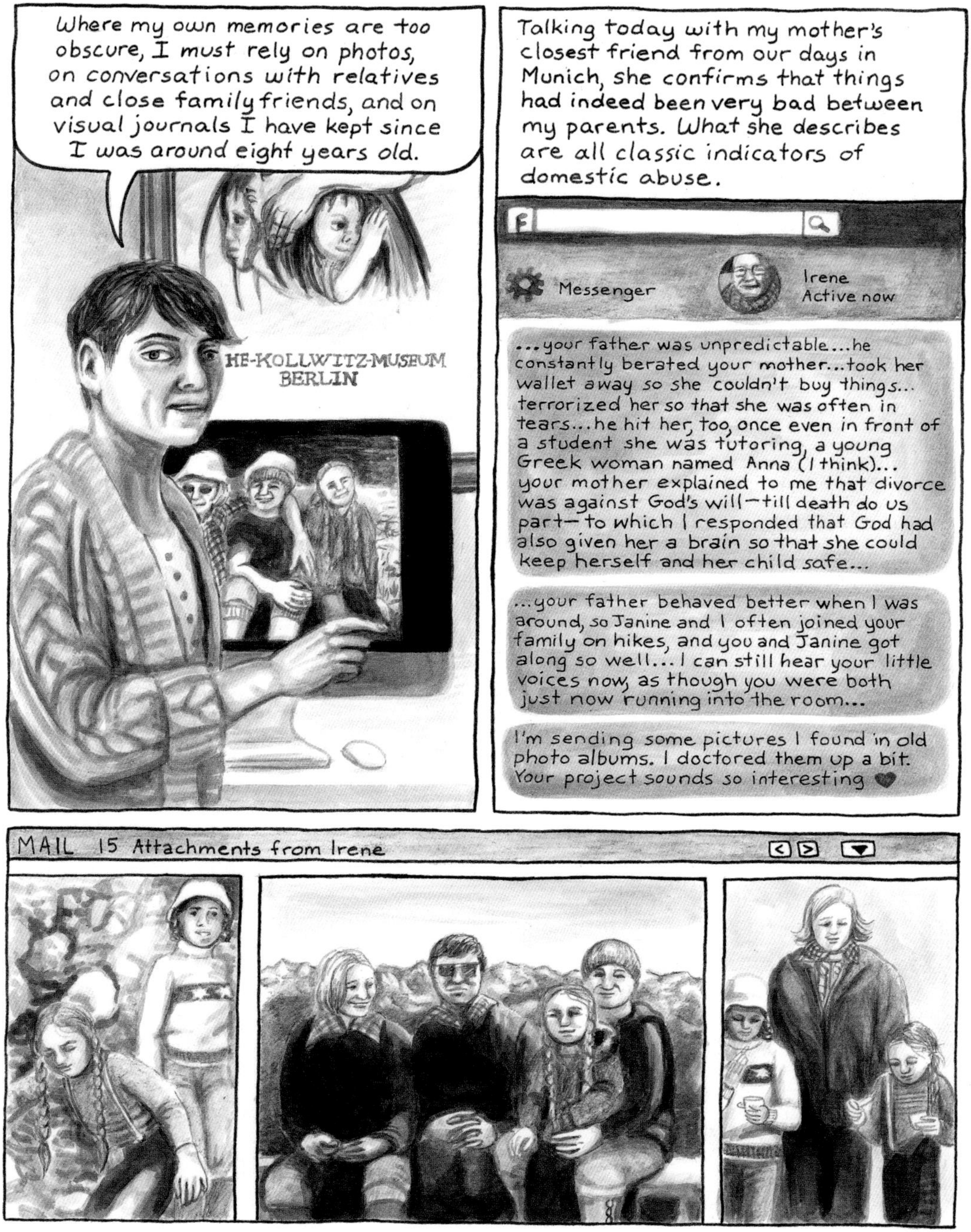

Where my own memories are too obscure, I must rely on photos, on conversations with relatives and close family friends, and on visual journals I have kept since I was around eight years old.
HE-KOLLWITZ-MUSEUM BERLIN
Talking today with my mother's closest friend from our days in Munich, she confirms that things had indeed been very bad between my parents. What she describes are all classic indicators of domestic abuse.
Messenger
Irene
Active now
...your father was unpredictable...he constantly berated your mother...took her wallet away so she couldn't buy things... terrorized her so that she was often in tears...he hit her, too, once even in front of a student she was tutoring, a young Greek woman named Anna (I think)... your mother explained to me that divorce was against God's will—till death do us part—to which I responded that God had also given her a brain so that she could keep herself and her child safe...
...your father behaved better when I was around, so Janine and I often joined your family on hikes, and you and Janine got along so well... I can still hear your little voices now, as though you were both just now running into the room...
I'm sending some pictures I found in old photo albums. I doctored them up a bit. Your project sounds so interesting
MAIL 15 Attachments from Irene

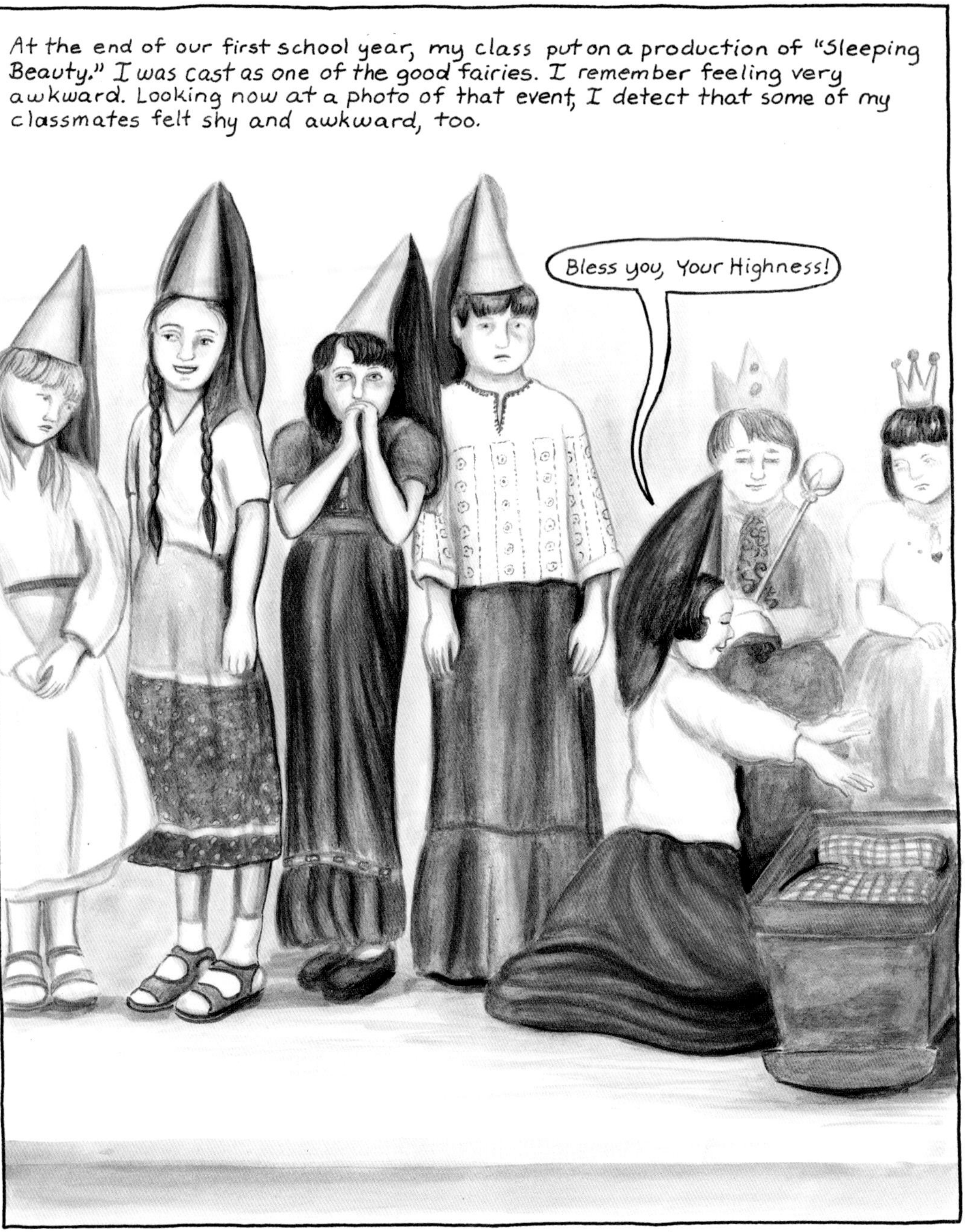
At the end of our first school year, my class put on a production of "Sleeping Beauty." I was cast as one of the good fairies. I remember feeling very awkward. Looking now at a photo of that event, I detect that some of my classmates felt shy and awkward, too.
Bless you, Your Highness!

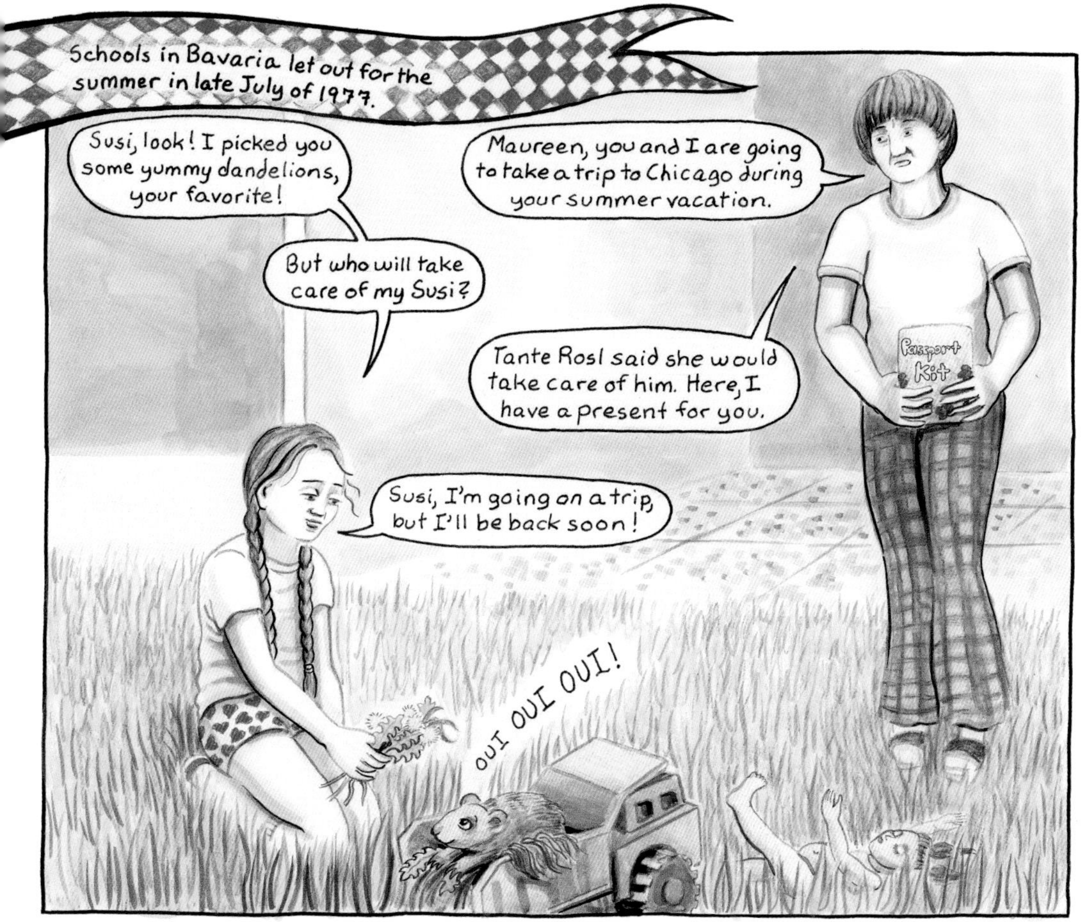
Schools in Bavaria let out for the summer in late July of 1977.
Susi, look! I picked you some yummy dandelions, your favorite!
But who will take care of my Susi?
Maureen, you and I are going to take a trip to Chicago during your summer vacation.
Tante Rosl said she would take care of him. Here, I have a present for you.
Passport Kit
Susi, I'm going on a trip, but I'll be back soon!
OUI OUI OUI!

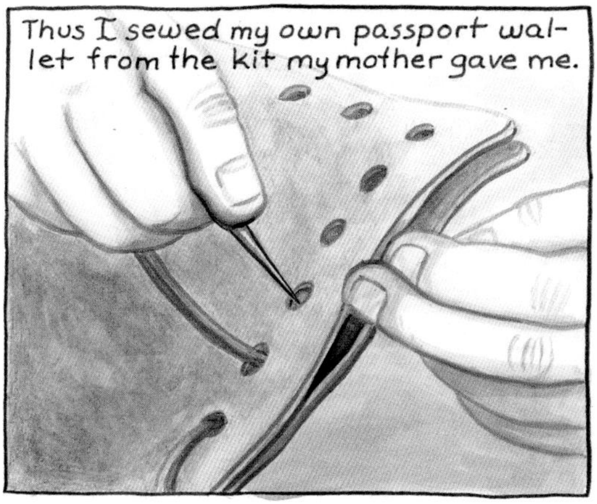
Thus I sewed my own passport wallet from the kit my mother gave me.

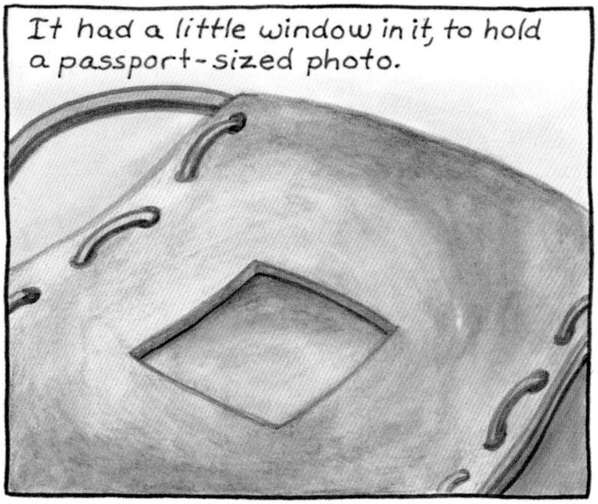
It had a little window in it, to hold a passport-sized photo.

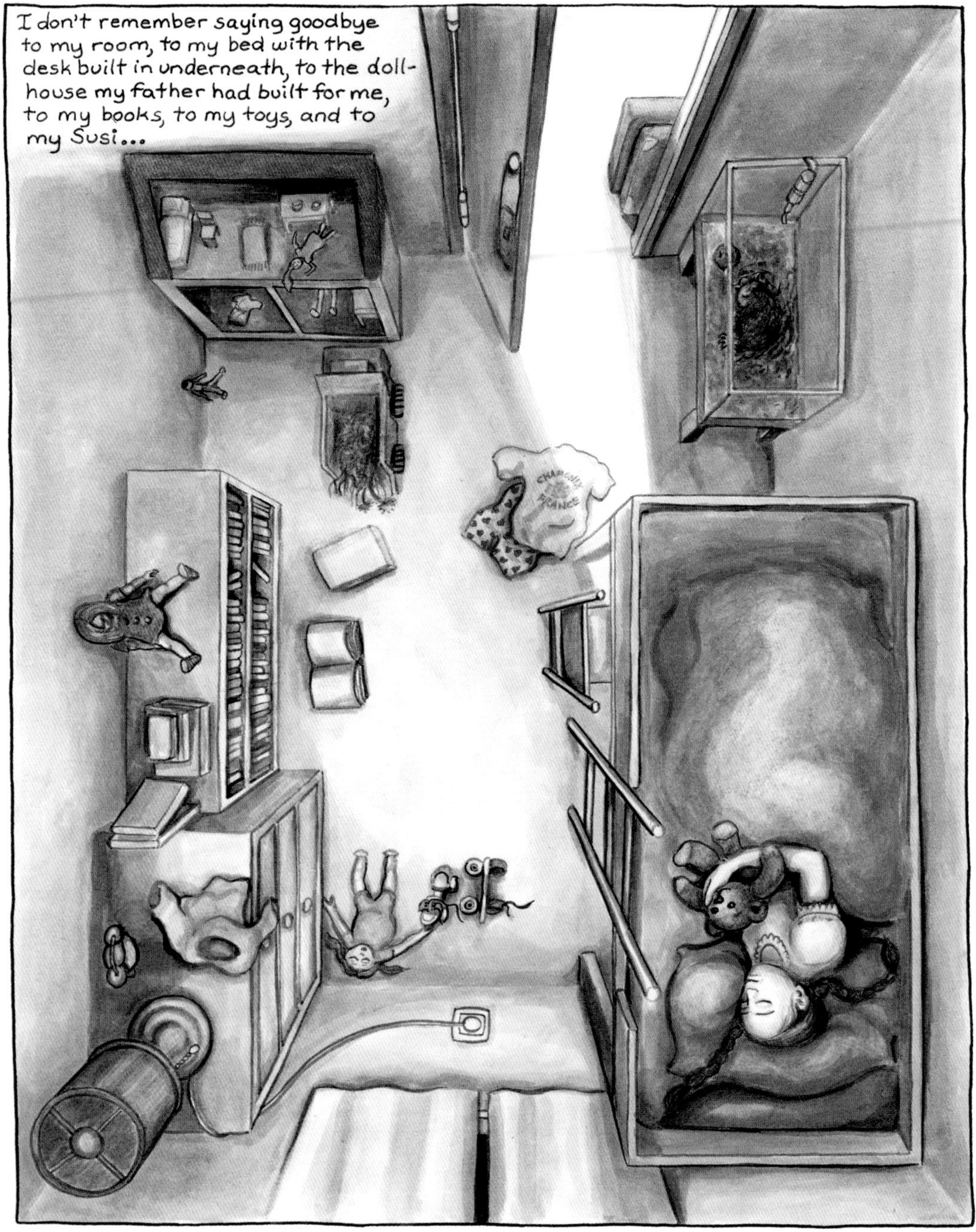
I don't remember saying goodbye to my room, to my bed with the desk built in underneath, to the doll-house my father had built for me, to my books, to my toys, and to my Susi...

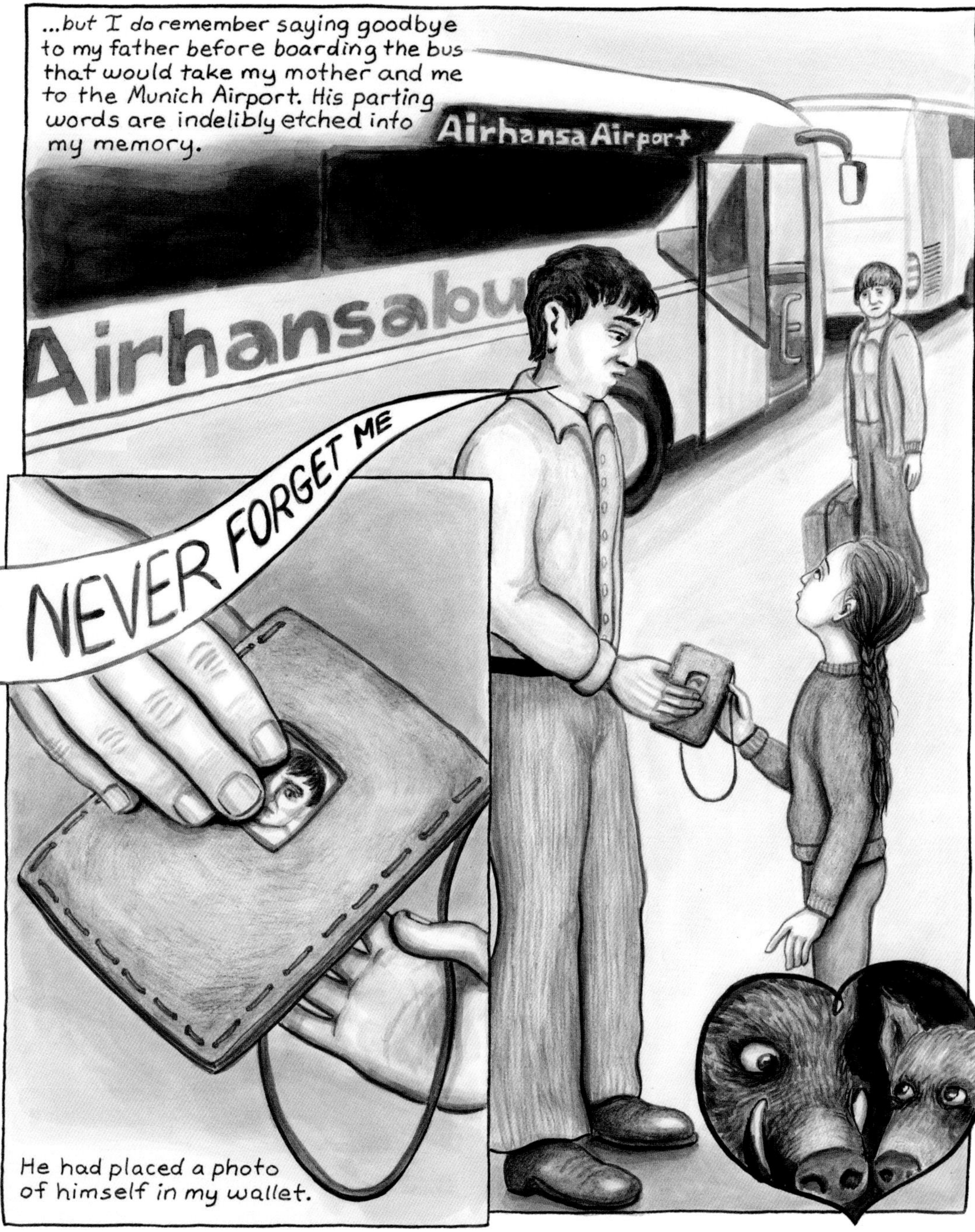
...but I do remember saying goodbye to my father before boarding the bus that would take my mother and me to the Munich Airport. His parting words are indelibly etched into my memory.
Airhansa Airport
Airhansabu
NEVER FORGET ME
He had placed a photo of himself in my wallet.

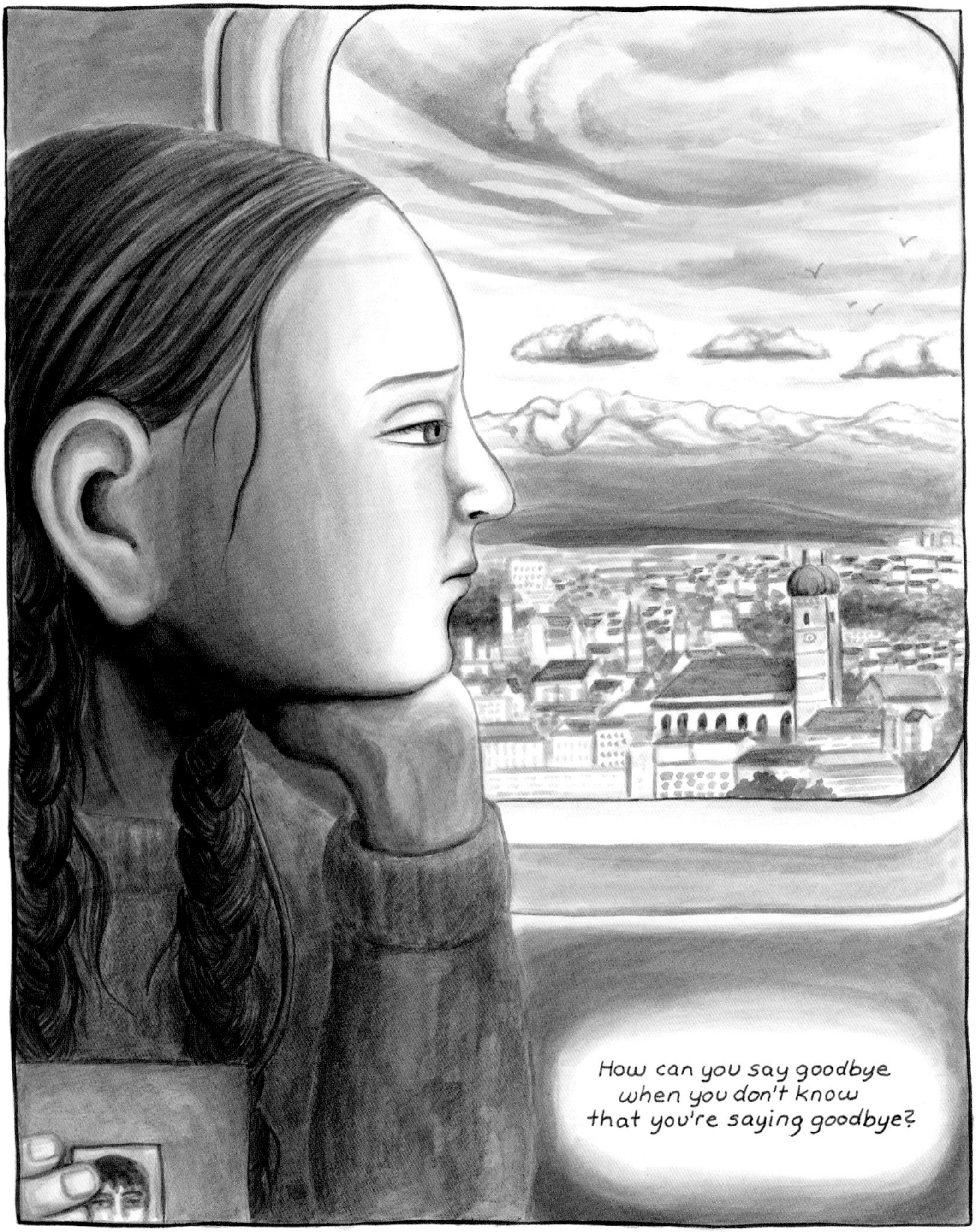
How can you say goodbye
when you don't know
that you're saying goodbye?

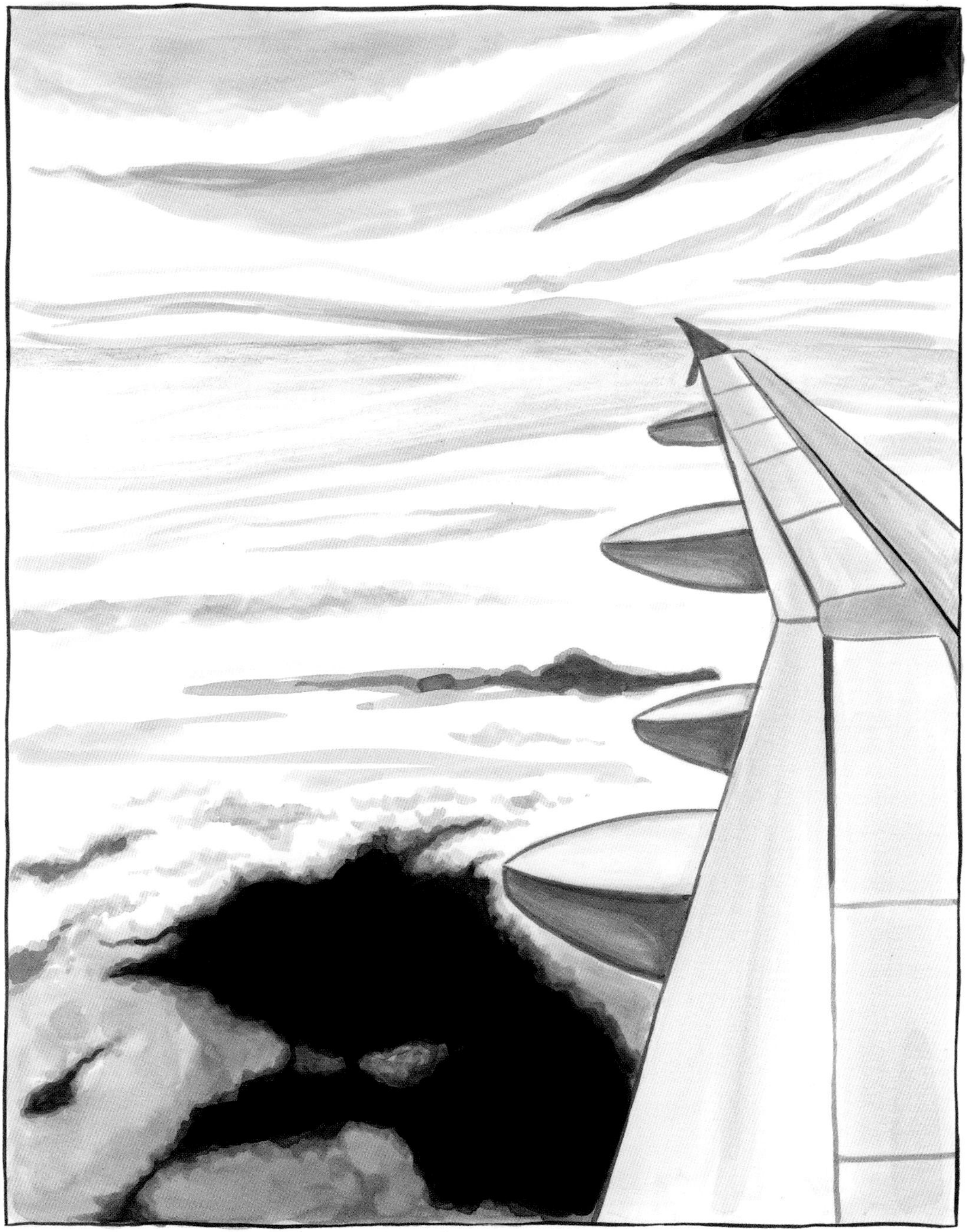

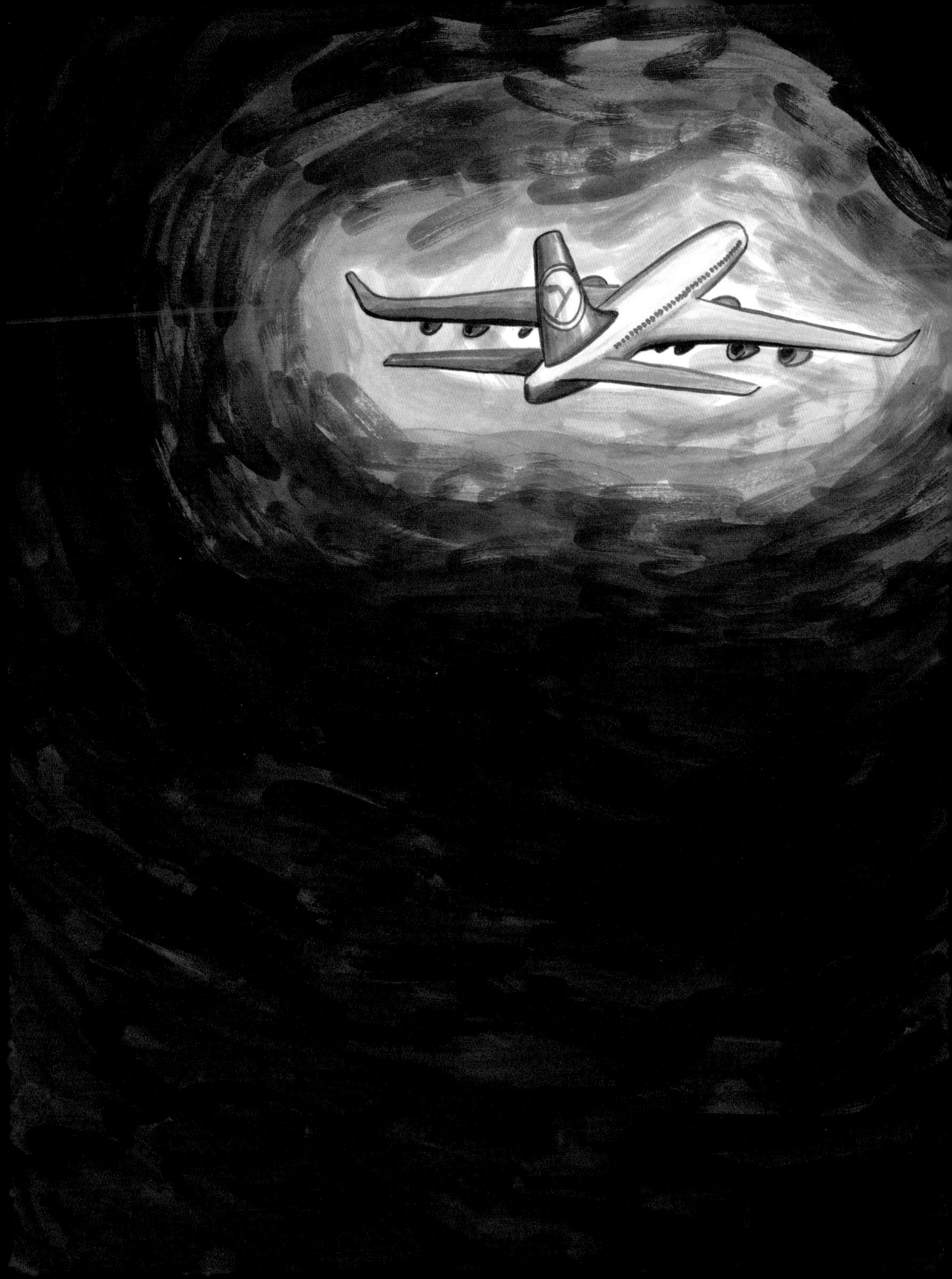

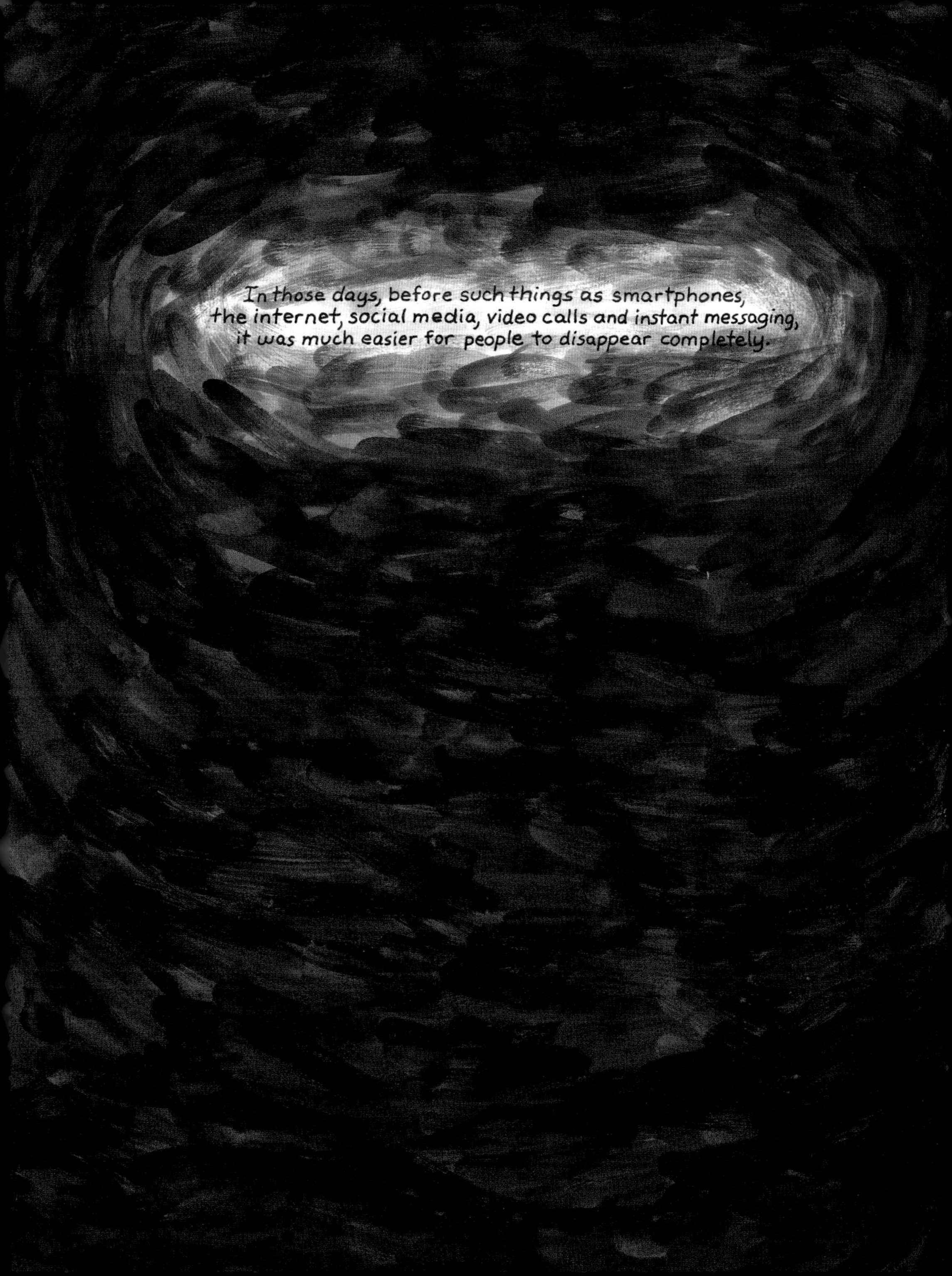
In those days, before such things as smartphones, the internet, social media, video calls and instant messaging, it was much easier for people to disappear completely.

Hear that lonesome whippoorwill,
He sounds too blue to fly.
The midnight train is whining low,
I'm so lonesome I could cry.

~Hank Williams

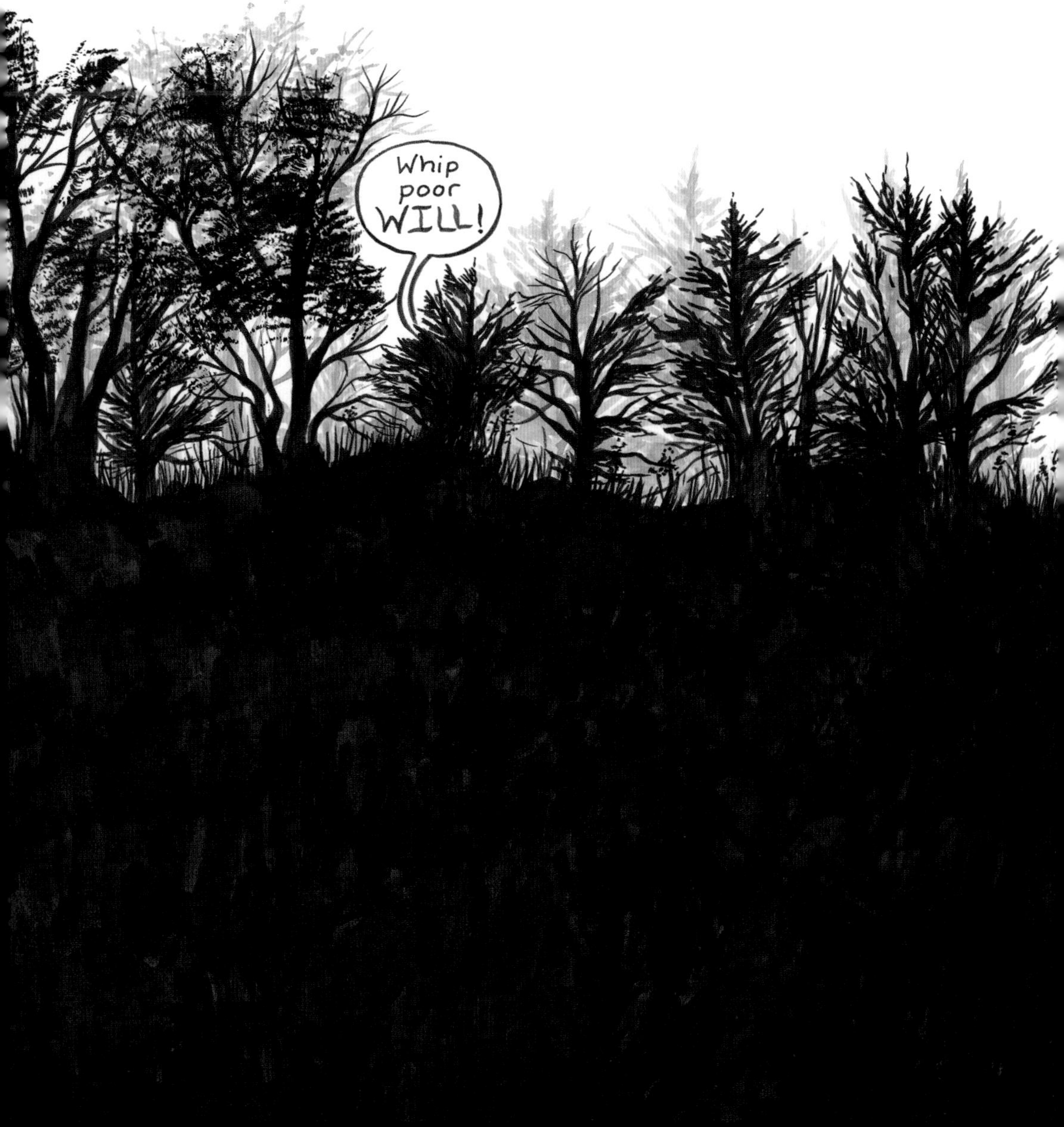
Whip poor WILL!

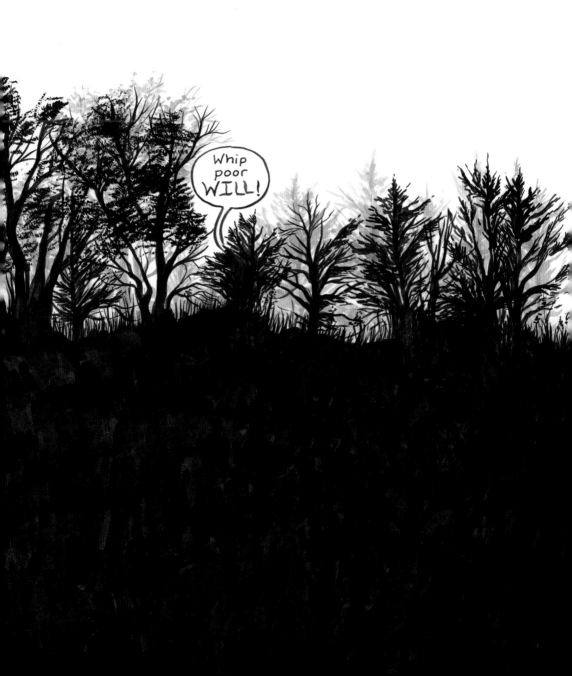

Part Two

WHIPPOORWILL'S REQUIEM

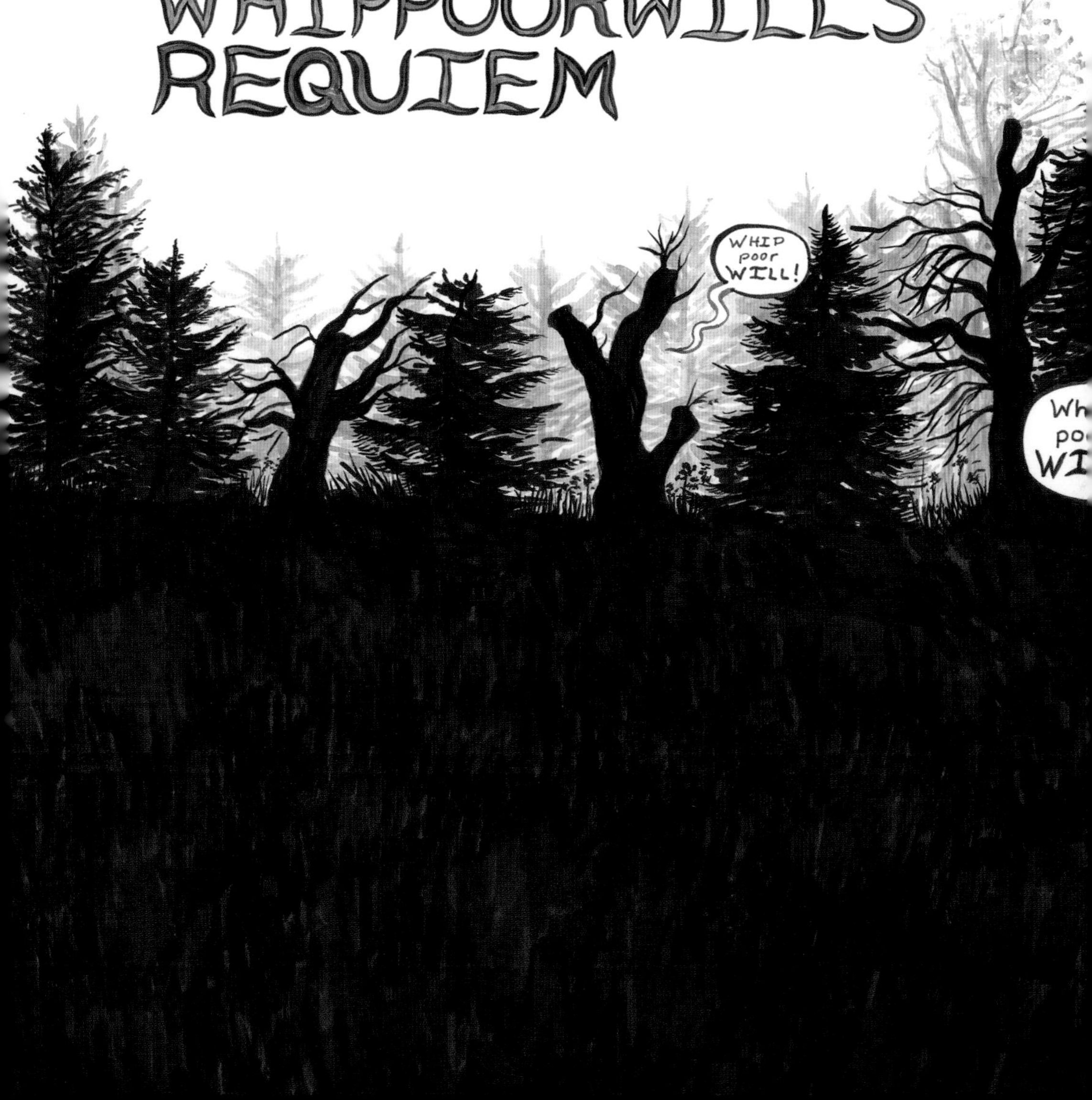
WHIP poor WILL!

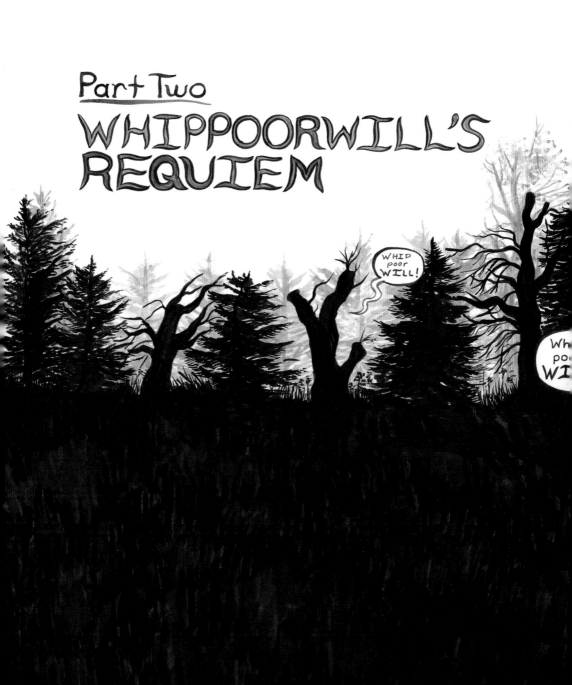

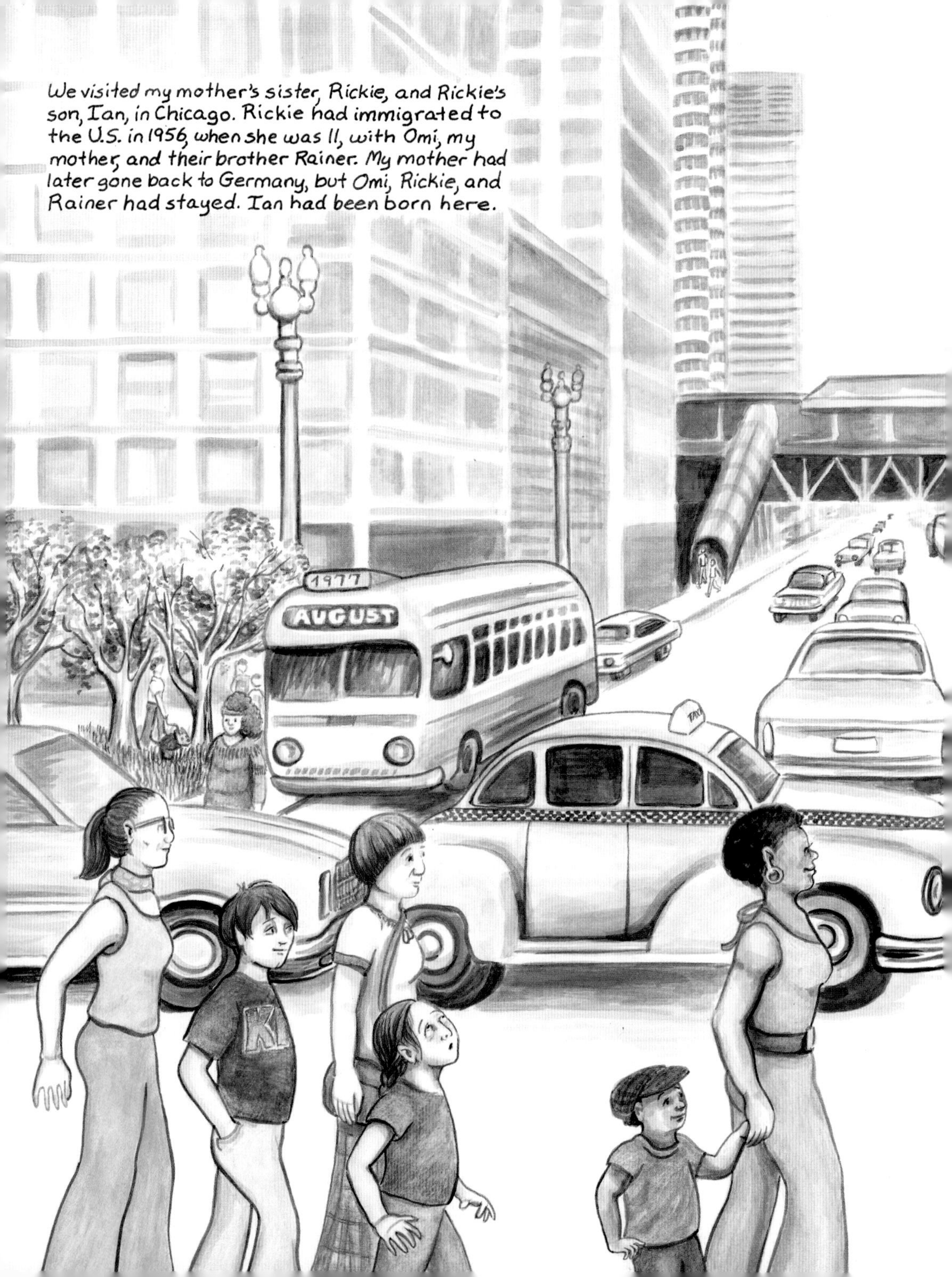
We visited my mother's sister, Rickie, and Rickie's son, Ian, in Chicago. Rickie had immigrated to the U.S. in 1956, when she was 11, with Omi, my mother, and their brother Rainer. My mother had later gone back to Germany, but Omi, Rickie, and Rainer had stayed. Ian had been born here.
1977
AUGUST

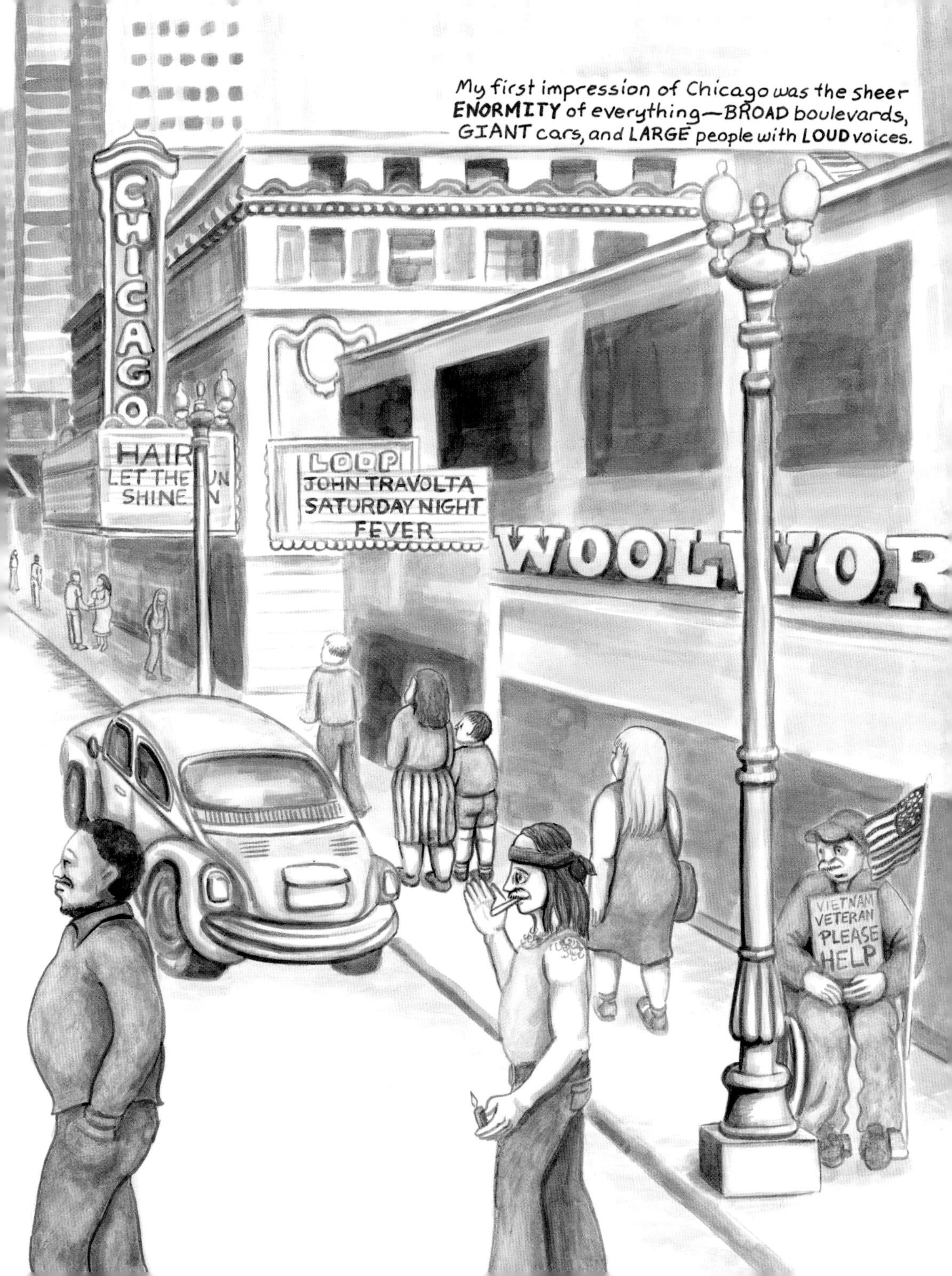
My first impression of Chicago was the sheer ENORMITY of everything—BROAD boulevards, GIANT cars, and LARGE people with LOUD voices.
CHICAGO
HAIR
LET THE UN
SHINE N
LOOP
JOHN TRAVOLTA
SATURDAY NIGHT
FEVER
WOOLWOR
VIETNAM VETERAN PLEASE HELP

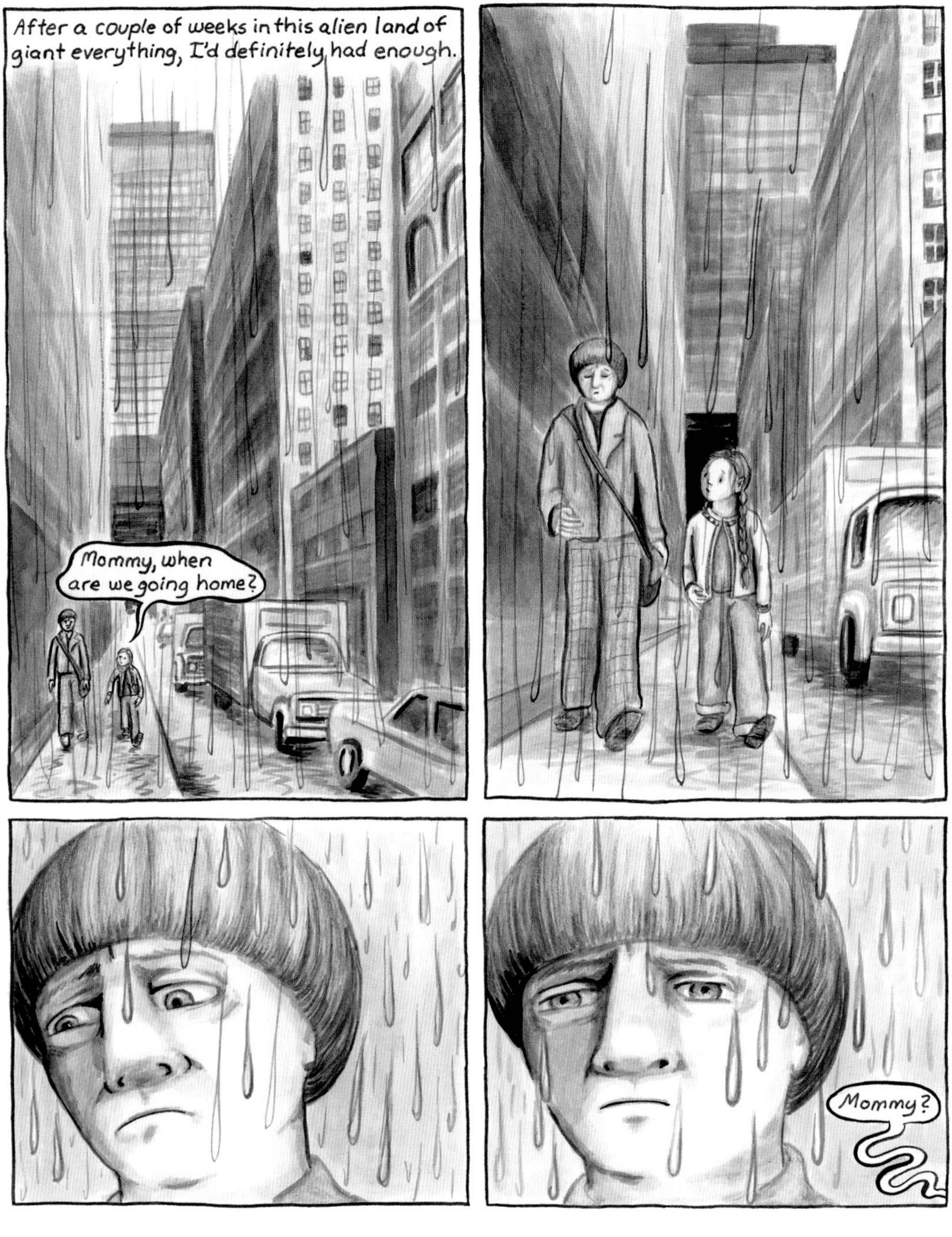
After a couple of weeks in this alien land of giant everything, I'd definitely had enough.
Mommy, when are we going home?
Mommy?

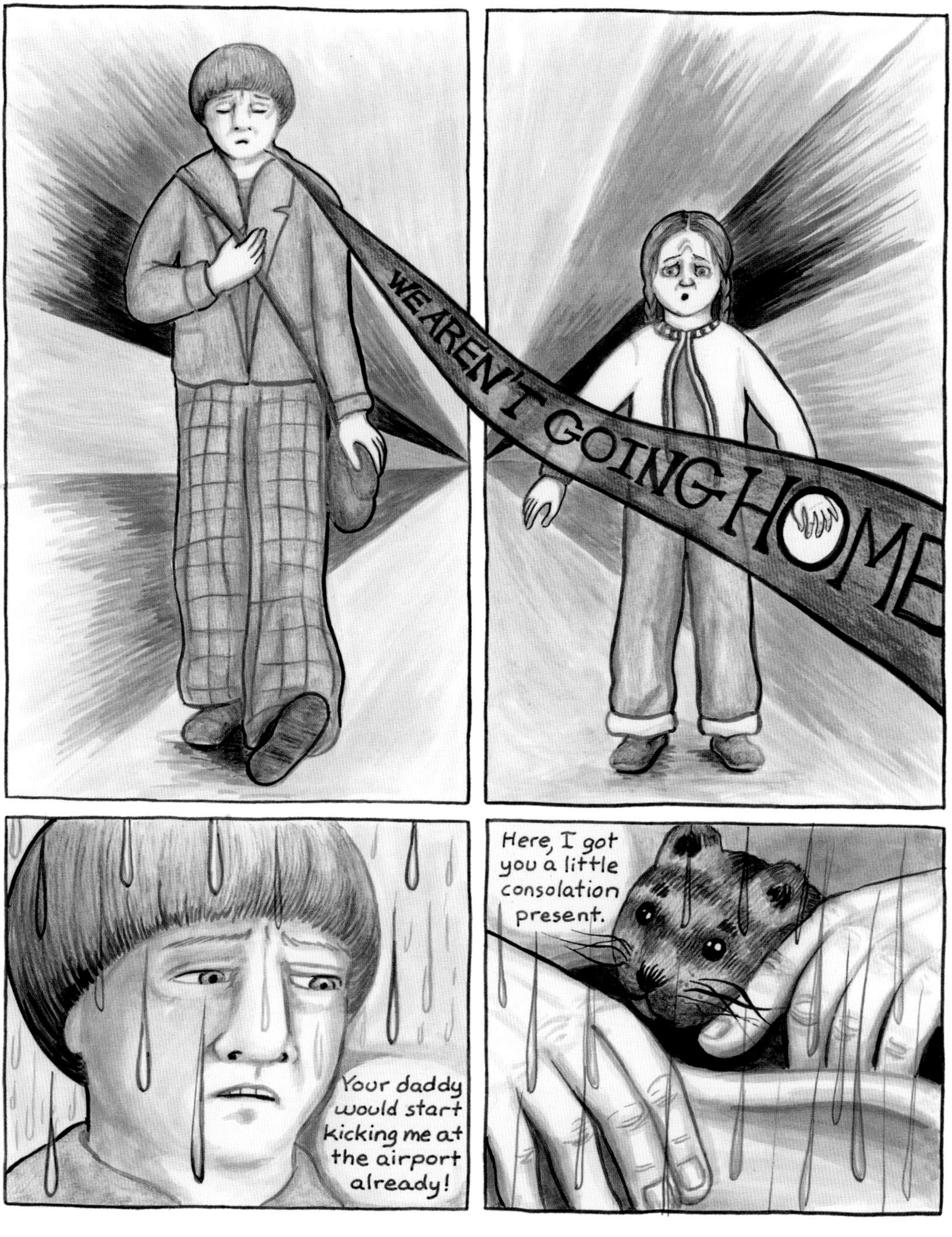
WE AREN'T GOING HOME
Your daddy would start kicking me at the airport already!
Here, I got you a little consolation present.

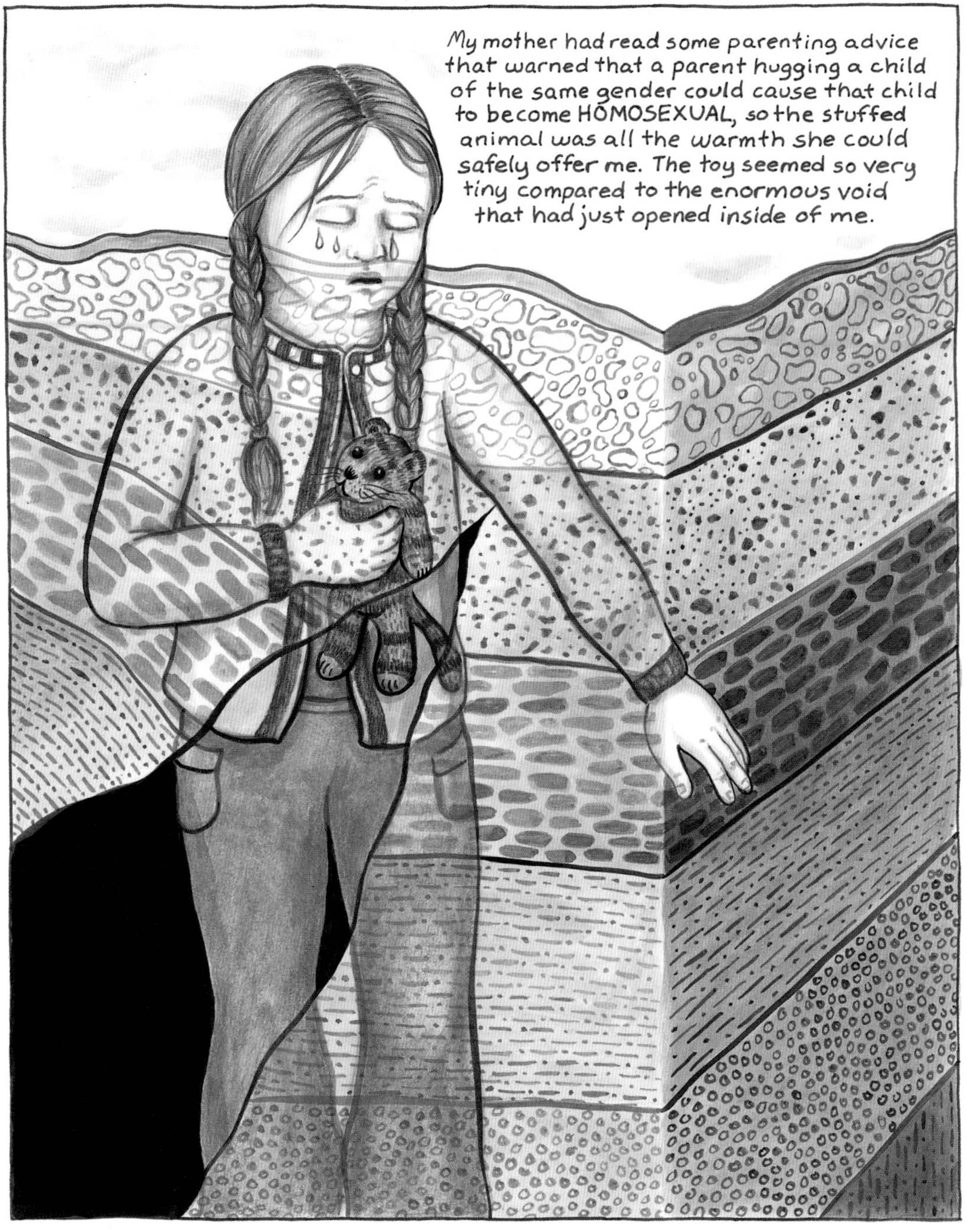
My mother had read some parenting advice
that warned that a parent hugging a child
of the same gender could cause that child
to become HOMOSEXUAL, so the stuffed
animal was all the warmth she could
safely offer me. The toy seemed so very
tiny compared to the enormous void
that had just opened inside of me.

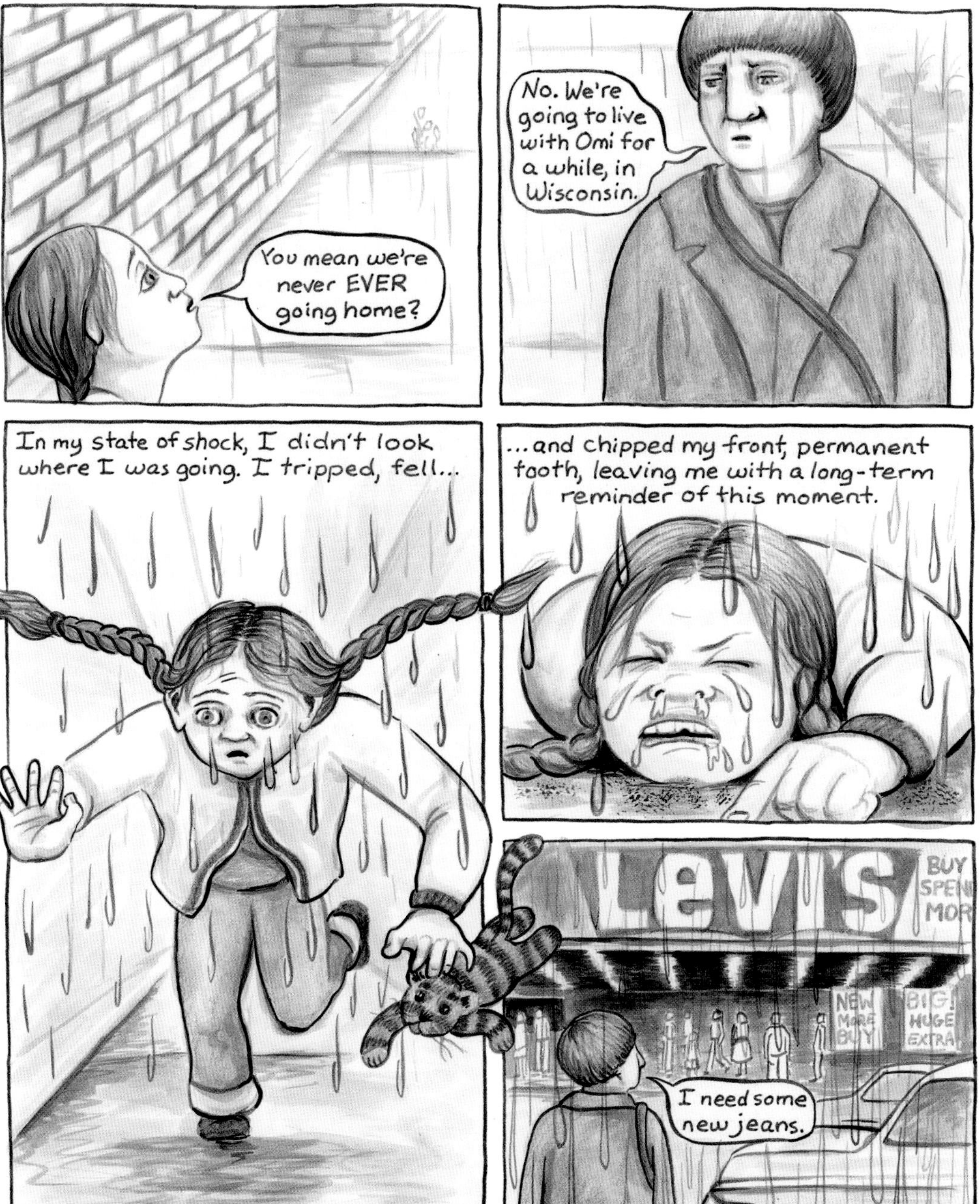
You mean we're never EVER going home?
No. We're going to live with Omi for a while, in Wisconsin.
In my state of shock, I didn't look where I was going. I tripped, fell...
...and chipped my front, permanent tooth, leaving me with a long-term reminder of this moment.
LEVI'S
BUY
NEW MORE BUY
BIG! HUGE EXTRA
I need some new jeans.

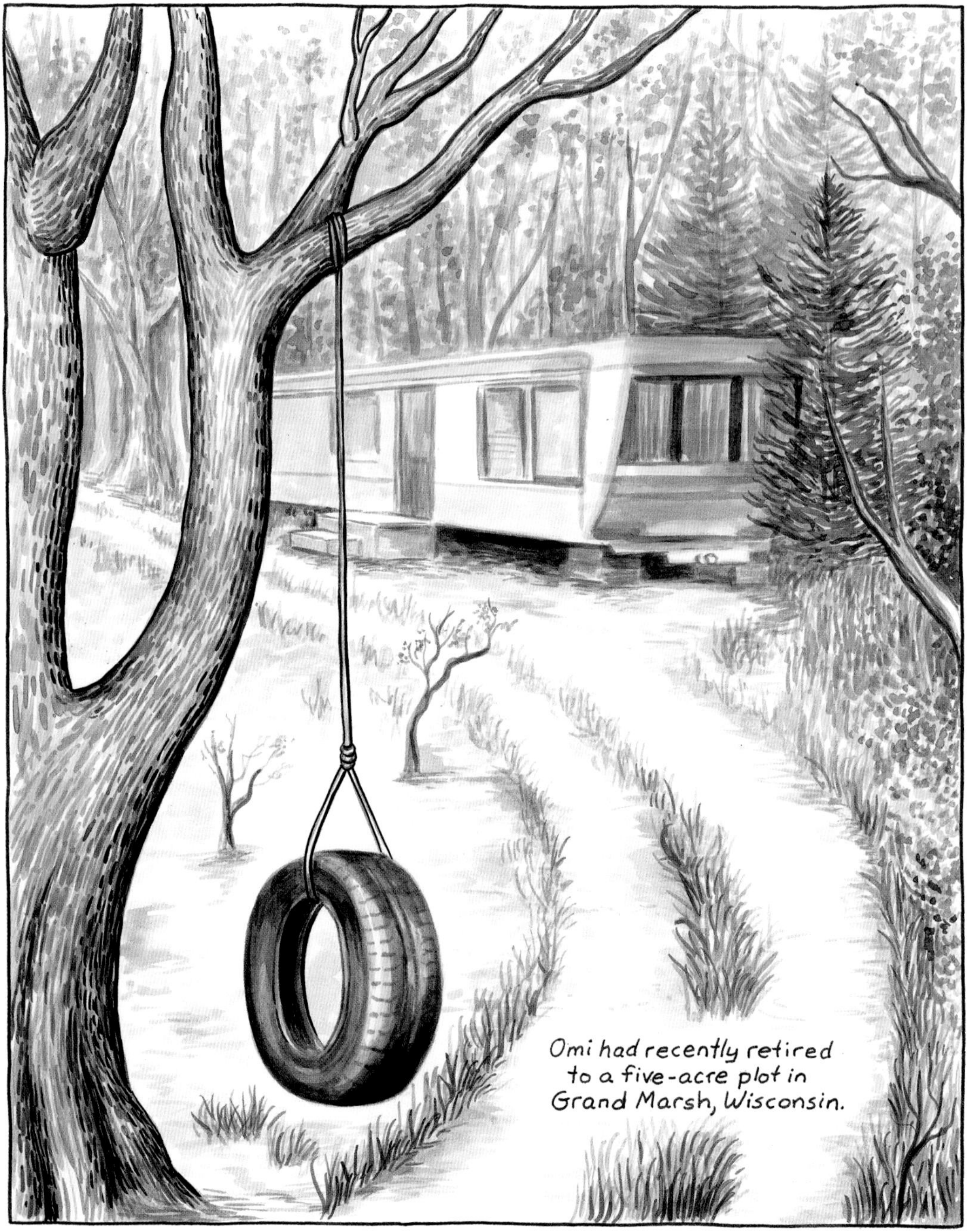
Omi had recently retired to a five-acre plot in Grand Marsh, Wisconsin.

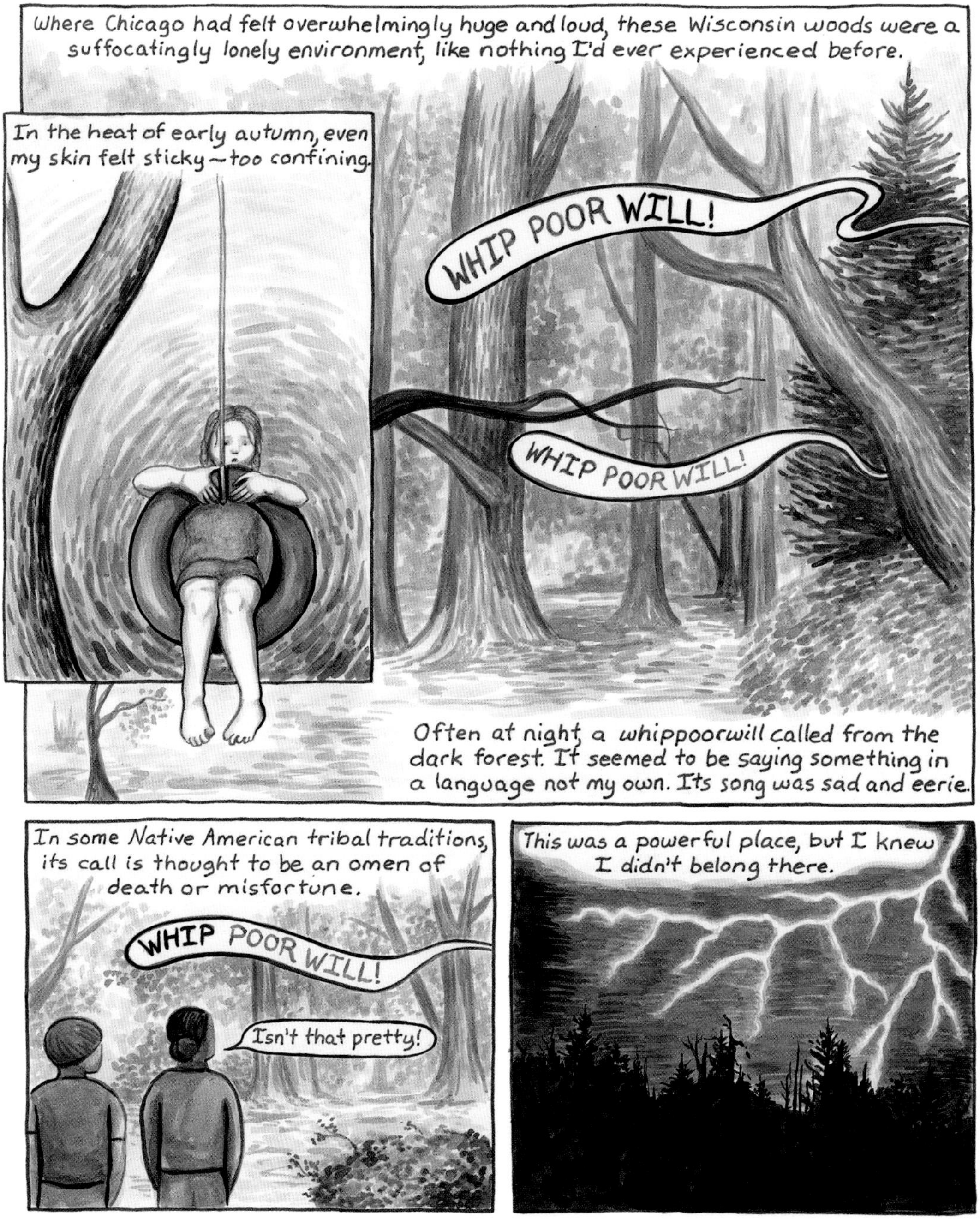
Where Chicago had felt overwhelmingly huge and loud, these Wisconsin woods were a suffocatingly lonely environment, like nothing I'd ever experienced before.
In the heat of early autumn, even my skin felt sticky—too confining.
WHIP POOR WILL!
WHIP POOR WILL!
Often at night, a whippoorwill called from the dark forest. It seemed to be saying something in a language not my own. Its song was sad and eerie.
In some Native American tribal traditions, its call is thought to be an omen of death or misfortune.
WHIP POOR WILL!
Isn't that pretty!
This was a powerful place, but I knew I didn't belong there.

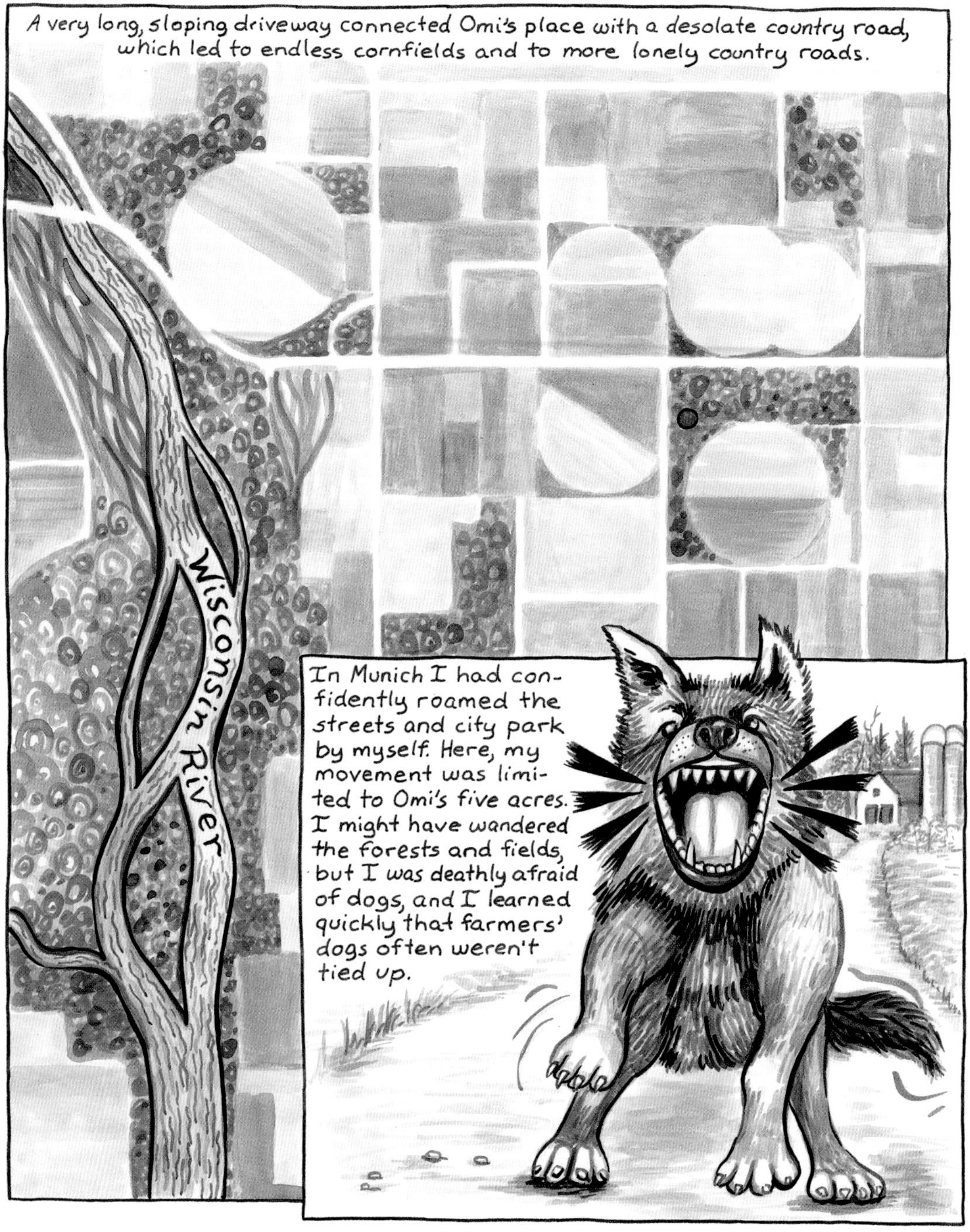
A very long, sloping driveway connected Omi's place with a desolate country road, which led to endless cornfields and to more lonely country roads.
Wisconsin River
In Munich I had confidently roamed the streets and city park by myself. Here, my movement was limited to Omi's five acres. I might have wandered the forests and fields, but I was deathly afraid of dogs, and I learned quickly that farmers' dogs often weren't tied up.

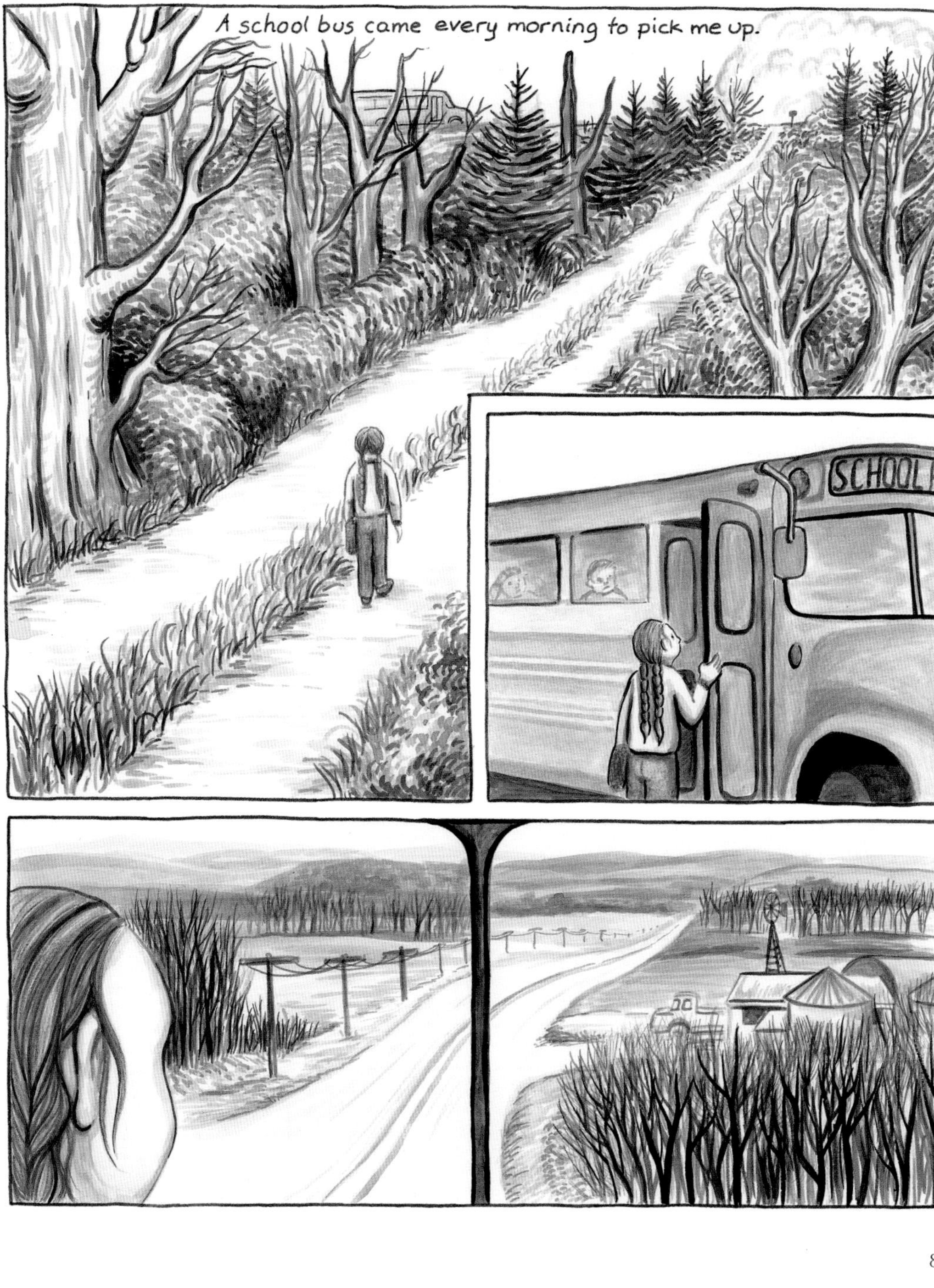
A school bus came every morning to pick me up.
SCHOOL B

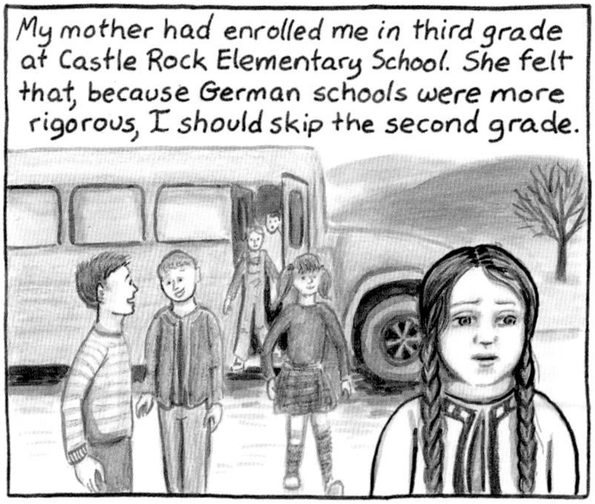
My mother had enrolled me in third grade at Castle Rock Elementary School. She felt that, because German schools were more rigorous, I should skip the second grade.

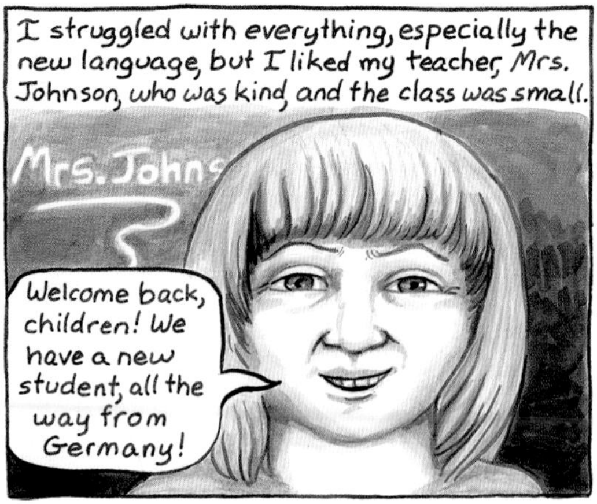
I struggled with everything, especially the new language, but I liked my teacher, Mrs. Johnson, who was kind, and the class was small.
Mrs. Johns
Welcome back, children! We have a new student, all the way from Germany!

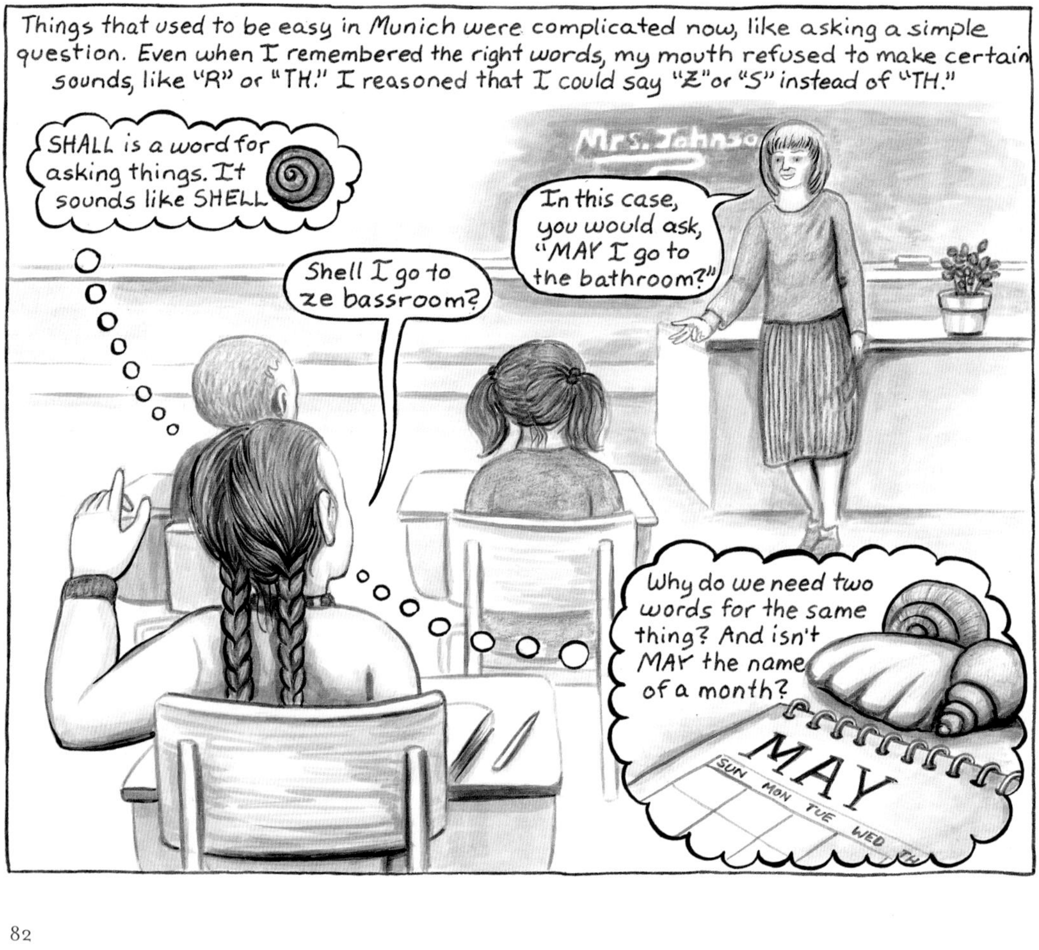
Things that used to be easy in Munich were complicated now, like asking a simple question. Even when I remembered the right words, my mouth refused to make certain sounds, like "R" or "TH." I reasoned that I could say "Z" or "S" instead of "TH."
Mrs. Johnso
SHALL is a word for asking things. It sounds like SHELL
In this case, you would ask, "MAY I go to the bathroom?"
Shell I go to ze bassroom?
Why do we need two words for the same thing? And isn't MAY the name of a month?
MAY
SUN MON TUE WED TH

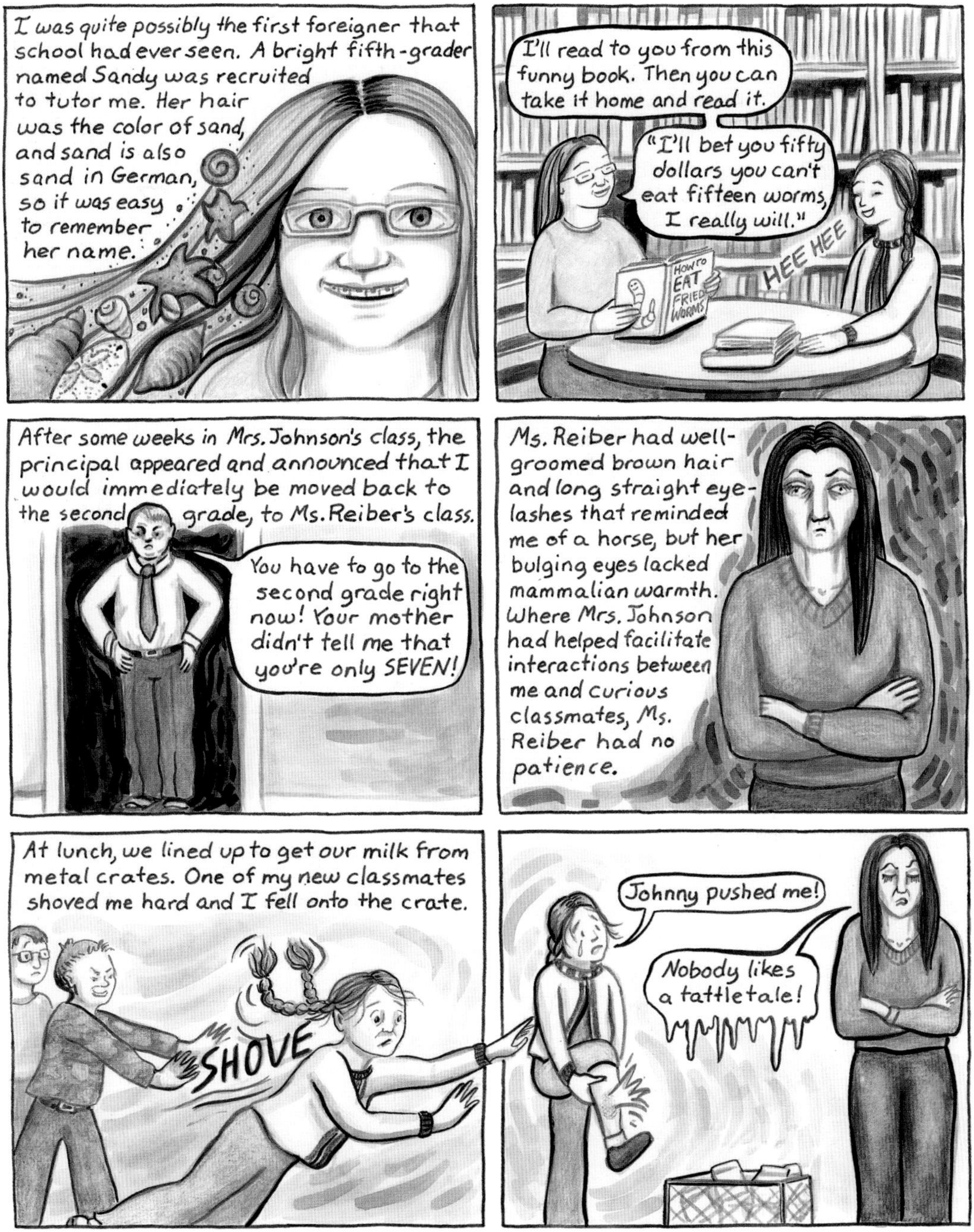

I was quite possibly the first foreigner that school had ever seen. A bright fifth-grader named Sandy was recruited to tutor me. Her hair was the color of sand, and sand is also sand in German, so it was easy to remember her name.
I'll read to you from this funny book. Then you can take it home and read it.
"I'll bet you fifty dollars you can't eat fifteen worms, I really will."
HOW TO EAT FRIED WORMS
HEE HEE
After some weeks in Mrs. Johnson's class, the principal appeared and announced that I would immediately be moved back to the second grade, to Ms. Reiber's class.
You have to go to the second grade right now! Your mother didn't tell me that you're only SEVEN!
Ms. Reiber had well-groomed brown hair and long straight eye-lashes that reminded me of a horse, but her bulging eyes lacked mammalian warmth. Where Mrs. Johnson had helped facilitate interactions between me and curious classmates, Ms. Reiber had no patience.
At lunch, we lined up to get our milk from metal crates. One of my new classmates shoved me hard and I fell onto the crate.
SHOVE
Johnny pushed me!
Nobody likes a tattletale!

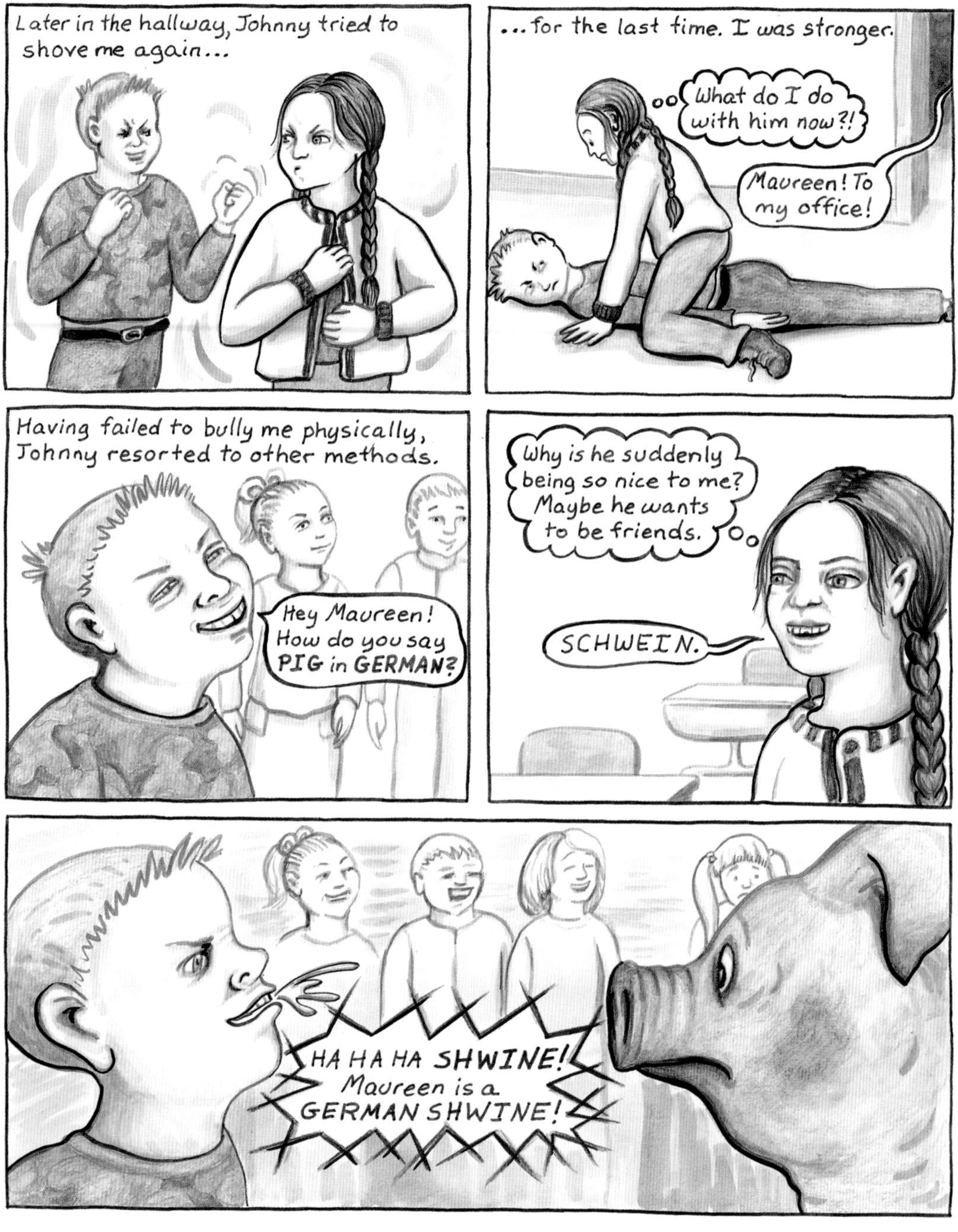
Later in the hallway, Johnny tried to shove me again...
...for the last time. I was stronger.
What do I do with him now?!
Maureen! To my office!
Having failed to bully me physically, Johnny resorted to other methods.
Hey Maureen! How do you say PIG in GERMAN?
Why is he suddenly being so nice to me? Maybe he wants to be friends.
SCHWEIN.
HA HA HA SHWINE! Maureen is a GERMAN SHWINE!

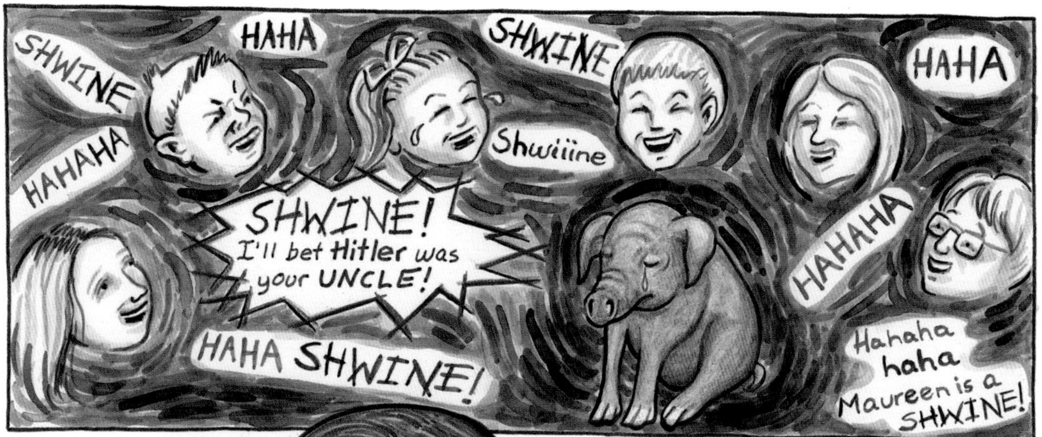
SHWINE
HAHA
SHWINE
HAHA
HAHAHA
Shwiiine
SHWINE! I'll bet Hitler was your UNCLE!
HAHAHA
HAHA SHWINE!
Hahaha haha Maureen is a SHWINE!

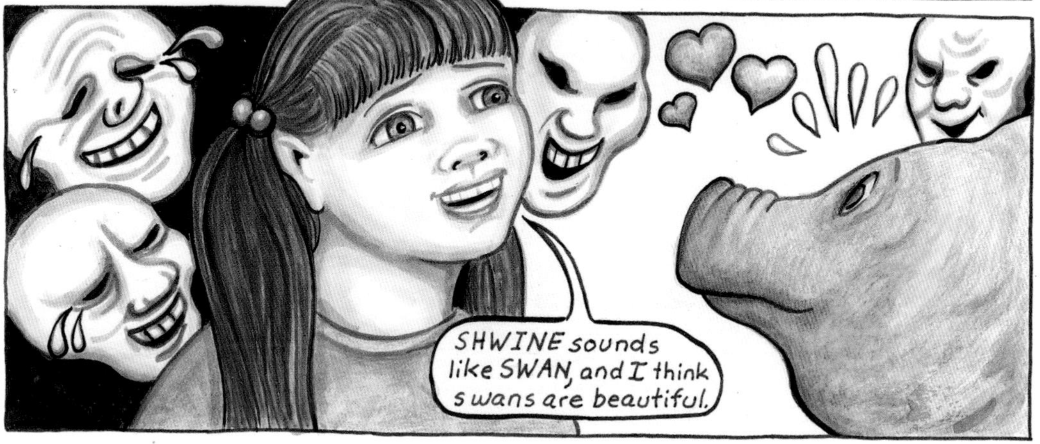
SHWINE sounds like SWAN, and I think swans are beautiful.

Kelly's brave, compassionate gesture has stayed with me all these years.

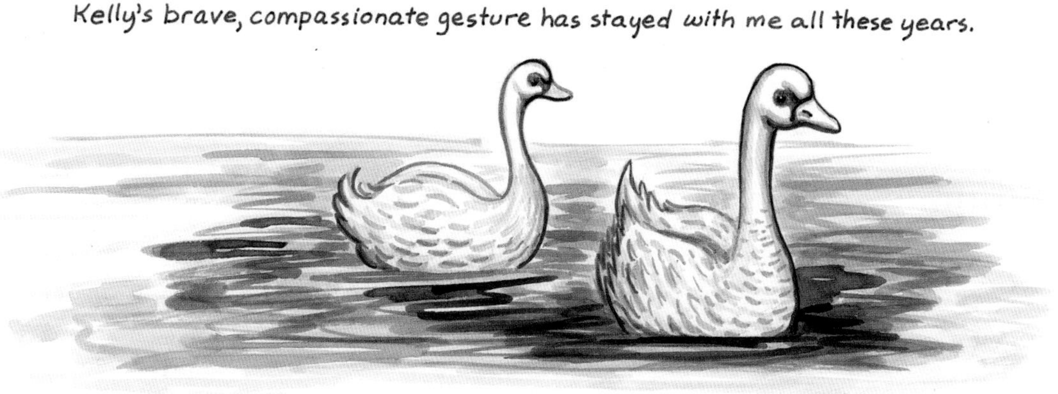

At home, I found little sympathy.

There you sit, making such a long face, as though YOU had anything to complain about!

The children in my new class are so mean. They said Hitler was my uncle!

Your problem is that you're spoiled. You have no idea what real hardship is, what the likes of **us** had to endure! Hitler did a lot of good. He built highways and created jobs. My sister Hildegard married Hitler's bodyguard, Kurt Gildisch, a **fabulous** man from a **very** good family...

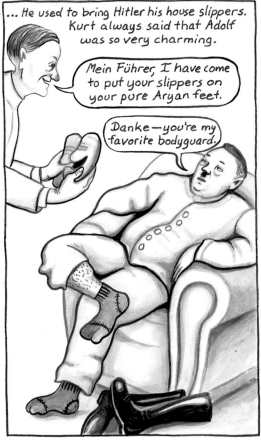

... He used to bring Hitler his house slippers. Kurt always said that Adolf was so very charming.

Mein Führer, I have come to put your slippers on your pure Aryan feet.

Danke—you're my favorite bodyguard.

A family photo confirms

"Hild. + Kurt G. on their wedding day"

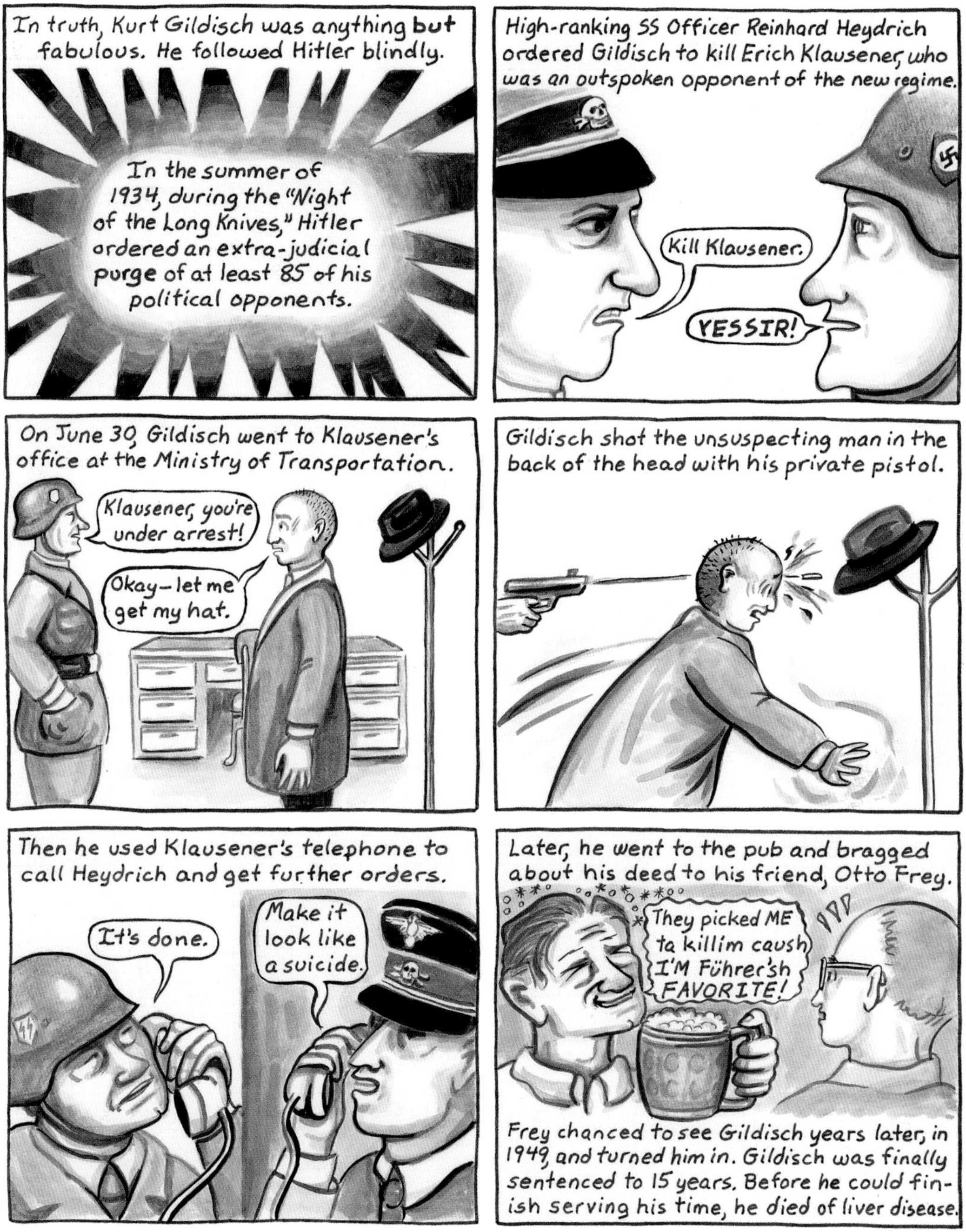
In truth, Kurt Gildisch was anything but fabulous. He followed Hitler blindly.
In the summer of 1934, during the "Night of the Long Knives," Hitler ordered an extra-judicial purge of at least 85 of his political opponents.
High-ranking SS Officer Reinhard Heydrich ordered Gildisch to kill Erich Klausener, who was an outspoken opponent of the new regime.
Kill Klausener.
YESSIR!
On June 30, Gildisch went to Klausener's office at the Ministry of Transportation.
Klausener, you're under arrest!
Okay—let me get my hat.
Gildisch shot the unsuspecting man in the back of the head with his private pistol.
Then he used Klausener's telephone to call Heydrich and get further orders.
It's done.
Make it look like a suicide.
Later, he went to the pub and bragged about his deed to his friend, Otto Frey.
They picked ME ta killim caush I'M Führer'sh FAVORITE!
Frey chanced to see Gildisch years later, in 1949, and turned him in. Gildisch was finally sentenced to 15 years. Before he could finish serving his time, he died of liver disease.

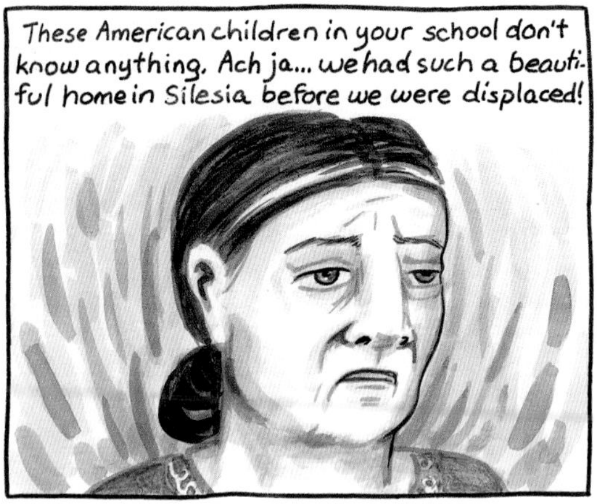
These American children in your school don't know anything. Ach ja... we had such a beautiful home in Silesia before we were displaced!

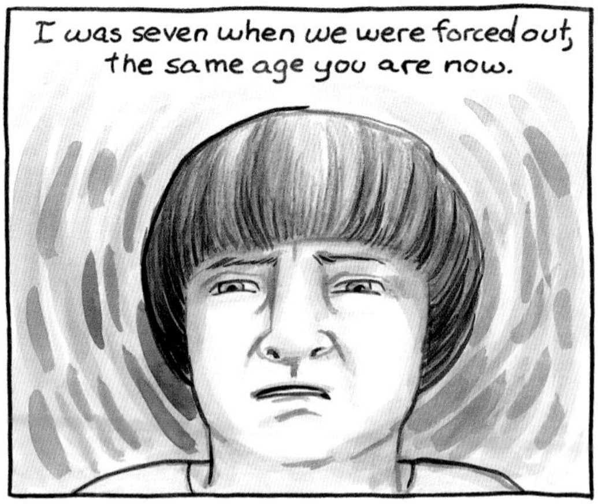
I was seven when we were forced out, the same age you are now.

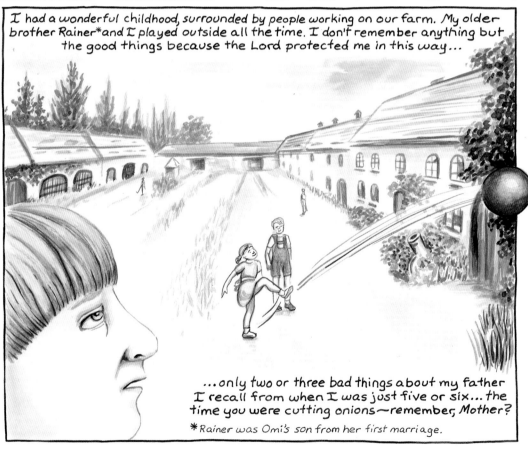

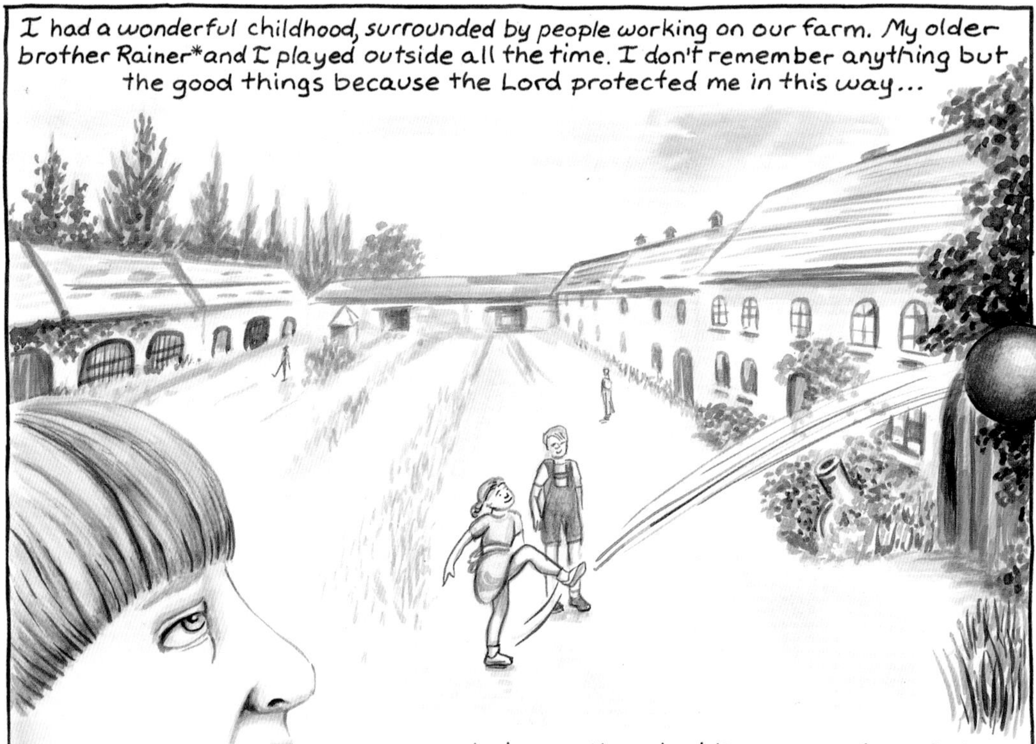
I had a wonderful childhood, surrounded by people working on our farm. My older brother Rainer* and I played outside all the time. I don't remember anything but the good things because the Lord protected me in this way...
...only two or three bad things about my father I recall from when I was just five or six... the time you were cutting onions—remember, Mother?
*Rainer was Omi's son from her first marriage.

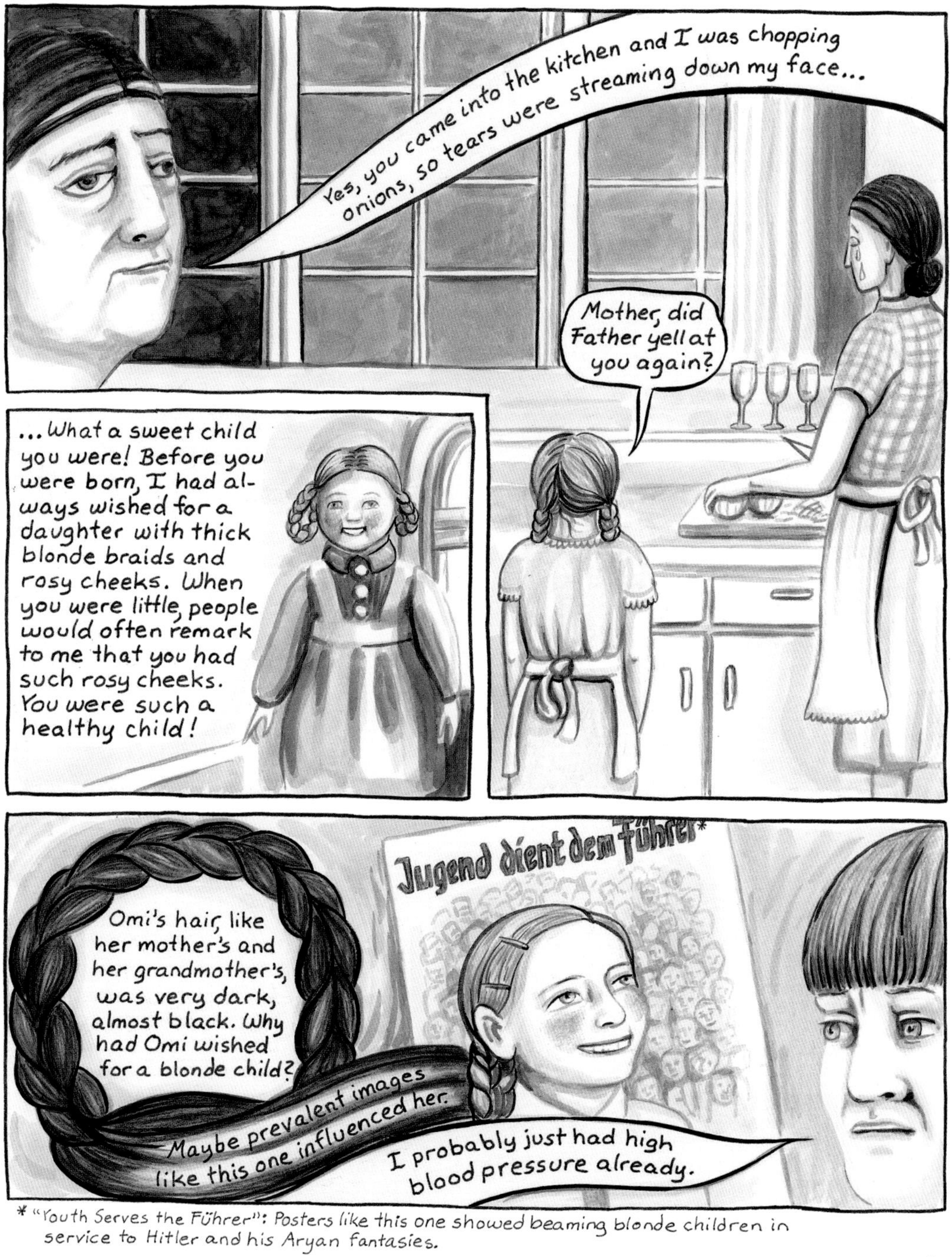
Yes, you came into the kitchen and I was chopping onions, so tears were streaming down my face...
Mother, did Father yell at you again?
...What a sweet child you were! Before you were born, I had always wished for a daughter with thick blonde braids and rosy cheeks. When you were little, people would often remark to me that you had such rosy cheeks. You were such a healthy child!
Jugend dient dem Führer*
Omi's hair, like her mother's and her grandmother's, was very dark, almost black. Why had Omi wished for a blonde child?
Maybe prevalent images like this one influenced her.
I probably just had high blood pressure already.

* "Youth Serves the Führer": Posters like this one showed beaming blonde children in service to Hitler and his Aryan fantasies.

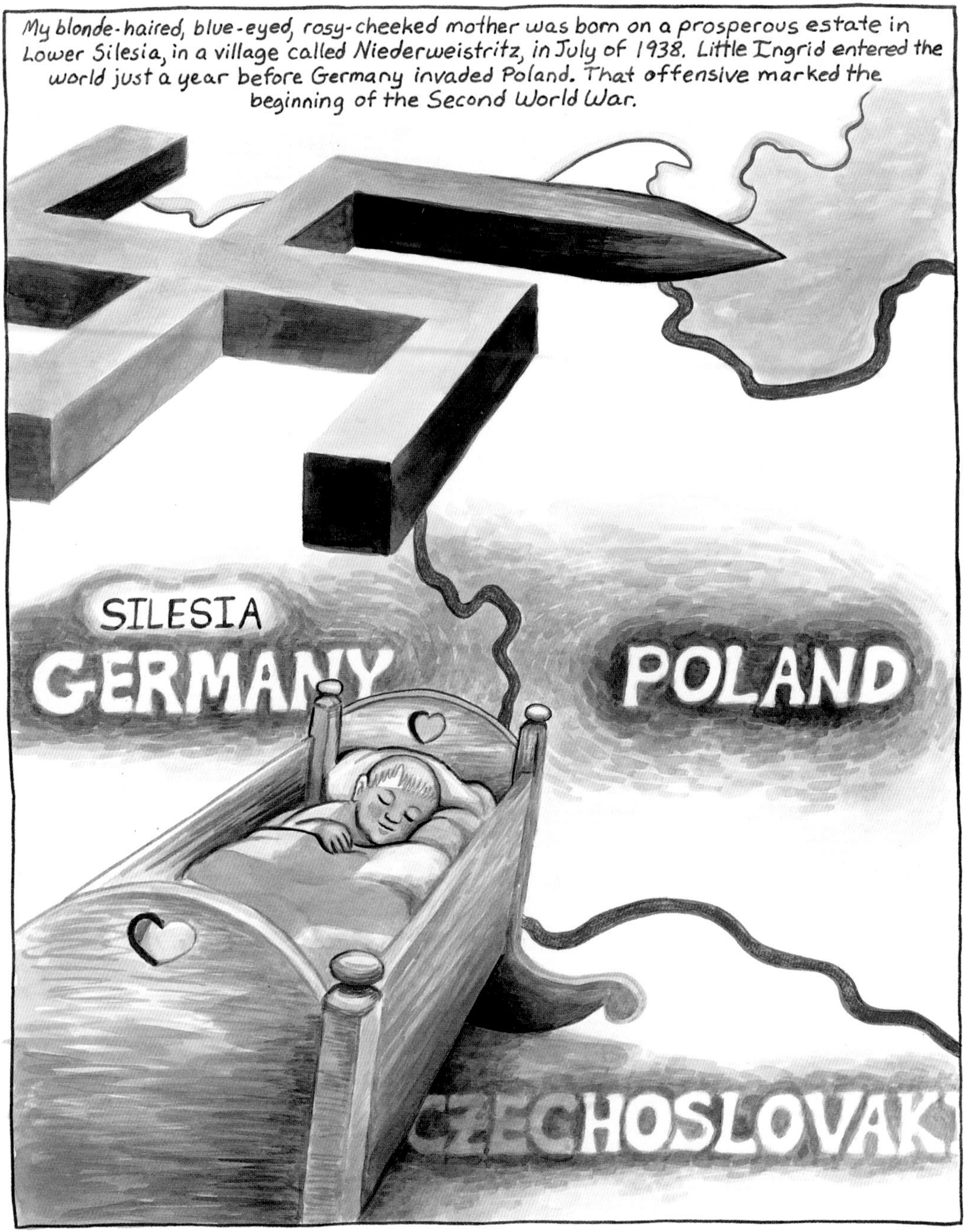
My blonde-haired, blue-eyed, rosy-cheeked mother was born on a prosperous estate in Lower Silesia, in a village called Niederweistritz, in July of 1938. Little Ingrid entered the world just a year before Germany invaded Poland. That offensive marked the beginning of the Second World War.
SILESIA
GERMANY
POLAND
CZECHOSLOVAKI

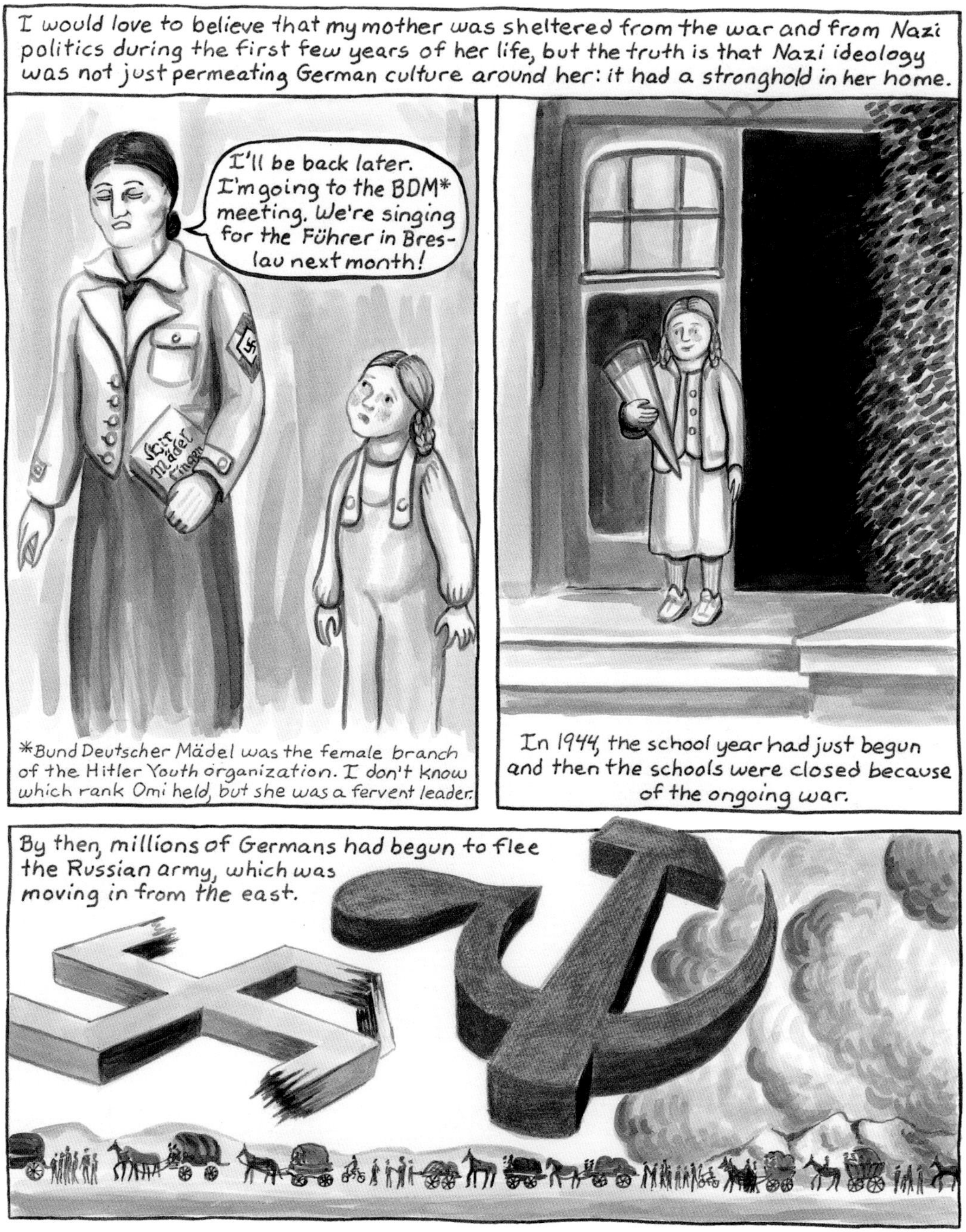
I would love to believe that my mother was sheltered from the war and from Nazi politics during the first few years of her life, but the truth is that Nazi ideology was not just permeating German culture around her: it had a stronghold in her home.
I'll be back later. I'm going to the BDM* meeting. We're singing for the Führer in Breslau next month!
*Bund Deutscher Mädel was the female branch of the Hitler Youth organization. I don't know which rank Omi held, but she was a fervent leader.
In 1944, the school year had just begun and then the schools were closed because of the ongoing war.
By then, millions of Germans had begun to flee the Russian army, which was moving in from the east.

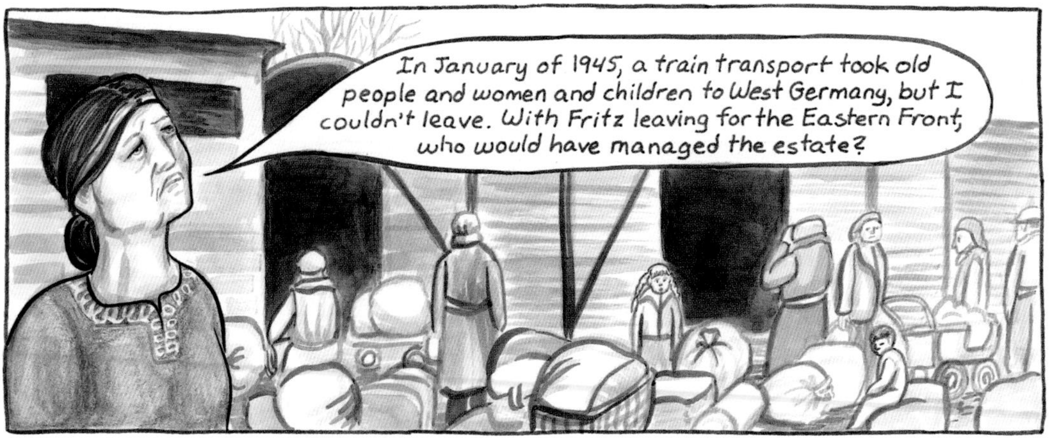
In January of 1945, a train transport took old people and women and children to West Germany, but I couldn't leave. With Fritz leaving for the Eastern Front, who would have managed the estate?

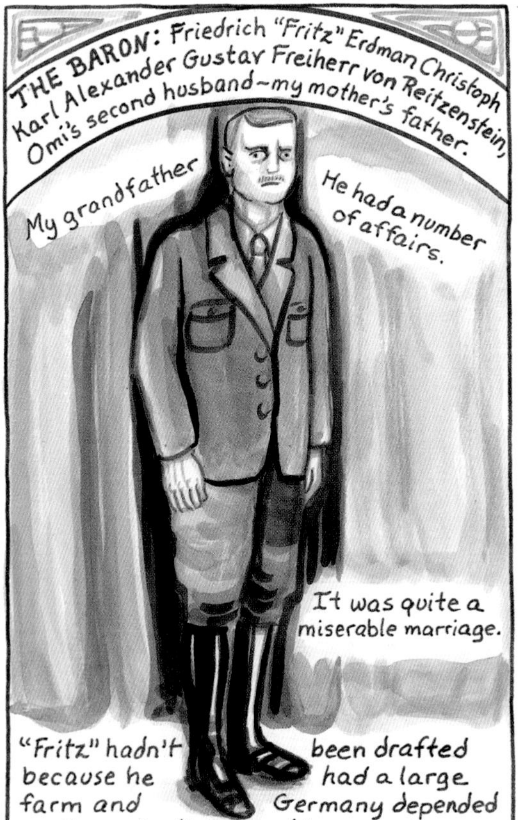
THE BARON: Friedrich "Fritz" Erdman Christoph Karl Alexander Gustav Freiherr von Reitzenstein, Omi's second husband—my mother's father.
My grandfather
He had a number of affairs.
It was quite a miserable marriage.
"Fritz" hadn't been drafted because he had a large farm and Germany depended on its agriculture (and because he was wealthy and well-connected).

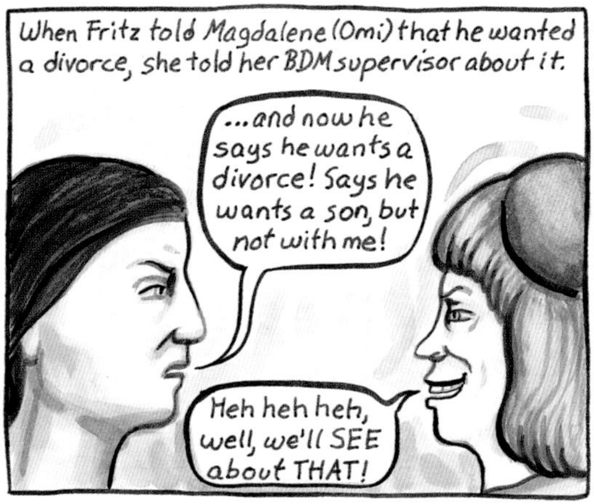
When Fritz told Magdalene (Omi) that he wanted a divorce, she told her BDM supervisor about it.
...and now he says he wants a divorce! Says he wants a son, but not with me!
Heh heh heh, well, we'll SEE about THAT!

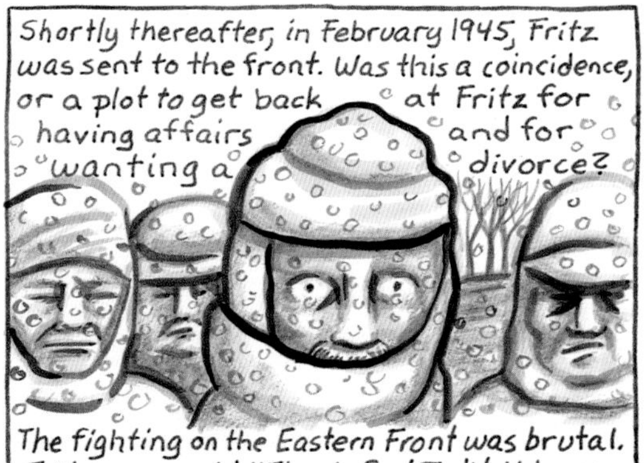
Shortly thereafter, in February 1945, Fritz was sent to the front. Was this a coincidence, or a plot to get back at Fritz for having affairs and for wanting a divorce?
The fighting on the Eastern Front was brutal. Fritz once said, "Thank God I didn't have to kill anyone." Maybe that's true...

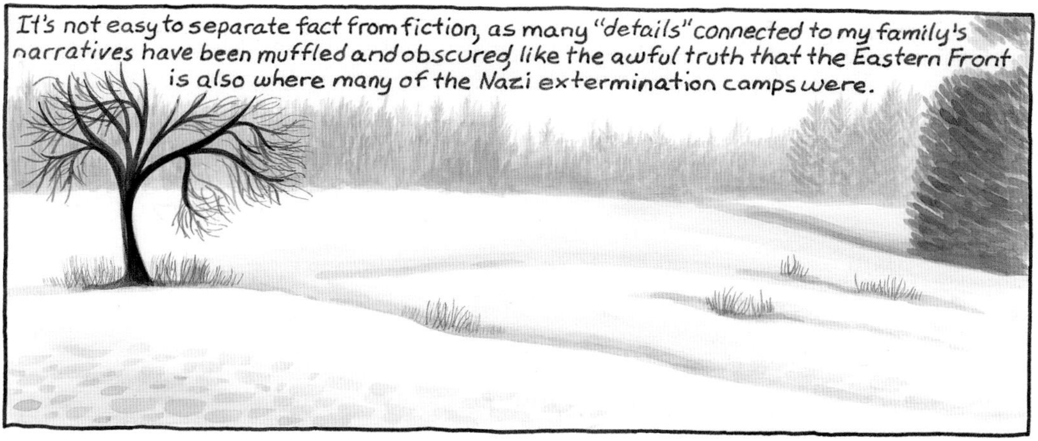
It's not easy to separate fact from fiction, as many "details" connected to my family's narratives have been muffled and obscured, like the awful truth that the Eastern Front is also where many of the Nazi extermination camps were.

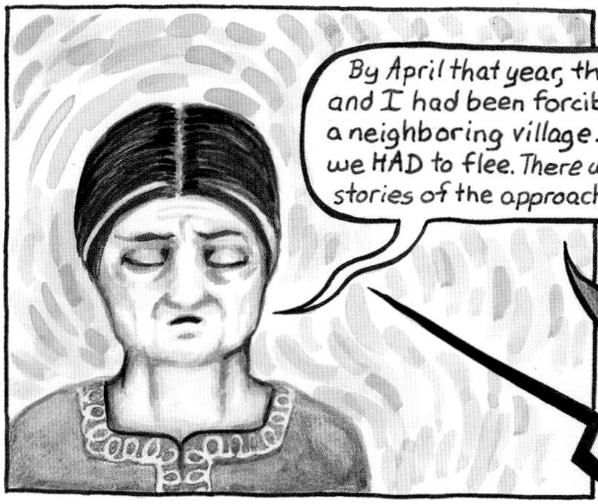
By April that year, the children and I had been forcibly moved to a neighboring village. I realized we HAD to flee. There were horrible stories of the approaching Russians!

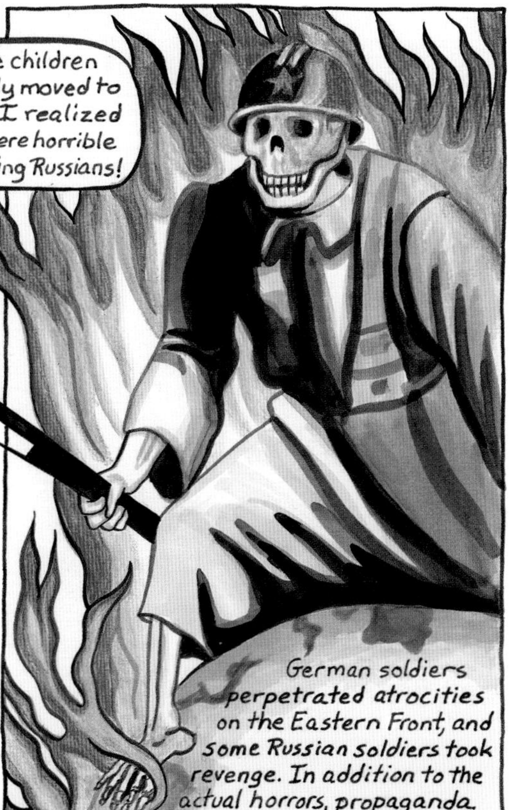
German soldiers perpetrated atrocities on the Eastern Front, and some Russian soldiers took revenge. In addition to the actual horrors, propaganda like this anti-Soviet poster must have amplified the dread.

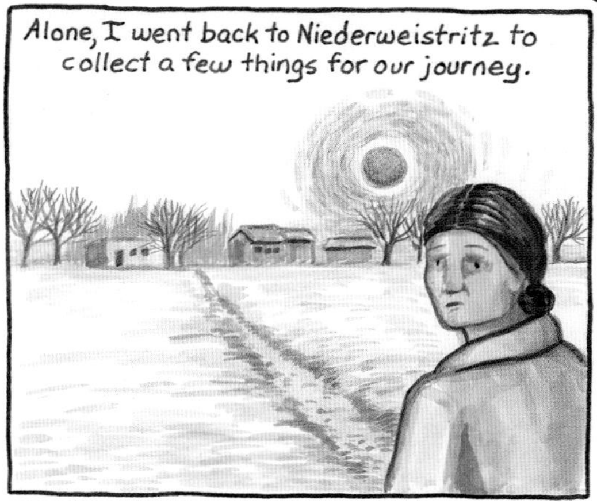
Alone, I went back to Niederweistritz to collect a few things for our journey.

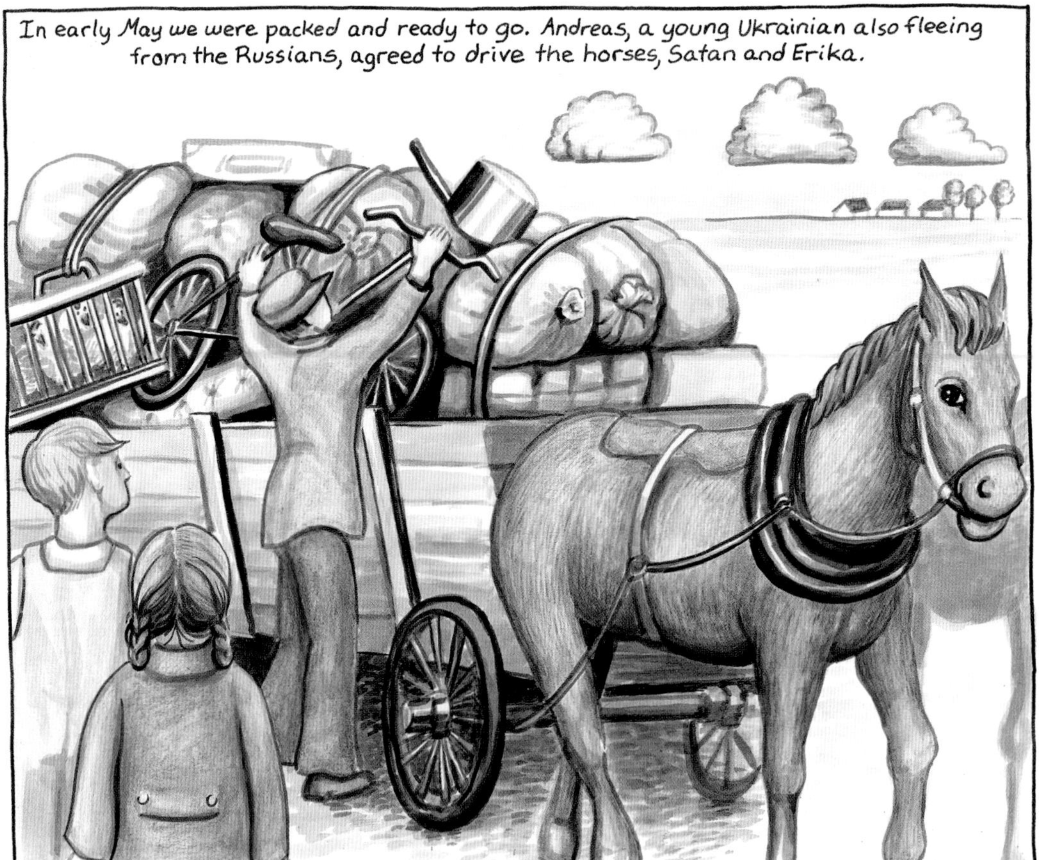
In early May we were packed and ready to go. Andreas, a young Ukrainian also fleeing from the Russians, agreed to drive the horses, Satan and Erika.

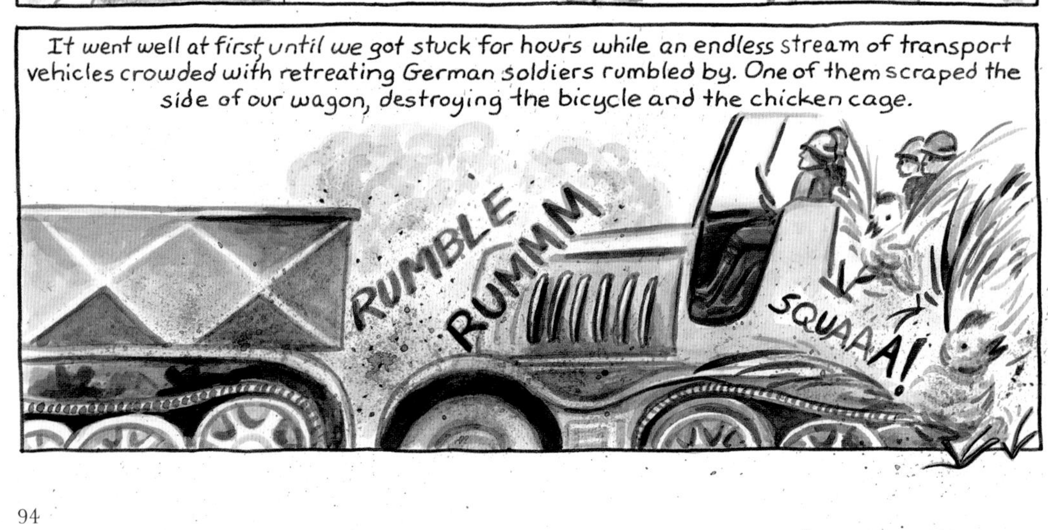
It went well at first, until we got stuck for hours while an endless stream of transport vehicles crowded with retreating German soldiers rumbled by. One of them scraped the side of our wagon, destroying the bicycle and the chicken cage.
RUMBLE
RUMMM
SQUAAA!

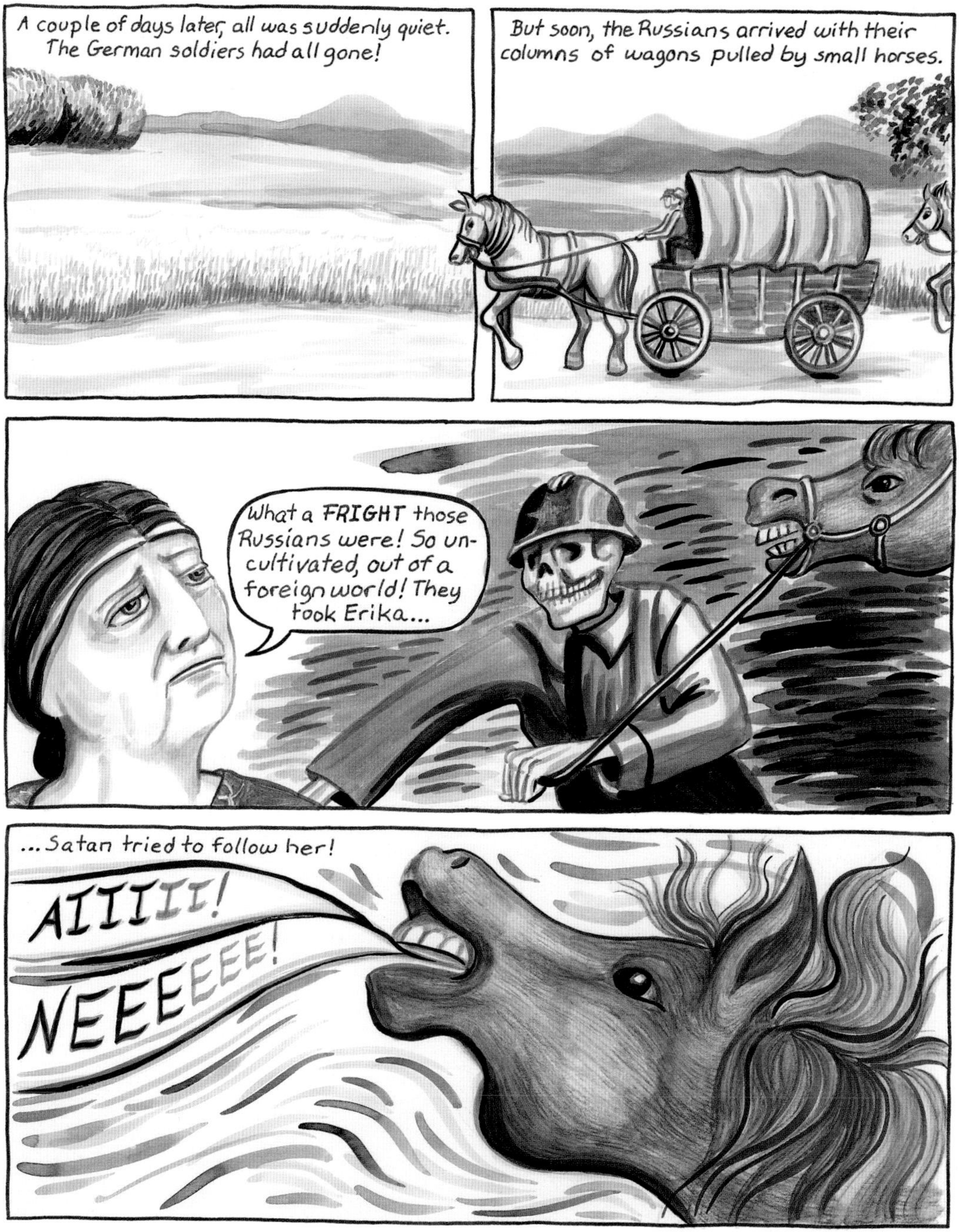
A couple of days later, all was suddenly quiet. The German soldiers had all gone!
But soon, the Russians arrived with their columns of wagons pulled by small horses.
What a FRIGHT those Russians were! So uncultivated, out of a foreign world! They took Erika...
...Satan tried to follow her!
AIIIII!
NEEEEEE!

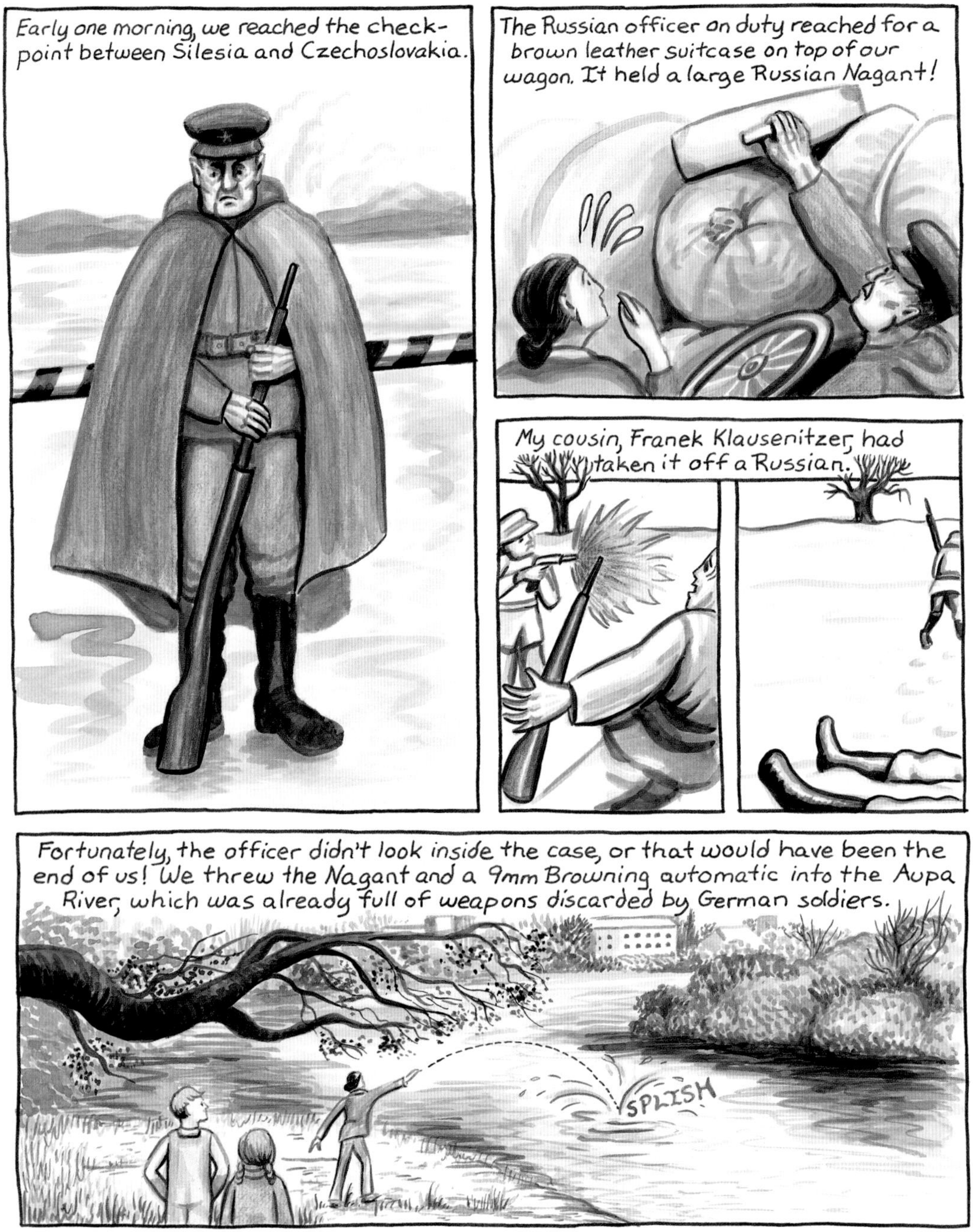
Early one morning, we reached the check-point between Silesia and Czechoslovakia.
The Russian officer on duty reached for a brown leather suitcase on top of our wagon. It held a large Russian Nagant!
My cousin, Franek Klausenitzer, had taken it off a Russian.
Fortunately, the officer didn't look inside the case, or that would have been the end of us! We threw the Nagant and a 9mm Browning automatic into the Aupa River, which was already full of weapons discarded by German soldiers.
SPLISH

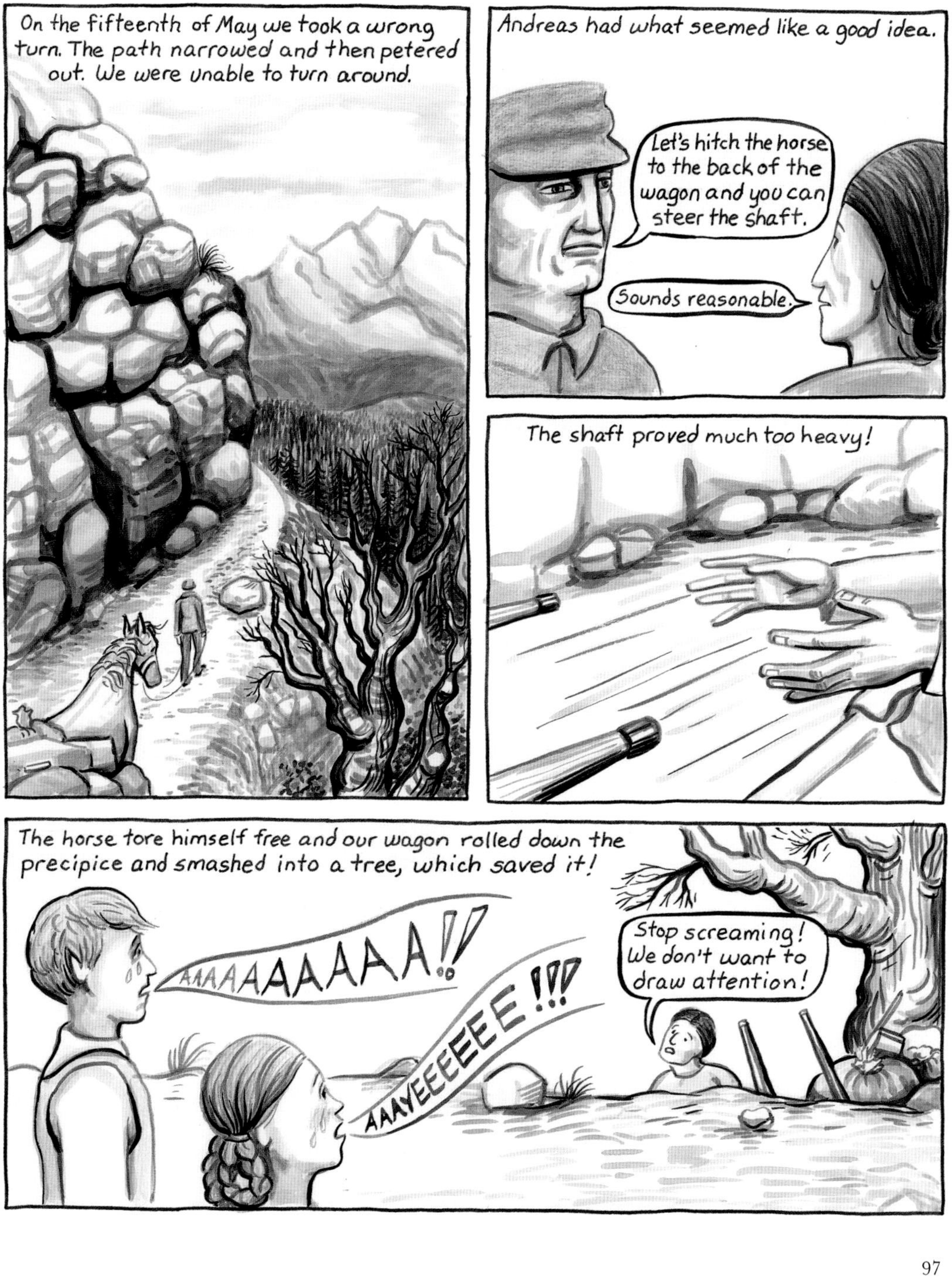
On the fifteenth of May we took a wrong turn. The path narrowed and then petered out. We were unable to turn around.
Andreas had what seemed like a good idea.
Let's hitch the horse to the back of the wagon and you can steer the shaft.
Sounds reasonable.
The shaft proved much too heavy!
The horse tore himself free and our wagon rolled down the precipice and smashed into a tree, which saved it!
AAAAAAAAAA!!
AAAYEEEEEEE!!!
Stop screaming! We don't want to draw attention!

As a child, I did not receive Omi's stories as a tidy linear narrative. Instead, I inherited shards of stories ~MEMORY SHRAPNEL~ and these fragments were often repetitive.

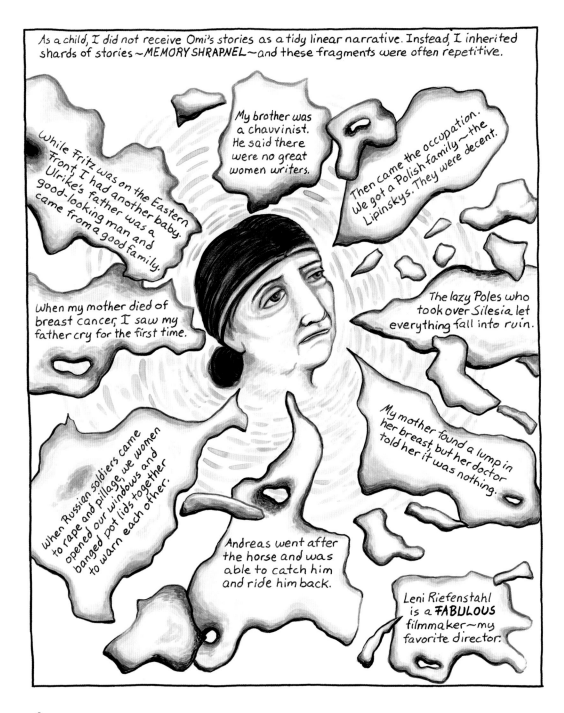

My brother was a chauvinist. He said there were no great women writers.

Then came the occupation. We got a Polish family ~the Lipinskys. They were decent.

While Fritz was on the Eastern Front, I had another baby. Ulrike's father was a good-looking man and came from a good family.

When my mother died of breast cancer, I saw my father cry for the first time.

The lazy Poles who took over Silesia let everything fall into ruin.

My mother found a lump in her breast but her doctor told her it was nothing.

When Russian soldiers came to rape and pillage, we women opened our windows and banged pot lids together to warn each other.

Andreas went after the horse and was able to catch him and ride him back.

Leni Riefenstahl is a **FABULOUS** filmmaker ~my favorite director.

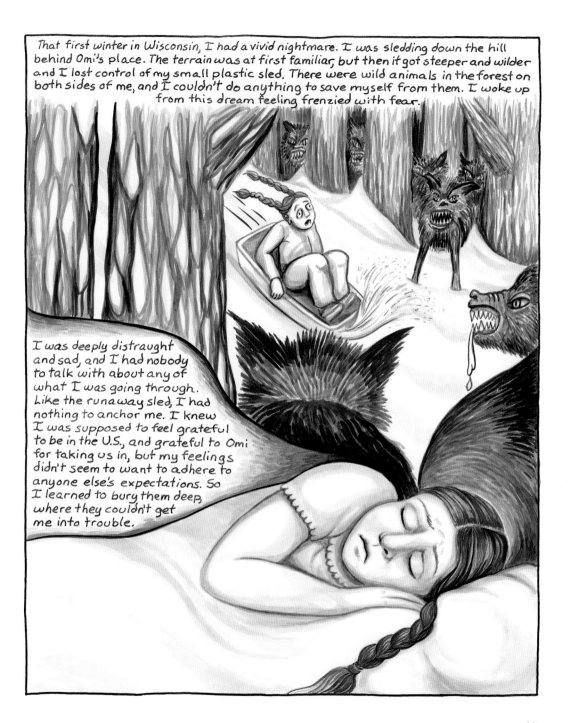

That first winter in Wisconsin, I had a vivid nightmare. I was sledding down the hill behind Omi's place. The terrain was at first familiar, but then it got steeper and wilder and I lost control of my small plastic sled. There were wild animals in the forest on both sides of me, and I couldn't do anything to save myself from them. I woke up from this dream feeling frenzied with fear.

I was deeply distraught and sad, and I had nobody to talk with about any of what I was going through. Like the runaway sled, I had nothing to anchor me. I knew I was supposed to feel grateful to be in the U.S., and grateful to Omi for taking us in, but my feelings didn't seem to want to adhere to anyone else's expectations. So I learned to bury them deep, where they couldn't get me into trouble.

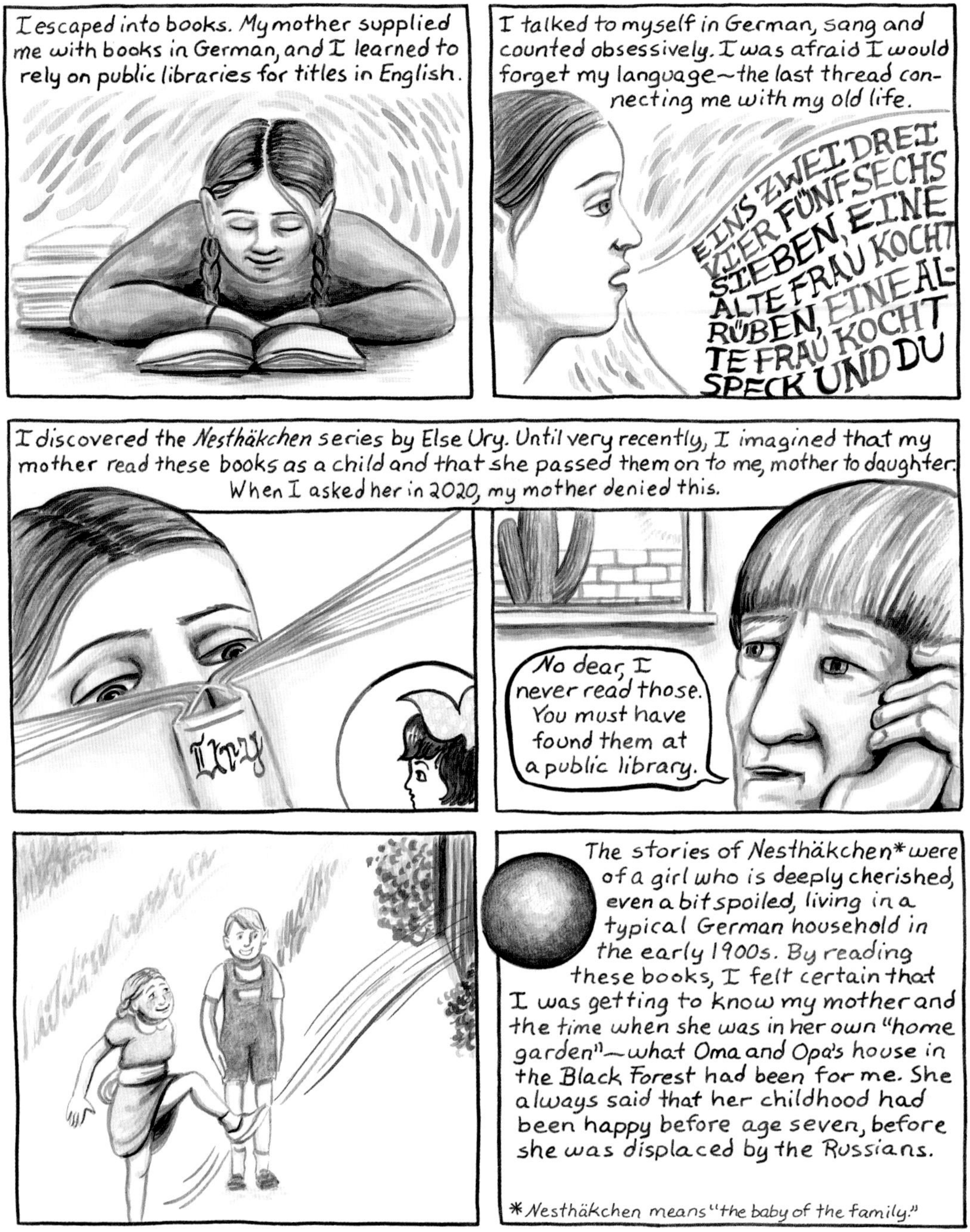
I escaped into books. My mother supplied me with books in German, and I learned to rely on public libraries for titles in English.
I talked to myself in German, sang and counted obsessively. I was afraid I would forget my language—the last thread connecting me with my old life.
EINS ZWEI DREI
VIER FÜNF SECHS
SIEBEN, EINE
ALTE FRAU KOCHT
RÜBEN, EINE AL-
TE FRAU KOCHT
SPECK UND DU
I discovered the *Nesthäkchen* series by Else Ury. Until very recently, I imagined that my mother read these books as a child and that she passed them on to me, mother to daughter. When I asked her in 2020, my mother denied this.
Ury
No dear, I never read those. You must have found them at a public library.
The stories of *Nesthäkchen** were of a girl who is deeply cherished, even a bit spoiled, living in a typical German household in the early 1900s. By reading these books, I felt certain that I was getting to know my mother and the time when she was in her own "home garden"—what Oma and Opa's house in the Black Forest had been for me. She always said that her childhood had been happy before age seven, before she was displaced by the Russians.
* *Nesthäkchen* means "the baby of the family."

ELSE URY, the author of the *Nesthäkchen* stories, was a massively popular children's book writer. She was born in 1877 in Berlin to well-educated and financially successful German Jewish parents.

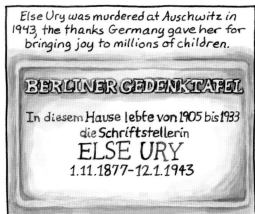

Else Ury was murdered at Auschwitz in 1943, the thanks Germany gave her for bringing joy to millions of children.

BERLINER GEDENKTAFEL

In diesem Hause lebte von 1905 bis 1933 die Schriftstellerin
ELSE URY
1.11.1877–12.1.1943

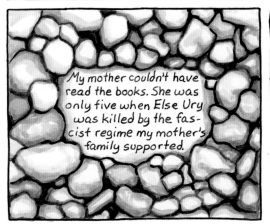

My mother couldn't have read the books. She was only five when *Else Ury* was killed by the fascist regime my mother's family supported.

Moreover, my mother couldn't remember when she learned to read. It was some time after the war had ended... after her family had fled from the Russian army.

When I read the series, I had no idea that the author was Jewish, or that she had died in a concentration camp.

Omi talked about Germans as victims of the war. She didn't discuss the Holocaust except to deny its occurrence or magnitude.

If there **were** any Jews killed, it was maybe a few thousand, certainly not millions.

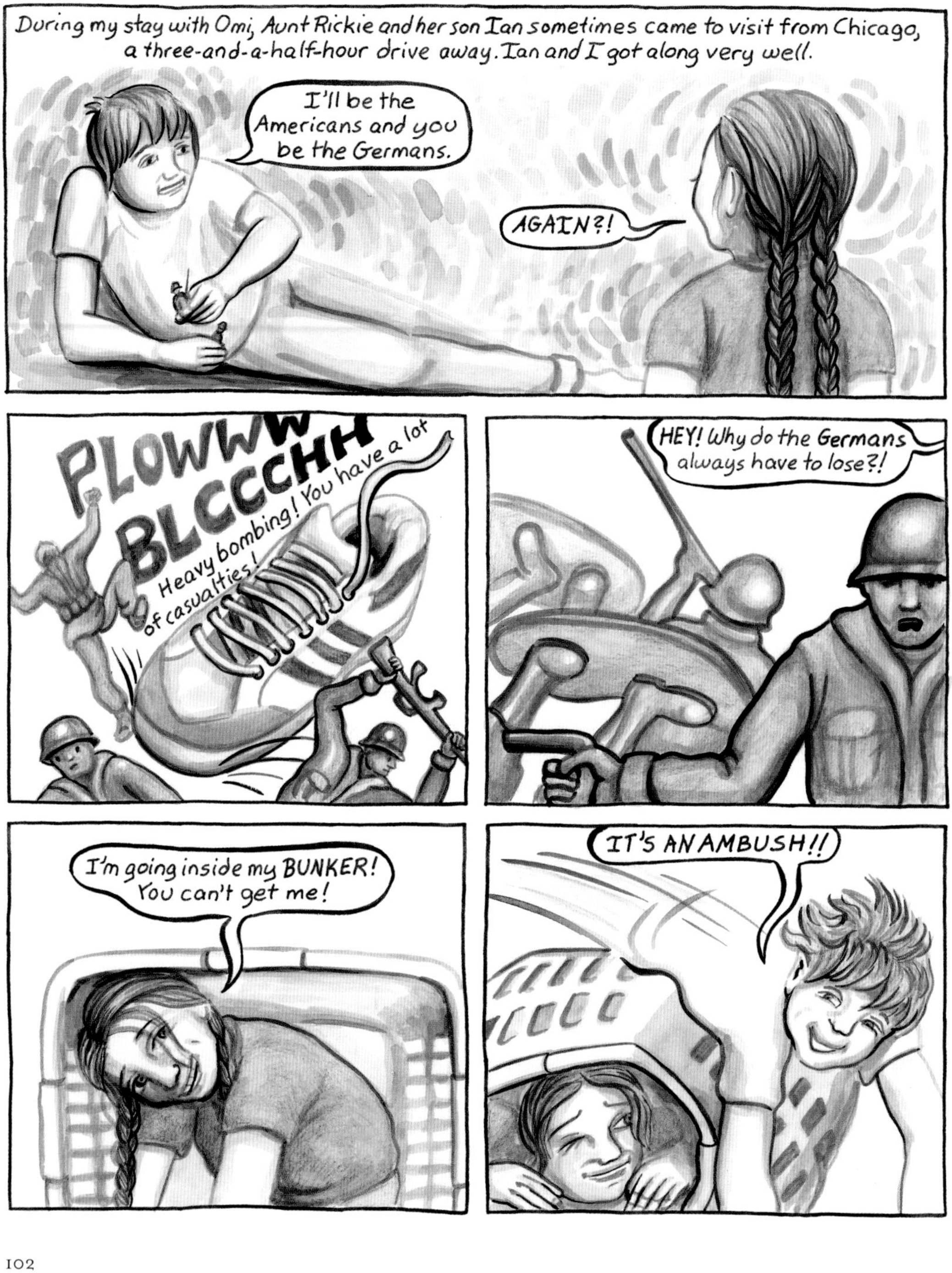
During my stay with Omi, Aunt Rickie and her son Ian sometimes came to visit from Chicago, a three-and-a-half-hour drive away. Ian and I got along very well.
I'll be the Americans and you be the Germans.
AGAIN?!
PLOWWW BLCCCHH
Heavy bombing! You have a lot of casualties!
HEY! Why do the Germans always have to lose?!
I'm going inside my BUNKER! You can't get me!
IT'S AN AMBUSH!!

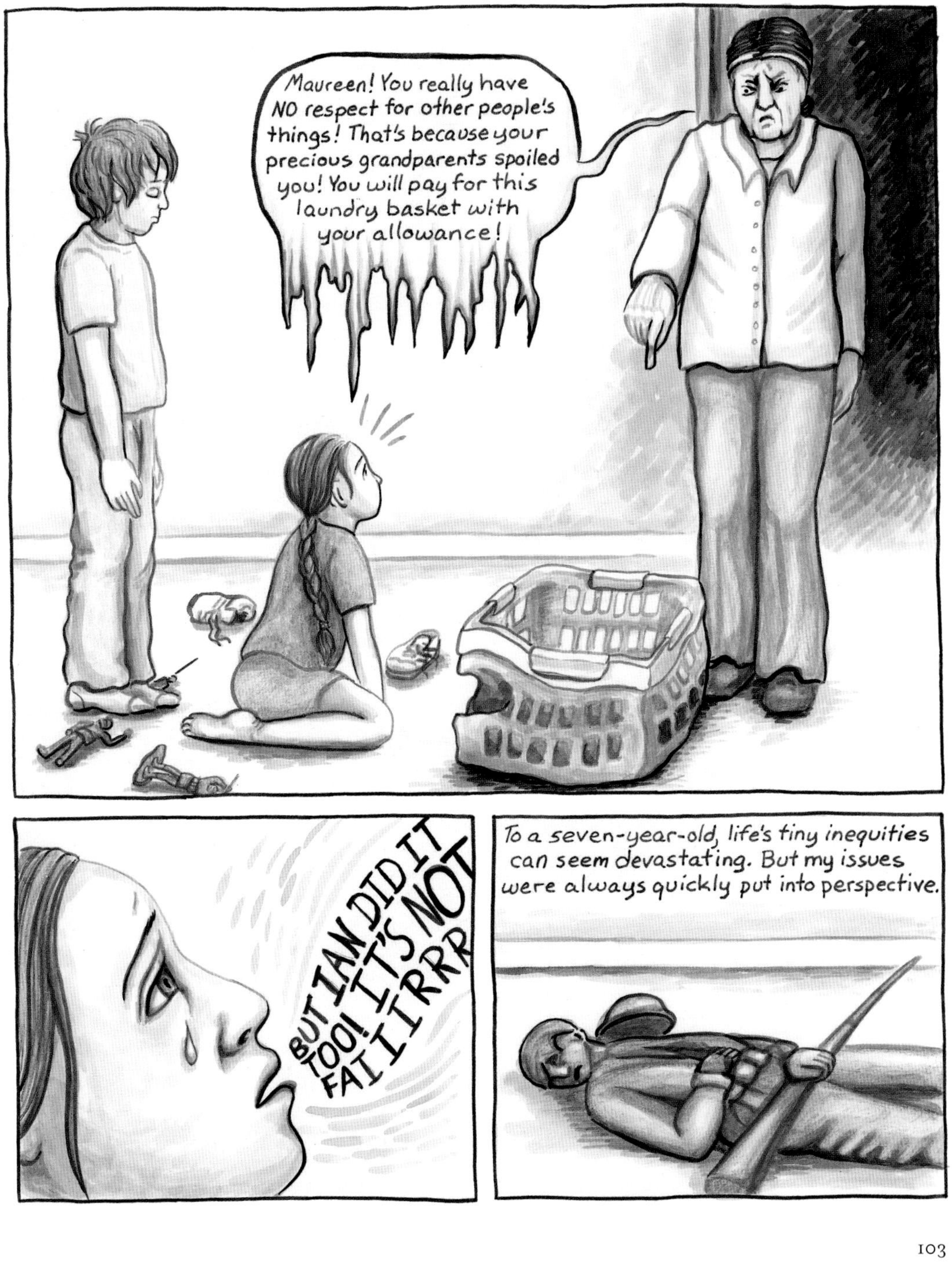
Maureen! You really have NO respect for other people's things! That's because your precious grandparents spoiled you! You will pay for this laundry basket with your allowance!
BUT IAN DID IT TOO! IT'S NOT FAIIIRRR
To a seven-year-old, life's tiny inequities can seem devastating. But my issues were always quickly put into perspective.

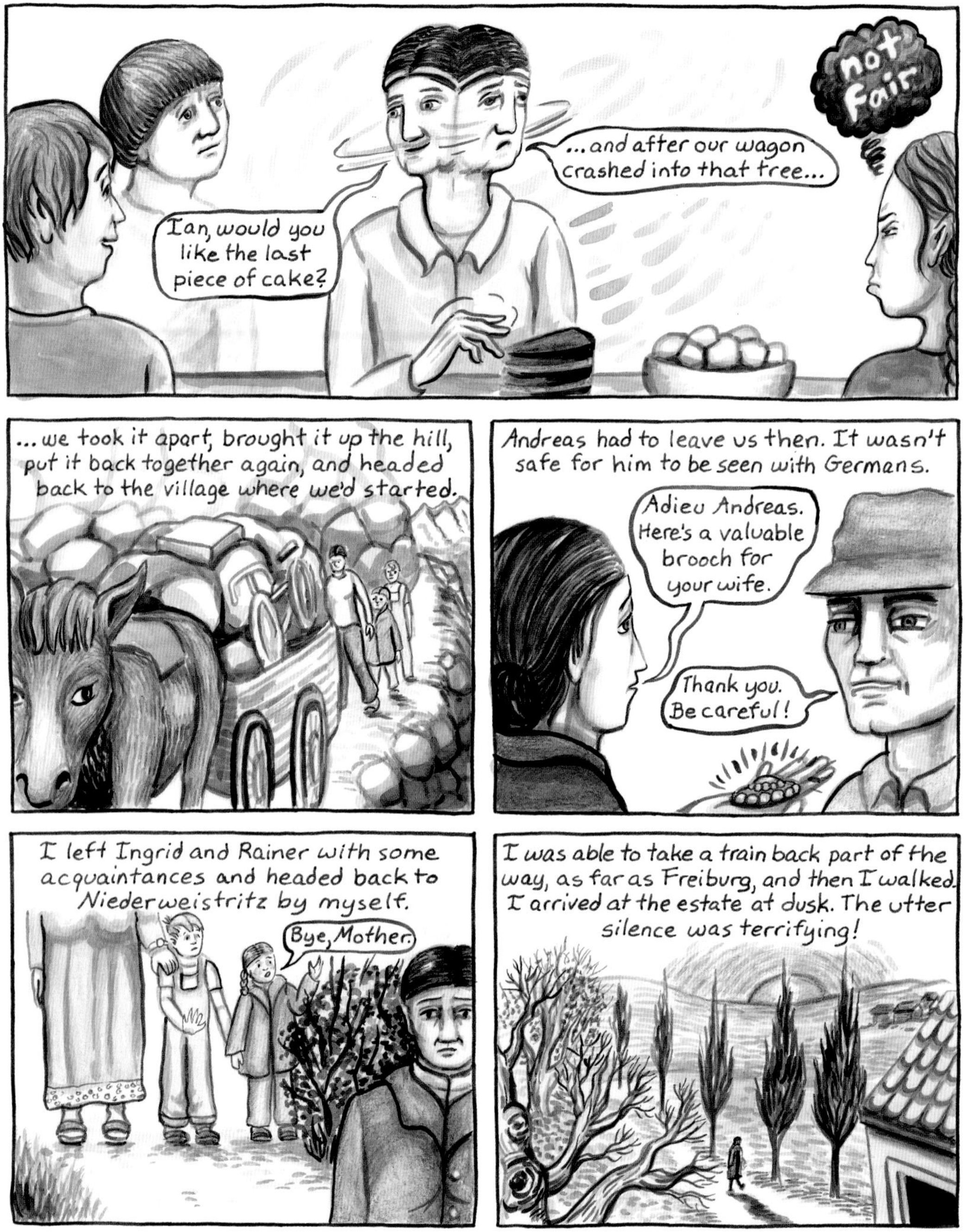
not fair
Ian, would you like the last piece of cake?
...and after our wagon crashed into that tree...
...we took it apart, brought it up the hill, put it back together again, and headed back to the village where we'd started.
Andreas had to leave us then. It wasn't safe for him to be seen with Germans.
Adieu Andreas. Here's a valuable brooch for your wife.
Thank you. Be careful!
I left Ingrid and Rainer with some acquaintances and headed back to Niederweistritz by myself.
Bye, Mother.
I was able to take a train back part of the way, as far as Freiburg, and then I walked. I arrived at the estate at dusk. The utter silence was terrifying!

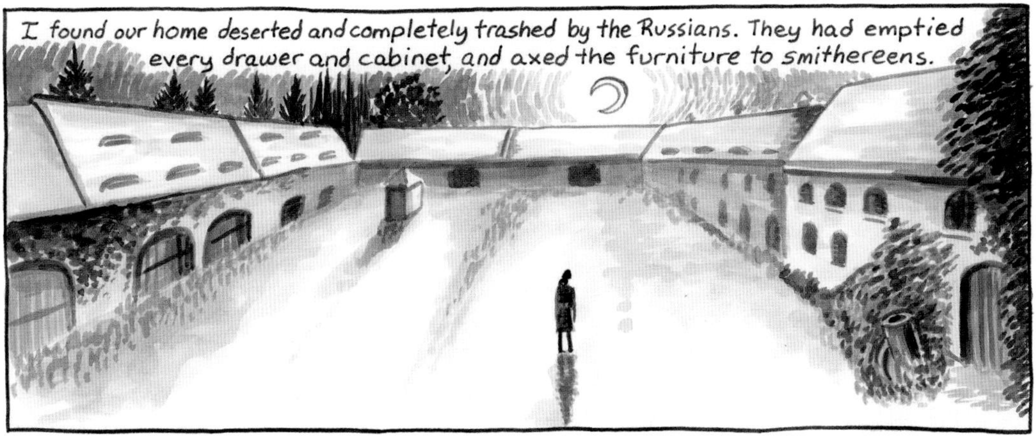
I found our home deserted and completely trashed by the Russians. They had emptied every drawer and cabinet, and axed the furniture to smithereens.

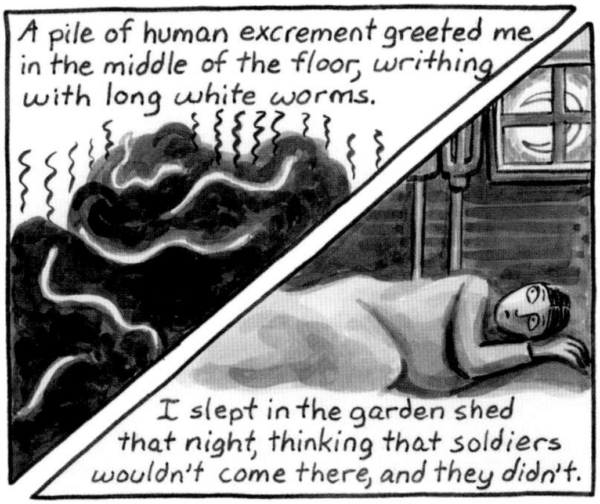
A pile of human excrement greeted me in the middle of the floor, writhing with long white worms.
I slept in the garden shed that night, thinking that soldiers wouldn't come there, and they didn't.

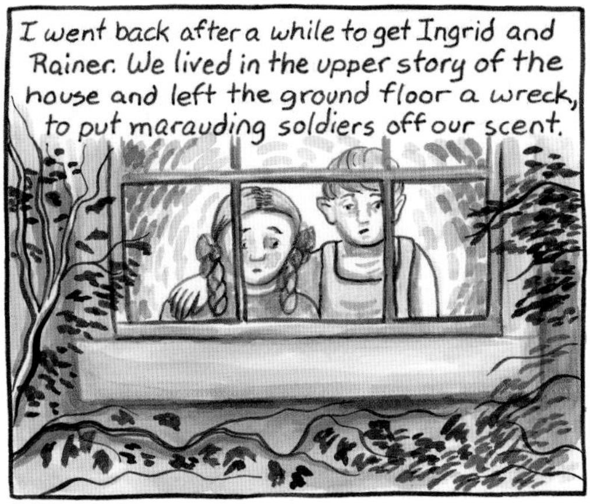
I went back after a while to get Ingrid and Rainer. We lived in the upper story of the house and left the ground floor a wreck, to put marauding soldiers off our scent.

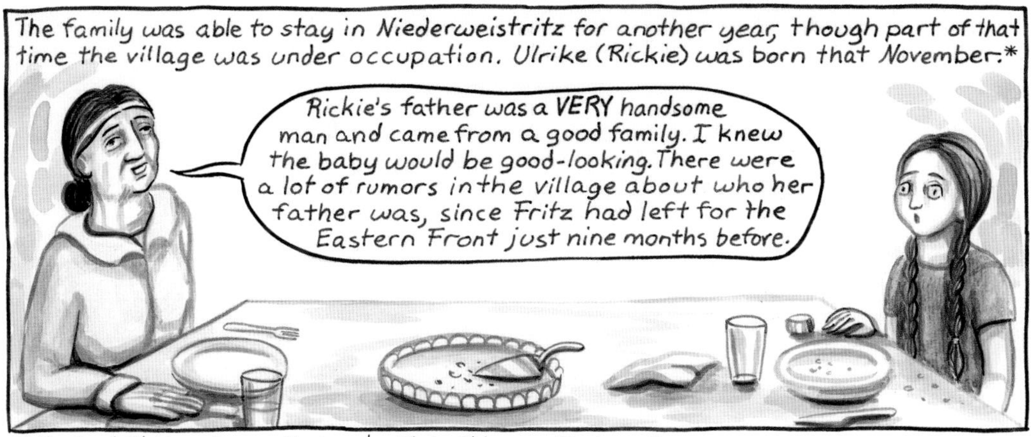
The family was able to stay in Niederweistritz for another year, though part of that time the village was under occupation. Ulrike (Rickie) was born that November.*
Rickie's father was a VERY handsome man and came from a good family. I knew the baby would be good-looking. There were a lot of rumors in the village about who her father was, since Fritz had left for the Eastern Front just nine months before.

*My Aunt Rickie, whom we'd stayed with in Chicago—Ian's mother.

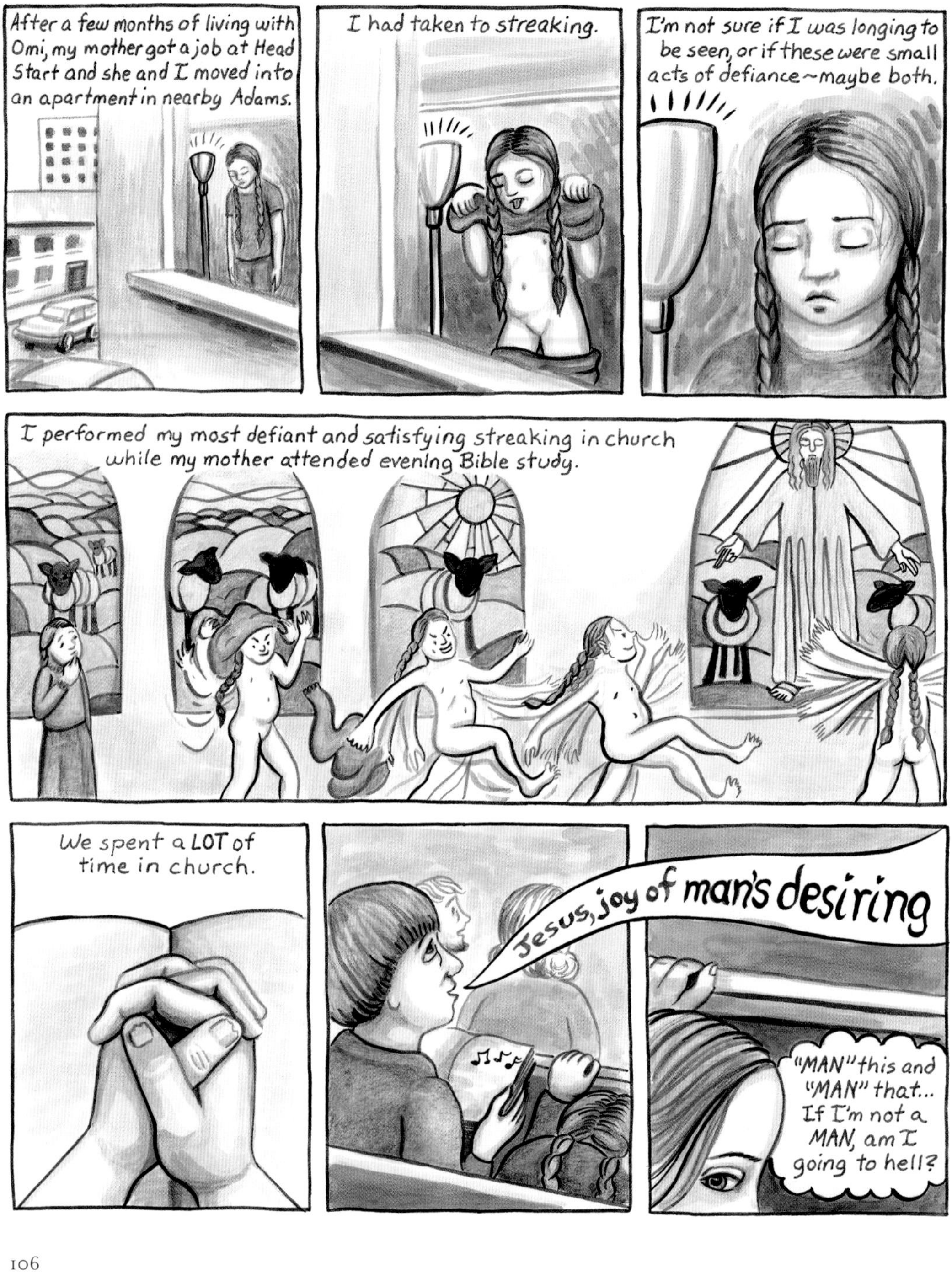

After a few months of living with Omi, my mother got a job at Head Start and she and I moved into an apartment in nearby Adams.
I had taken to streaking.
I'm not sure if I was longing to be seen, or if these were small acts of defiance~maybe both.
I performed my most defiant and satisfying streaking in church while my mother attended evening Bible study.
We spent a LOT of time in church.
Jesus, joy of man's desiring
"MAN" this and "MAN" that... If I'm not a MAN, am I going to hell?

Homesickness and loneliness had leached through my skin and into my muscle tissue.

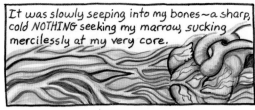

It was slowly seeping into my bones ~ a sharp, cold NOTHING seeking my marrow, sucking mercilessly at my very core.

One day on the bus ride home, I thought the girl next to me had fallen asleep with her head against my shoulder.

I felt her warmth against my arm.

The sensation was so comforting...

...so wonderful.

I didn't dare peek.

I sat very still for the longest time...

...afraid to move.

I didn't want to wake her.

When I finally looked, I saw I'd imagined it.

I did start to make some friends during my year at Castle Rock. There was Karen.

HAHAAA! Maureen is a LESBIAN!

Karen wouldn't talk to me anymore after that.

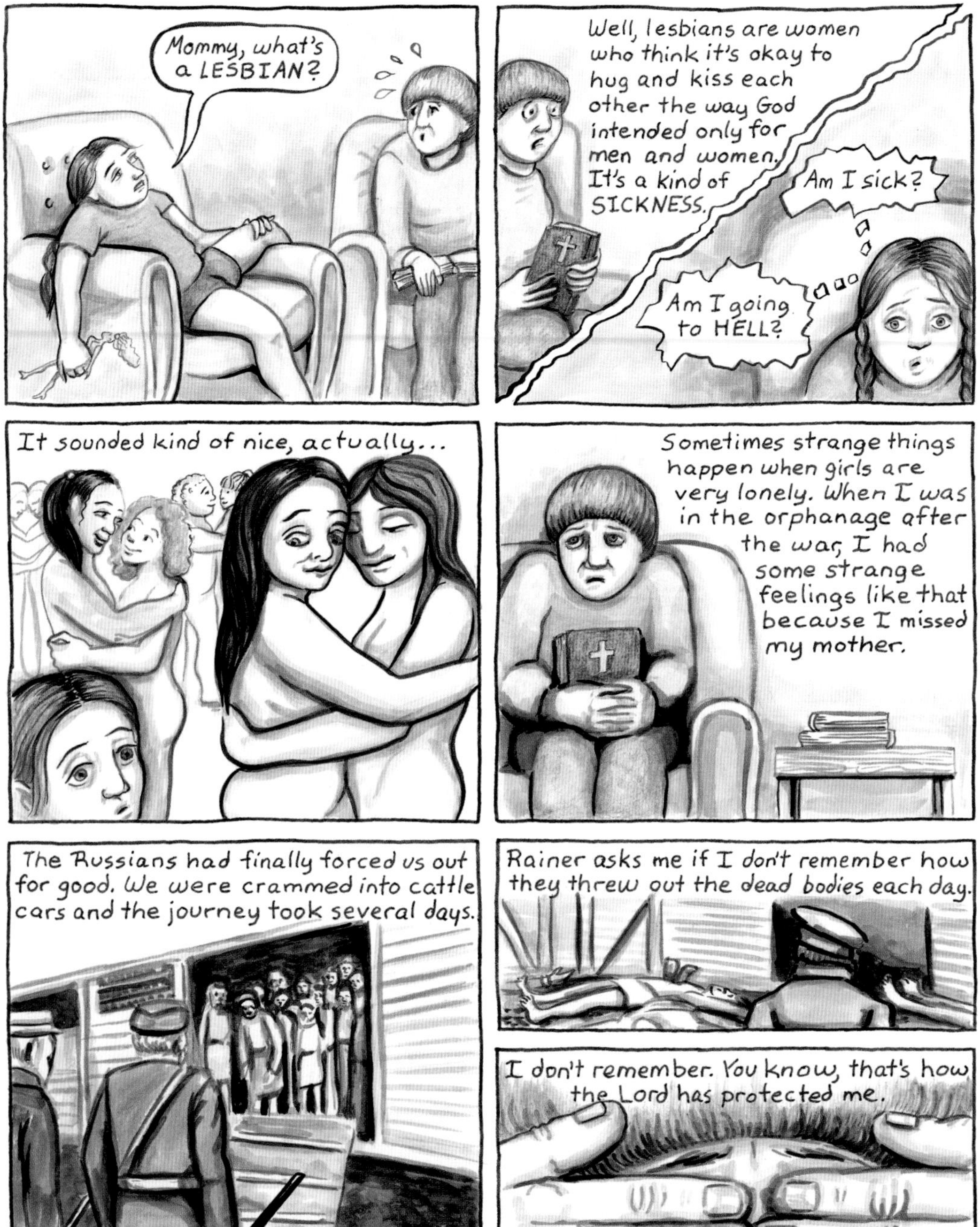
Mommy, what's a LESBIAN?
Well, lesbians are women who think it's okay to hug and kiss each other the way God intended only for men and women. It's a kind of SICKNESS.
Am I sick?
Am I going to HELL?
It sounded kind of nice, actually...
Sometimes strange things happen when girls are very lonely. When I was in the orphanage after the war, I had some strange feelings like that because I missed my mother.
The Russians had finally forced us out for good. We were crammed into cattle cars and the journey took several days.
Rainer asks me if I don't remember how they threw out the dead bodies each day.
I don't remember. You know, that's how the Lord has protected me.

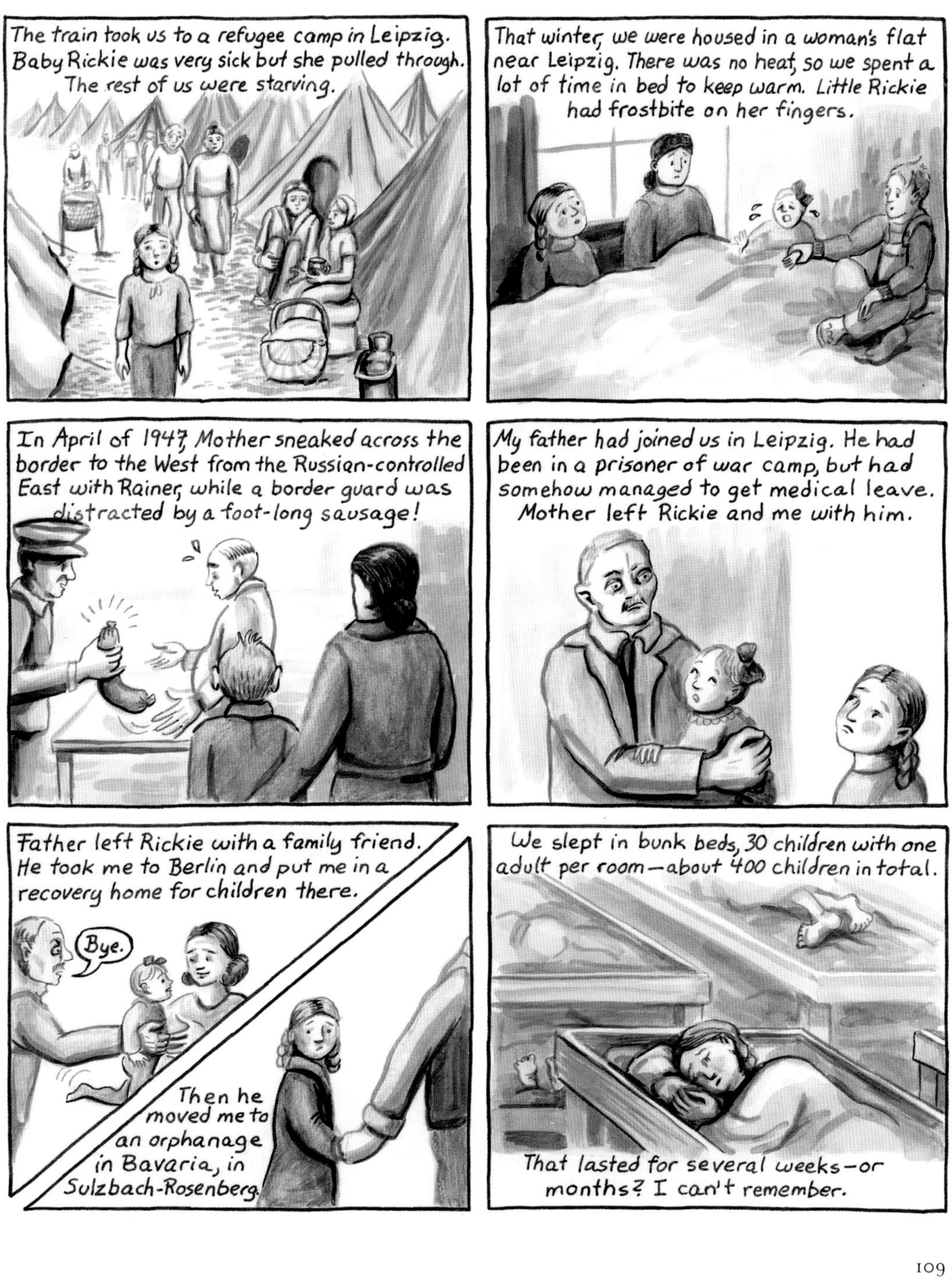
The train took us to a refugee camp in Leipzig. Baby Rickie was very sick but she pulled through. The rest of us were starving.
That winter, we were housed in a woman's flat near Leipzig. There was no heat, so we spent a lot of time in bed to keep warm. Little Rickie had frostbite on her fingers.
In April of 1947, Mother sneaked across the border to the West from the Russian-controlled East with Rainer, while a border guard was distracted by a foot-long sausage!
My father had joined us in Leipzig. He had been in a prisoner of war camp, but had somehow managed to get medical leave. Mother left Rickie and me with him.
Father left Rickie with a family friend. He took me to Berlin and put me in a recovery home for children there.
Bye.
Then he moved me to an orphanage in Bavaria, in Sulzbach-Rosenberg.
We slept in bunk beds, 30 children with one adult per room—about 400 children in total.
That lasted for several weeks—or months? I can't remember.

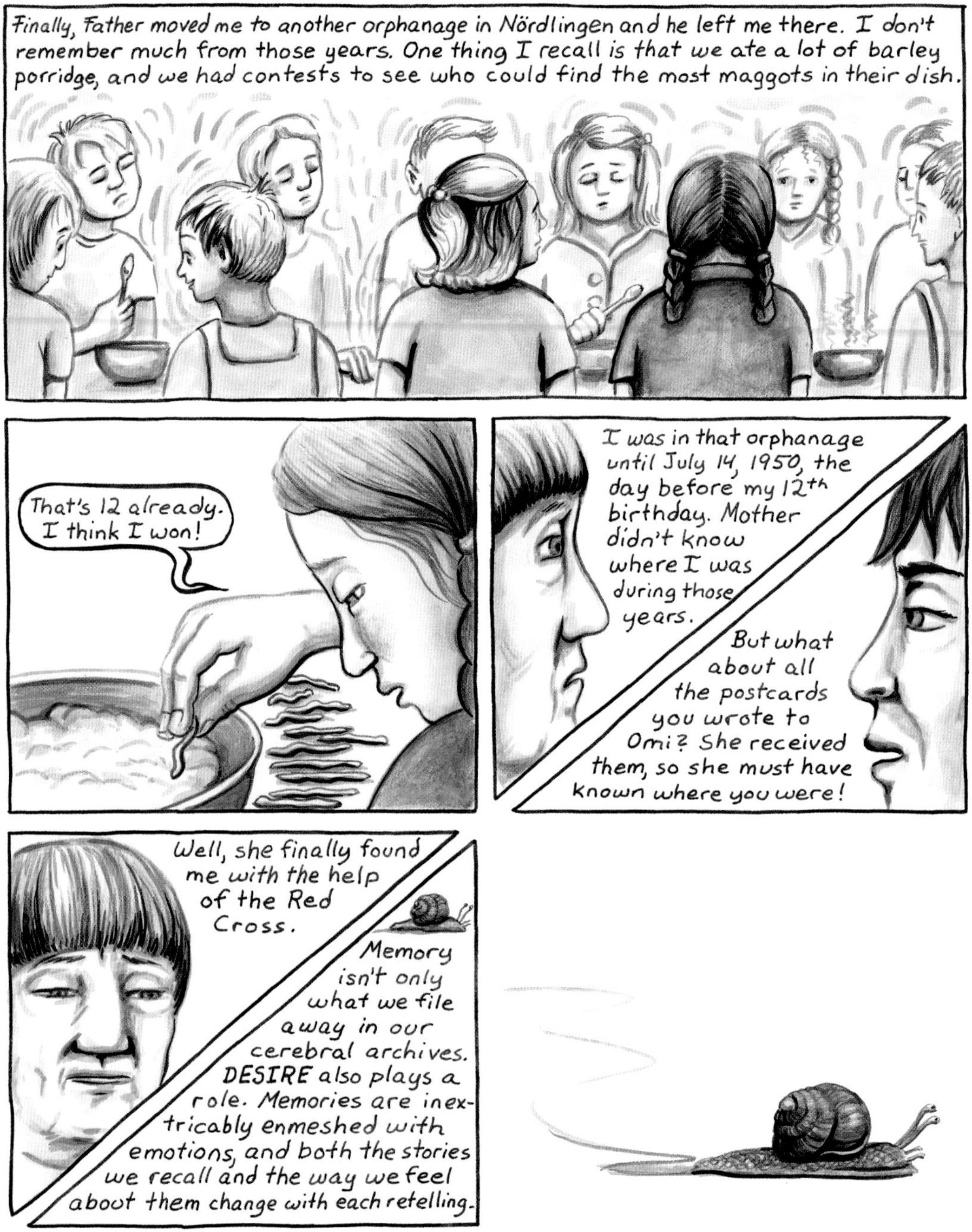

Finally, Father moved me to another orphanage in Nördlingen and he left me there. I don't remember much from those years. One thing I recall is that we ate a lot of barley porridge, and we had contests to see who could find the most maggots in their dish.
That's 12 already. I think I won!
I was in that orphanage until July 14, 1950, the day before my 12th birthday. Mother didn't know where I was during those years.
But what about all the postcards you wrote to Omi? She received them, so she must have known where you were!
Well, she finally found me with the help of the Red Cross.
Memory isn't only what we file away in our cerebral archives. DESIRE also plays a role. Memories are inextricably enmeshed with emotions, and both the stories we recall and the way we feel about them change with each retelling.

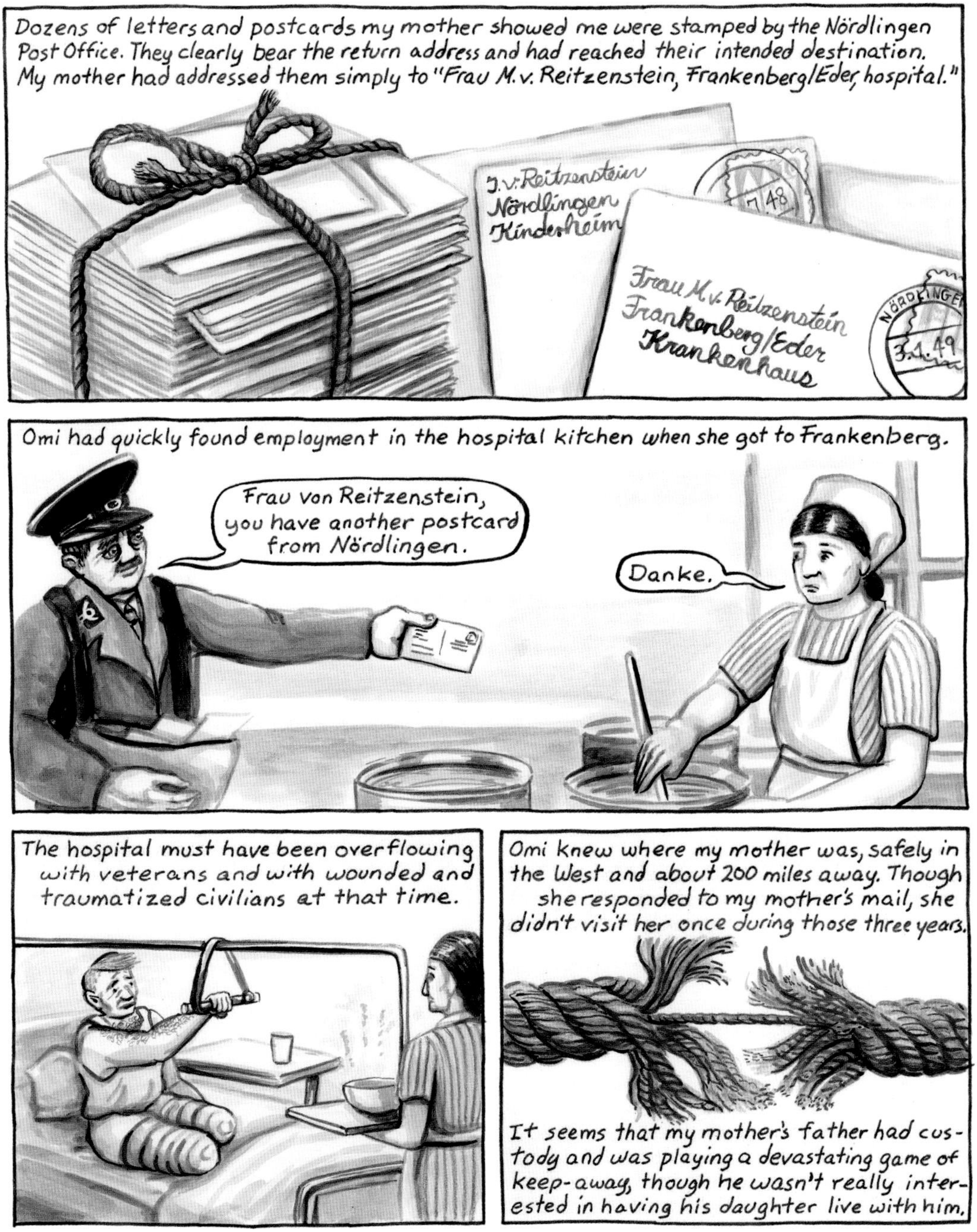
Dozens of letters and postcards my mother showed me were stamped by the Nördlingen Post Office. They clearly bear the return address and had reached their intended destination. My mother had addressed them simply to "Frau M.v. Reitzenstein, Frankenberg/Eder, hospital."
I.v. Reitzenstein
Nördlingen
Kinderheim
Frau M.v. Reitzenstein
Frankenberg/Eder
Krankenhaus
7.48
NÖRDLINGEN
3.1.49
Omi had quickly found employment in the hospital kitchen when she got to Frankenberg.
Frau von Reitzenstein, you have another postcard from Nördlingen.
Danke.
The hospital must have been overflowing with veterans and with wounded and traumatized civilians at that time.
Omi knew where my mother was, safely in the West and about 200 miles away. Though she responded to my mother's mail, she didn't visit her once during those three years.
It seems that my mother's father had custody and was playing a devastating game of keep-away, though he wasn't really interested in having his daughter live with him.

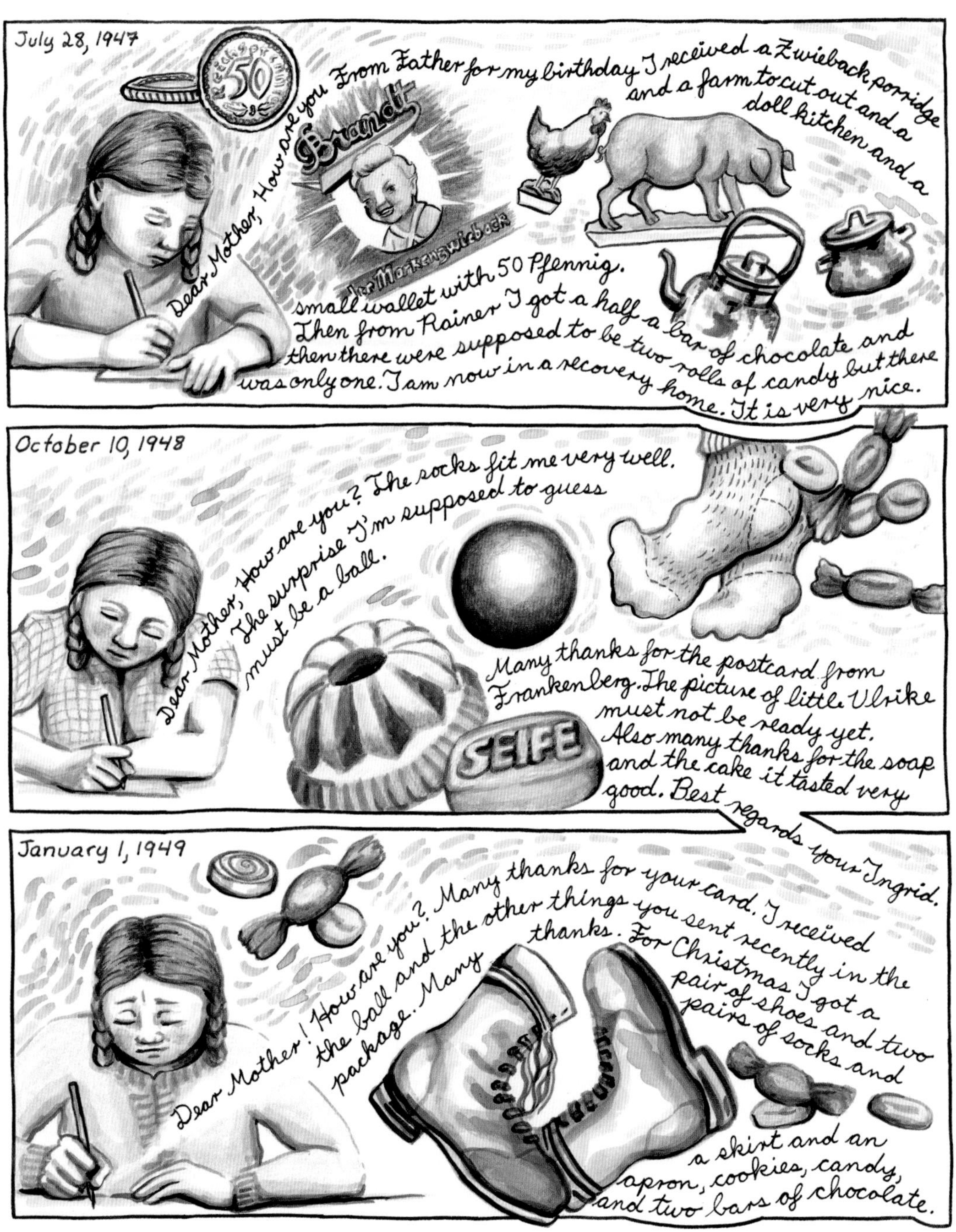
July 28, 1947
50
Brandt
Dear Mother, How are you From Father for my birthday I received a Zwieback porridge
and a farm to cut out and a
doll kitchen and a
small wallet with 50 Pfennig.
Then from Rainer I got a half a bar of chocolate and
then there were supposed to be two rolls of candy but there
was only one. I am now in a recovery home. It is very nice.
October 10, 1948
Dear Mother, How are you? The socks fit me very well.
The surprise I'm supposed to guess
must be a ball.
SEIFE
Many thanks for the postcard from
Frankenberg. The picture of little Ulrike
must not be ready yet.
Also many thanks for the soap
and the cake it tasted very
good. Best regards your Ingrid.
January 1, 1949
Dear Mother! How are you? Many thanks for your card. I received
the ball and the other things you sent recently in the
package. Many thanks. For Christmas I got a
pair of shoes and two
pairs of socks and
a skirt and an
apron, cookies, candy,
and two bars of chocolate.

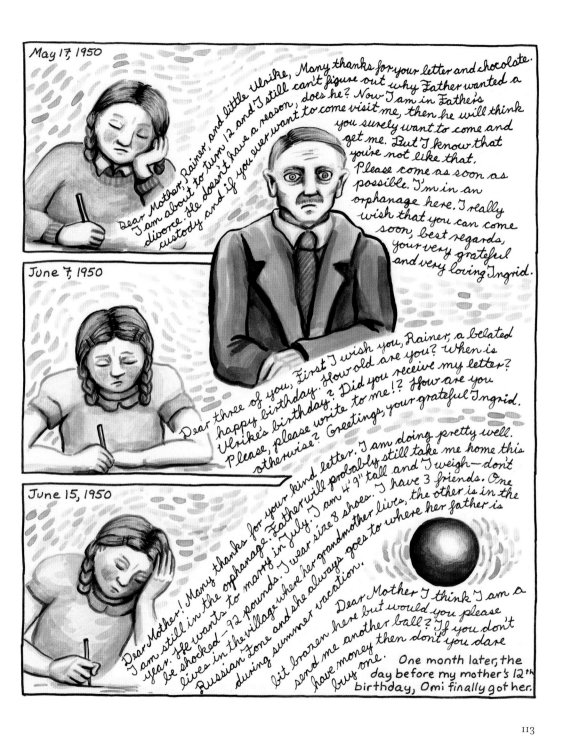

May 17, 1950

Dear Mother, Rainer and little Ulrike, Many thanks for your letter and chocolate. I am about to turn 12 and I still can't figure out why Father wanted a divorce. He doesn't have a reason, does he? Now I am in Father's custody and if you ever want to come visit me, then he will think you surely want to come and get me. But I know that you're not like that.
Please come as soon as possible. I'm in an orphanage here. I really wish that you can come soon, best regards, your very grateful and very loving Ingrid.

June 7, 1950

Dear three of you, First I wish you, Rainer, a belated happy birthday. How old are you? When is Ulrike's birthday? Did you receive my letter? How are you otherwise? Greetings, your grateful Ingrid. Please, please write to me!? How are you

June 15, 1950

Dear Mother! Many thanks for your kind letter. I am doing pretty well. I am still in the orphanage. Father will probably still take me home this year. He wants to marry in July. I am 4'9" tall and I weigh—don't be shocked—92 pounds. I wear size 8 shoes. I have 3 friends. One lives in the village where her grandmother lives, the other is in the Russian Zone and she always goes to where her father is during summer vacation.

Dear Mother I think I am a bit brazen here but would you please send me another ball? If you don't have money then don't you dare buy one. One month later, the day before my mother's 12th birthday, Omi finally got her.

113

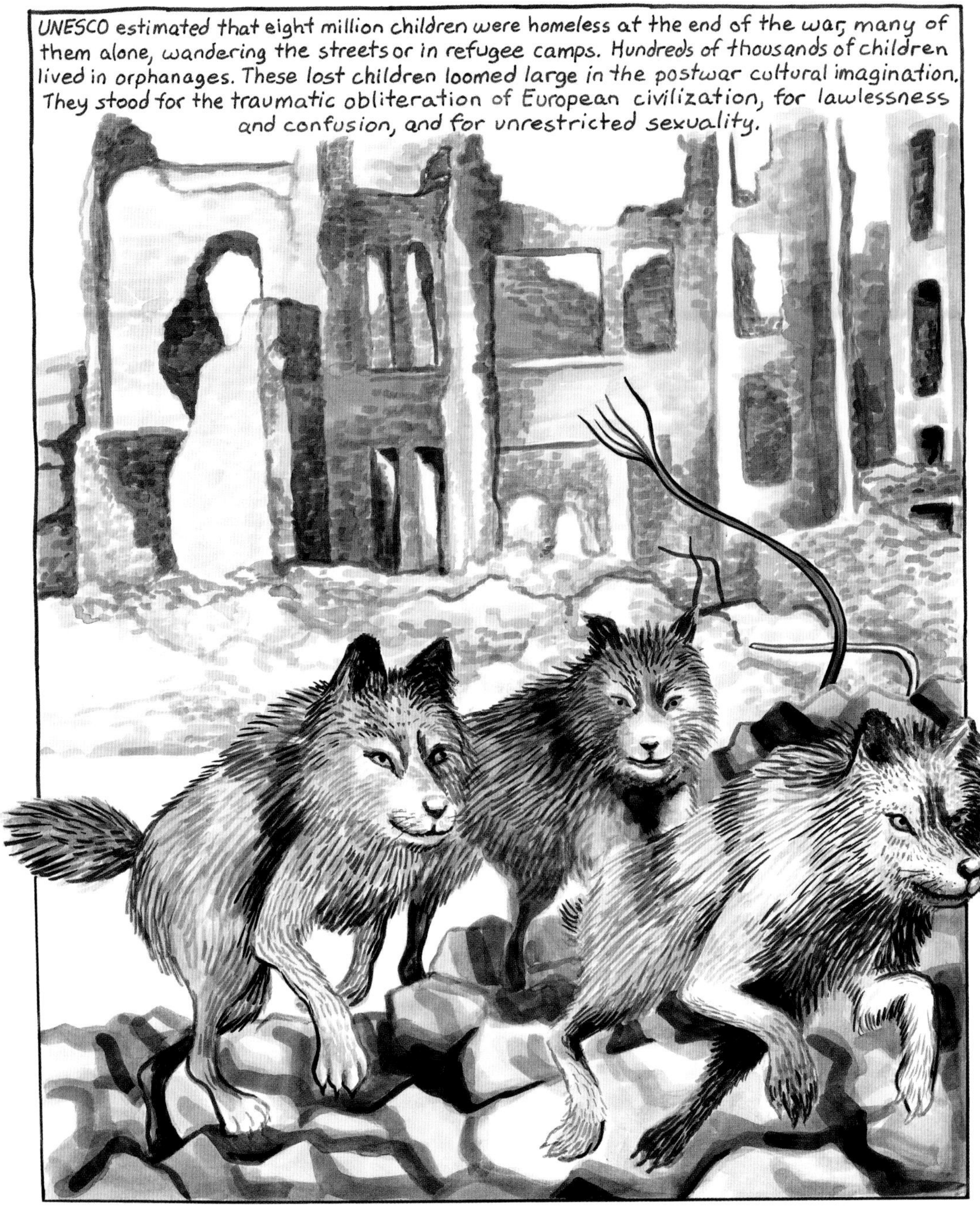
UNESCO estimated that eight million children were homeless at the end of the war, many of them alone, wandering the streets or in refugee camps. Hundreds of thousands of children lived in orphanages. These lost children loomed large in the postwar cultural imagination. They stood for the traumatic obliteration of European civilization, for lawlessness and confusion, and for unrestricted sexuality.

Seeing this extreme situation right after the war, people in the Western world, like British-American author Alice Bailey, were shocked that such a total collapse could happen in the West.

Those peculiar and wild children of Europe and of China to whom the name "wolf children" has been given...have known no parental authority; they run in packs like wolves; they lack all moral sense and have no civilized values and know no sexual restrictions; they know no laws save the law of self-preservation.

My mother is without a doubt a *kriegskind,* a "war child," and she was doubly lost. She'd witnessed and experienced horrible things and, while she was fortunate to still have two living parents, it seems she was also the collateral damage in her parents' divorce drama.

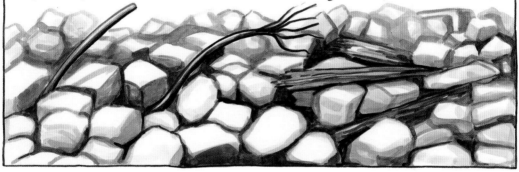

I think my mother has confused Jesus with Somnus, the Roman god of sleep. It wasn't Jesus who protected her, but her own closed eyes. Maybe opening them would have hurt too much.

What can I say? I wasn't born in 1938. I have the opposite problem— *in*Somnia. I can't seem to keep my eyes closed.

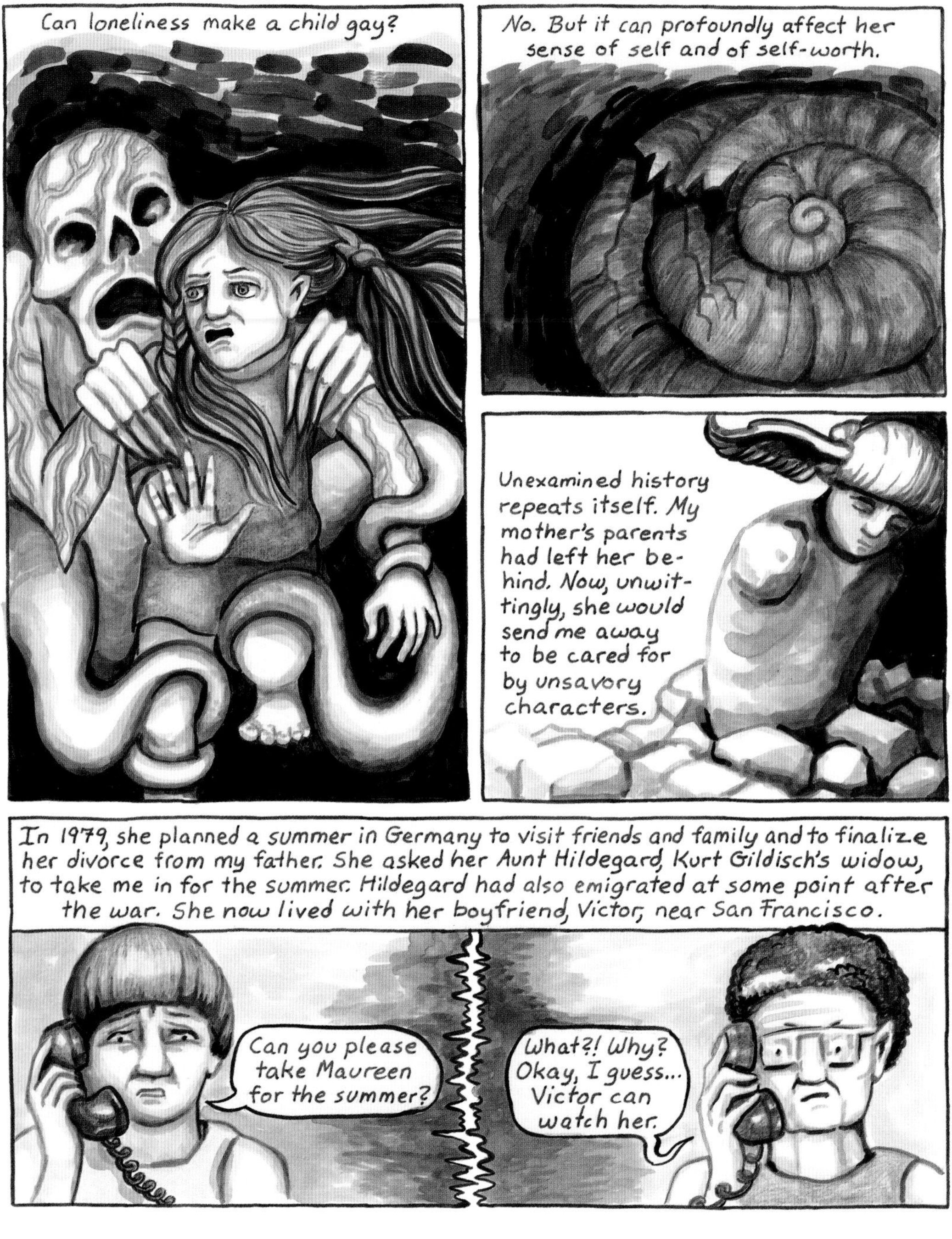
Can loneliness make a child gay?
No. But it can profoundly affect her sense of self and of self-worth.
Unexamined history repeats itself. My mother's parents had left her behind. Now, unwittingly, she would send me away to be cared for by unsavory characters.
In 1979, she planned a summer in Germany to visit friends and family and to finalize her divorce from my father. She asked her Aunt Hildegard, Kurt Gildisch's widow, to take me in for the summer. Hildegard had also emigrated at some point after the war. She now lived with her boyfriend, Victor, near San Francisco.
Can you please take Maureen for the summer?
What?! Why? Okay, I guess... Victor can watch her.

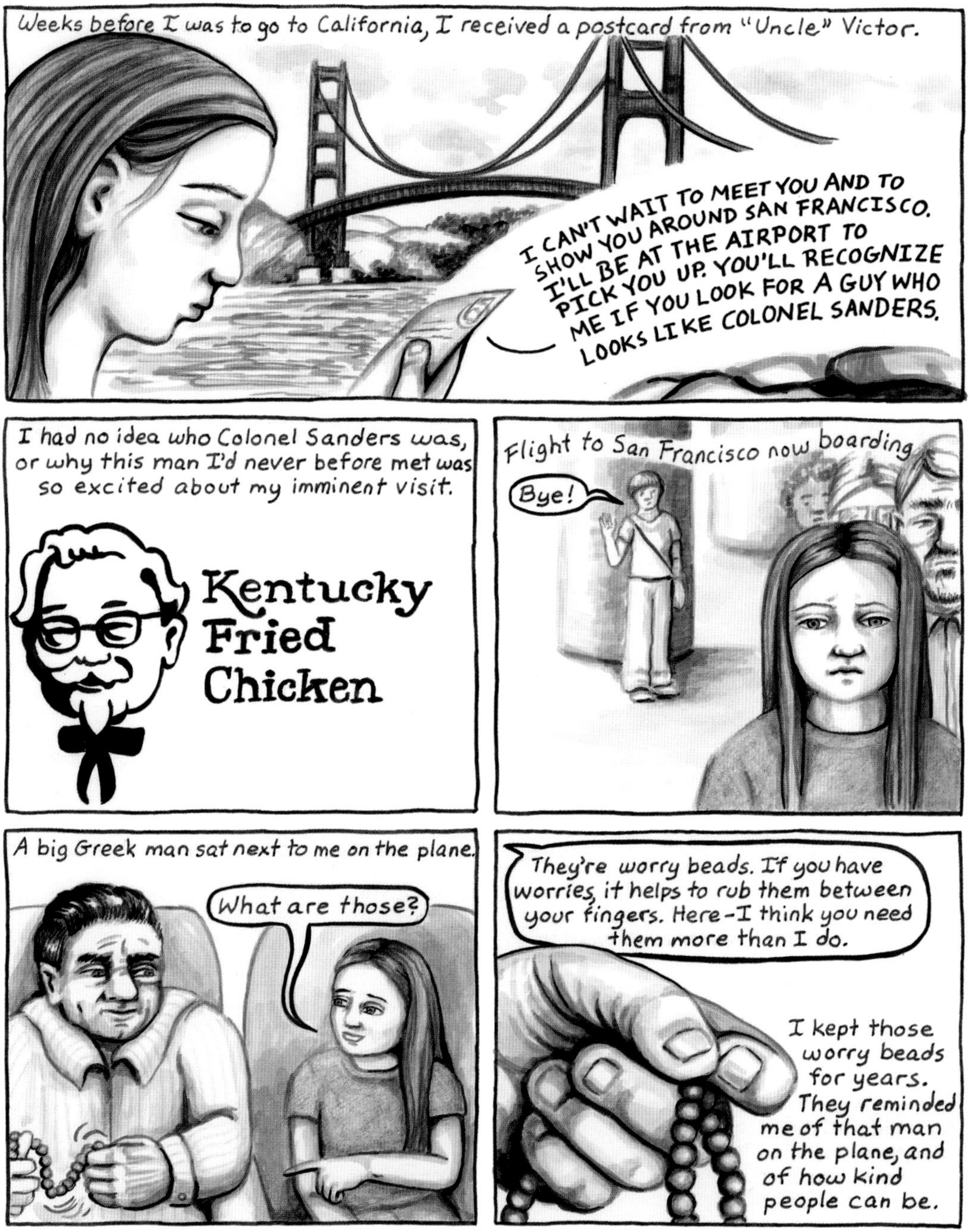
Weeks before I was to go to California, I received a postcard from "Uncle" Victor.
I CAN'T WAIT TO MEET YOU AND TO SHOW YOU AROUND SAN FRANCISCO. I'LL BE AT THE AIRPORT TO PICK YOU UP. YOU'LL RECOGNIZE ME IF YOU LOOK FOR A GUY WHO LOOKS LIKE COLONEL SANDERS.
I had no idea who Colonel Sanders was, or why this man I'd never before met was so excited about my imminent visit.
Kentucky Fried Chicken
Flight to San Francisco now boarding
Bye!
A big Greek man sat next to me on the plane.
What are those?
They're worry beads. If you have worries, it helps to rub them between your fingers. Here-I think you need them more than I do.
I kept those worry beads for years. They reminded me of that man on the plane, and of how kind people can be.

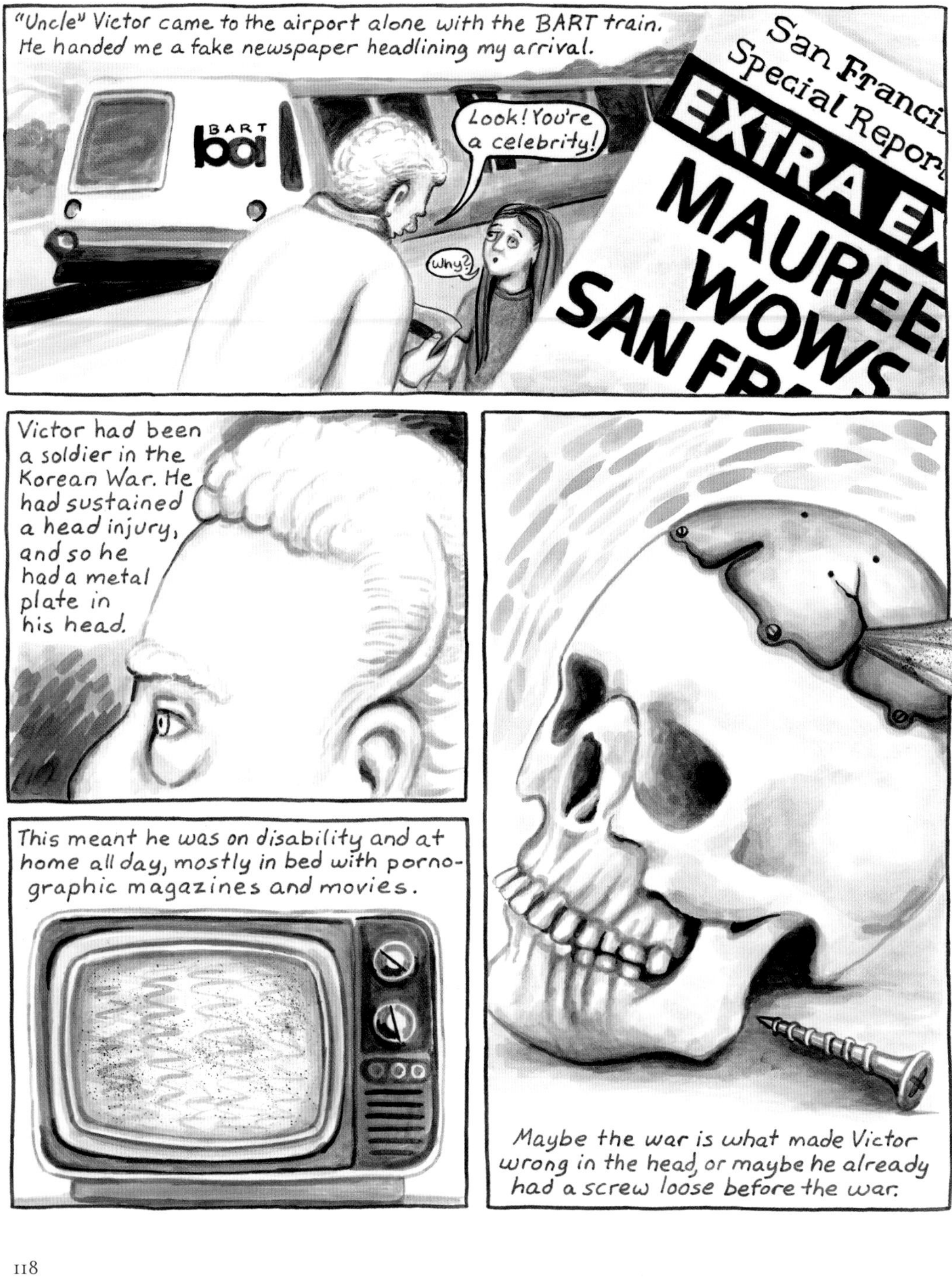

"Uncle" Victor came to the airport alone with the BART train. He handed me a fake newspaper headlining my arrival.
BART
Look! You're a celebrity!
Why?
San Franci
Special Repor
EXTRA EX
MAUREE
WOWS
Victor had been a soldier in the Korean War. He had sustained a head injury, and so he had a metal plate in his head.
This meant he was on disability and at home all day, mostly in bed with porno-graphic magazines and movies.
Maybe the war is what made Victor wrong in the head, or maybe he already had a screw loose before the war.

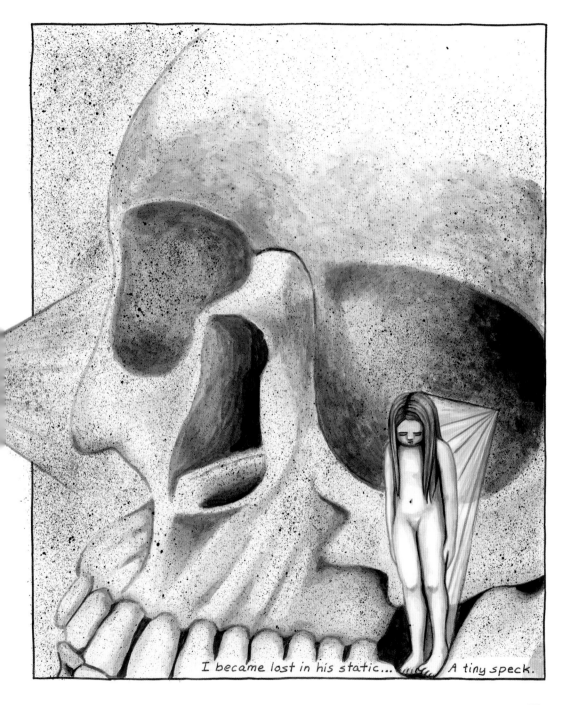

I became lost in his static... A tiny speck.

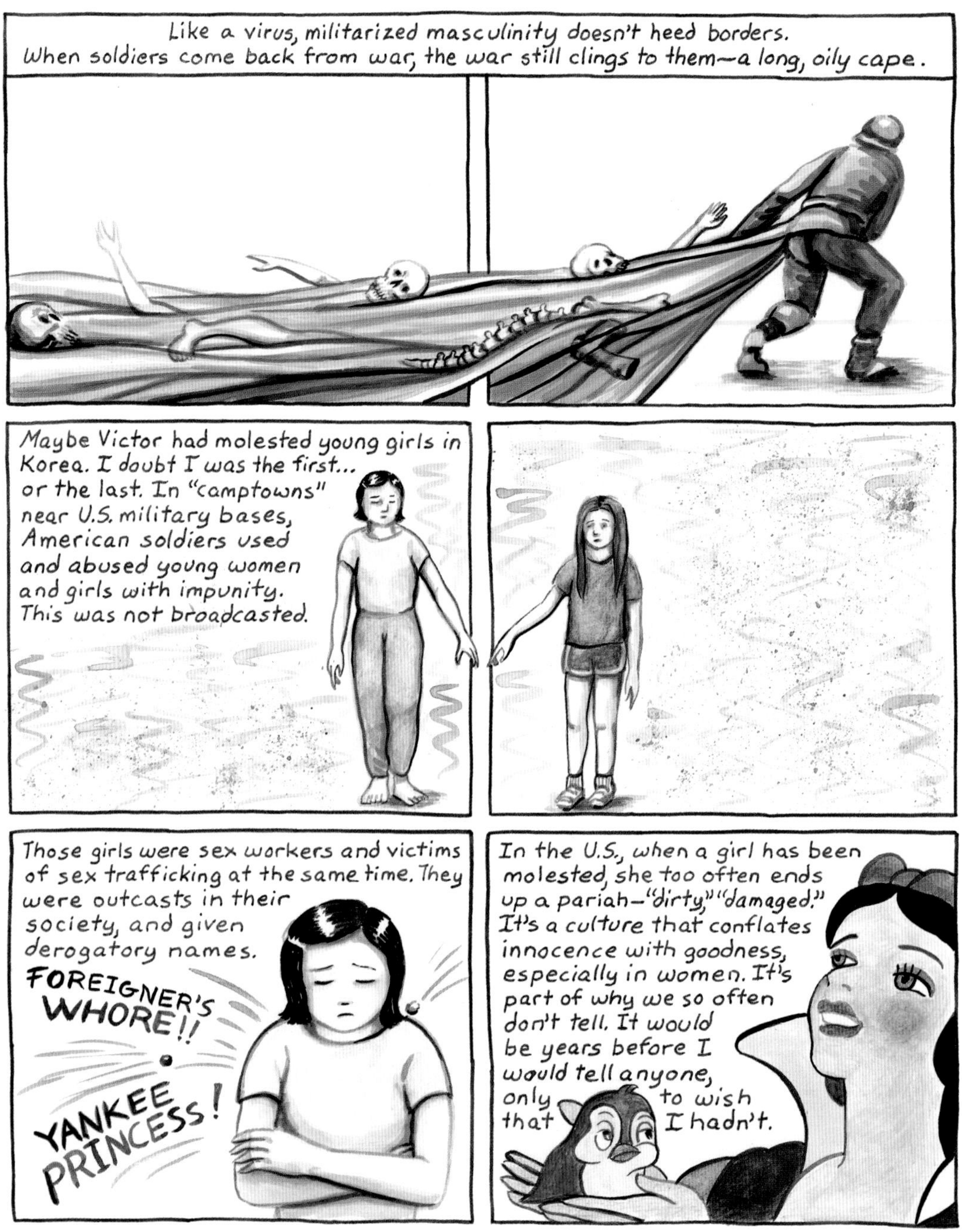
Like a virus, militarized masculinity doesn't heed borders.
When soldiers come back from war, the war still clings to them—a long, oily cape.
Maybe Victor had molested young girls in Korea. I doubt I was the first... or the last. In "camptowns" near U.S. military bases, American soldiers used and abused young women and girls with impunity. This was not broadcasted.
Those girls were sex workers and victims of sex trafficking at the same time. They were outcasts in their society, and given derogatory names.
FOREIGNER'S WHORE!!
YANKEE PRINCESS!
In the U.S., when a girl has been molested, she too often ends up a pariah—"dirty," "damaged." It's a culture that conflates innocence with goodness, especially in women. It's part of why we so often don't tell. It would be years before I would tell anyone, only to wish that I hadn't.

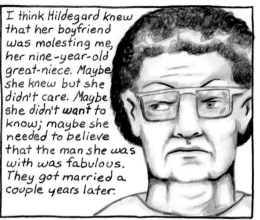

I think Hildegard knew that her boyfriend was molesting me, her nine-year-old great-niece. Maybe she knew but she didn't care. Maybe she didn't **want** to know; maybe she needed to believe that the man she was with was fabulous. They got married a couple years later.

Apparently she had been quite a vamp back in the day ~ fetching enough to attract "fabulous" men like Kurt Gildisch... Here she is, wearing her cap and apron, from a photo stamped December 15, 1947, Berlin. She'd been a midwife.

If she knew, maybe Hildegard blamed me instead of Victor for the things he did to me while she was at work every day.

You're so dirty!

OUCH!

SCRUB RUB

THAT'S NOT DIRT! MY SKIN IS SUPPOSED TO BE THAT COLOR!!

Some nights, Hildegard would bake a chicken for herself and Victor, but I was only allowed to eat the skin. The meat was for them.

When we went out by ourselves, Victor bought me things ~ chocolate, a Wonder Woman bathing suit...

Hey, how'd you feel if I gave you a whole lot of kisses right here in public? HAHAHA Hershey's kisses.

121

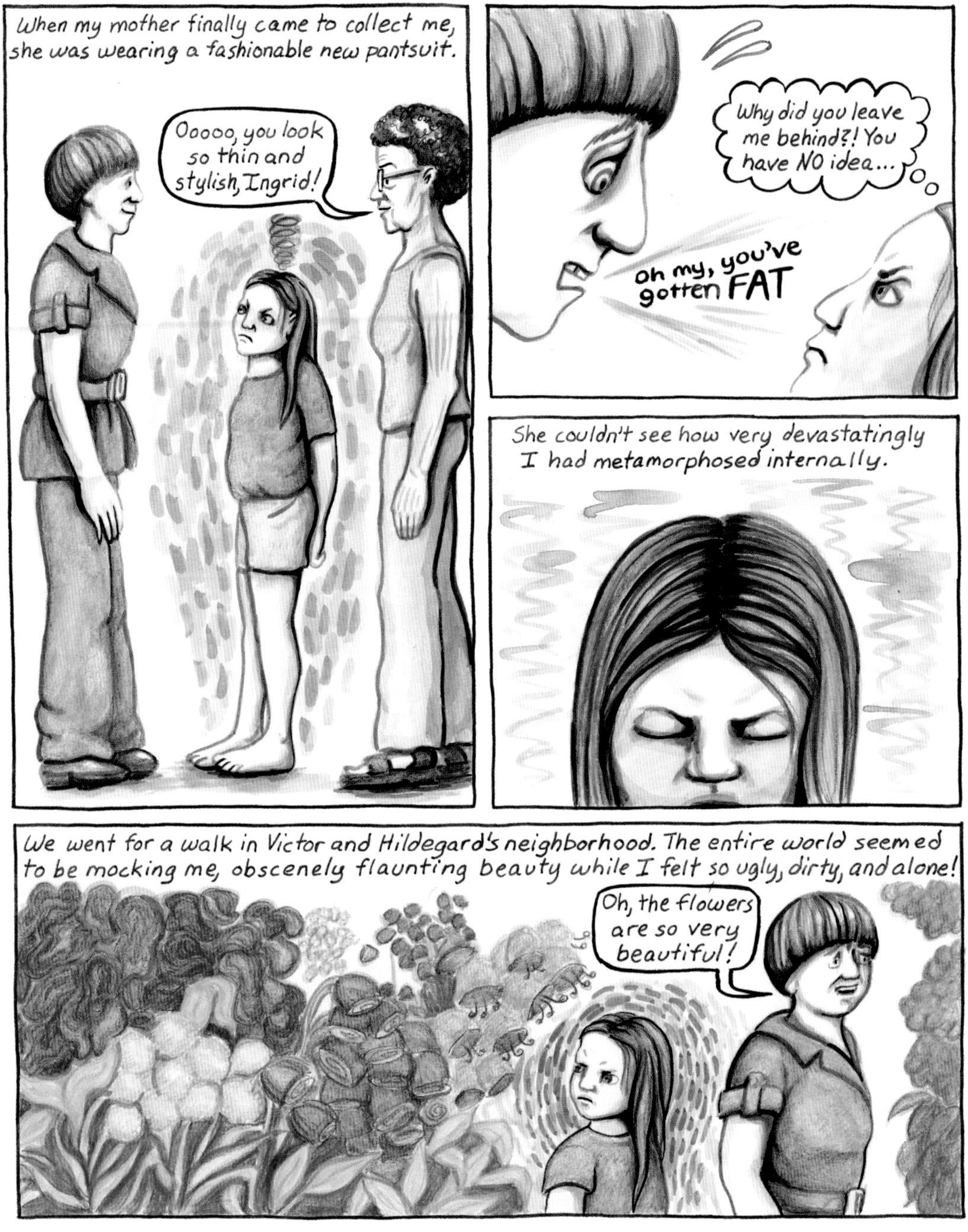
When my mother finally came to collect me, she was wearing a fashionable new pantsuit.
Ooooo, you look so thin and stylish, Ingrid!
Why did you leave me behind?! You have NO idea...
Oh my, you've gotten FAT
She couldn't see how very devastatingly I had metamorphosed internally.
We went for a walk in Victor and Hildegard's neighborhood. The entire world seemed to be mocking me, obscenely flaunting beauty while I felt so ugly, dirty, and alone!
Oh, the flowers are so very beautiful!

After that summer, my nightmares became more intense and frequent. I often woke up in a panic, crying and soaked with sweat.

A recurring theme was a man who came to saw or chop off my feet or legs, and I was unable to run away.

This strange phobia started affecting me during waking hours, too.

If I move, the **thing** from under the couch will come out and bite off my feet!

When I was home alone, my fears always became unbearable.

AAAAAAAAAAAOOOOOOOO
AAAAAOOOOOOOO

At some point, a neighbor must have heard my howls and called social services. A social worker came. She pronounced me a "forgotten child."

AAAOOOOOOOOOO
AAA
ZAOO

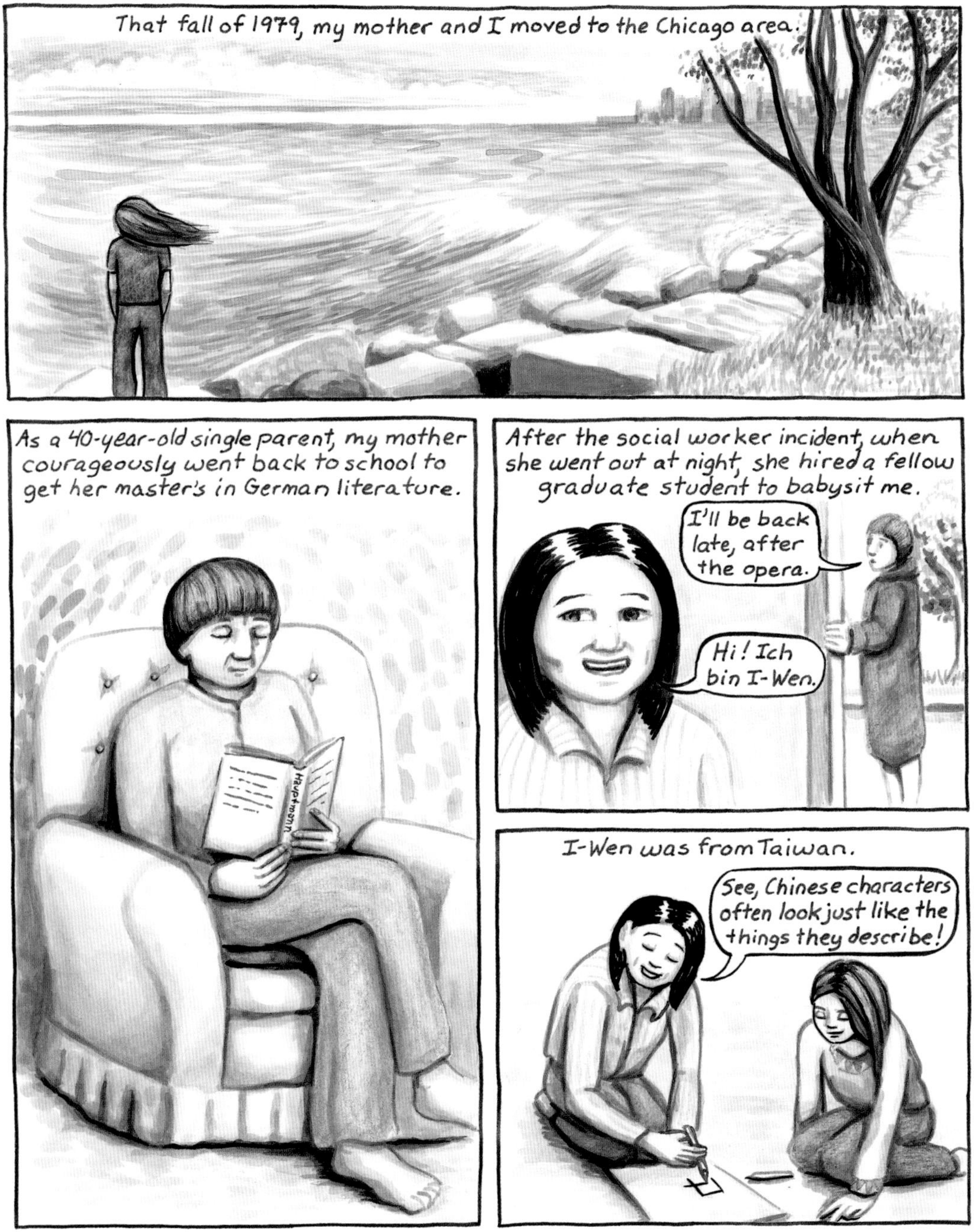
That fall of 1979, my mother and I moved to the Chicago area.
As a 40-year-old single parent, my mother courageously went back to school to get her master's in German literature.
Hauptmann
After the social worker incident, when she went out at night, she hired a fellow graduate student to babysit me.
I'll be back late, after the opera.
Hi! Ich bin I-Wen.
I-Wen was from Taiwan.
See, Chinese characters often look just like the things they describe!

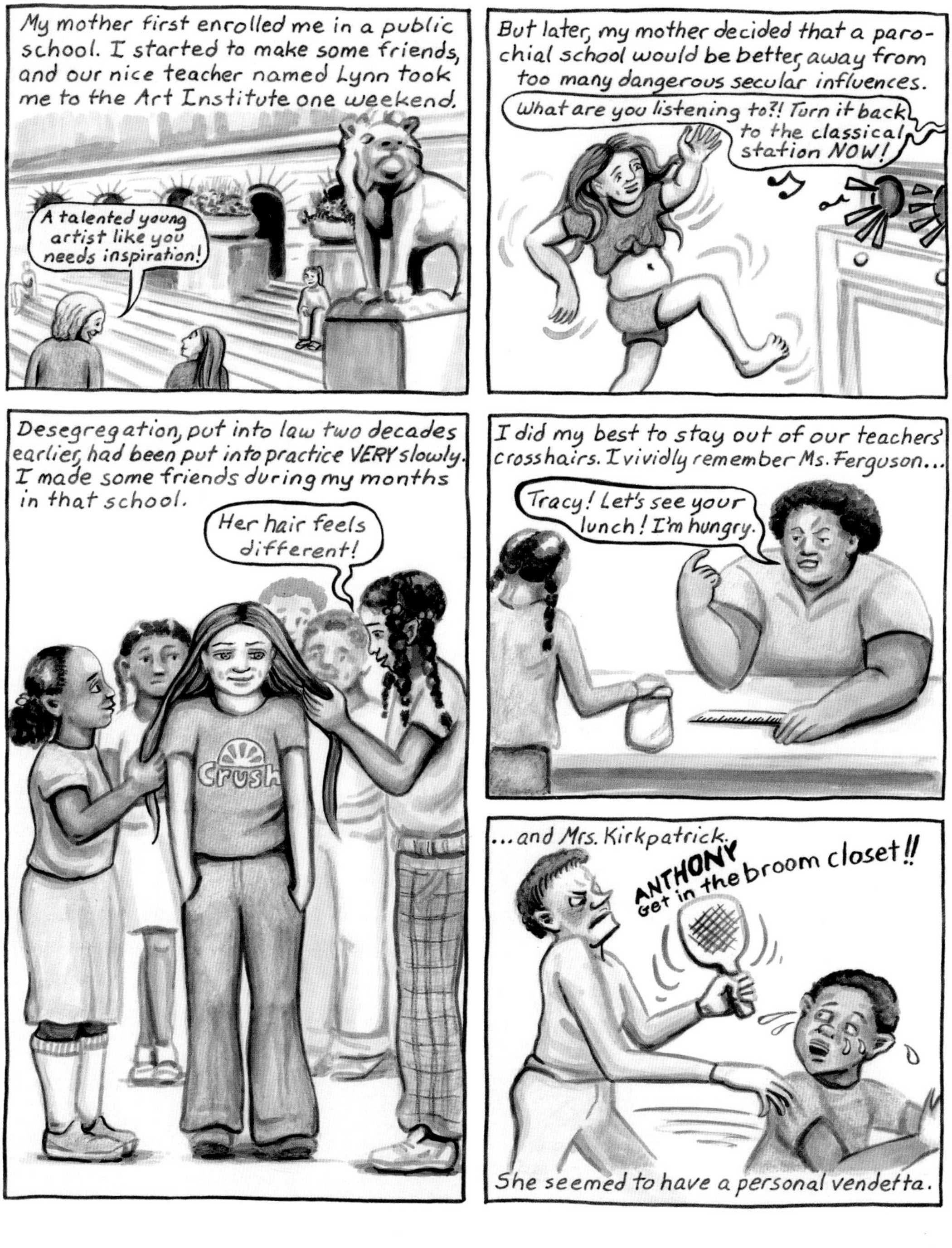
My mother first enrolled me in a public school. I started to make some friends, and our nice teacher named Lynn took me to the Art Institute one weekend.
A talented young artist like you needs inspiration!
But later, my mother decided that a parochial school would be better, away from too many dangerous secular influences.
What are you listening to?! Turn it back to the classical station NOW!
Desegregation, put into law two decades earlier, had been put into practice VERY slowly. I made some friends during my months in that school.
Her hair feels different!
Crush
I did my best to stay out of our teachers' crosshairs. I vividly remember Ms. Ferguson...
Tracy! Let's see your lunch! I'm hungry.
...and Mrs. Kirkpatrick.
ANTHONY Get in the broom closet!!
She seemed to have a personal vendetta.

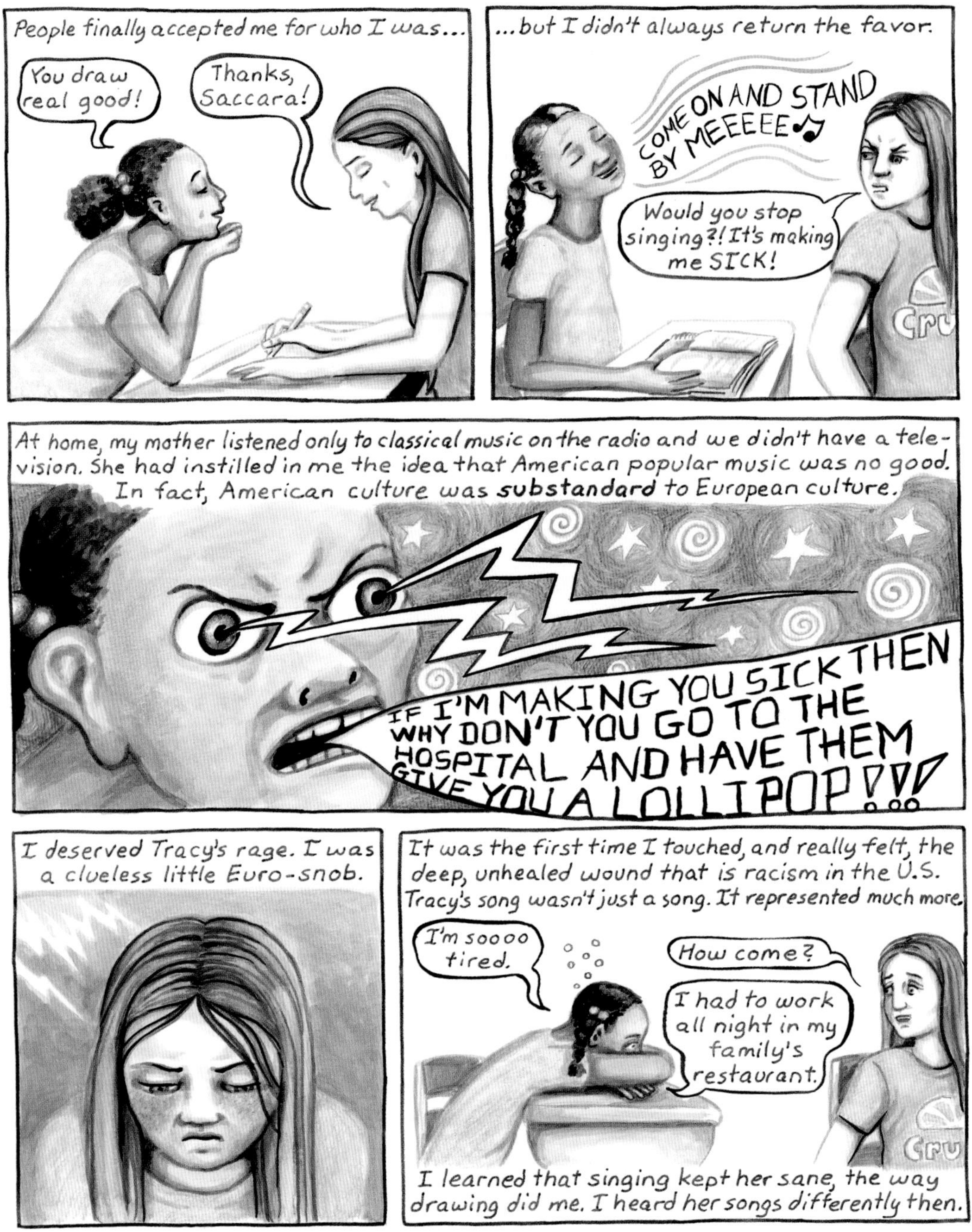
People finally accepted me for who I was...
You draw real good!
Thanks, Saccara!
...but I didn't always return the favor.
COME ON AND STAND BY MEEEEE♪
Would you stop singing?! It's making me SICK!
At home, my mother listened only to classical music on the radio and we didn't have a television. She had instilled in me the idea that American popular music was no good. In fact, American culture was **substandard** to European culture.
IF I'M MAKING YOU SICK THEN WHY DON'T YOU GO TO THE HOSPITAL AND HAVE THEM GIVE YOU A LOLLIPOP!!!
I deserved Tracy's rage. I was a clueless little Euro-snob.
It was the first time I touched, and really felt, the deep, unhealed wound that is racism in the U.S. Tracy's song wasn't just a song. It represented much more.
I'm soooo tired.
How come?
I had to work all night in my family's restaurant.
I learned that singing kept her sane, the way drawing did me. I heard her songs differently then.

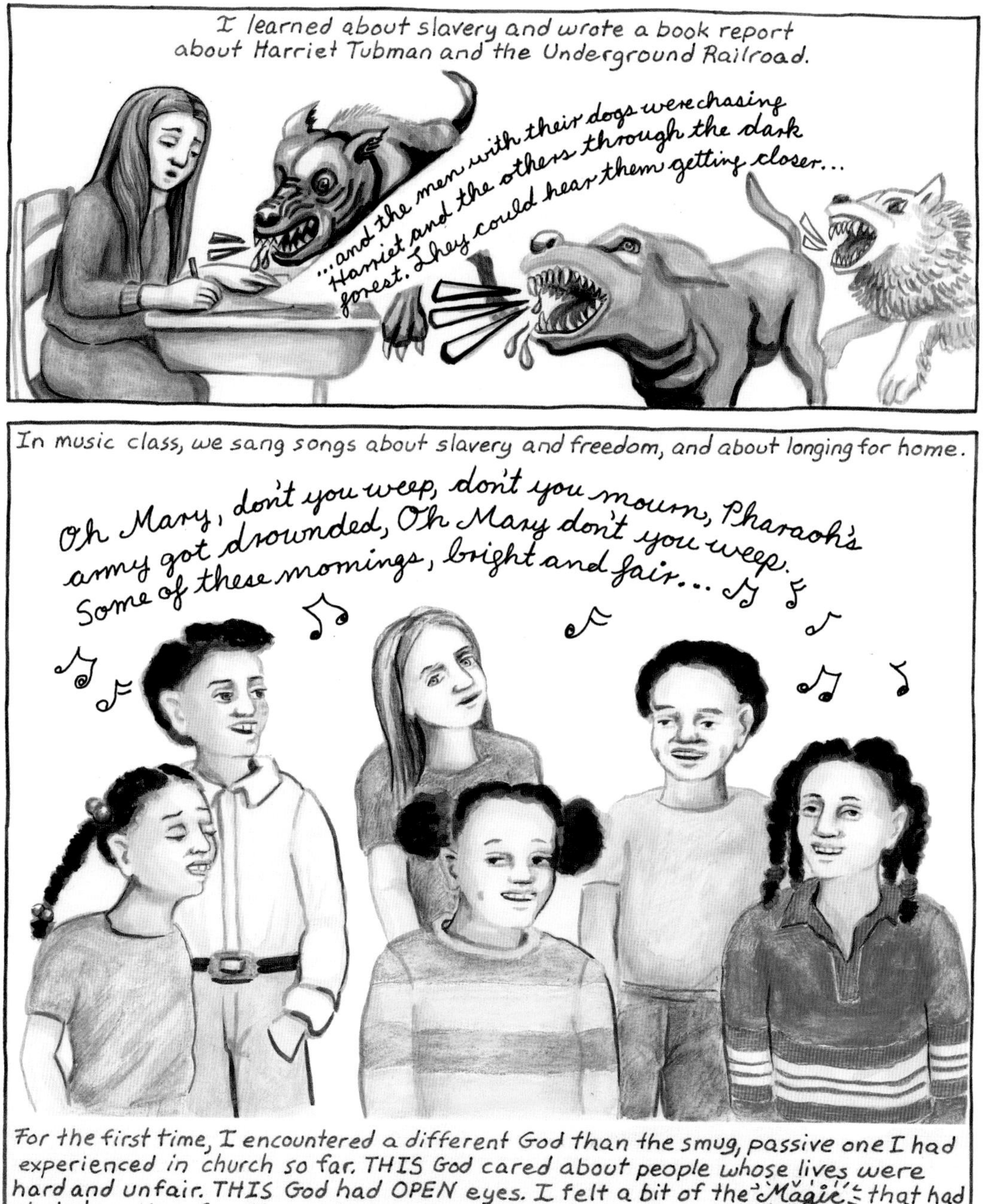
I learned about slavery and wrote a book report about Harriet Tubman and the Underground Railroad.
...and the men with their dogs were chasing Harriet and the others through the dark forest. They could hear them getting closer...
In music class, we sang songs about slavery and freedom, and about longing for home.
Oh Mary, don't you weep, don't you mourn, Pharaoh's army got drowned, Oh Mary don't you weep. Some of these mornings, bright and fair...
For the first time, I encountered a different God than the smug, passive one I had experienced in church so far. THIS God cared about people whose lives were hard and unfair. THIS God had OPEN eyes. I felt a bit of the "Magic" that had eluded me thus far. The next year, my mother moved me to another, all white, school.

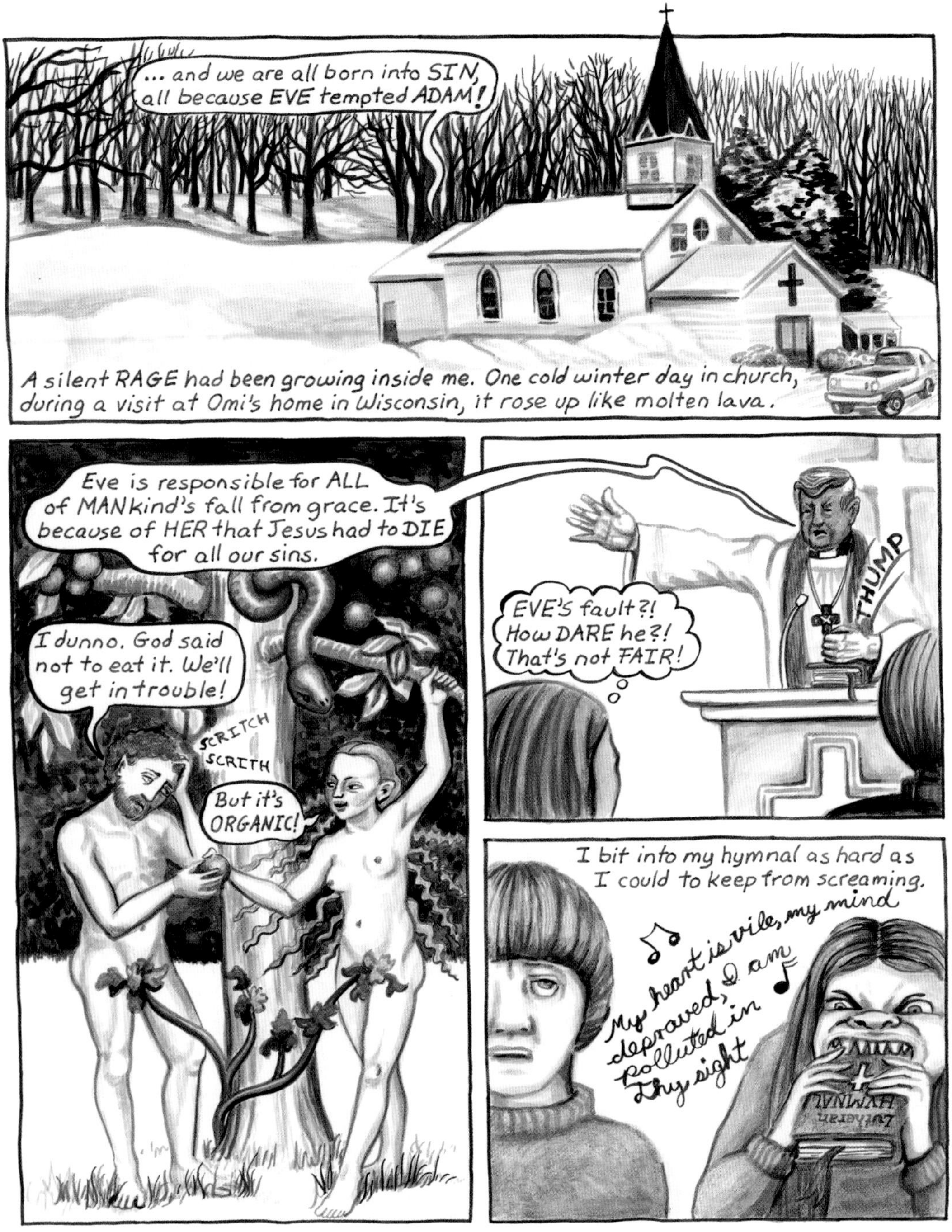
... and we are all born into SIN, all because EVE tempted ADAM!
A silent RAGE had been growing inside me. One cold winter day in church, during a visit at Omi's home in Wisconsin, it rose up like molten lava.
Eve is responsible for ALL of MANkind's fall from grace. It's because of HER that Jesus had to DIE for all our sins.
I dunno. God said not to eat it. We'll get in trouble!
SCRITCH
SCRITCH
But it's ORGANIC!
THUMP
EVE'S fault?! How DARE he?! That's not FAIR!
I bit into my hymnal as hard as I could to keep from screaming.
My heart is vile, my mind depraved, I am polluted in Thy sight

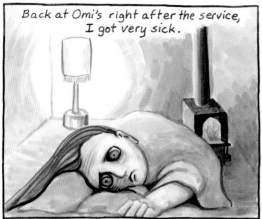

Back at Omi's right after the service, I got very sick.

Why are the walls BREATHING?

Is this my punishment for getting mad in church?!

I didn't know it at that time, but I had tapped into a store of feminist rage that day in church.

Oh God! I think I'm possessed by Satan!

My feminist awakening just happened to coincide with a very NASTY case of the flu!

She has a VERY high fever!

Am I... possessed?

No, dear.

129

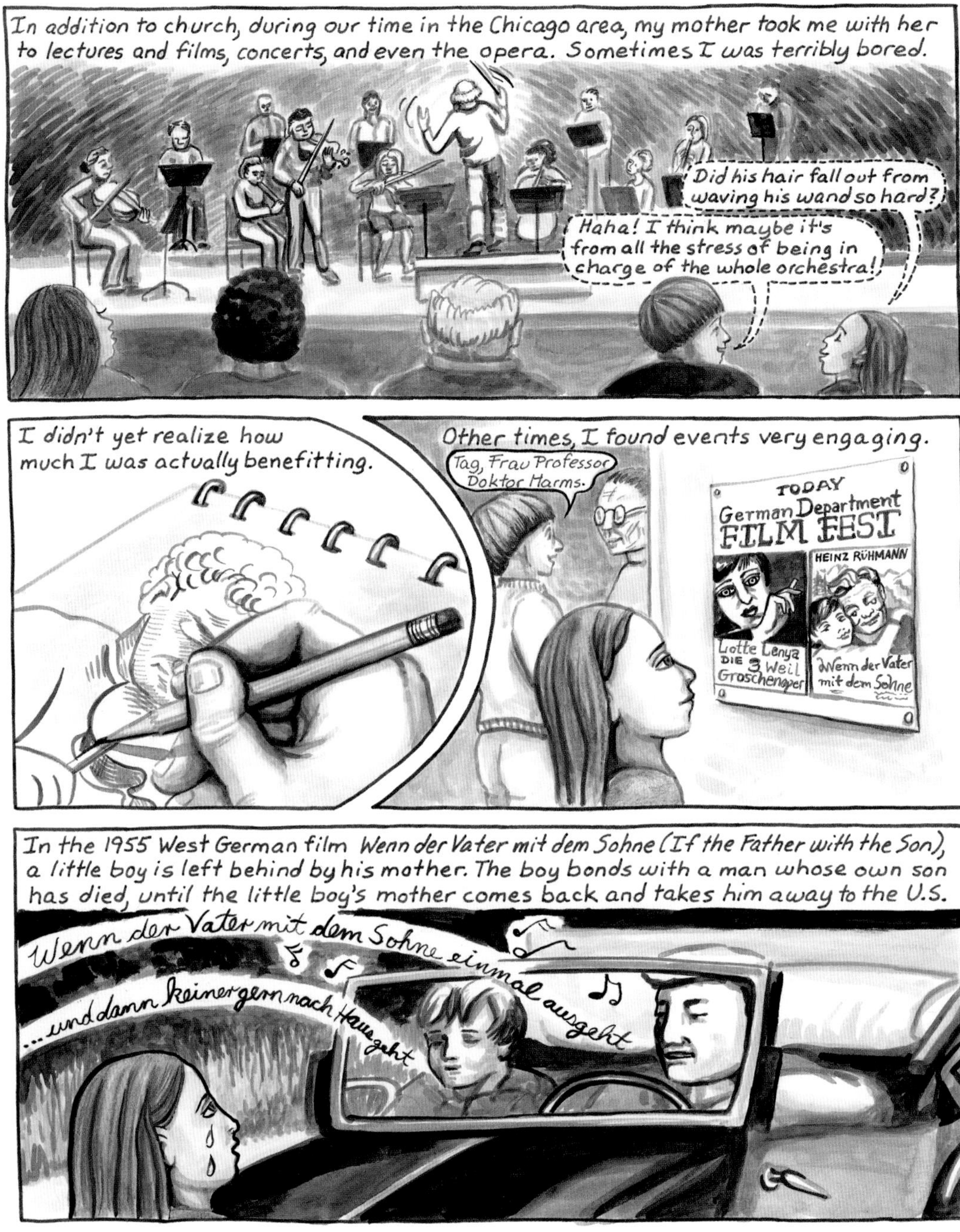
In addition to church, during our time in the Chicago area, my mother took me with her to lectures and films, concerts, and even the opera. Sometimes I was terribly bored.
Did his hair fall out from waving his wand so hard?
Haha! I think maybe it's from all the stress of being in charge of the whole orchestra!
I didn't yet realize how much I was actually benefitting.
Other times, I found events very engaging.
Tag, Frau Professor Doktor Harms.
TODAY
German Department
FILM FEST
HEINZ RÜHMANN
Lotte Lenya
DIE 3 Groschenoper
Weill
Wenn der Vater mit dem Sohne
In the 1955 West German film Wenn der Vater mit dem Sohne (If the Father with the Son), a little boy is left behind by his mother. The boy bonds with a man whose own son has died, until the little boy's mother comes back and takes him away to the U.S.
Wenn der Vater mit dem Sohne einmal ausgeht
... und dann keiner gern nach Hause geht

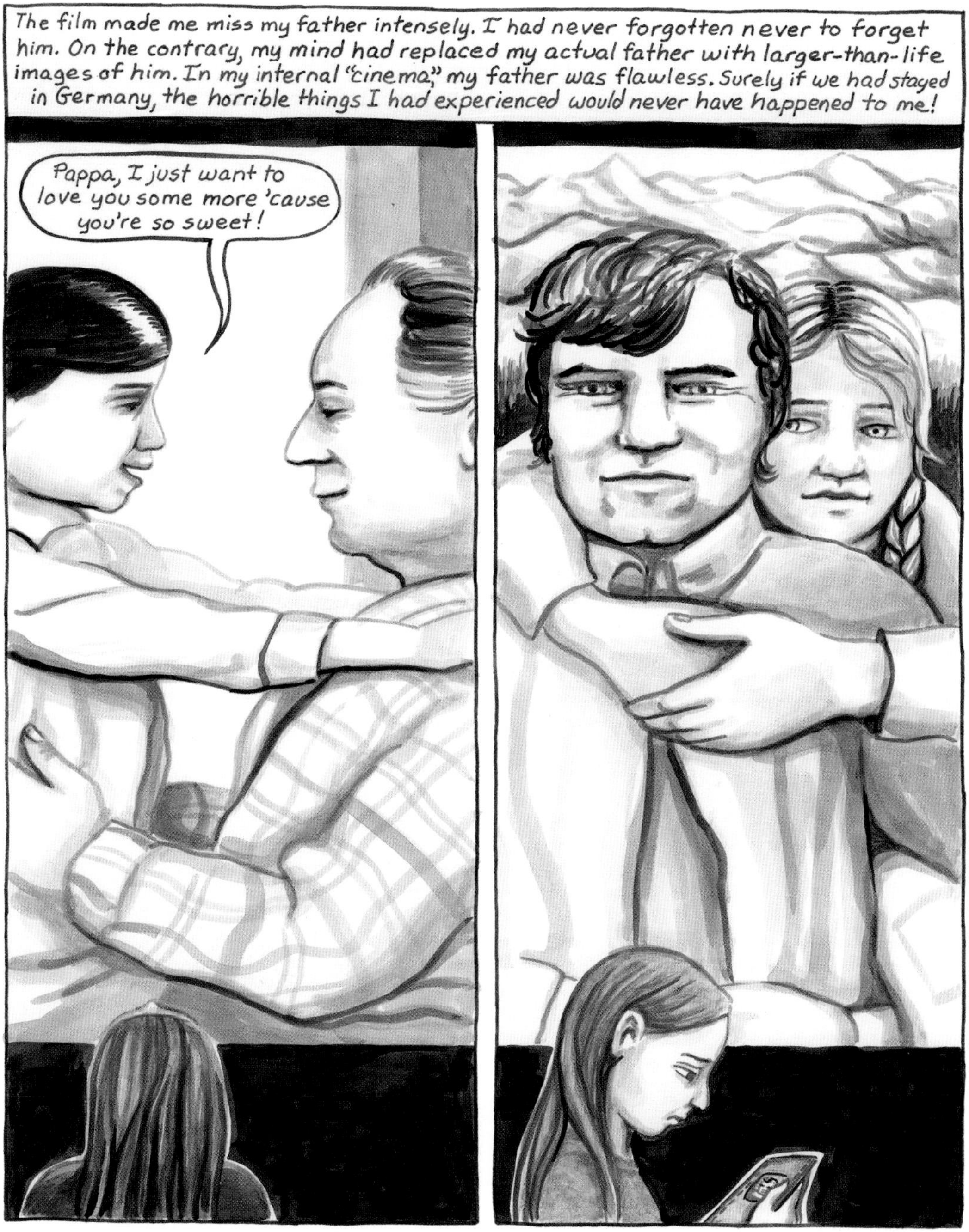
The film made me miss my father intensely. I had never forgotten never to forget him. On the contrary, my mind had replaced my actual father with larger-than-life images of him. In my internal "cinema," my father was flawless. Surely if we had stayed in Germany, the horrible things I had experienced would never have happened to me!
Pappa, I just want to love you some more 'cause you're so sweet!

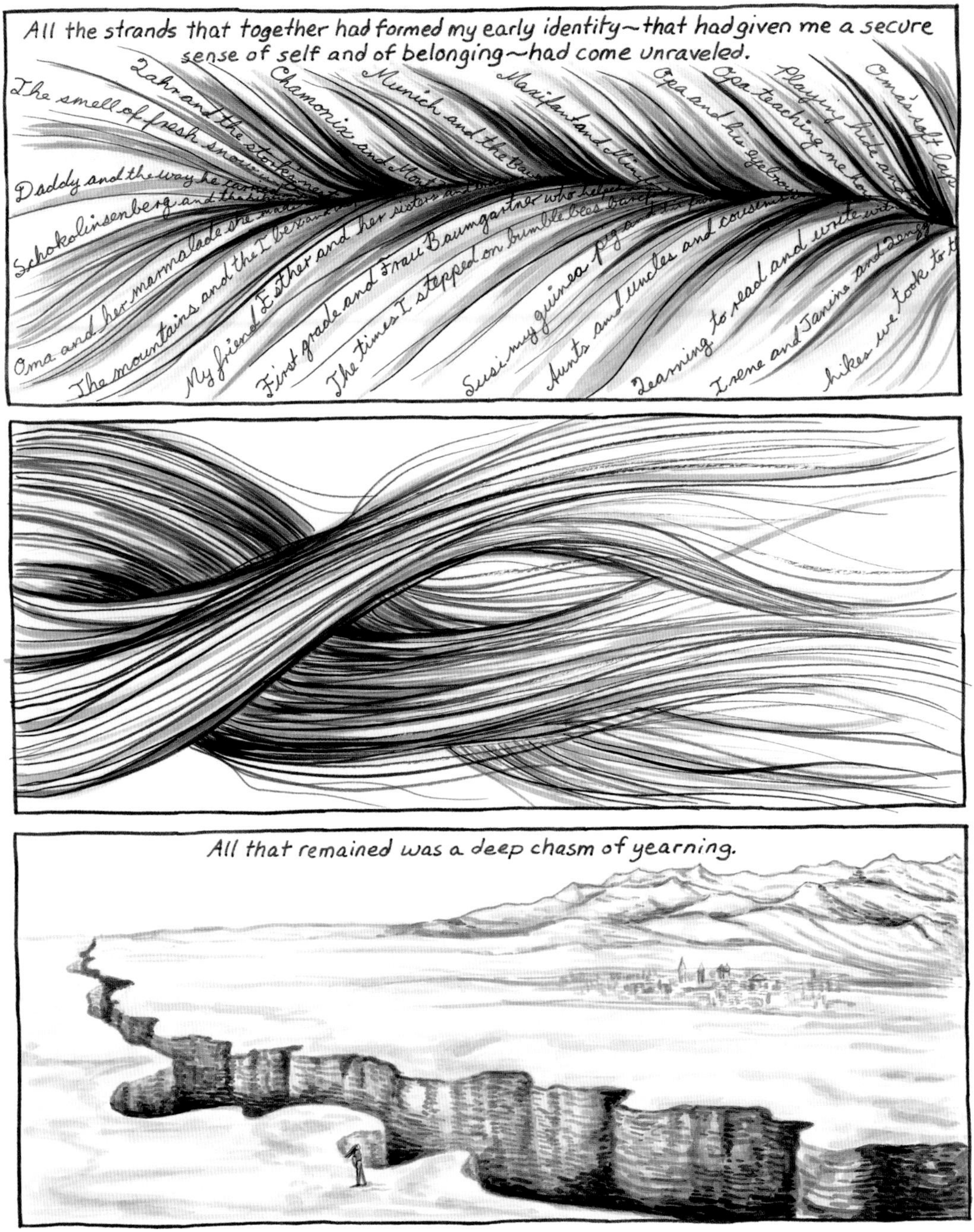
All the strands that together had formed my early identity—that had given me a secure sense of self and of belonging—had come unraveled.
The smell of fresh snow
Zahr and the storks
Chamonix and Mont
Munich and the
Maxifant and
Opa and his
Opa teaching me how
Playing hide and
Oma's soft lap
Daddy and the way he carried me
Schokolinsenberg and the
Oma and her marmalade she made
The mountains and the
My friend Esther and her sisters and
First grade and Frau Baumgartner who helped
The times I stepped on bumble bees barefoot
Susi my guinea pig and
Aunts and uncles and cousins
Learning to read and write
Irene and Janine and
hikes we took to
All that remained was a deep chasm of yearning.

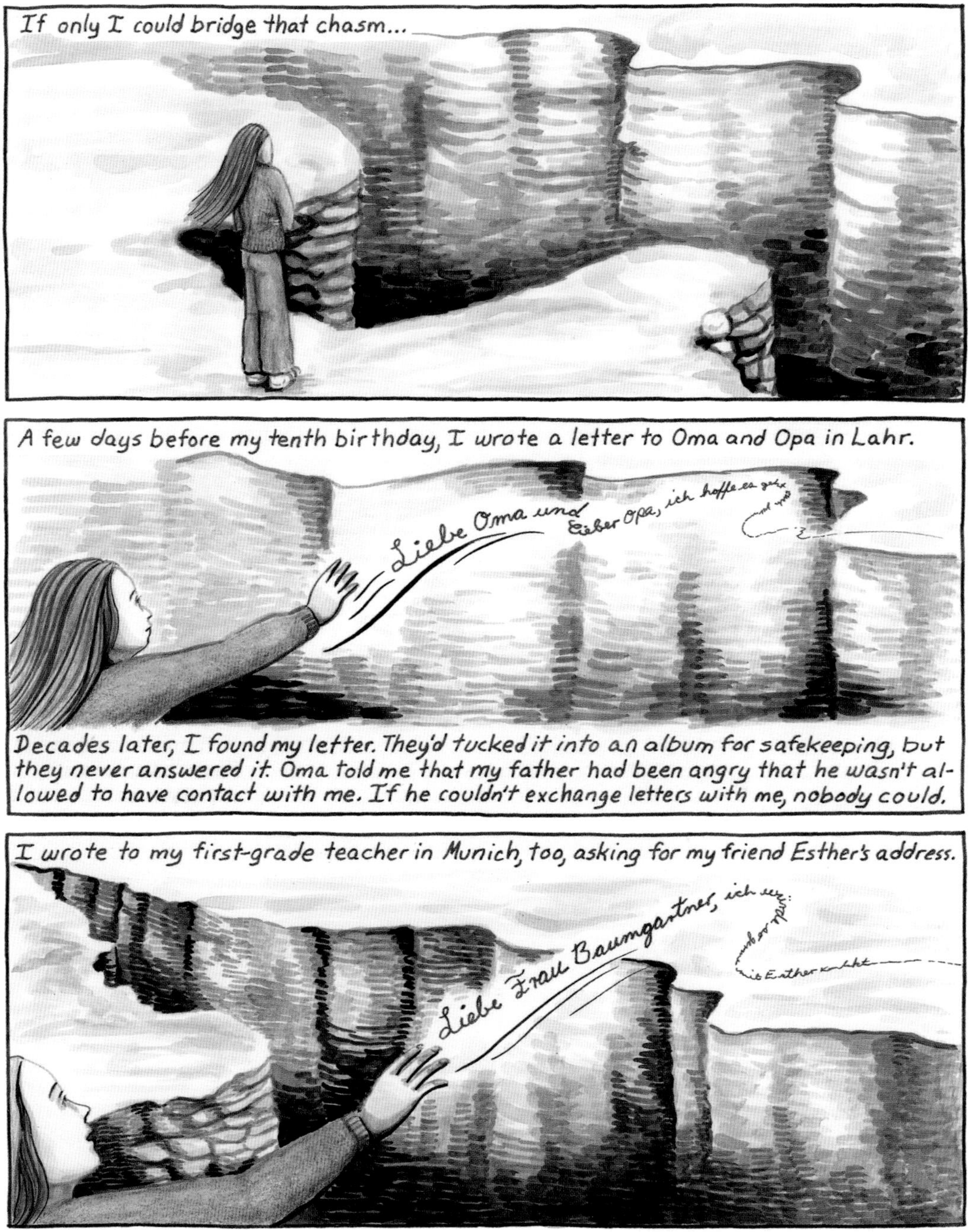
If only I could bridge that chasm...
A few days before my tenth birthday, I wrote a letter to Oma and Opa in Lahr.
Liebe Oma und
Decades later, I found my letter. They'd tucked it into an album for safekeeping, but they never answered it. Oma told me that my father had been angry that he wasn't allowed to have contact with me. If he couldn't exchange letters with me, nobody could.
I wrote to my first-grade teacher in Munich, too, asking for my friend Esther's address.
Liebe Frau Baumgartner,

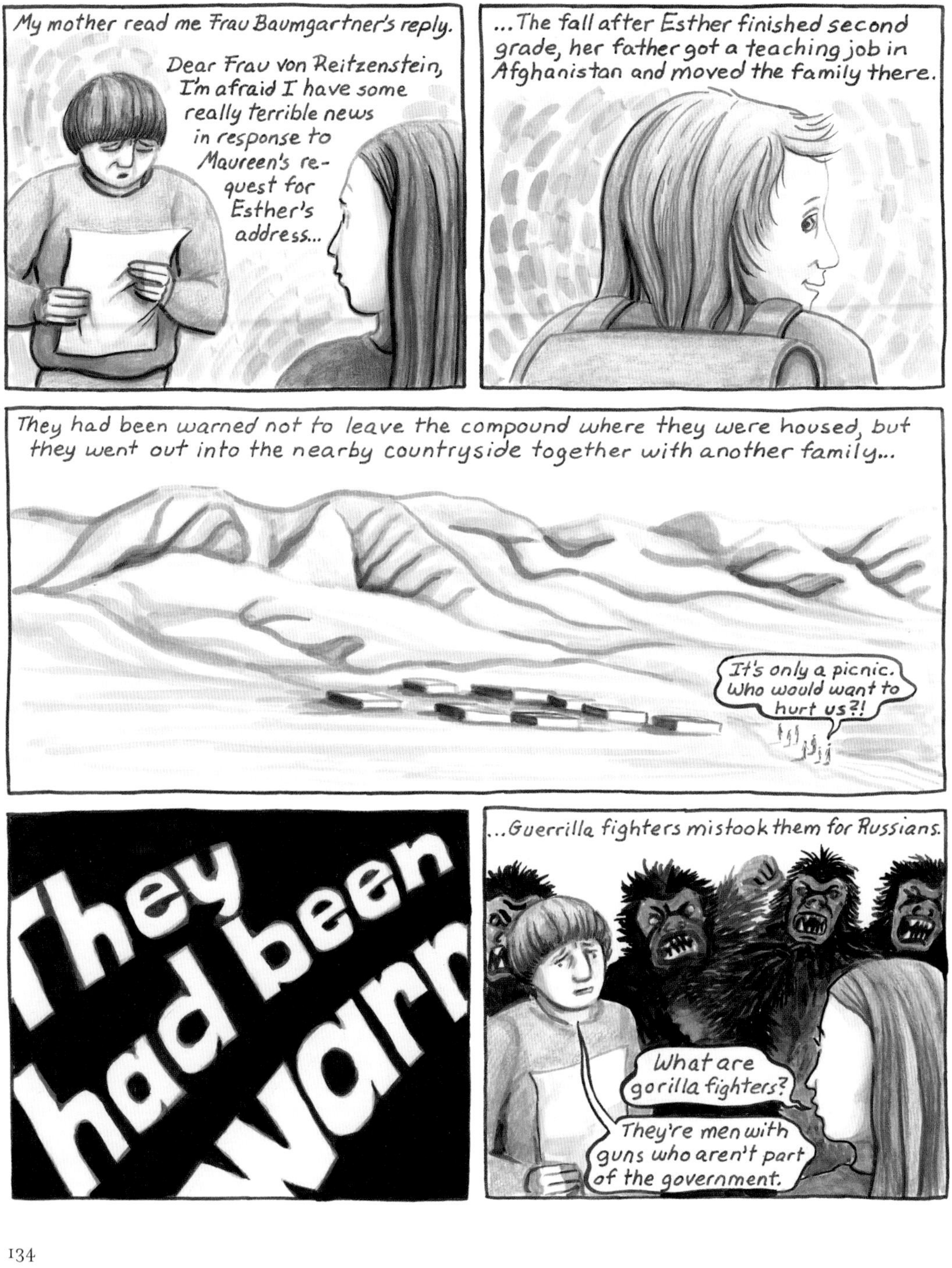
My mother read me Frau Baumgartner's reply.
Dear Frau von Reitzenstein, I'm afraid I have some really terrible news in response to Maureen's request for Esther's address...
...The fall after Esther finished second grade, her father got a teaching job in Afghanistan and moved the family there.
They had been warned not to leave the compound where they were housed, but they went out into the nearby countryside together with another family...
It's only a picnic. Who would want to hurt us?!
They had been warn
...Guerrilla fighters mistook them for Russians.
What are gorilla fighters?
They're men with guns who aren't part of the government.

They lined up both families, four parents and several children, and shot them all.

After my mother read me the letter, I couldn't stop wondering: did they shoot Esther first, so she didn't have to watch her parents, brothers, sisters, and friends die?

As far as I know, there is no monument or memorial anywhere for my friend Esther.

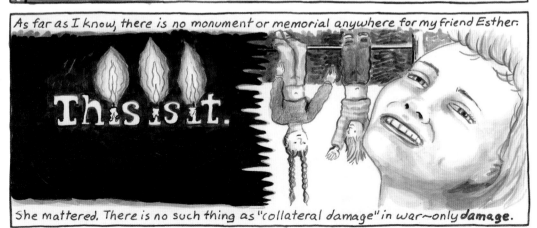

This is it.

She mattered. There is no such thing as "collateral damage" in war—only *damage*.

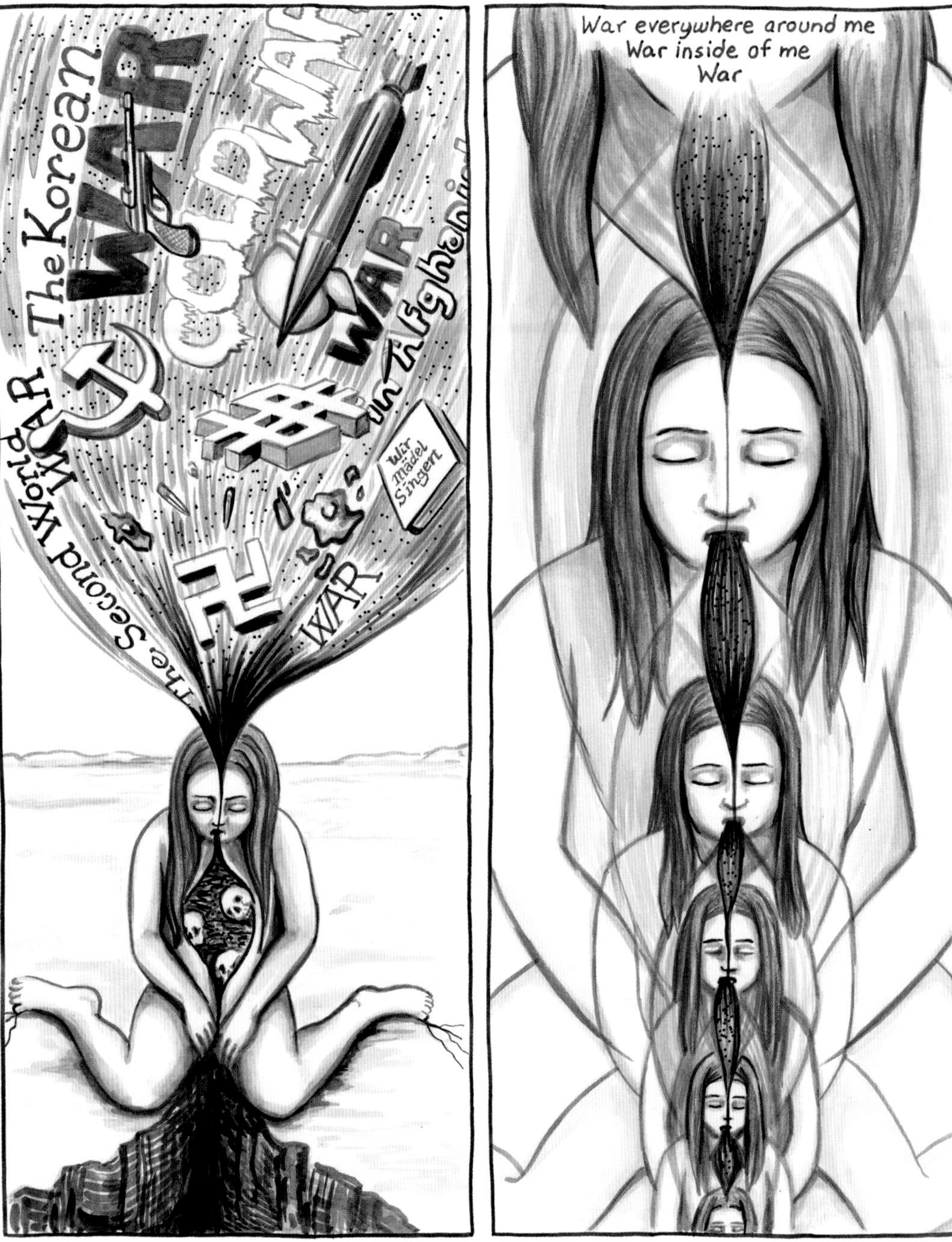
The Second World WAR
The Korean WAR
COLD WAR
WAR in Afghani
Wir mädel Singen
WAR
War everywhere around me
War inside of me
War

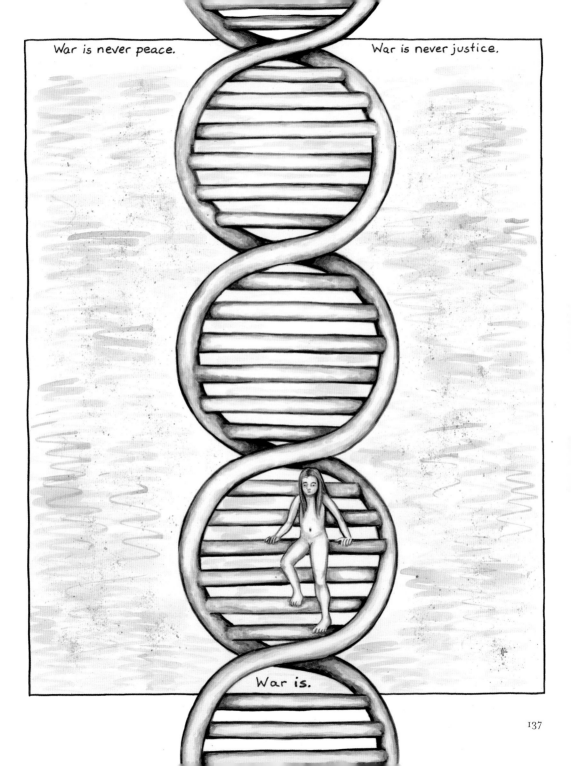

War is never peace.

War is never justice.

War is.

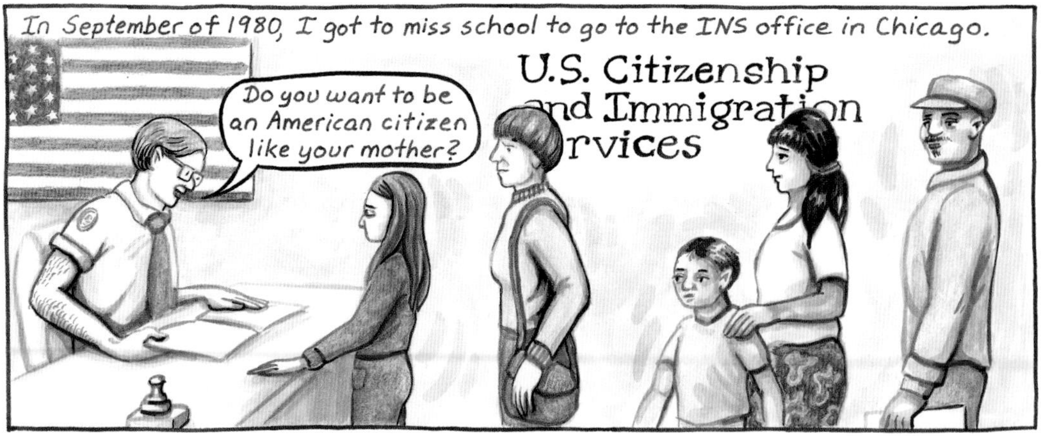
In September of 1980, I got to miss school to go to the INS office in Chicago.
U.S. Citizenship and Immigration Services
Do you want to be an American citizen like your mother?

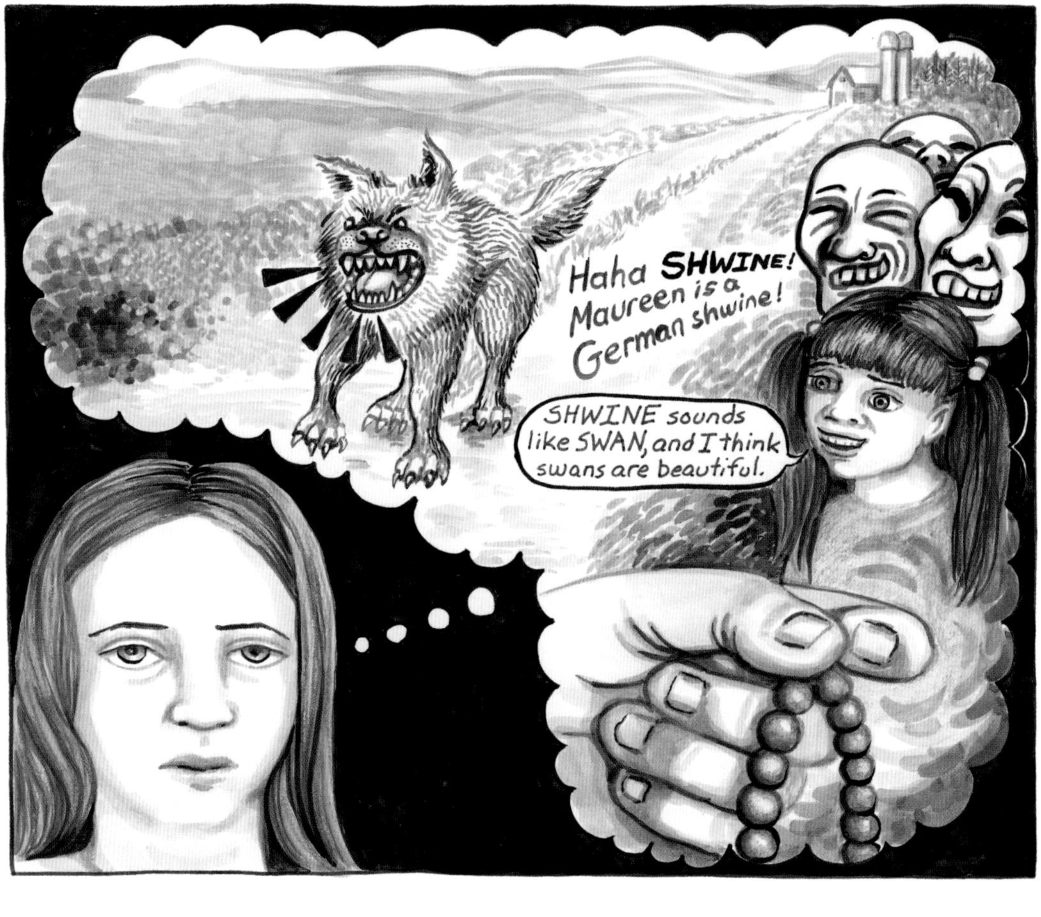
Haha SHWINE! Maureen is a German shwine!
SHWINE sounds like SWAN, and I think swans are beautiful.

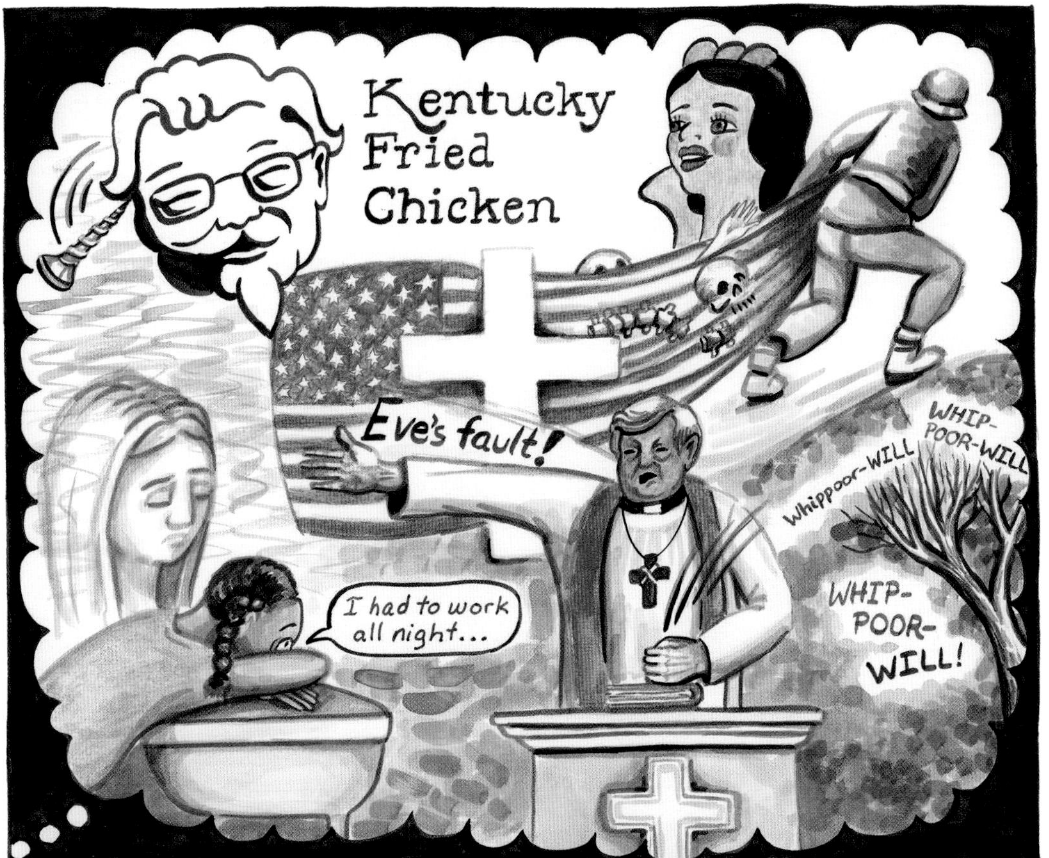
Kentucky
Fried
Chicken
Eve's fault!
I had to work all night...
Whippoor-WILL
WHIP-POOR-WILL
WHIP-POOR-WILL!

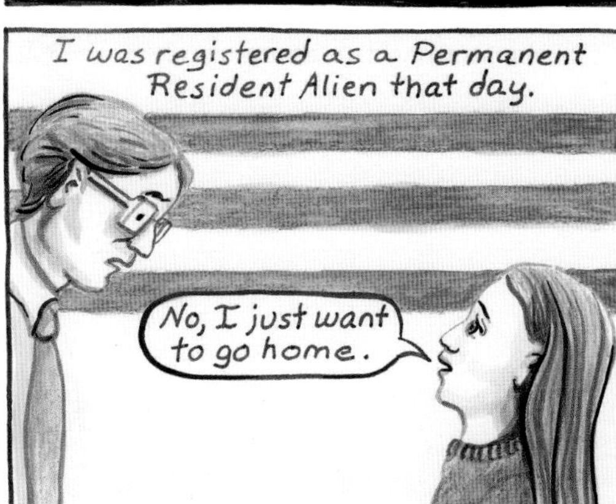
I was registered as a Permanent Resident Alien that day.
No, I just want to go home.

I didn't yet understand that home is not a place, and that no plane or train could ever take me there.

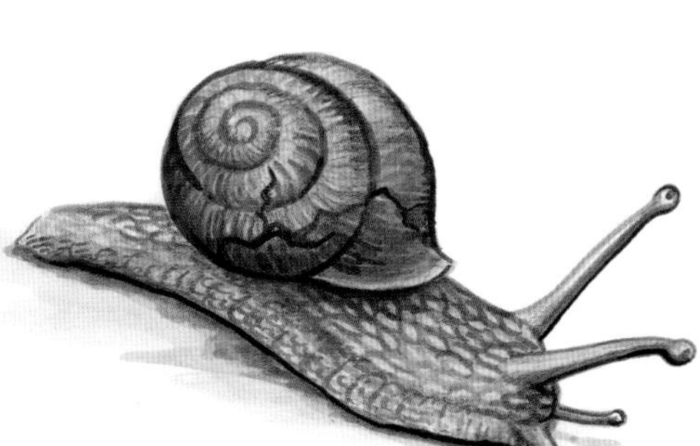

If you don't know where you are going,
any road will take you there.

~ The Cheshire Cat, *Alice in Wonderland*, Lewis Carroll

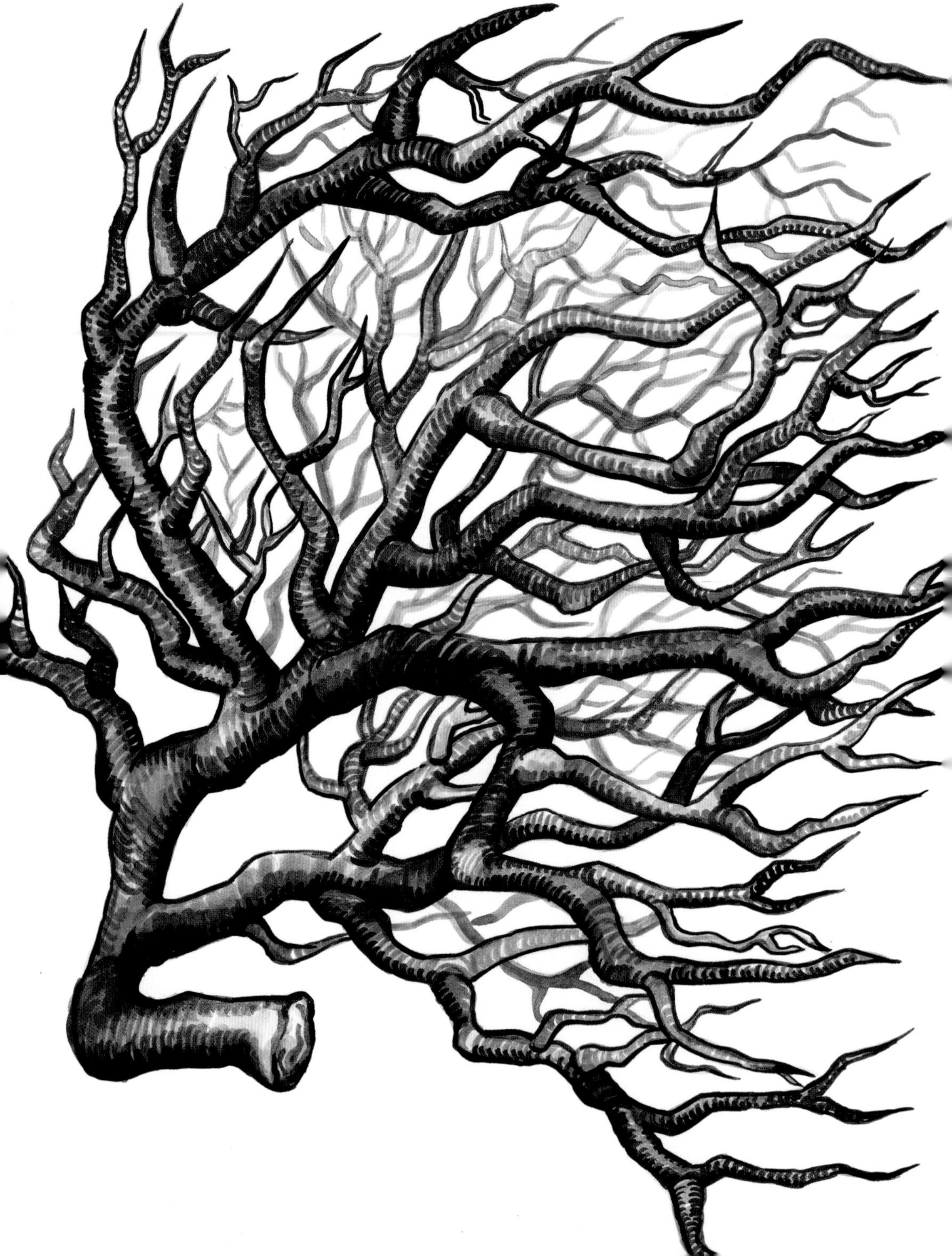

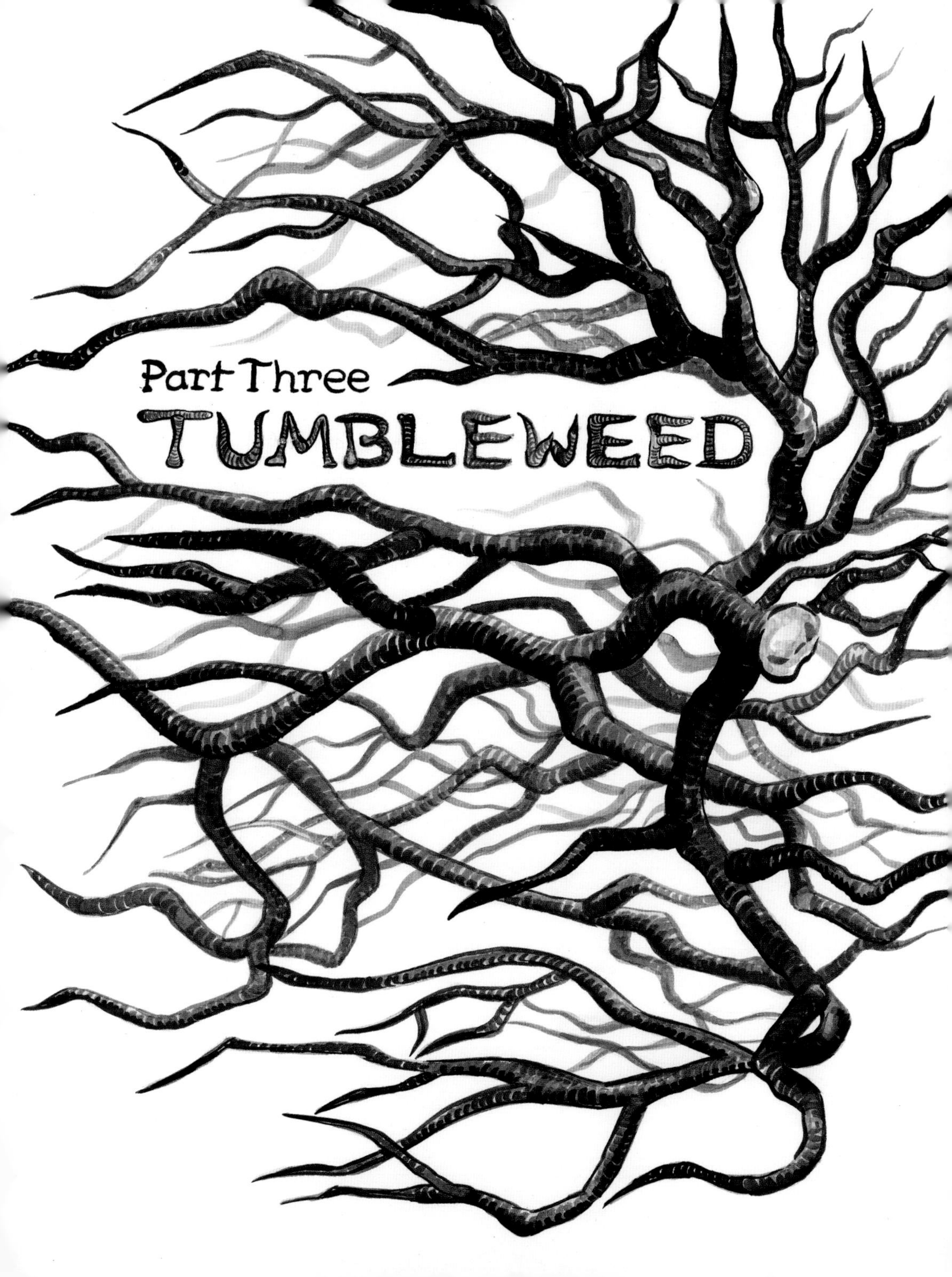
Part Three
TUMBLEWEED

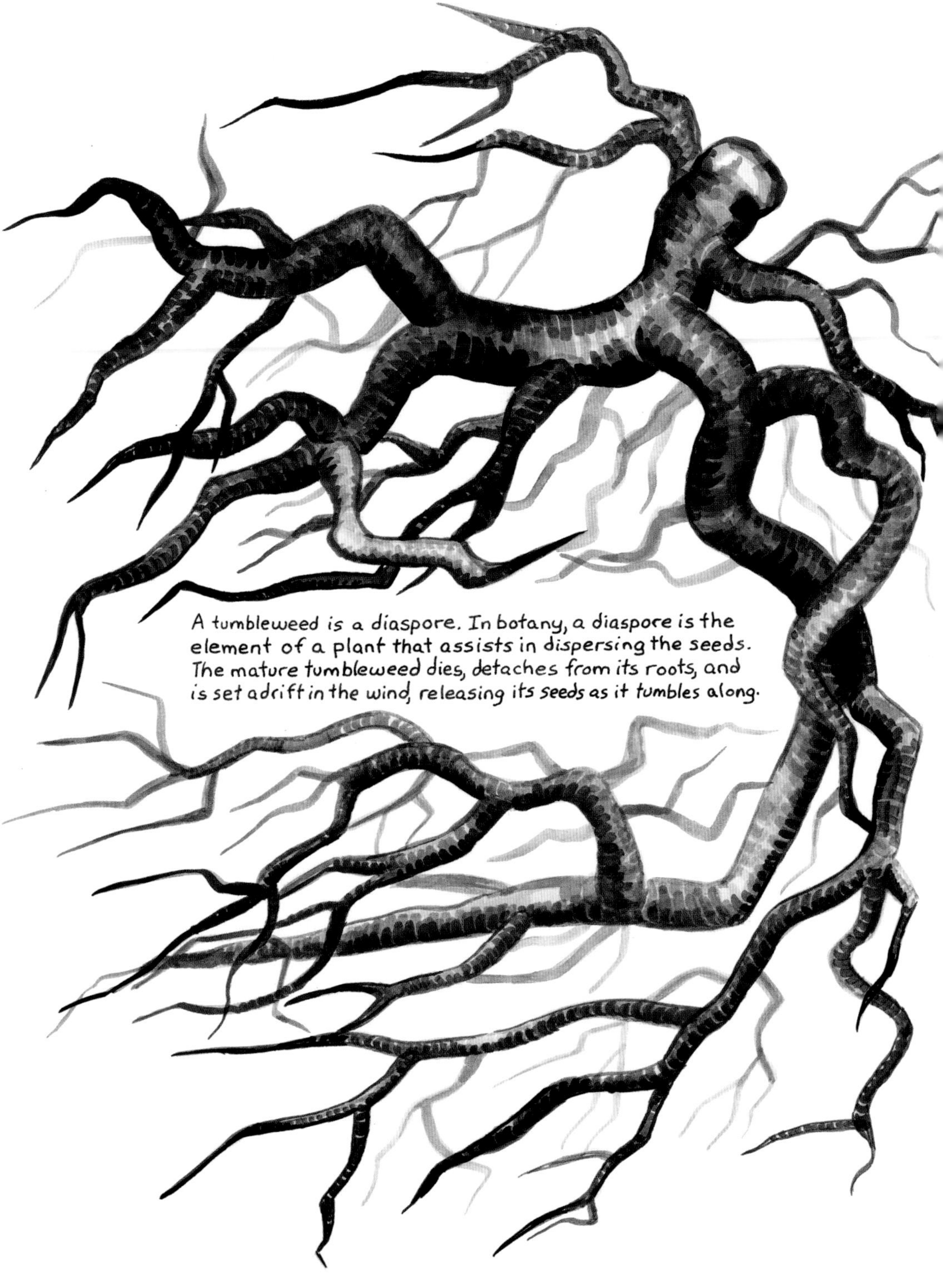
A tumbleweed is a diaspore. In botany, a diaspore is the element of a plant that assists in dispersing the seeds. The mature tumbleweed dies, detaches from its roots, and is set adrift in the wind, releasing its seeds as it tumbles along.

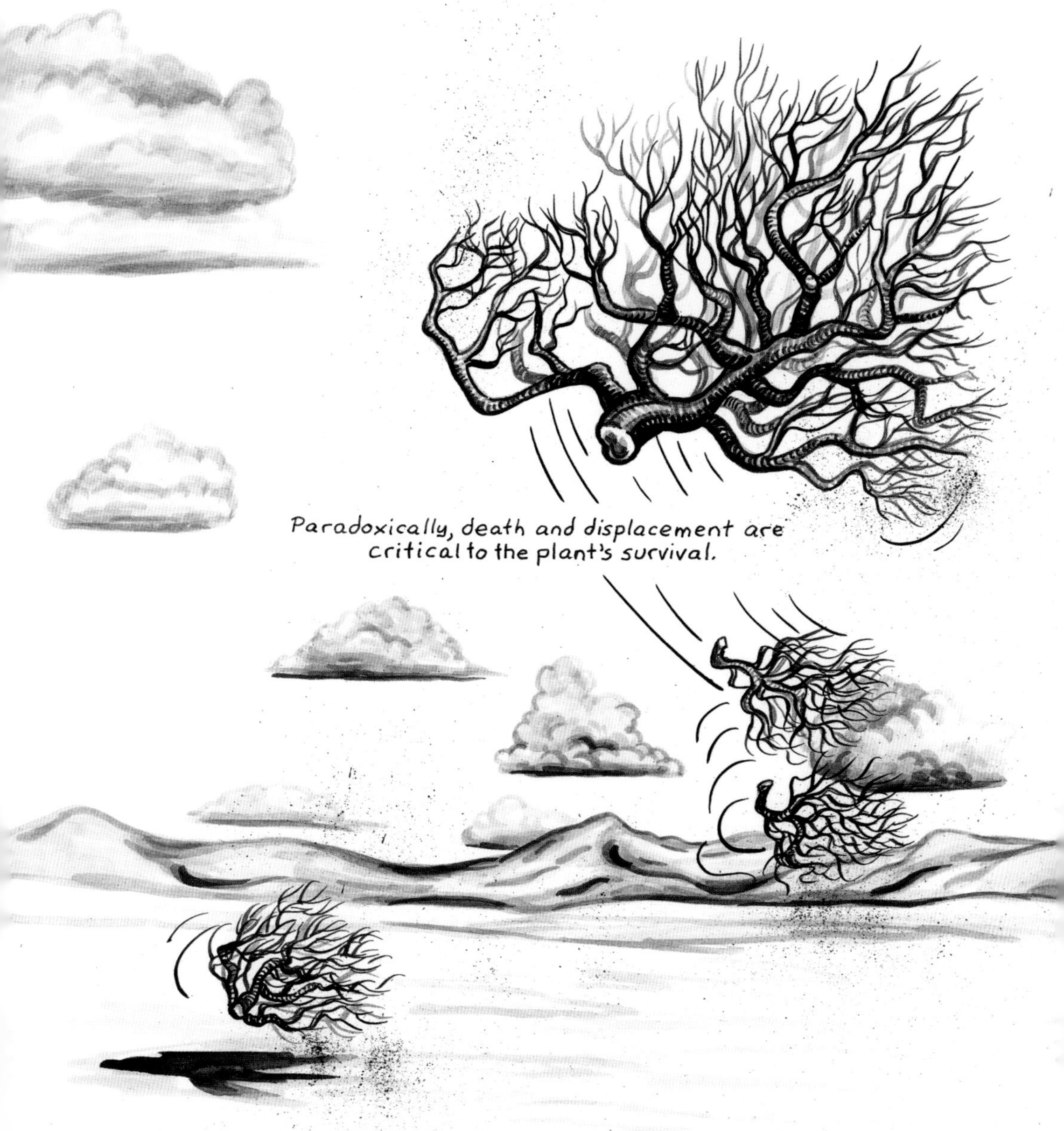
Paradoxically, death and displacement are critical to the plant's survival.

Sometimes, falling asleep at night

I felt myself shrinking

Shrinking to the size of a pea

Then a period

A speck of dust

Nothingness

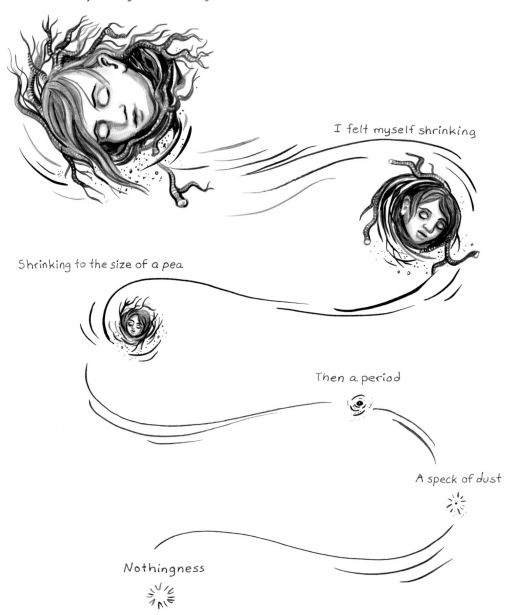

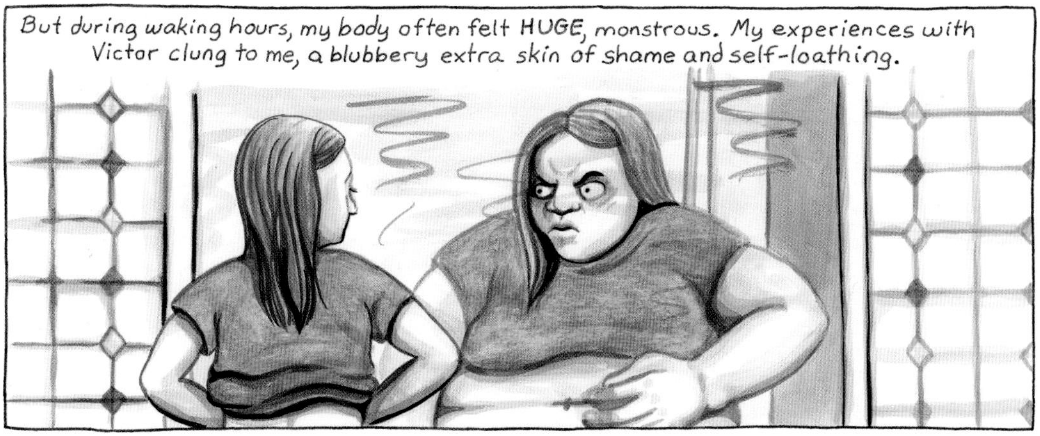
But during waking hours, my body often felt HUGE, monstrous. My experiences with Victor clung to me, a blubbery extra skin of shame and self-loathing.

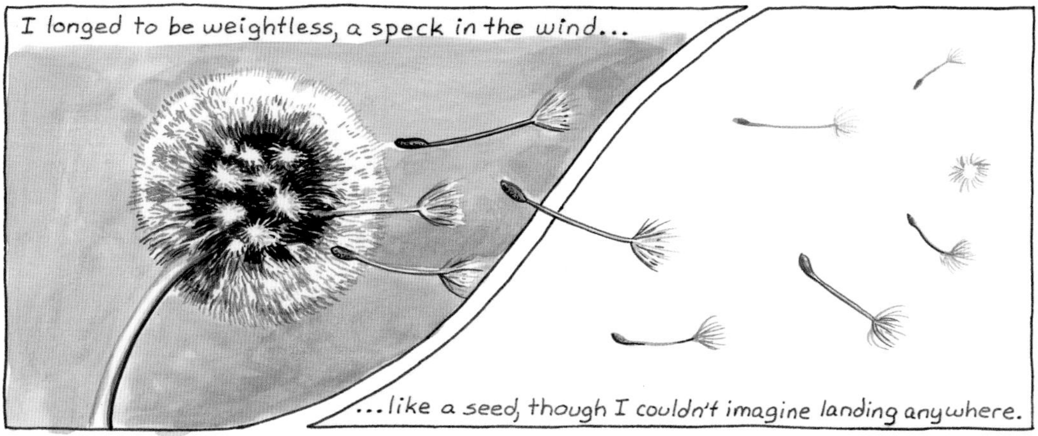
I longed to be weightless, a speck in the wind...
...like a seed, though I couldn't imagine landing anywhere.

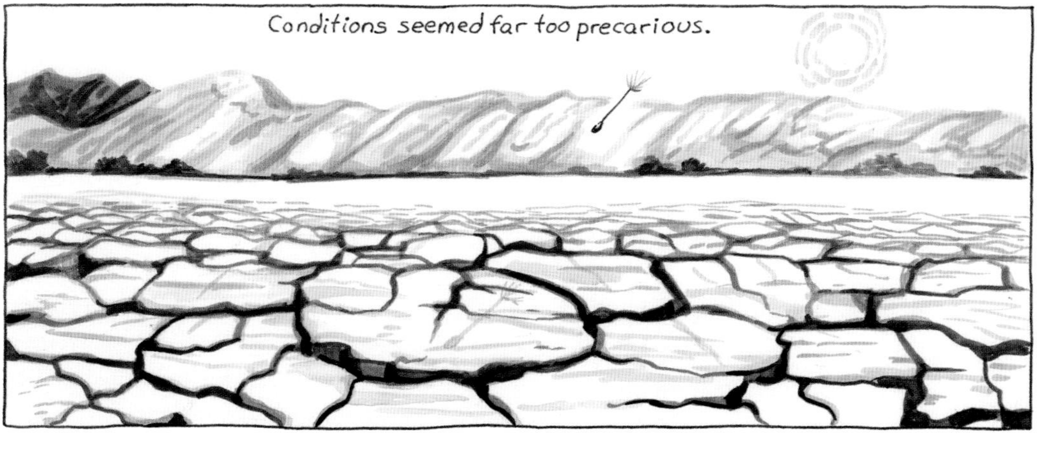
Conditions seemed far too precarious.

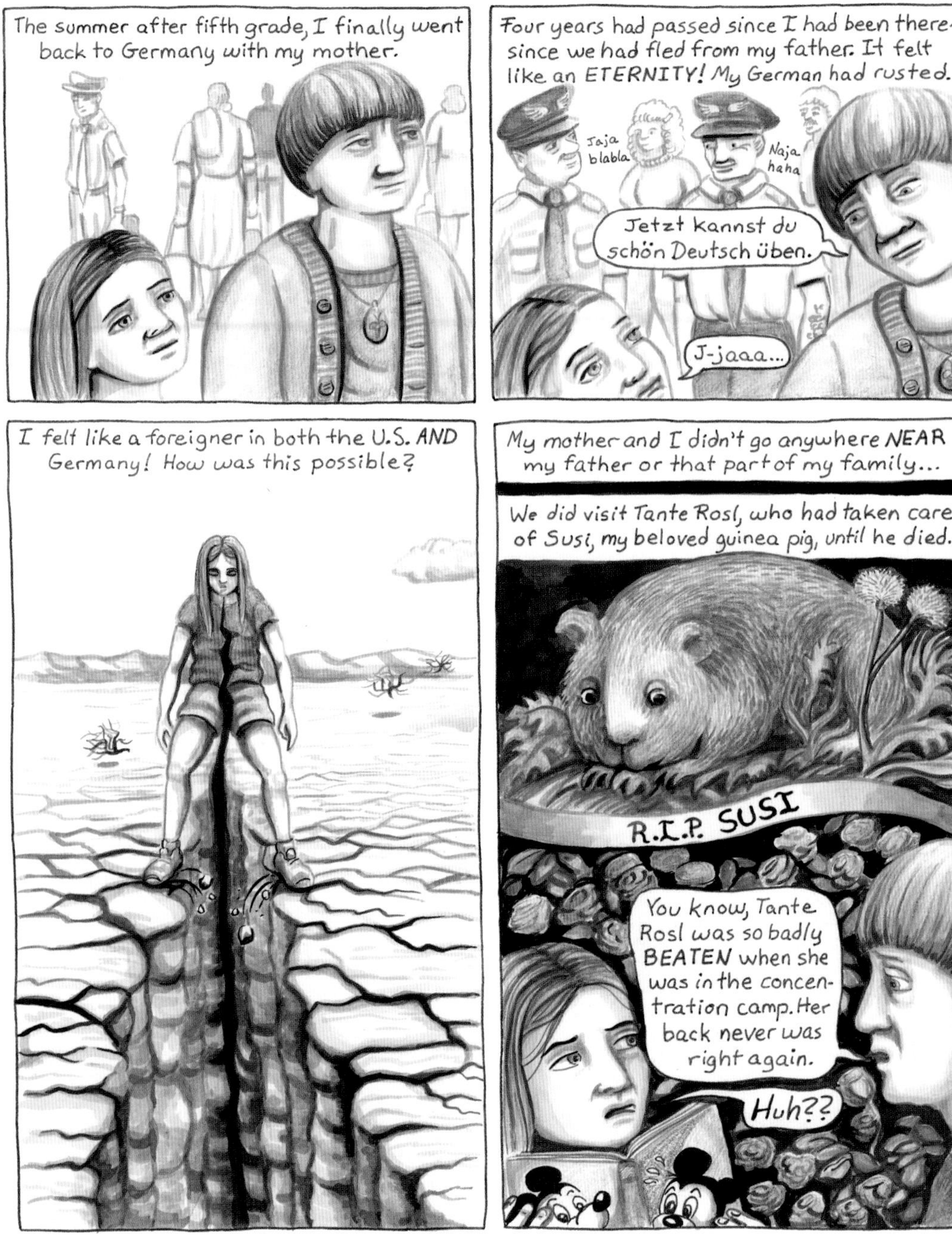
The summer after fifth grade, I finally went back to Germany with my mother.
Four years had passed since I had been there– since we had fled from my father. It felt like an ETERNITY! My German had rusted.
Jaja blabla
Naja haha
Jetzt kannst du schön Deutsch üben.
J-jaaa...
I felt like a foreigner in both the U.S. AND Germany! How was this possible?
My mother and I didn't go anywhere NEAR my father or that part of my family...
We did visit Tante Rosl, who had taken care of Susi, my beloved guinea pig, until he died.
R.I.P. SUSI
You know, Tante Rosl was so badly BEATEN when she was in the concentration camp. Her back never was right again.
Huh??

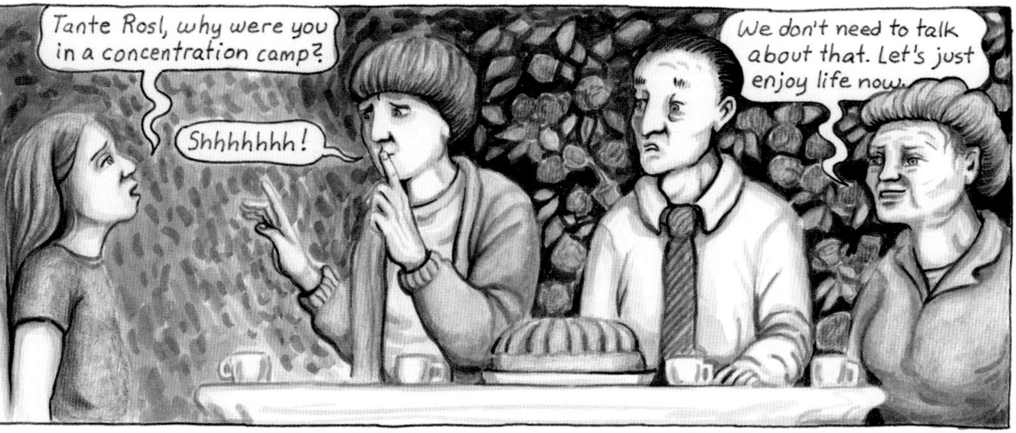
Tante Rosl, why were you in a concentration camp?
Shhhhhhh!
We don't need to talk about that. Let's just enjoy life now.

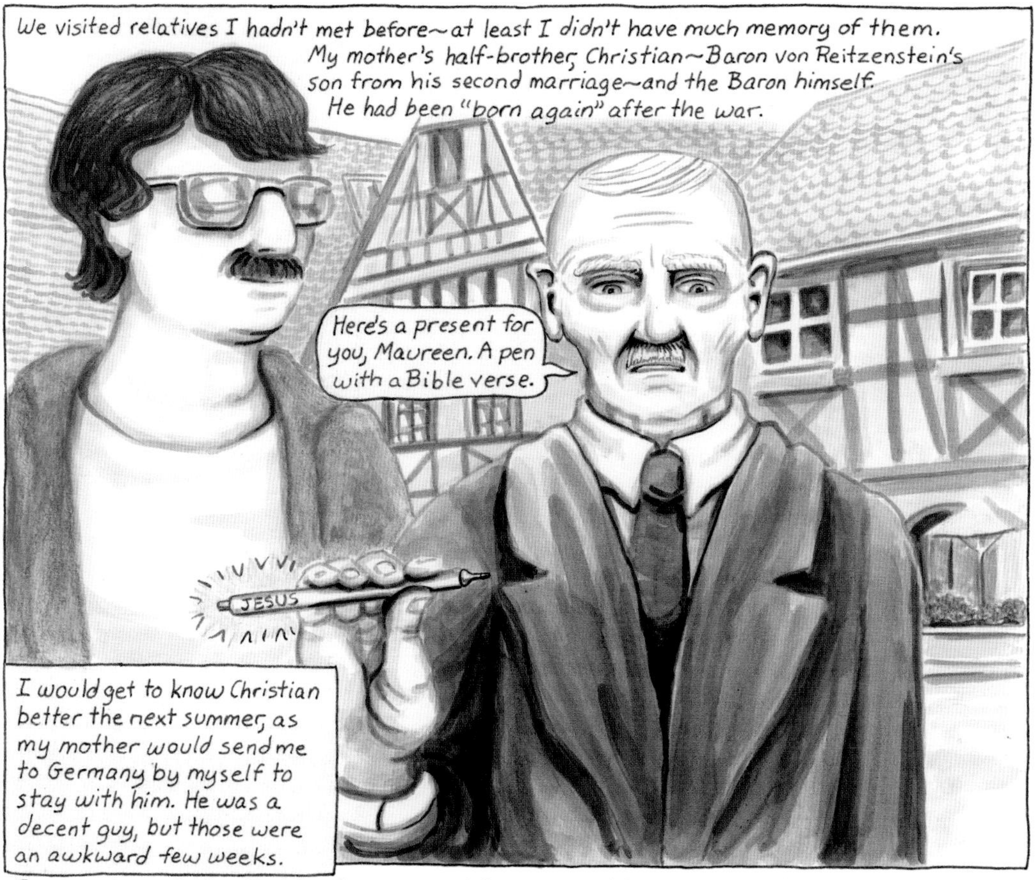
We visited relatives I hadn't met before~at least I didn't have much memory of them.
My mother's half-brother, Christian~Baron von Reitzenstein's son from his second marriage~and the Baron himself.
He had been "born again" after the war.
Here's a present for you, Maureen. A pen with a Bible verse.
JESUS
I would get to know Christian better the next summer, as my mother would send me to Germany by myself to stay with him. He was a decent guy, but those were an awkward few weeks.

I remember wishing that the Baron would die soon—not because I bore him any malice, but just because I hadn't yet experienced a dead relative, and he seemed both the most expendable and the closest to achieving that state without any outside help.

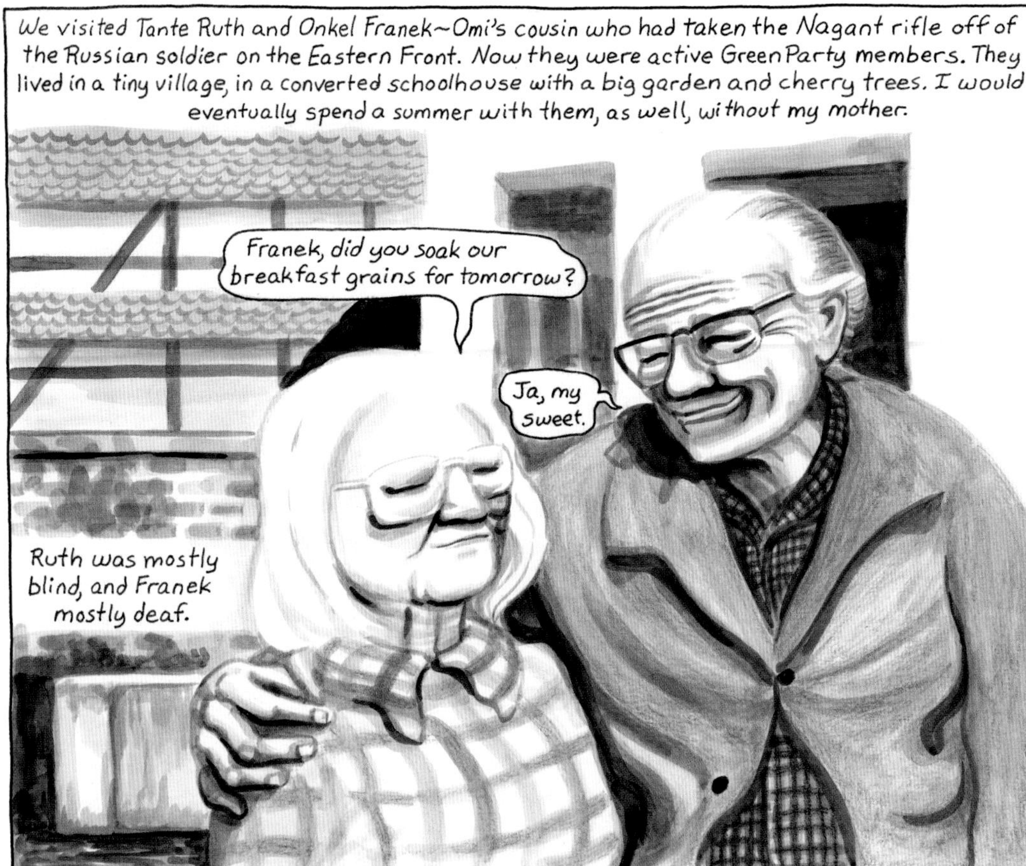
We visited Tante Ruth and Onkel Franek~Omi's cousin who had taken the Nagant rifle off of the Russian soldier on the Eastern Front. Now they were active Green Party members. They lived in a tiny village, in a converted schoolhouse with a big garden and cherry trees. I would eventually spend a summer with them, as well, without my mother.
Franek, did you soak our breakfast grains for tomorrow?
Ja, my sweet.
Ruth was mostly blind, and Franek mostly deaf.

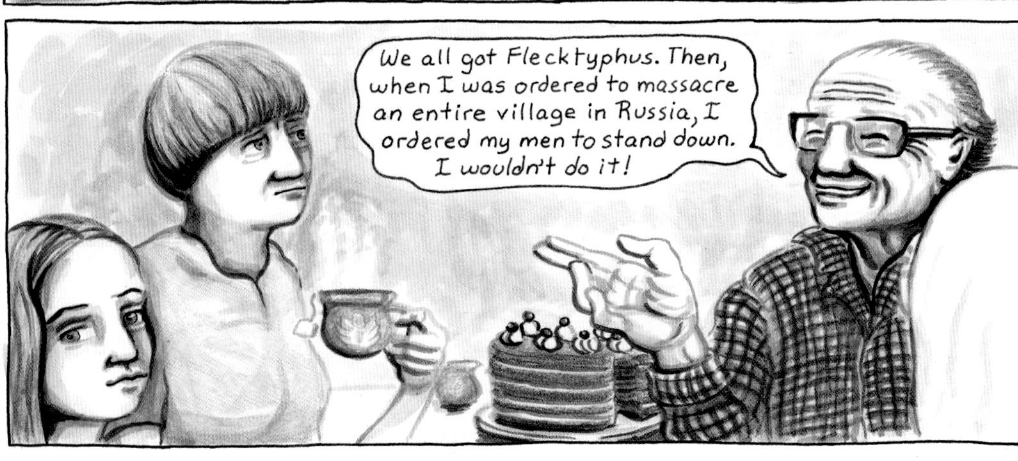
We all got Flecktyphus. Then, when I was ordered to massacre an entire village in Russia, I ordered my men to stand down. I wouldn't do it!

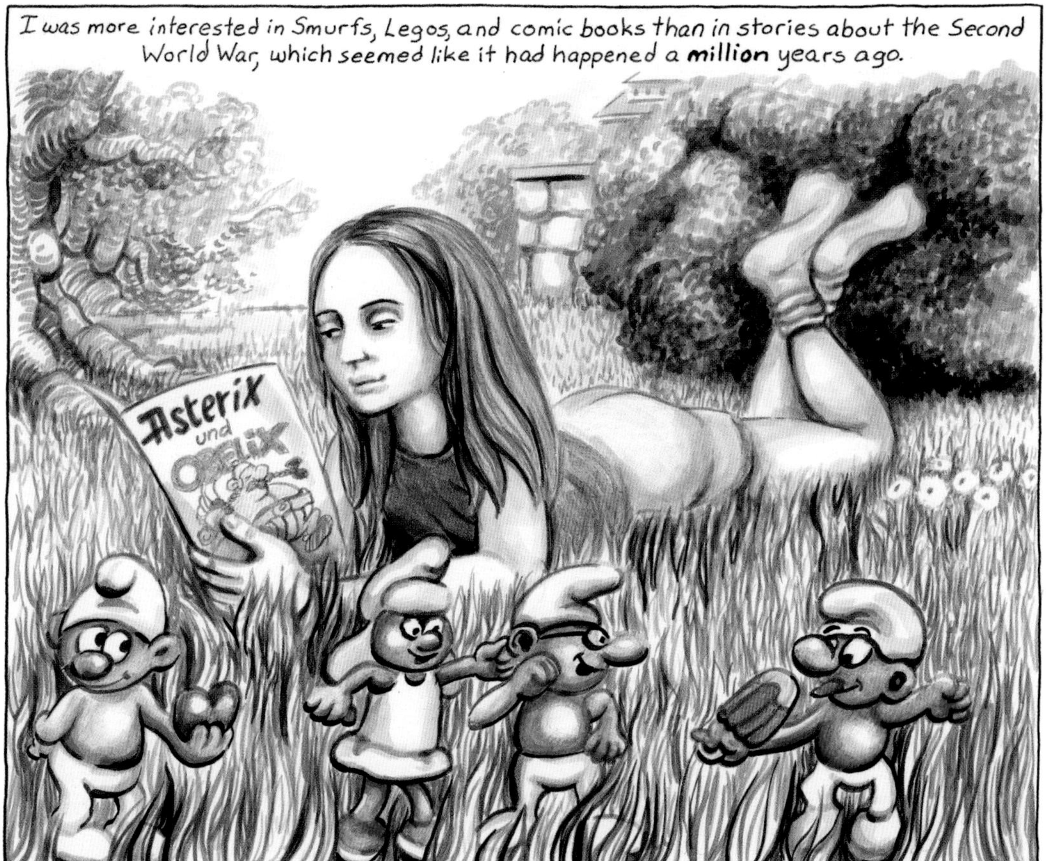
I was more interested in Smurfs, Legos, and comic books than in stories about the Second World War, which seemed like it had happened a **million** years ago.
Asterix und Obelix

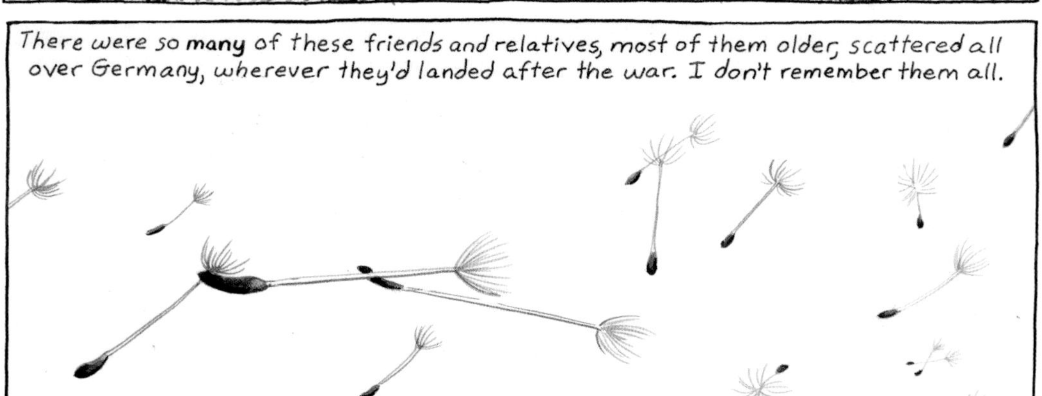
There were so **many** of these friends and relatives, most of them older, scattered all over Germany, wherever they'd landed after the war. I don't remember them all.

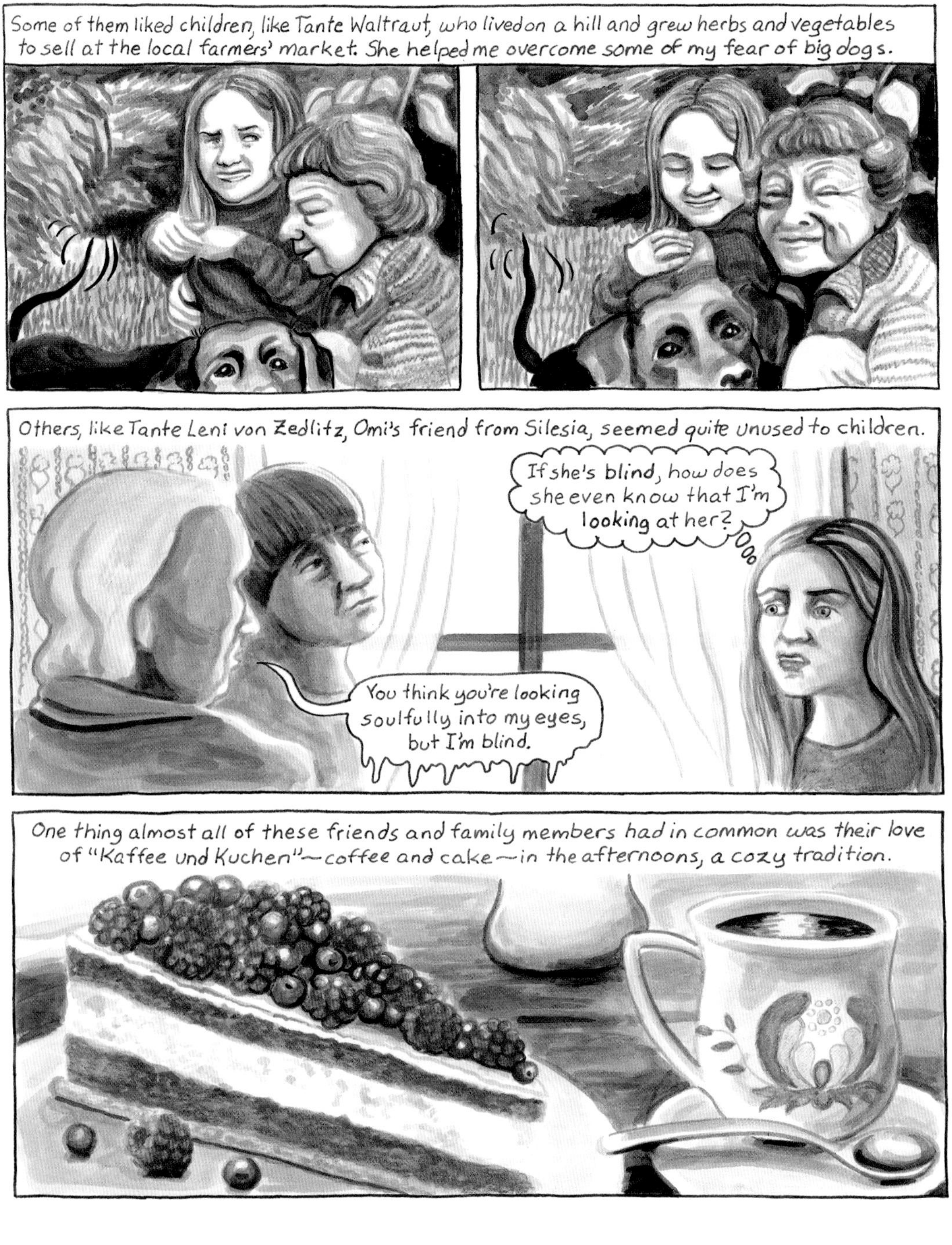
Some of them liked children, like Tante Waltraut, who livedon a hill and grew herbs and vegetables to sell at the local farmers' market. She helped me overcome some of my fear of big dogs.
Others, like Tante Leni von Zedlitz, Omi's friend from Silesia, seemed quite unused to children.
If she's blind, how does she even know that I'm looking at her?
You think you're looking soulfully into my eyes, but I'm blind.
One thing almost all of these friends and family members had in common was their love of "Kaffee und Kuchen"—coffee and cake—in the afternoons, a cozy tradition.

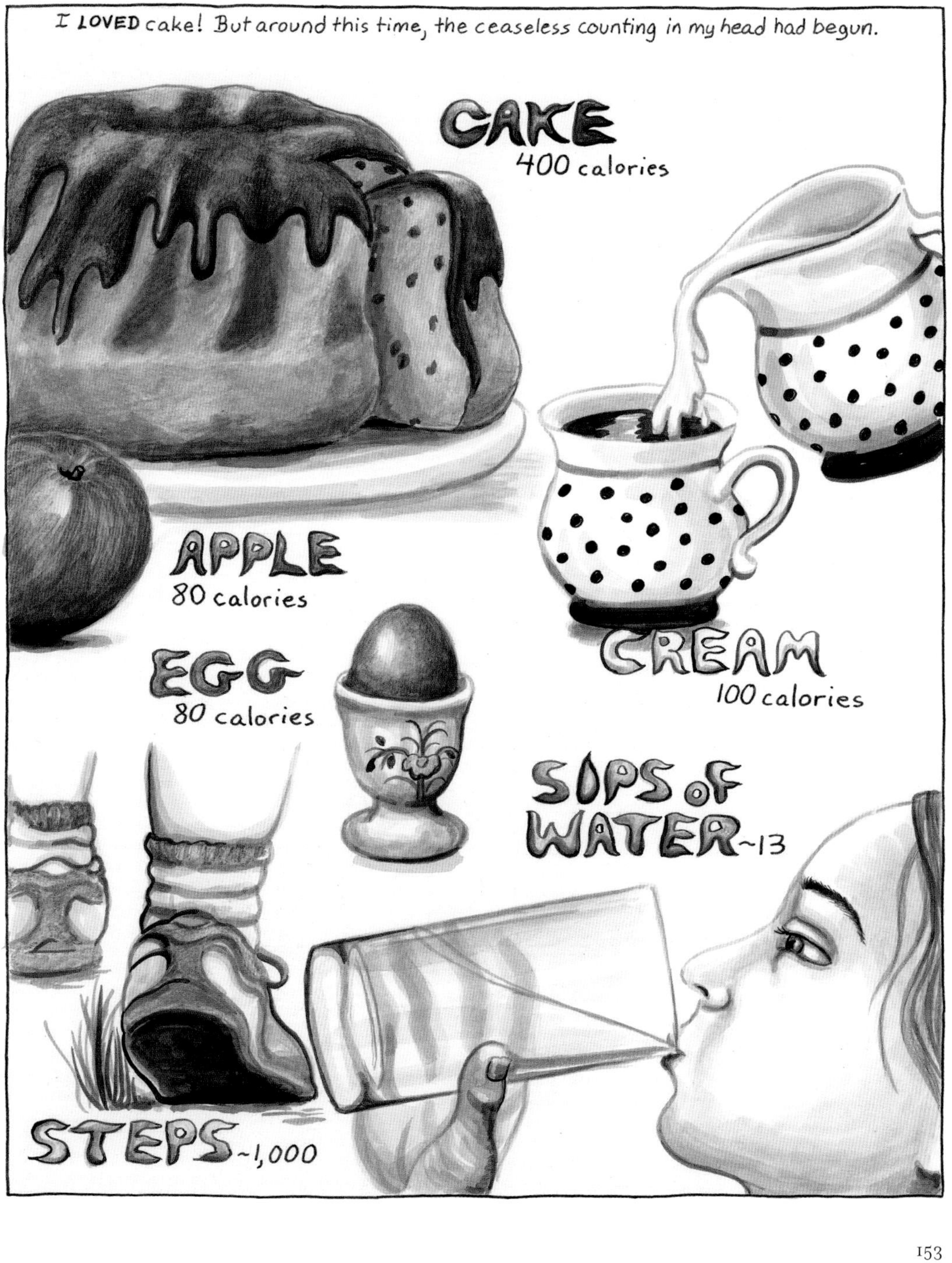
I LOVED cake! But around this time, the ceaseless counting in my head had begun.
CAKE
400 calories
APPLE
80 calories
CREAM
100 calories
EGG
80 calories
SIPS OF WATER ~13
STEPS ~1,000

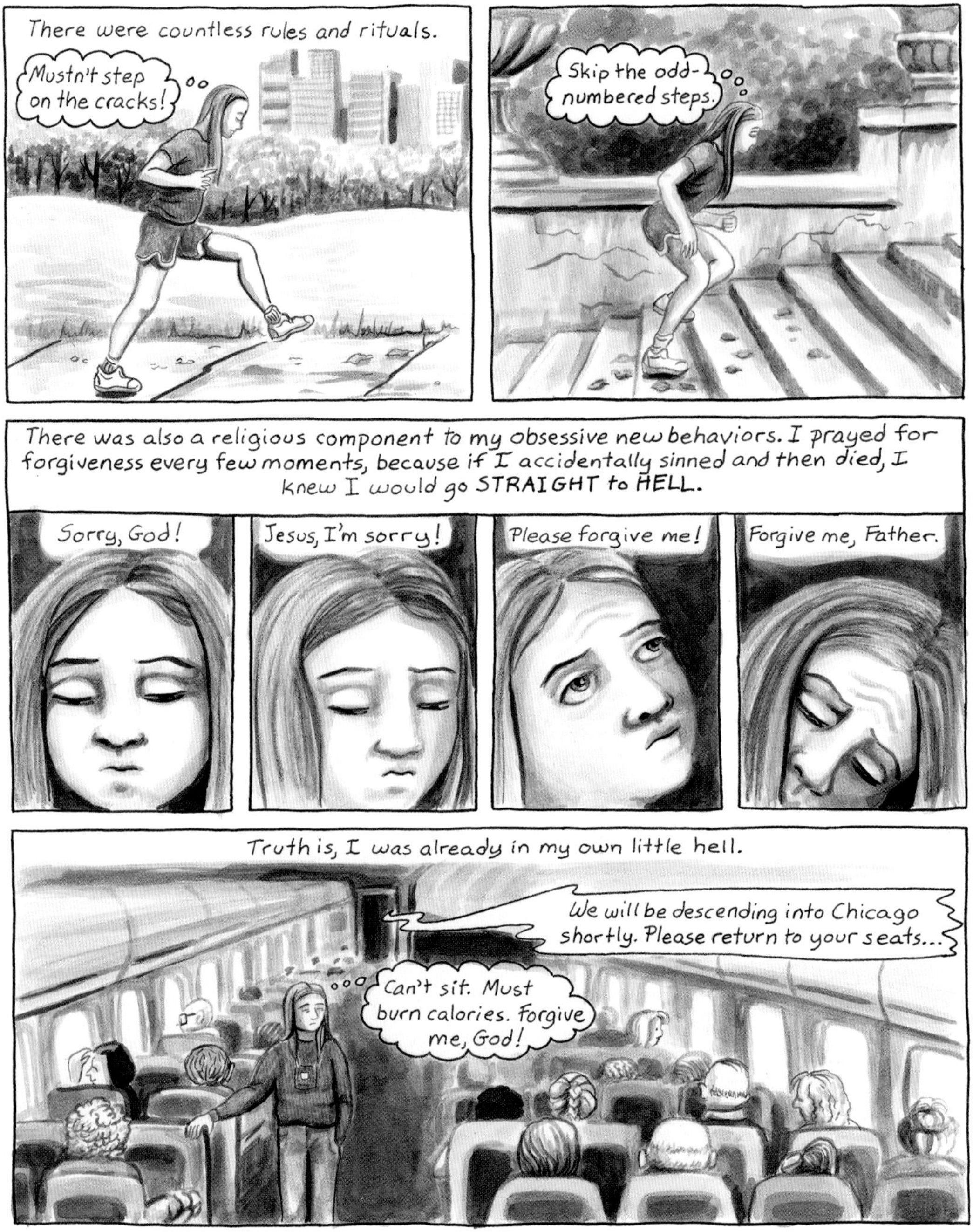
There were countless rules and rituals.
Mustn't step on the cracks!
Skip the odd-numbered steps.
There was also a religious component to my obsessive new behaviors. I prayed for forgiveness every few moments, because if I accidentally sinned and then died, I knew I would go STRAIGHT to HELL.
Sorry, God!
Jesus, I'm sorry!
Please forgive me!
Forgive me, Father.
Truth is, I was already in my own little hell.
We will be descending into Chicago shortly. Please return to your seats...
Can't sit. Must burn calories. Forgive me, God!

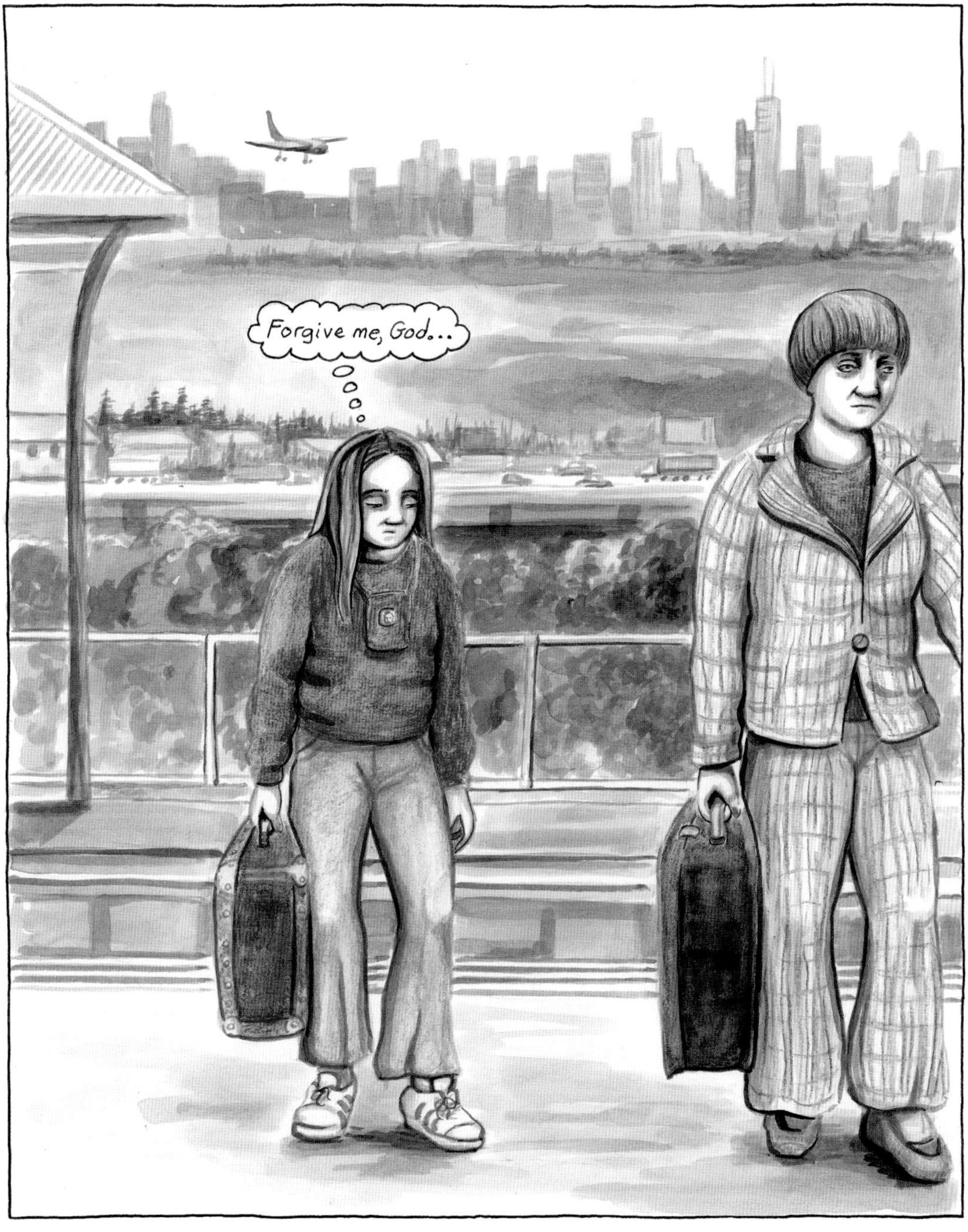
Forgive me, God...

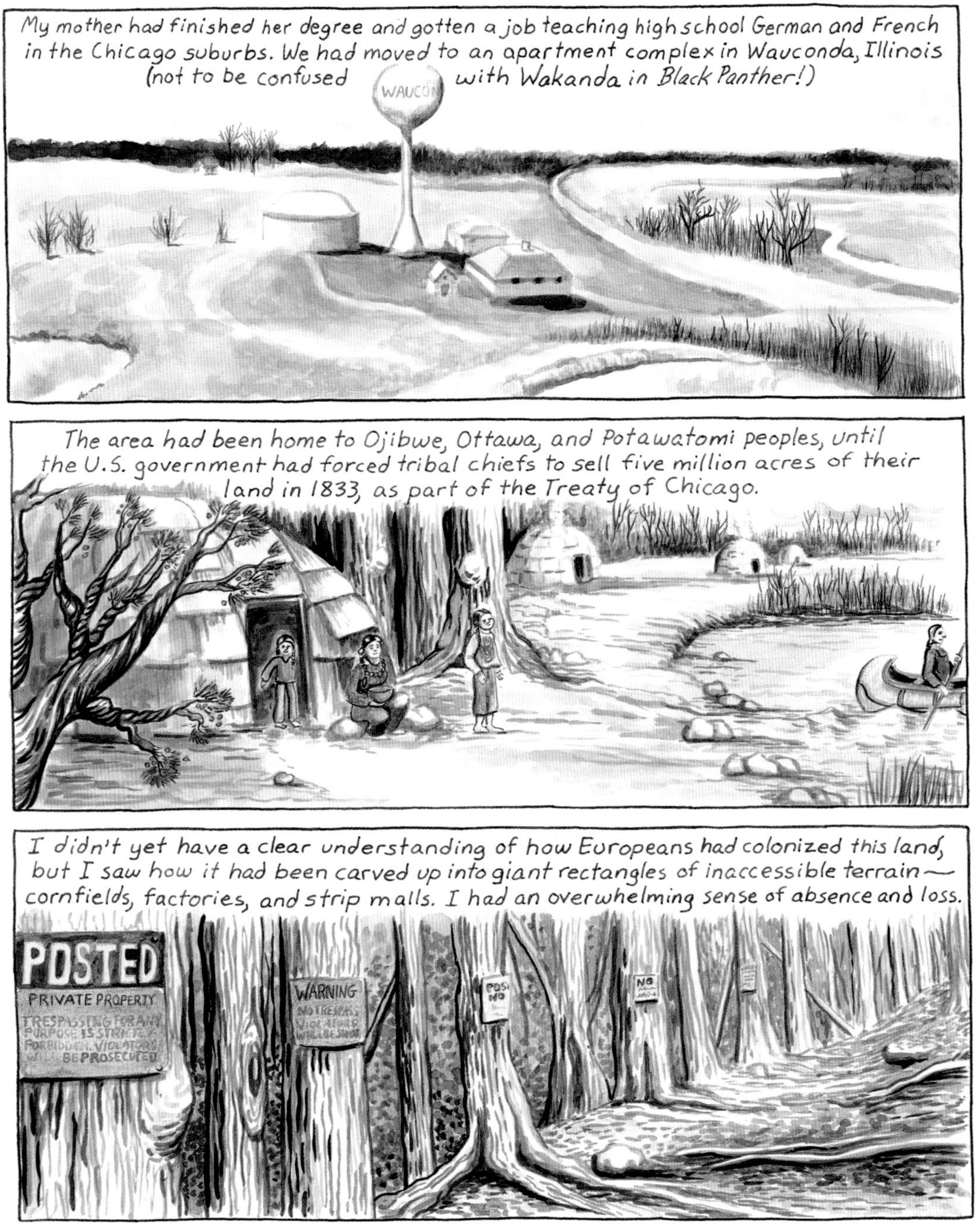
My mother had finished her degree and gotten a job teaching high school German and French in the Chicago suburbs. We had moved to an apartment complex in Wauconda, Illinois (not to be confused with Wakanda in *Black Panther*!)
WAUCON
The area had been home to Ojibwe, Ottawa, and Potawatomi peoples, until the U.S. government had forced tribal chiefs to sell five million acres of their land in 1833, as part of the Treaty of Chicago.
I didn't yet have a clear understanding of how Europeans had colonized this land, but I saw how it had been carved up into giant rectangles of inaccessible terrain — cornfields, factories, and strip malls. I had an overwhelming sense of absence and loss.
POSTED
PRIVATE PROPERTY
WARNING

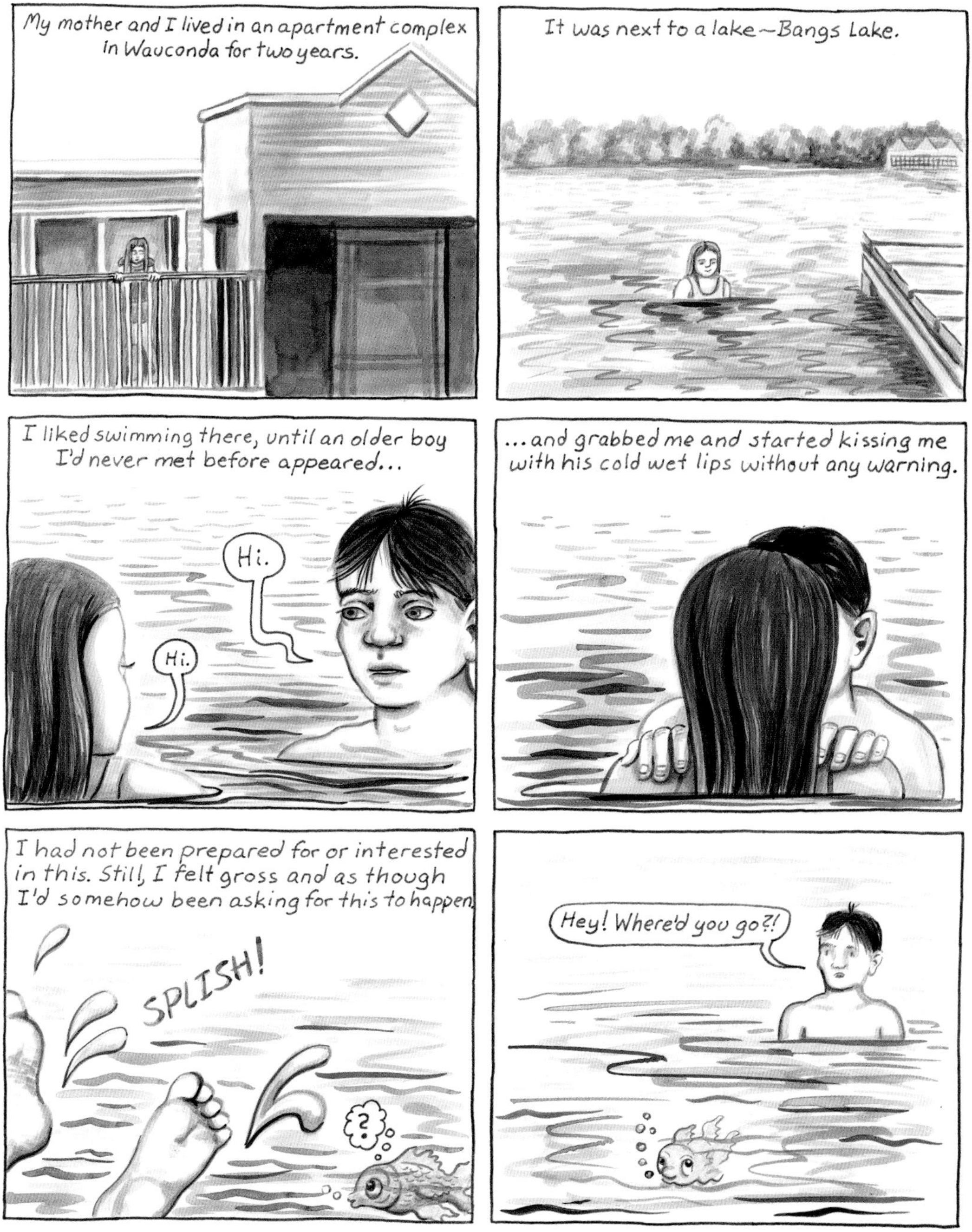
My mother and I lived in an apartment complex in Wauconda for two years.
It was next to a lake ~ Bangs Lake.
I liked swimming there, until an older boy I'd never met before appeared...
Hi.
Hi.
...and grabbed me and started kissing me with his cold wet lips without any warning.
I had not been prepared for or interested in this. Still, I felt gross and as though I'd somehow been asking for this to happen.
SPLISH!
?
Hey! Where'd you go?!

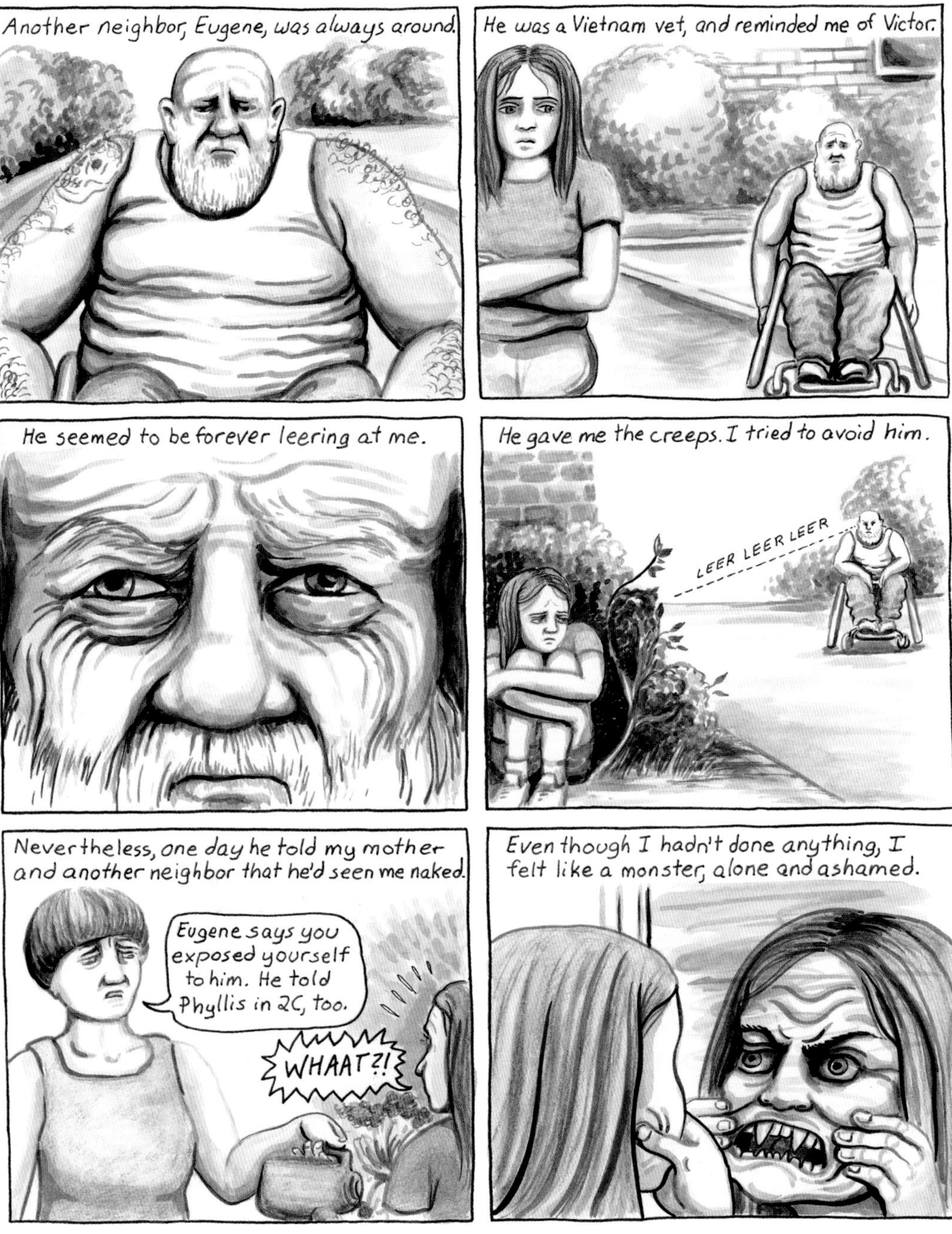
Another neighbor, Eugene, was always around.
He was a Vietnam vet, and reminded me of Victor.
He seemed to be forever leering at me.
He gave me the creeps. I tried to avoid him.
LEER LEER LEER
Nevertheless, one day he told my mother and another neighbor that he'd seen me naked.
Eugene says you exposed yourself to him. He told Phyllis in 2C, too.
WHAAT?!
Even though I hadn't done anything, I felt like a monster, alone and ashamed.

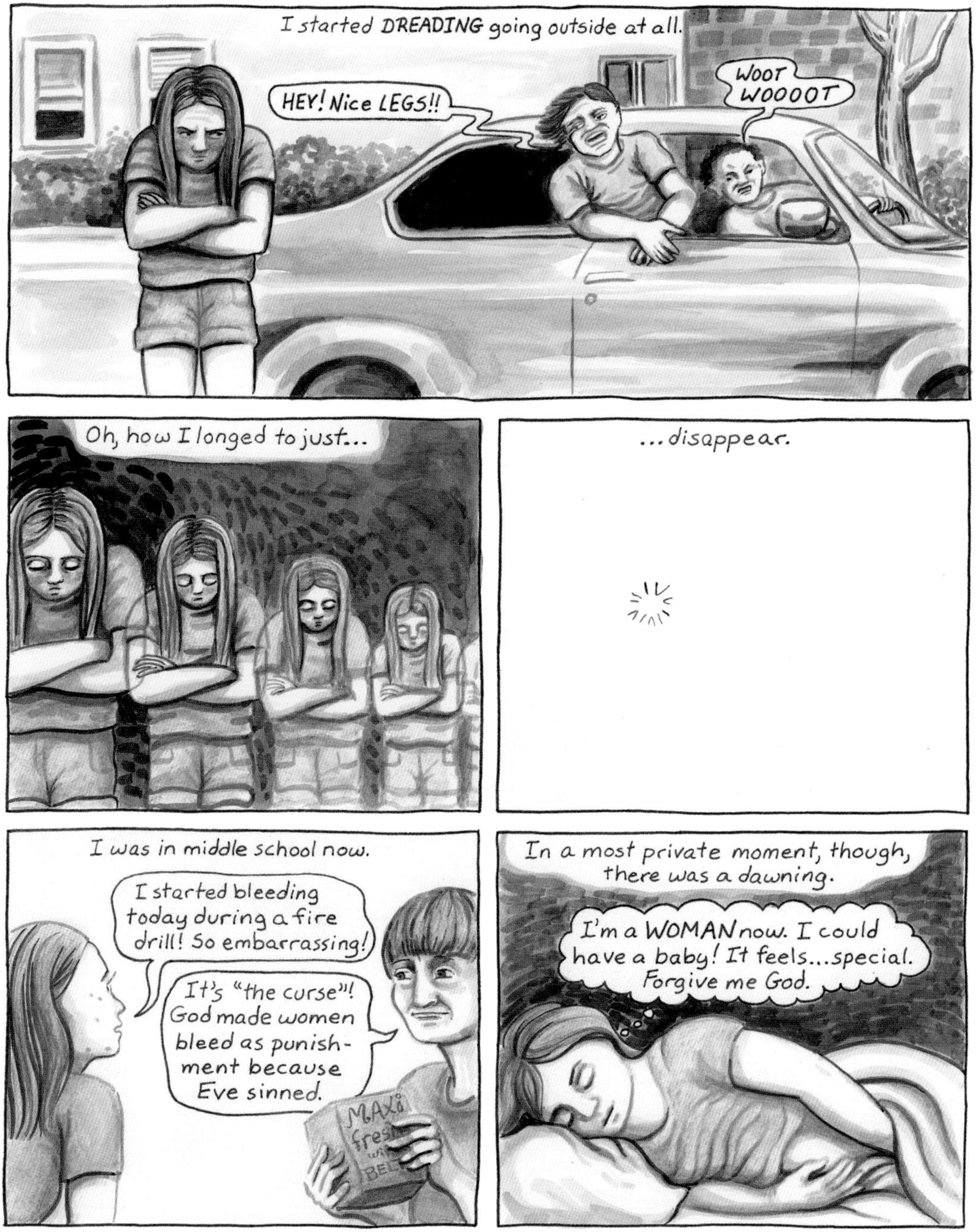
I started DREADING going outside at all.
HEY! Nice LEGS!!
WOOT WOOOOT
Oh, how I longed to just...
...disappear.
I was in middle school now.
I started bleeding today during a fire drill! So embarrassing!
It's "the curse"! God made women bleed as punish-ment because Eve sinned.
In a most private moment, though, there was a dawning.
I'm a WOMAN now. I could have a baby! It feels...special. Forgive me God.

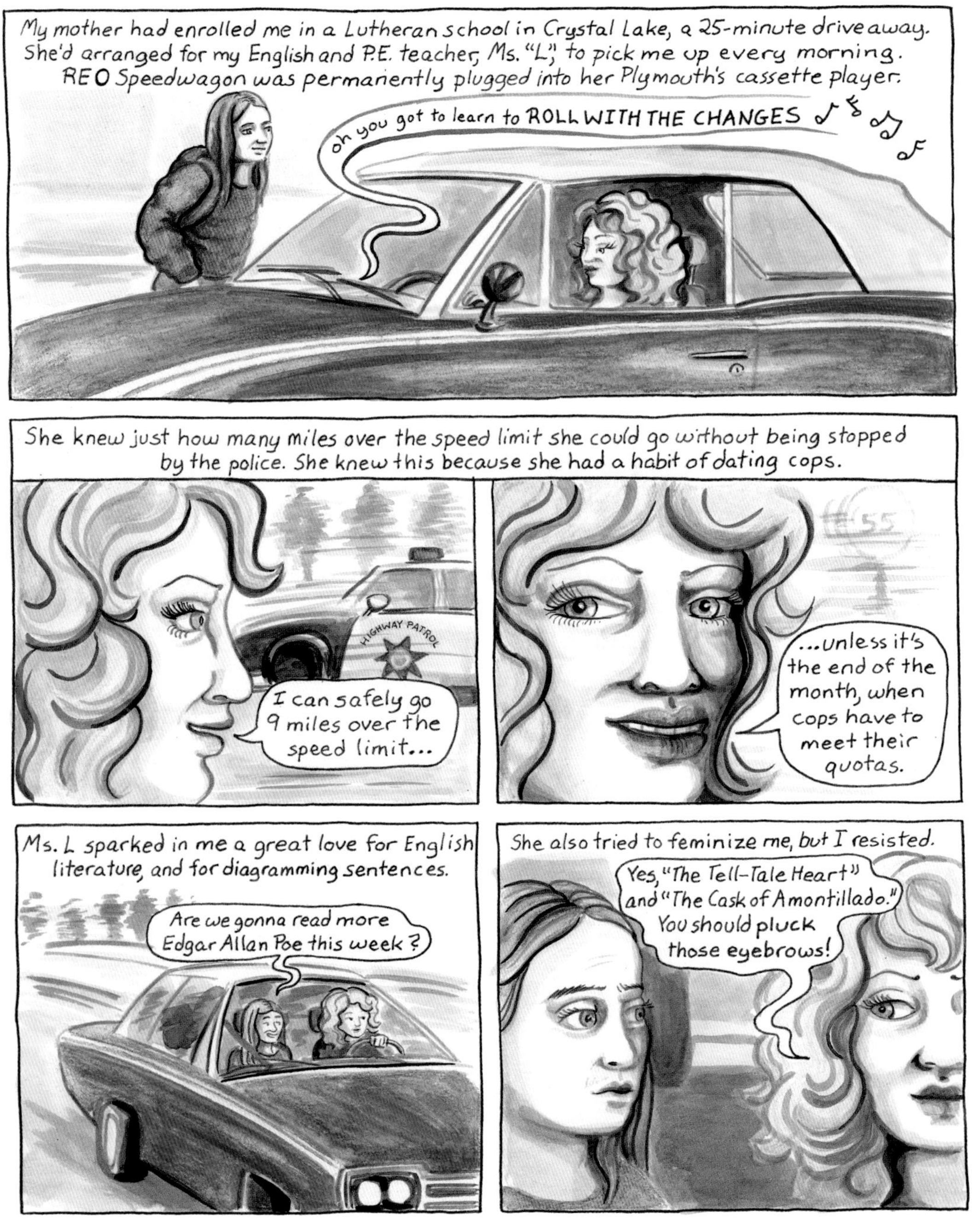
My mother had enrolled me in a Lutheran school in Crystal Lake, a 25-minute drive away. She'd arranged for my English and P.E. teacher, Ms. "L," to pick me up every morning. REO Speedwagon was permanently plugged into her Plymouth's cassette player.
oh you got to learn to ROLL WITH THE CHANGES
She knew just how many miles over the speed limit she could go without being stopped by the police. She knew this because she had a habit of dating cops.
HIGHWAY PATROL
I can safely go 9 miles over the speed limit...
55
...unless it's the end of the month, when cops have to meet their quotas.
Ms. L sparked in me a great love for English literature, and for diagramming sentences.
Are we gonna read more Edgar Allan Poe this week?
She also tried to feminize me, but I resisted.
Yes, "The Tell-Tale Heart" and "The Cask of Amontillado." You should pluck those eyebrows!

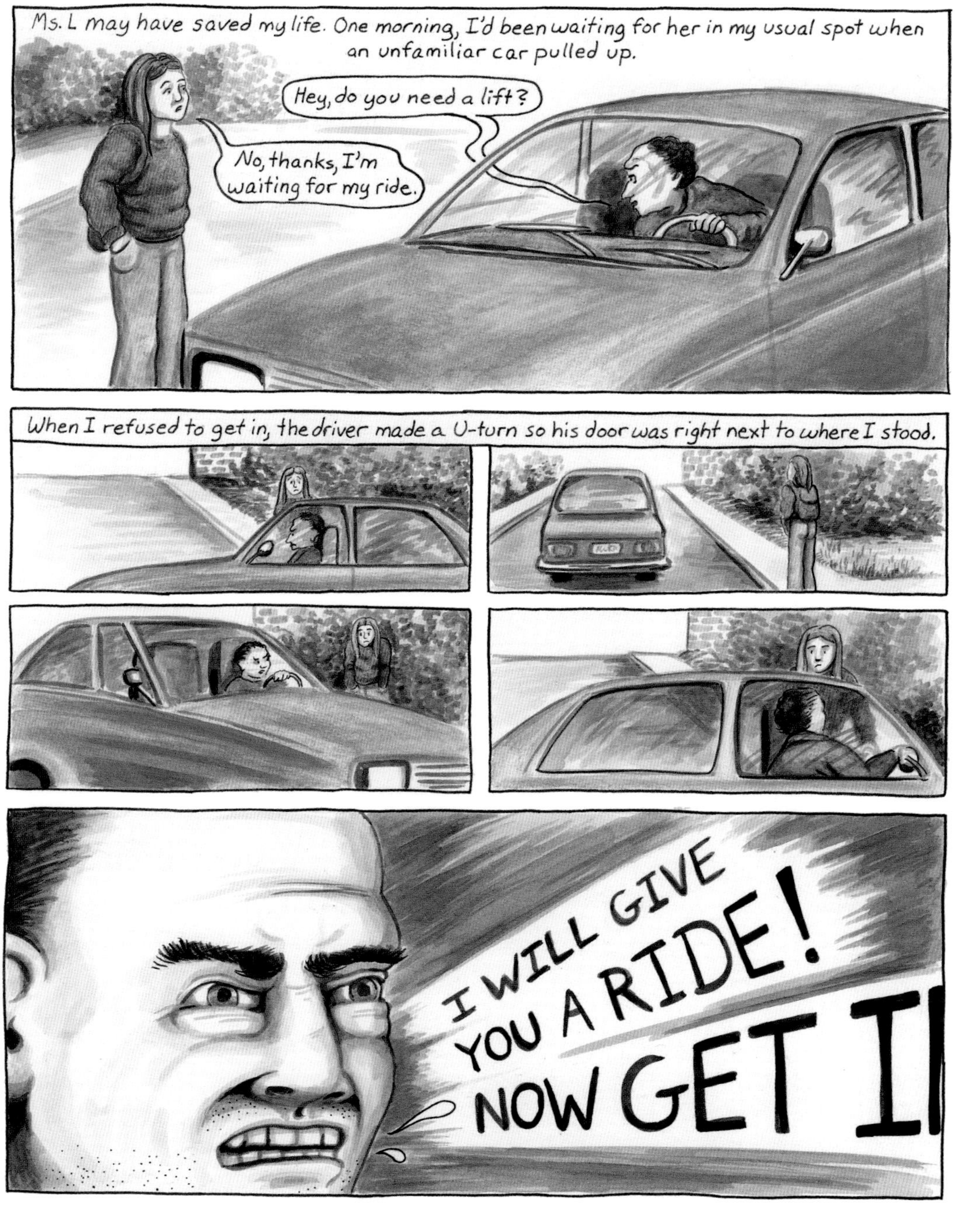
Ms. L may have saved my life. One morning, I'd been waiting for her in my usual spot when an unfamiliar car pulled up.
Hey, do you need a lift?
No, thanks, I'm waiting for my ride.
When I refused to get in, the driver made a U-turn so his door was right next to where I stood.
I WILL GIVE YOU A RIDE! NOW GET I

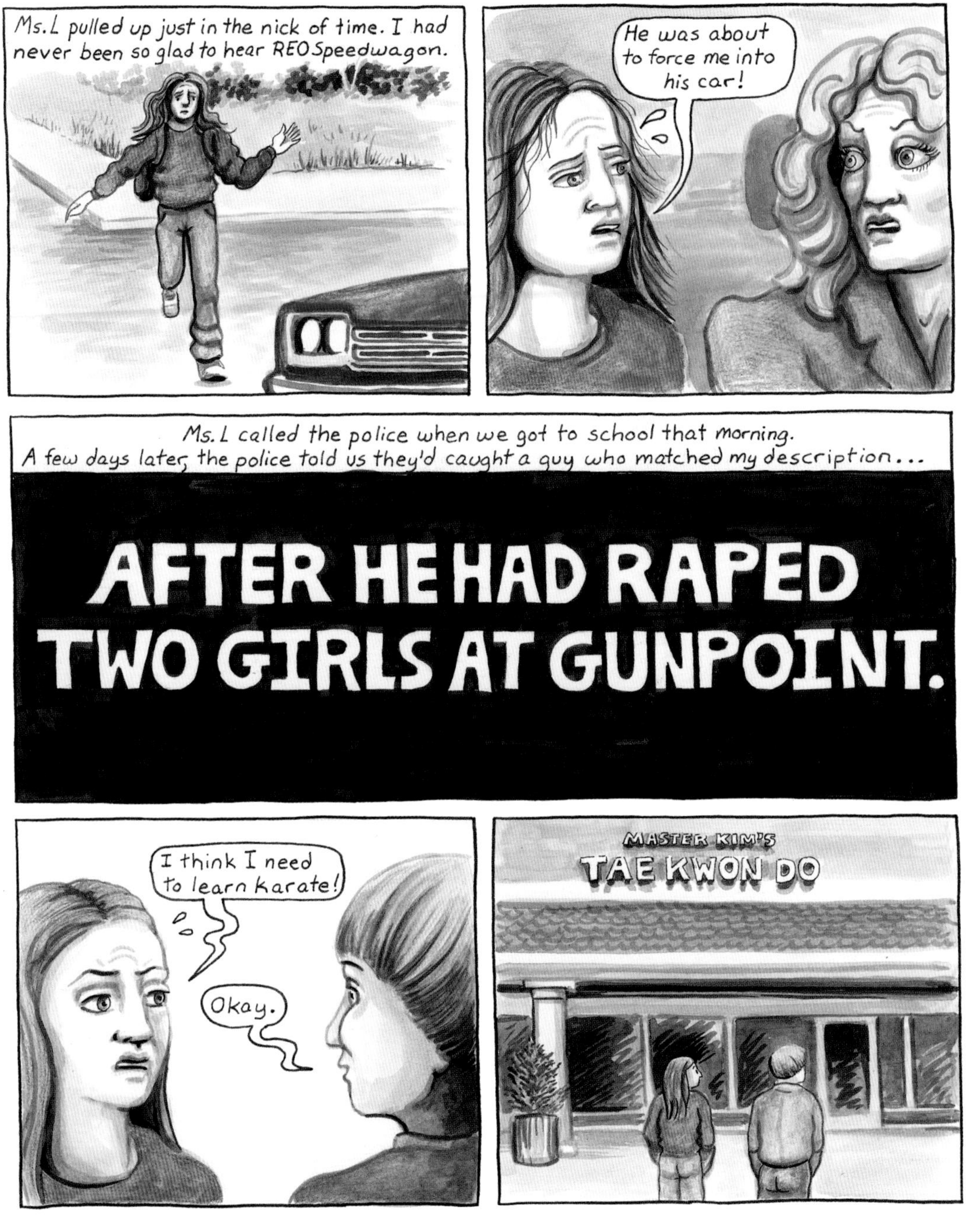
Ms. L pulled up just in the nick of time. I had never been so glad to hear REO Speedwagon.
He was about to force me into his car!
Ms. L called the police when we got to school that morning.
A few days later, the police told us they'd caught a guy who matched my description...
AFTER HE HAD RAPED TWO GIRLS AT GUNPOINT.
I think I need to learn karate!
Okay.
MASTER KIM'S
TAE KWON DO

My mother enrolled me in Taekwondo, a Korean martial art. She adored all things Korean after her years living in Seoul, where she'd taught after college.

ANNYEONG-HASEYO!

Mr. Kim was one of the kindest, most decent men I'd ever met.

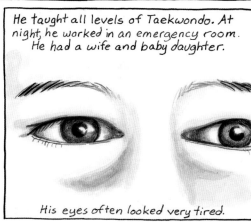

He taught all levels of Taekwondo. At night, he worked in an emergency room. He had a wife and baby daughter.

His eyes often looked very tired.

He was the first man since we'd emigrated who made me feel safe, and he was an immigrant, too! There were few females in the martial arts in the '80s, but Mr. Kim was respectful and encouraging.

WOW! You have very long legs! See how high you can kick?!

163

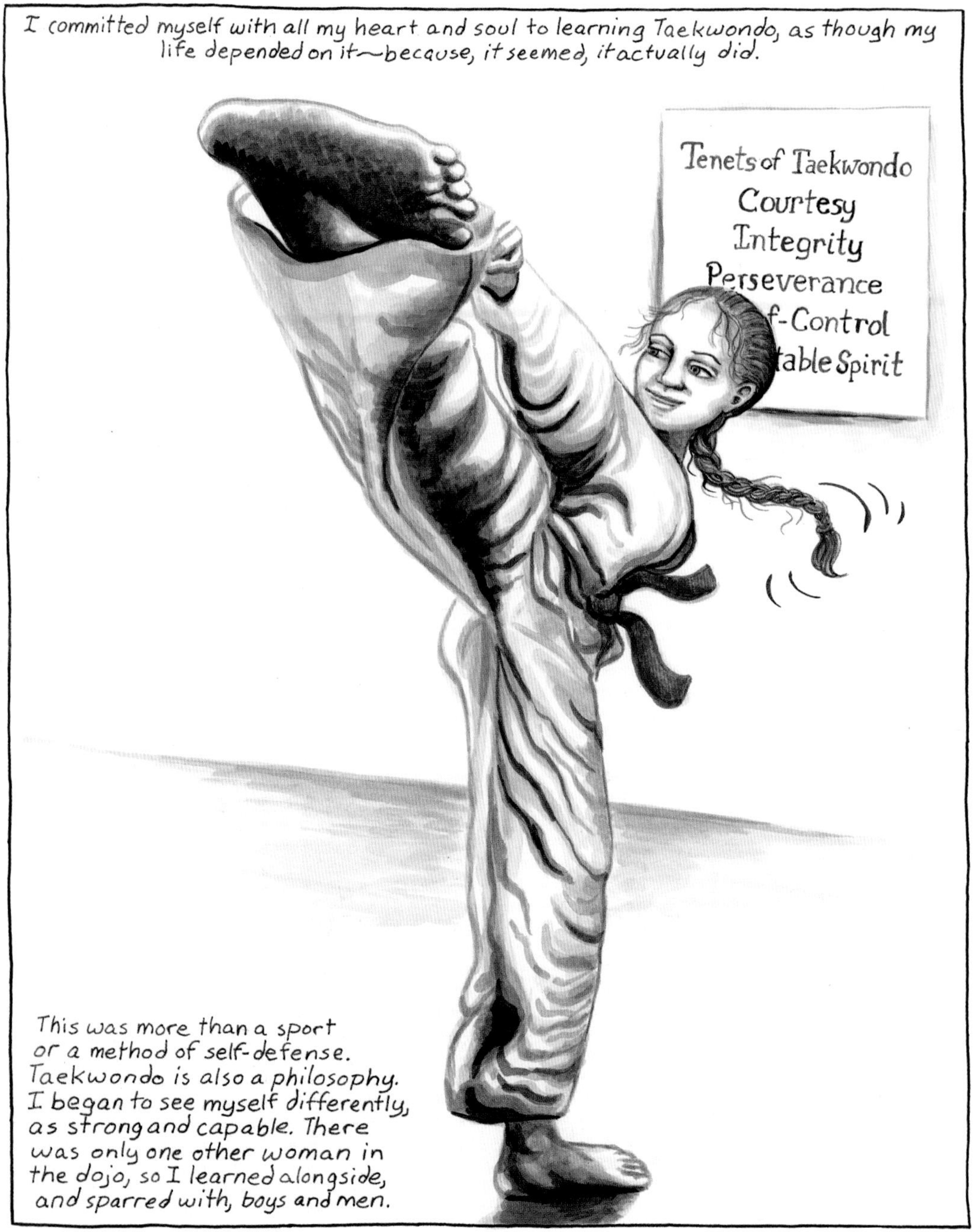
I committed myself with all my heart and soul to learning Taekwondo, as though my life depended on it—because, it seemed, it actually did.
Tenets of Taekwondo
Courtesy
Integrity
Perseverance
This was more than a sport or a method of self-defense. Taekwondo is also a philosophy. I began to see myself differently, as strong and capable. There was only one other woman in the dojo, so I learned alongside, and sparred with, boys and men.

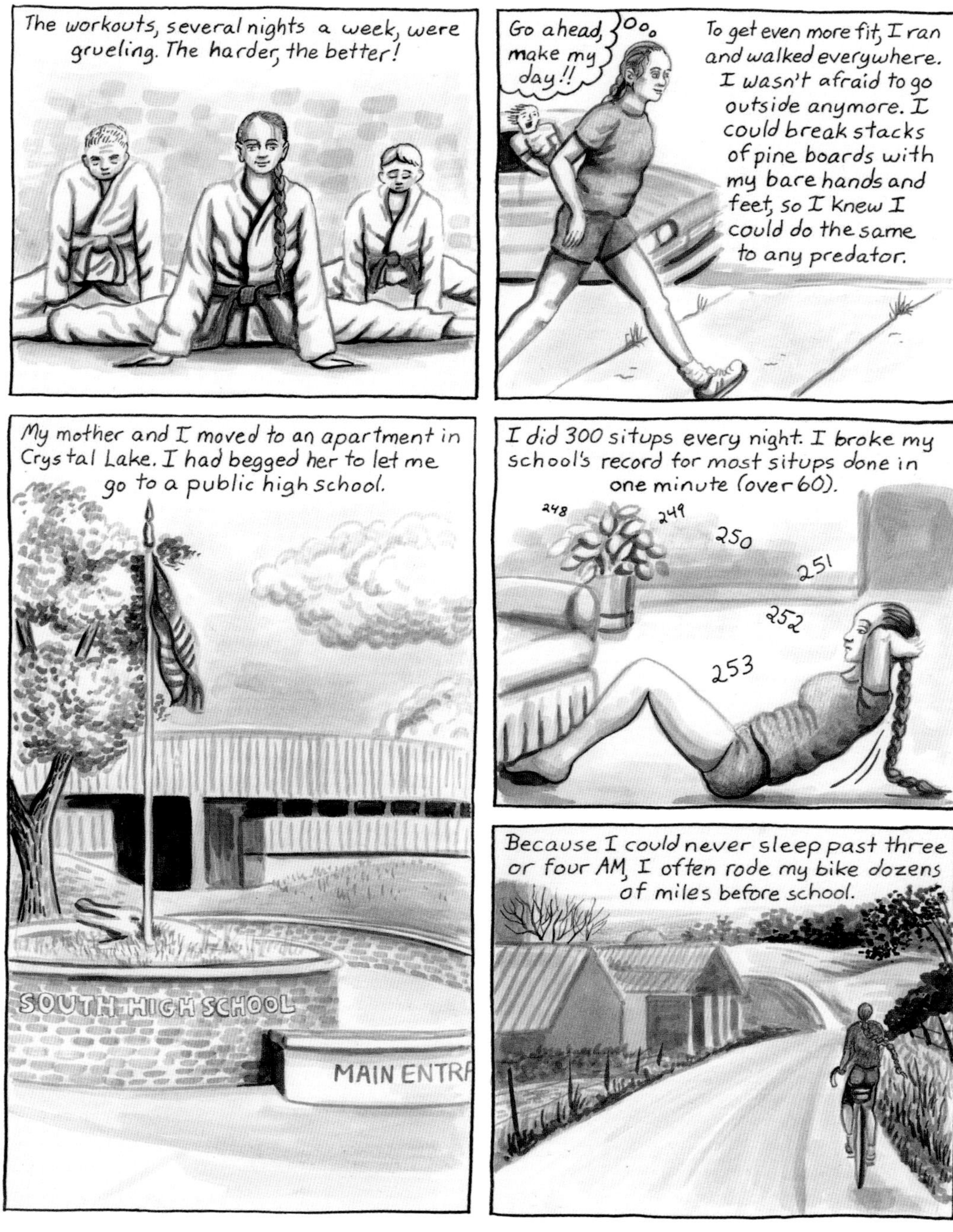
The workouts, several nights a week, were grueling. The harder, the better!
Go ahead, make my day!!
To get even more fit, I ran and walked everywhere. I wasn't afraid to go outside anymore. I could break stacks of pine boards with my bare hands and feet, so I knew I could do the same to any predator.
My mother and I moved to an apartment in Crystal Lake. I had begged her to let me go to a public high school.
SOUTH HIGH SCHOOL
MAIN ENTR
I did 300 situps every night. I broke my school's record for most situps done in one minute (over 60).
248
249
250
251
252
253
Because I could never sleep past three or four AM, I often rode my bike dozens of miles before school.

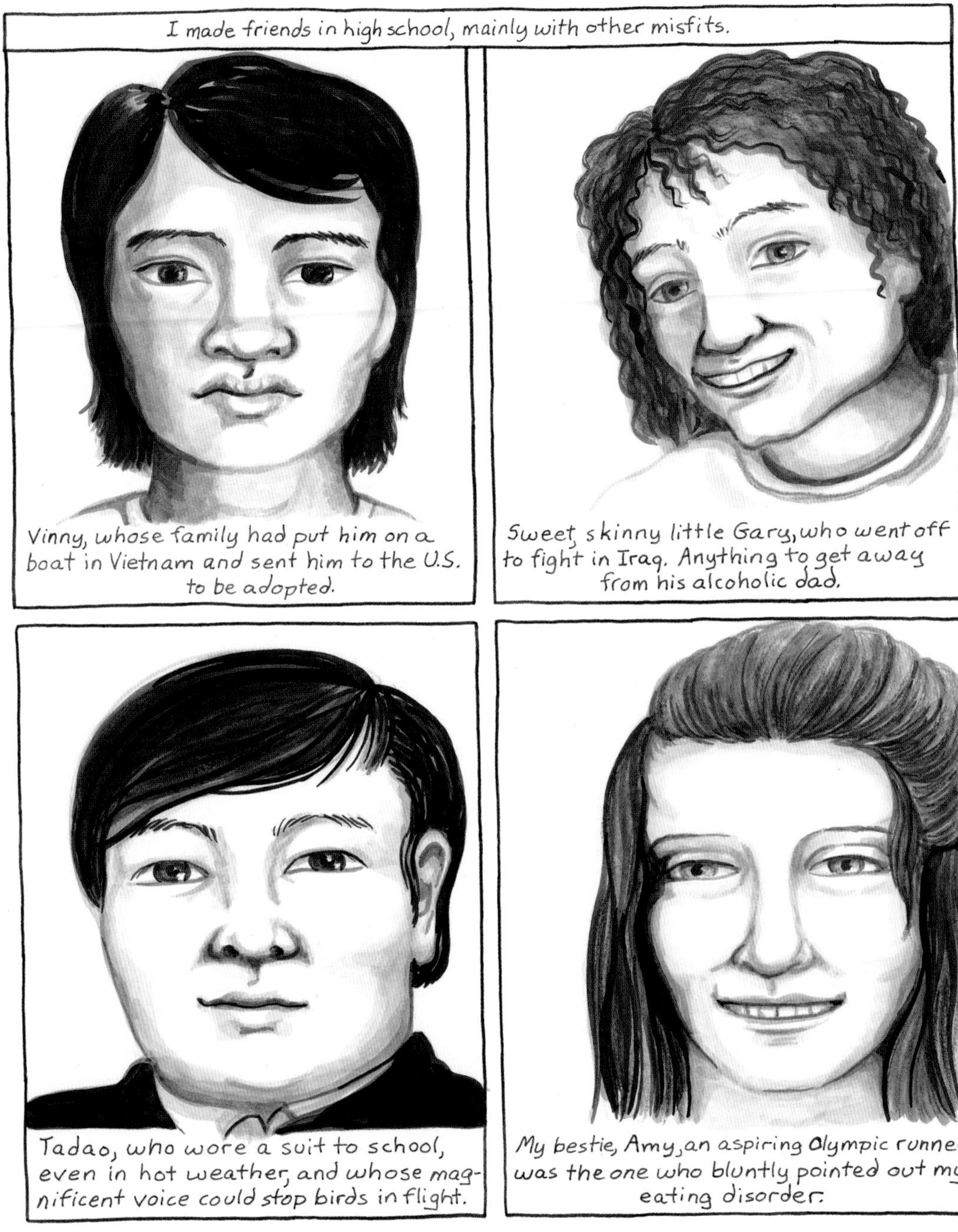
I made friends in high school, mainly with other misfits.
Vinny, whose family had put him on a boat in Vietnam and sent him to the U.S. to be adopted.
Sweet, skinny little Gary, who went off to fight in Iraq. Anything to get away from his alcoholic dad.
Tadao, who wore a suit to school, even in hot weather, and whose magnificent voice could stop birds in flight.
My bestie, Amy, an aspiring Olympic runner, was the one who bluntly pointed out my eating disorder.

Maureen, you look gross! Stop starving yourself!

I HAVE IT UNDER CONTROL!

I had become vegetarian and taught myself to cook by reading books from the public library.

AMERICAN WHOLEFOODS CUISINE

I had cut out sugar and all white flour.

SUGAR BLUES

I spent hours reading about nutrition and perusing grocery store shelves, reading labels and not buying anything.

The WHOLE WORLD is TOXIC... ooo

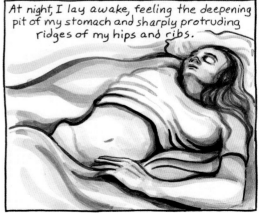

At night, I lay awake, feeling the deepening pit of my stomach and sharply protruding ridges of my hips and ribs.

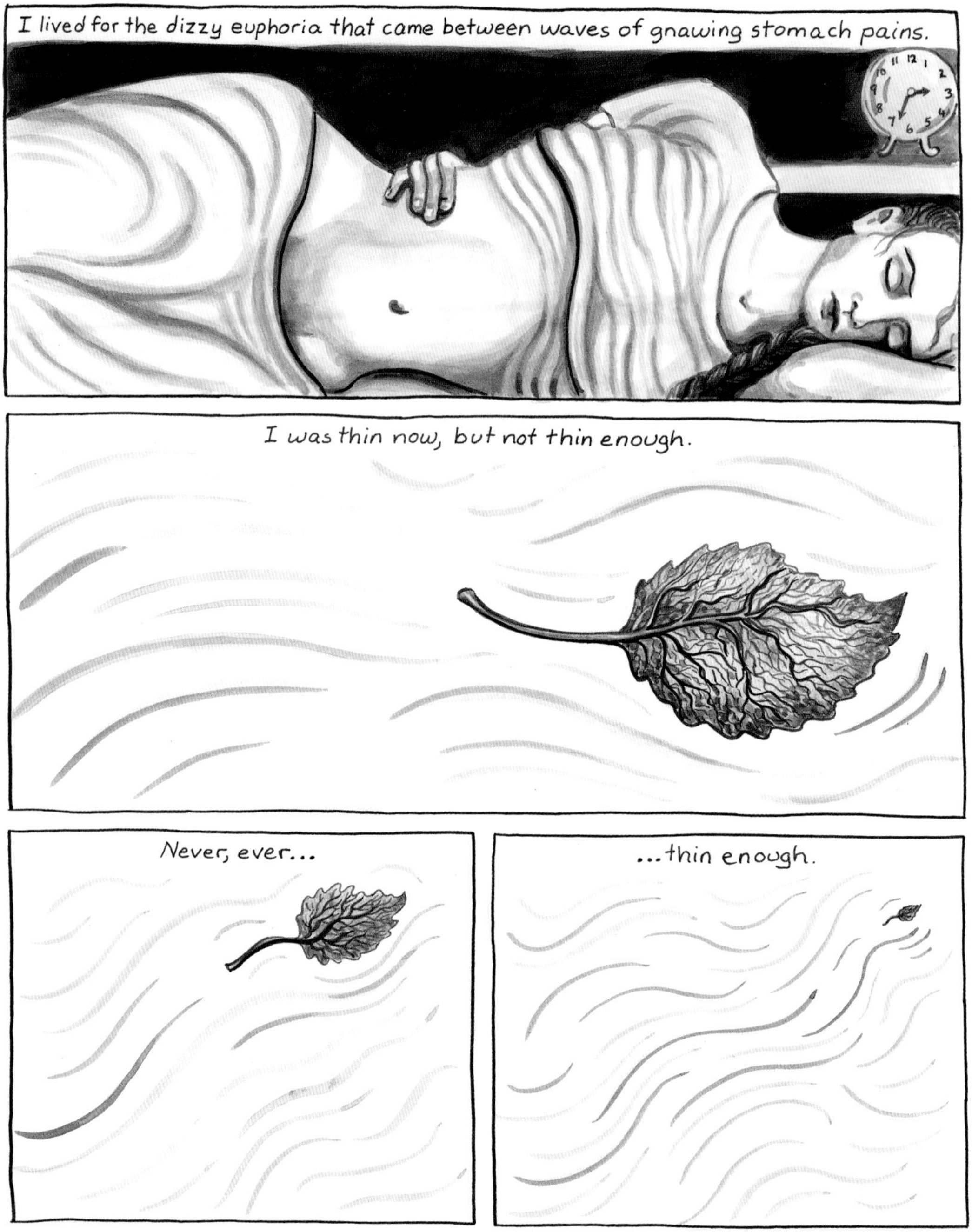
I lived for the dizzy euphoria that came between waves of gnawing stomach pains.
I was thin now, but not thin enough.
Never, ever...
...thin enough.

My mother took me to a doctor, a very rare occurrence reserved for true emergencies.

You're going to have big problems for the rest of your life if you don't stop this. You may never be able to have children.

I will see you in one month, and by then I expect you to gain at least FIVE POUNDS.

It was the last thing I wanted to hear. The thought of gaining even one pound was terrifying. The doctor's threat might not have affected many other anorexic girls, but I, having lost much of my family, wanted to have one more than anything.

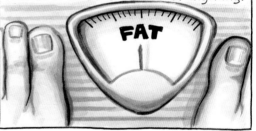

I figured I could trick the doctor by only gaining muscle, so I stepped up the exercise. In addition to Taekwondo and cycling, I often biked to a nearby park and walked for miles.

I never went back to that doctor, but over time, his words sunk in. I was lucky that his appeal to my young womb had the right effect. I wish someone had noticed that I was depressed.

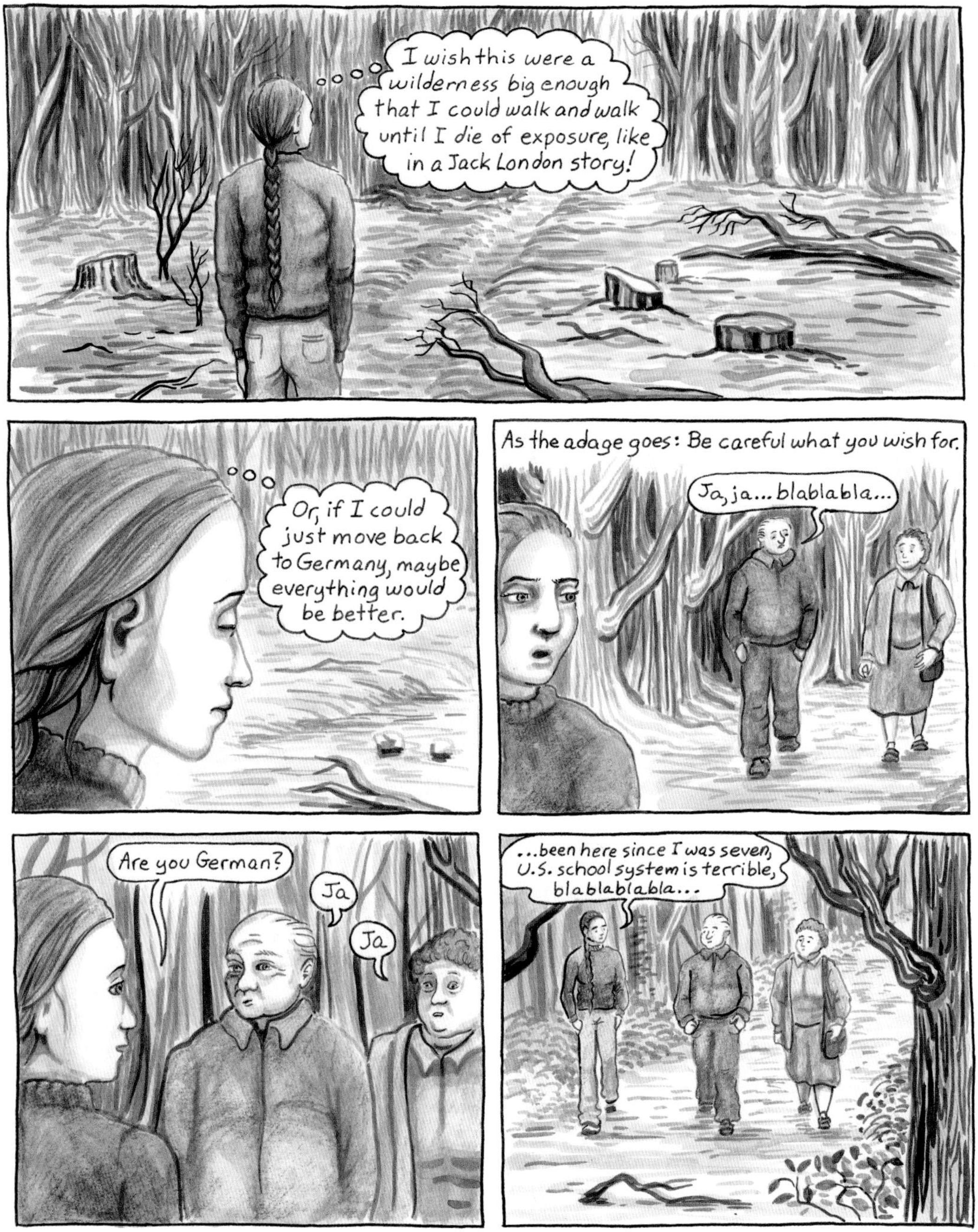
I wish this were a wilderness big enough that I could walk and walk until I die of exposure, like in a Jack London story!
Or, if I could just move back to Germany, maybe everything would be better.
As the adage goes: Be careful what you wish for.
Ja, ja... blablabla...
Are you German?
Ja
Ja
...been here since I was seven, U.S. school system is terrible, blablablabla...

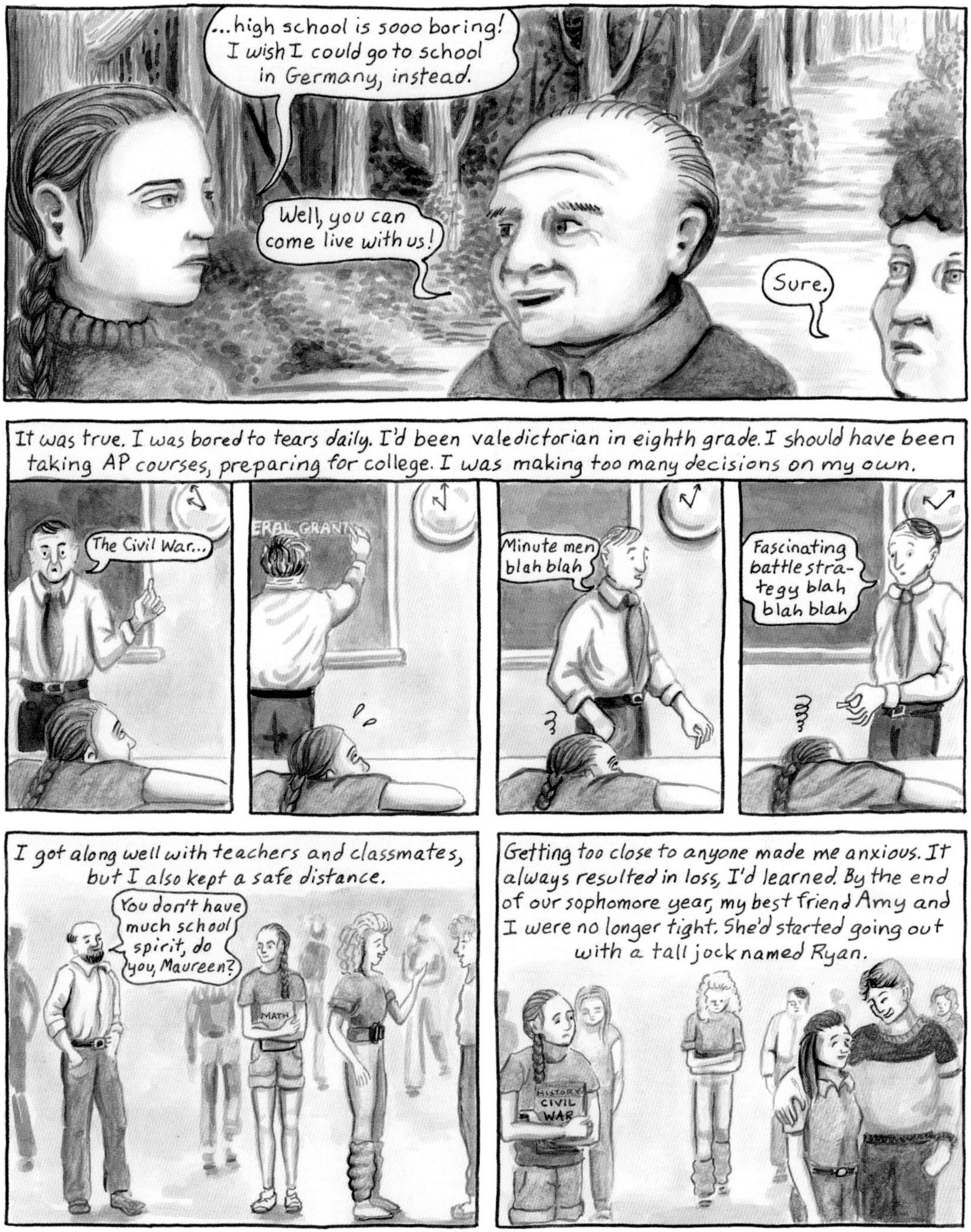
...high school is sooo boring! I wish I could go to school in Germany, instead.
Well, you can come live with us!
Sure.
It was true. I was bored to tears daily. I'd been valedictorian in eighth grade. I should have been taking AP courses, preparing for college. I was making too many decisions on my own.
The Civil War...
Minute men blah blah
Fascinating battle strategy blah blah blah
I got along well with teachers and classmates, but I also kept a safe distance.
You don't have much school spirit, do you, Maureen?
MATH
Getting too close to anyone made me anxious. It always resulted in loss, I'd learned. By the end of our sophomore year, my best friend Amy and I were no longer tight. She'd started going out with a tall jock named Ryan.
HISTORY CIVIL WAR

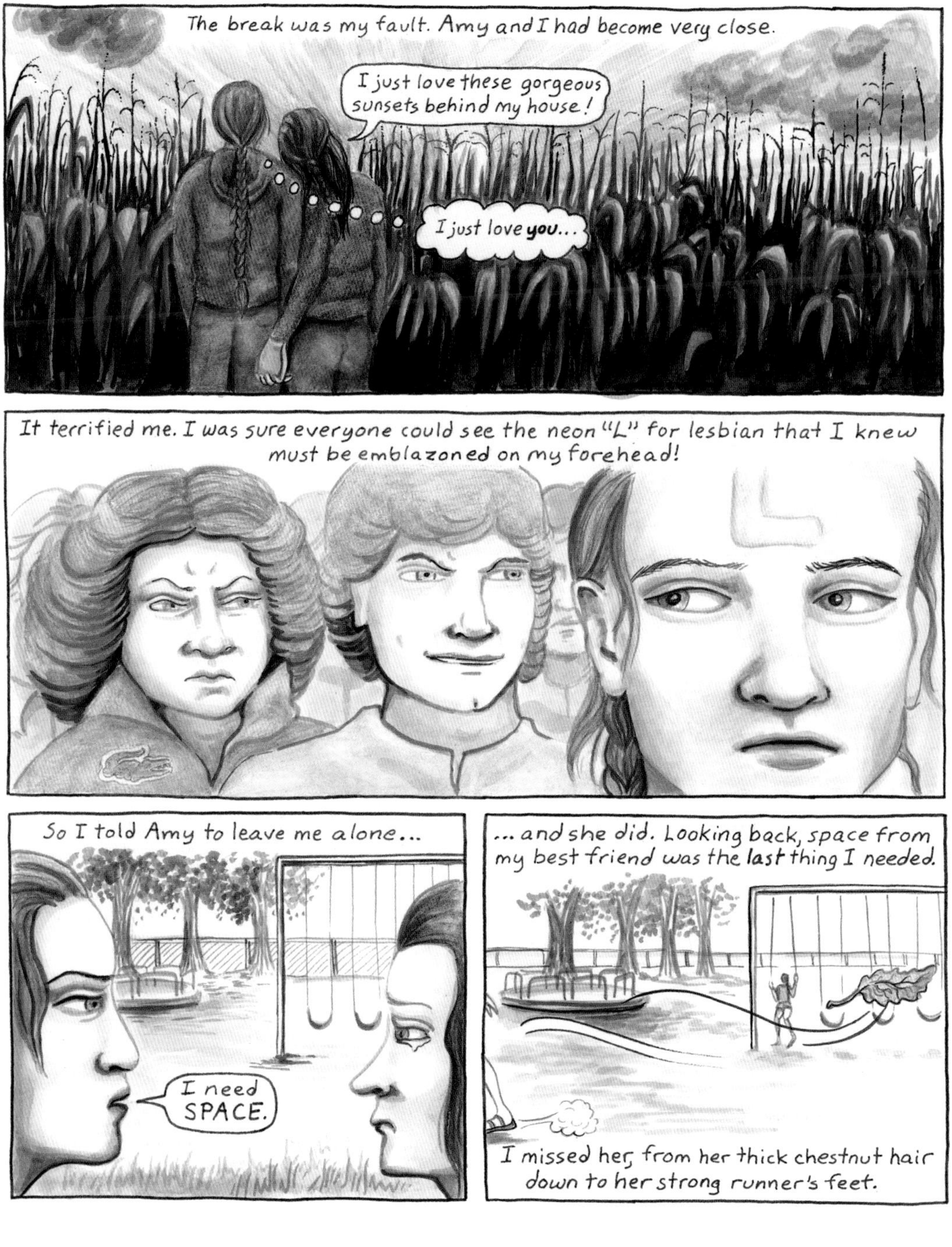
The break was my fault. Amy and I had become very close.
I just love these gorgeous sunsets behind my house!
I just love **you**...
It terrified me. I was sure everyone could see the neon "L" for lesbian that I knew must be emblazoned on my forehead!
So I told Amy to leave me alone...
I need SPACE.
...and she did. Looking back, space from my best friend was the **last** thing I needed.
I missed her, from her thick chestnut hair down to her strong runner's feet.

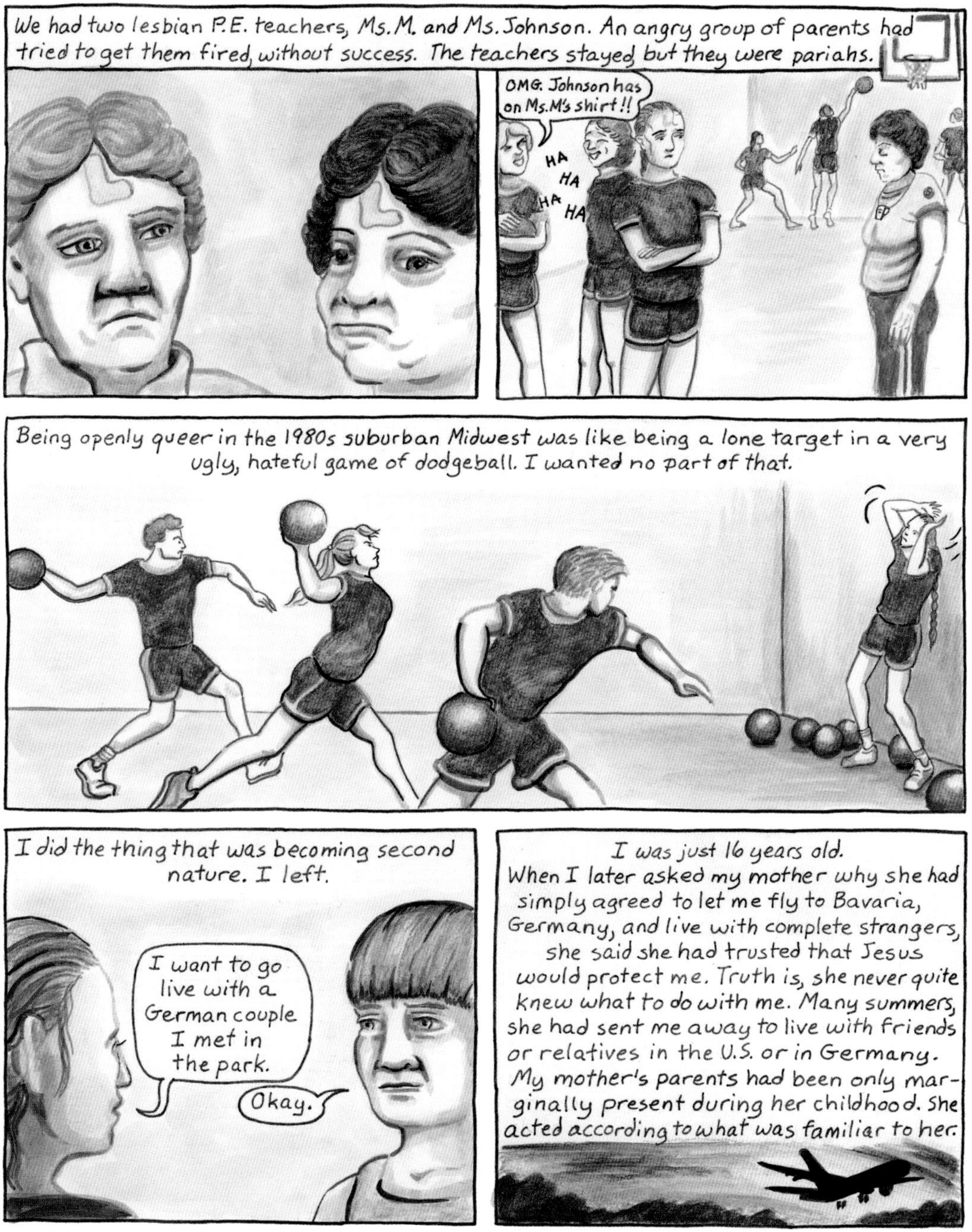
We had two lesbian P.E. teachers, Ms. M. and Ms. Johnson. An angry group of parents had tried to get them fired, without success. The teachers stayed, but they were pariahs.
OMG. Johnson has on Ms. M's shirt!!
HA HA HA HA
Being openly queer in the 1980s suburban Midwest was like being a lone target in a very ugly, hateful game of dodgeball. I wanted no part of that.
I did the thing that was becoming second nature. I left.
I want to go live with a German couple I met in the park.
Okay.
I was just 16 years old.
When I later asked my mother why she had simply agreed to let me fly to Bavaria, Germany, and live with complete strangers, she said she had trusted that Jesus would protect me. Truth is, she never quite knew what to do with me. Many summers, she had sent me away to live with friends or relatives in the U.S. or in Germany. My mother's parents had been only marginally present during her childhood. She acted according to what was familiar to her.

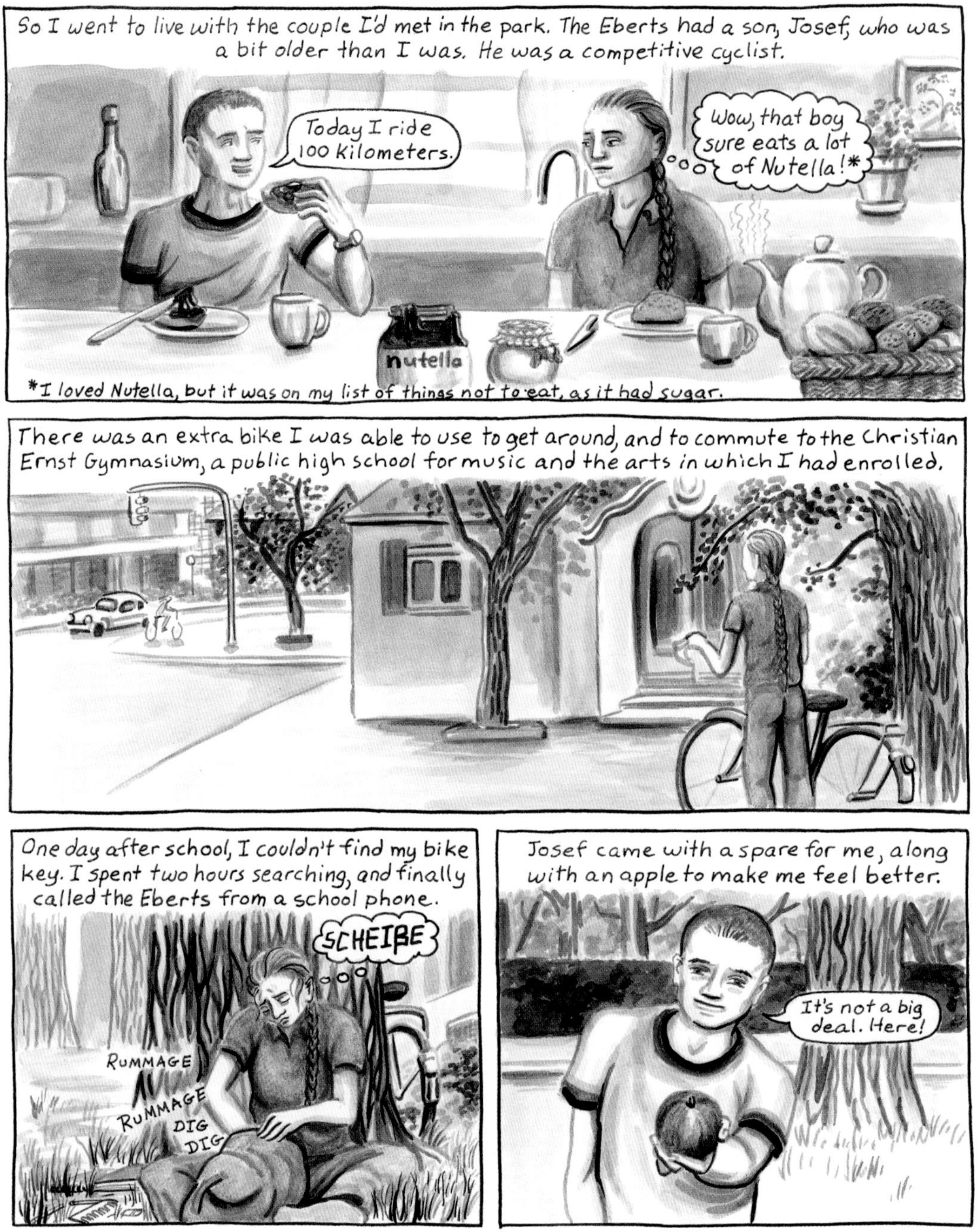
So I went to live with the couple I'd met in the park. The Eberts had a son, Josef, who was a bit older than I was. He was a competitive cyclist.
Today I ride 100 kilometers.
Wow, that boy sure eats a lot of Nutella!*
nutella
*I loved Nutella, but it was on my list of things not to eat, as it had sugar.
There was an extra bike I was able to use to get around, and to commute to the Christian Ernst Gymnasium, a public high school for music and the arts in which I had enrolled.
One day after school, I couldn't find my bike key. I spent two hours searching, and finally called the Eberts from a school phone.
SCHEIßE
RUMMAGE
RUMMAGE
DIG
DIG
Josef came with a spare for me, along with an apple to make me feel better.
It's not a big deal. Here!

Later, the key turned up at the bottom of my bag.

Haha! I found it! The whole time, it was just under stuff in my bag.

We know you just HID the key. You WANTED our son to come RESCUE you!

You're trying to SEDUCE our son!

Soon after, Frau Ebert had to go to the hospital for an extended time. Something to do with her "female parts," maybe a hysterectomy. That's when things got even weirder.

You don' know how to behave becaush you don' have a father. I will be extra shtrick with you—ish what you need!

hicks Love bloshoms like a ROSE... don' you unnershtand?

You are sho young, beautiful... you don' unnershtand yet...

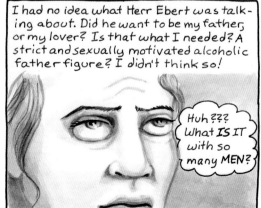

I had no idea what Herr Ebert was talking about. Did he want to be my father, or my lover? Is that what I needed? A strict and sexually motivated alcoholic father figure? I didn't think so!

Huh??? What IS IT with so many MEN?

175

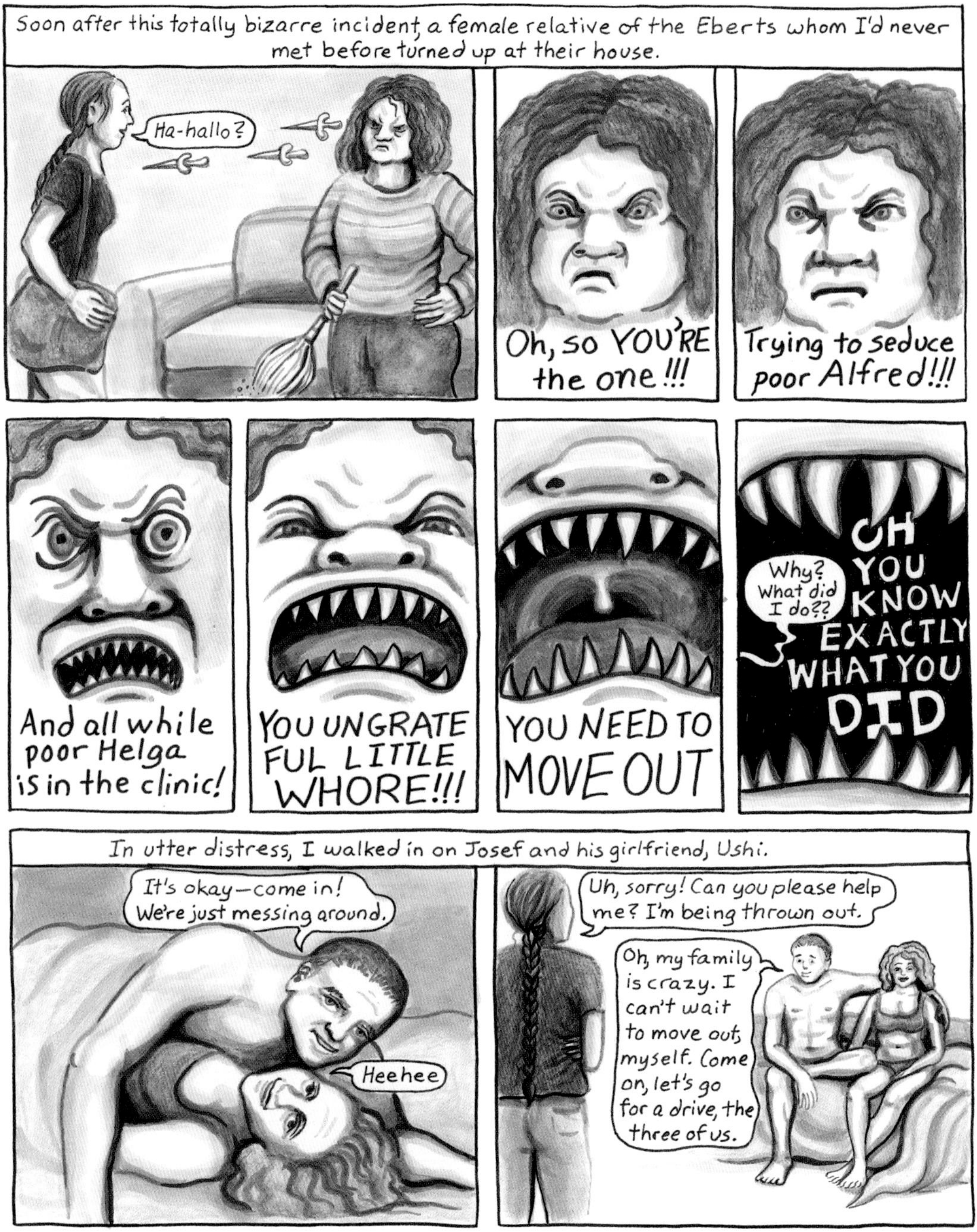
Soon after this totally bizarre incident, a female relative of the Eberts whom I'd never met before turned up at their house.
Ha-hallo?
Oh, so YOU'RE the one!!!
Trying to seduce poor Alfred!!!
And all while poor Helga is in the clinic!
YOU UNGRATEFUL LITTLE WHORE!!!
YOU NEED TO MOVE OUT
Why? What did I do??
OH YOU KNOW EXACTLY WHAT YOU DID
In utter distress, I walked in on Josef and his girlfriend, Ushi.
It's okay—come in! We're just messing around.
Heehee
Uh, sorry! Can you please help me? I'm being thrown out.
Oh, my family is crazy. I can't wait to move out, myself. Come on, let's go for a drive, the three of us.

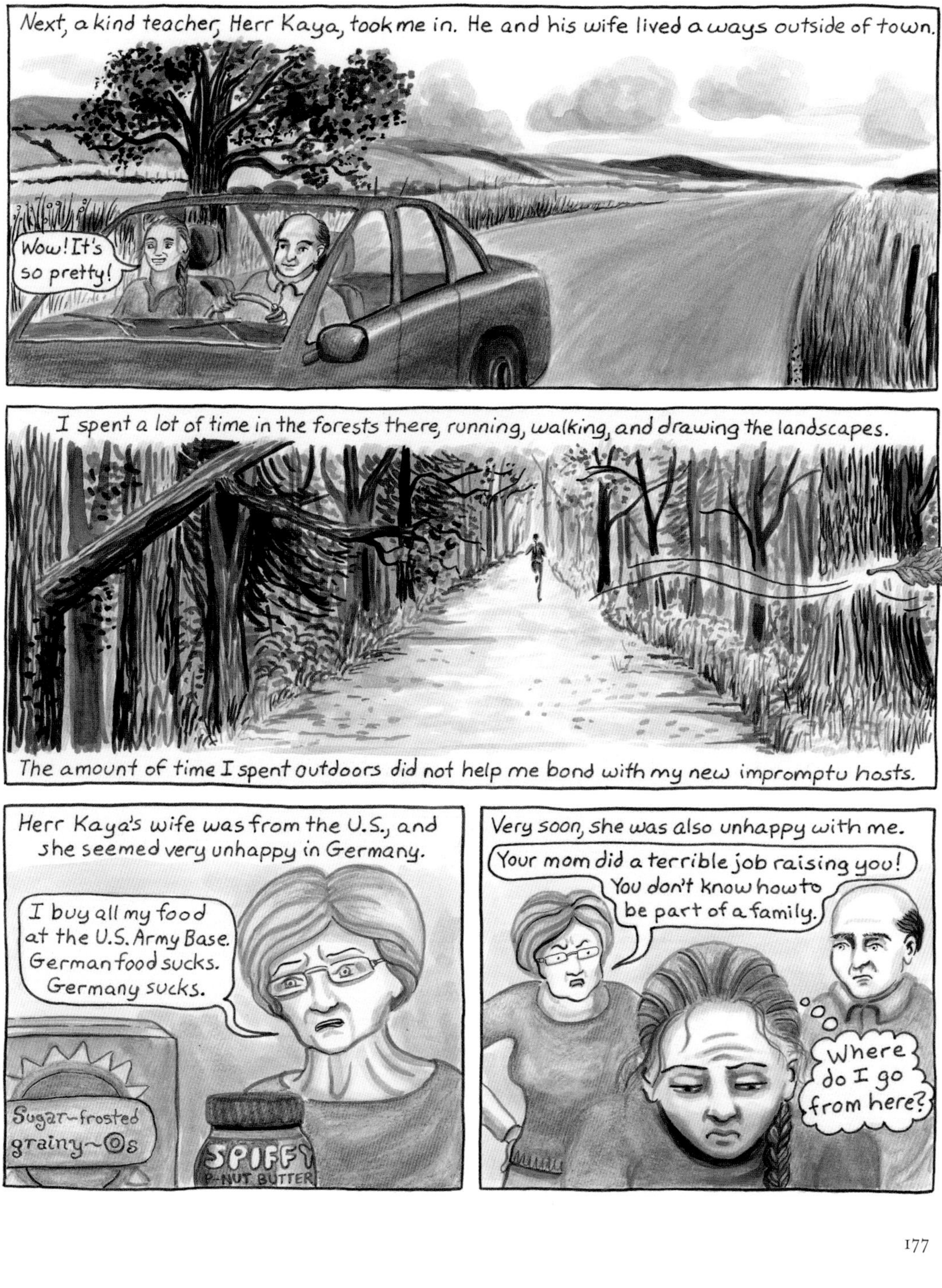
Next, a kind teacher, Herr Kaya, took me in. He and his wife lived a ways outside of town.
Wow! It's so pretty!
I spent a lot of time in the forests there, running, walking, and drawing the landscapes.
The amount of time I spent outdoors did not help me bond with my new impromptu hosts.
Herr Kaya's wife was from the U.S., and she seemed very unhappy in Germany.
I buy all my food at the U.S. Army Base. German food sucks. Germany sucks.
Sugar-frosted grainy-Os
SPIFFY P-NUT BUTTER
Very soon, she was also unhappy with me.
Your mom did a terrible job raising you! You don't know how to be part of a family.
Where do I go from here?

One of my new friends in school, Helga Müller, asked her parents if I could move in. Helga had large teeth and extremely smooth skin. She was a born-again Christian but her parents were atheists.

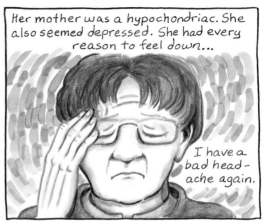

Her mother was a hypochondriac. She also seemed depressed. She had every reason to feel down...

I have a bad head-ache again.

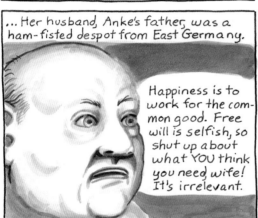

... Her husband, Anke's father, was a ham-fisted despot from East Germany.

Happiness is to work for the common good. Free will is selfish, so shut up about what YOU think you need, wife! It's irrelevant.

He was a die-hard communist, domestic abuser style.

WHAT ARE YOU BLATHER-ING ON ABOUT NOW, STUPID WOMAN?!

It was no wonder that Anke sought escape in her revivalist community. I joined her a few times. I so badly wanted to believe— to **BELONG!**

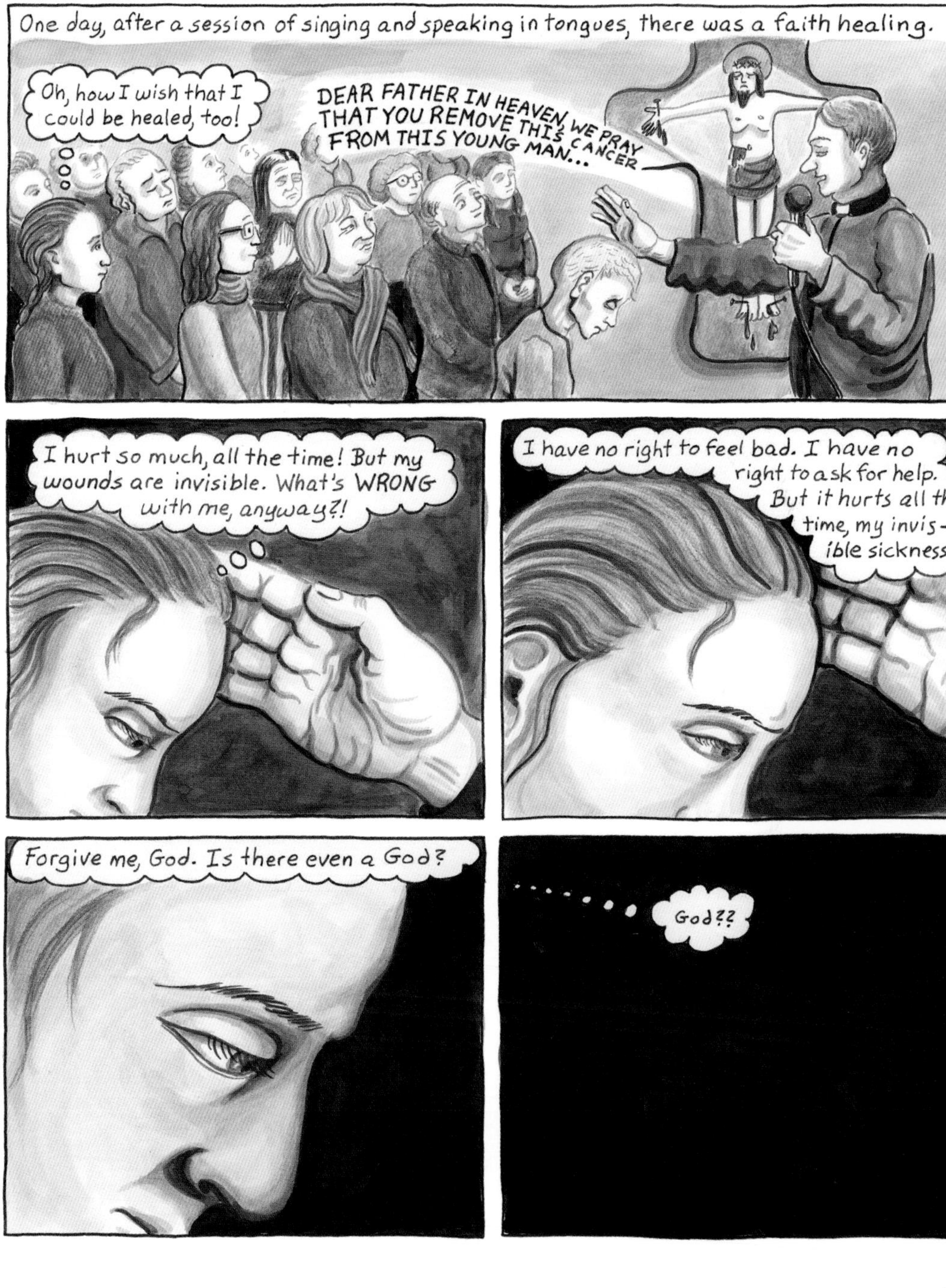
One day, after a session of singing and speaking in tongues, there was a faith healing.
Oh, how I wish that I could be healed, too!
DEAR FATHER IN HEAVEN, WE PRAY THAT YOU REMOVE THIS CANCER FROM THIS YOUNG MAN...
I hurt so much, all the time! But my wounds are invisible. What's WRONG with me, anyway?!
I have no right to feel bad. I have no right to ask for help. But it hurts all the time, my invis-ible sickness.
Forgive me, God. Is there even a God?
God??

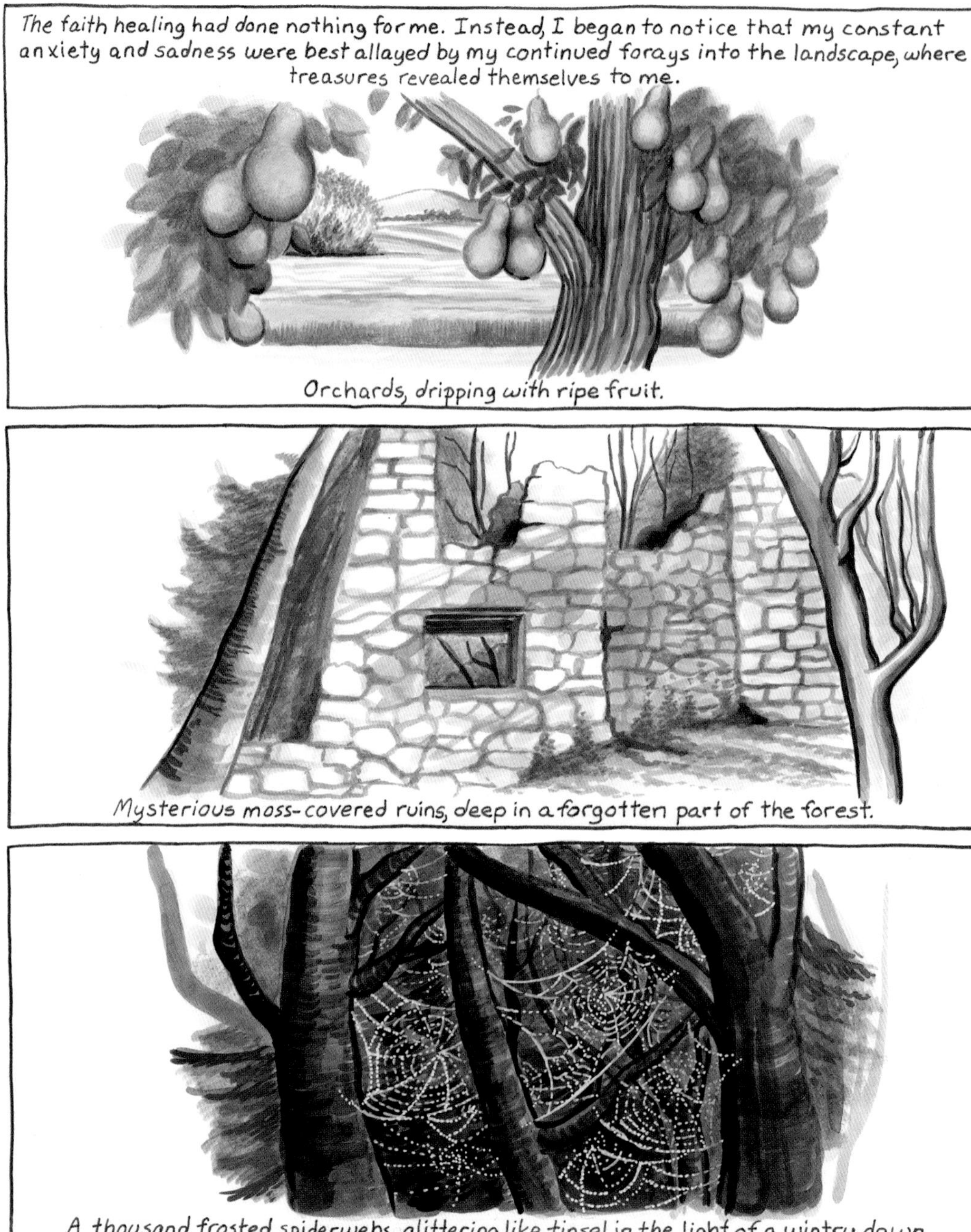
The faith healing had done nothing for me. Instead, I began to notice that my constant anxiety and sadness were best allayed by my continued forays into the landscape, where treasures revealed themselves to me.
Orchards, dripping with ripe fruit.
Mysterious moss-covered ruins, deep in a forgotten part of the forest.
A thousand frosted spiderwebs, glittering like tinsel in the light of a wintry dawn.

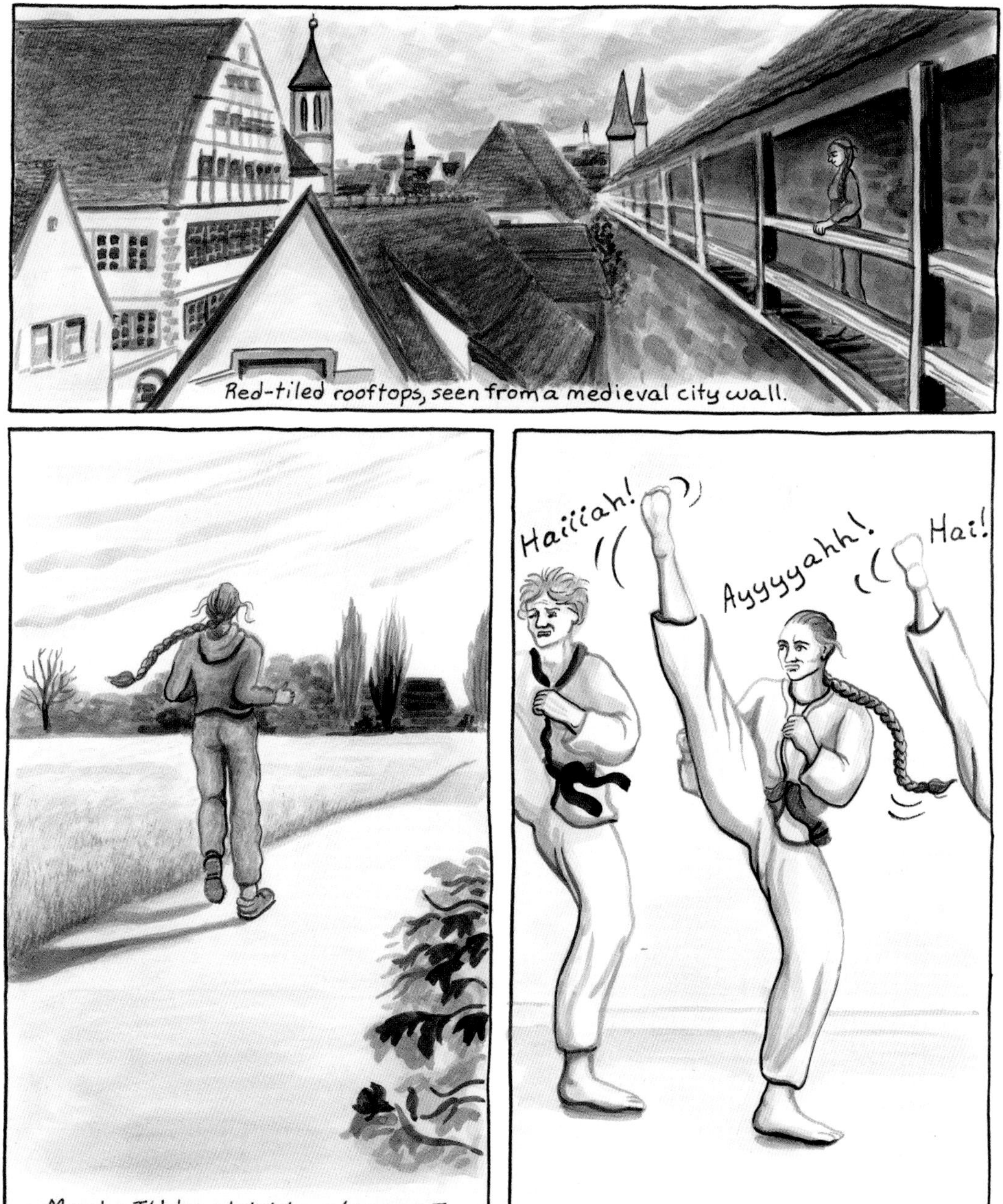
Red-tiled rooftops, seen from a medieval city wall.
Maybe I'd be alright, as long as I just kept moving...
Haiiiah!
Ayyyyahh!
Hai!
moving...

moving...
Ohhh nooo! There goes my black belt test next month...

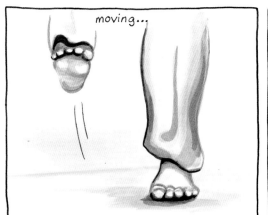

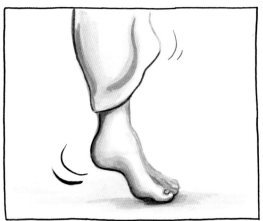

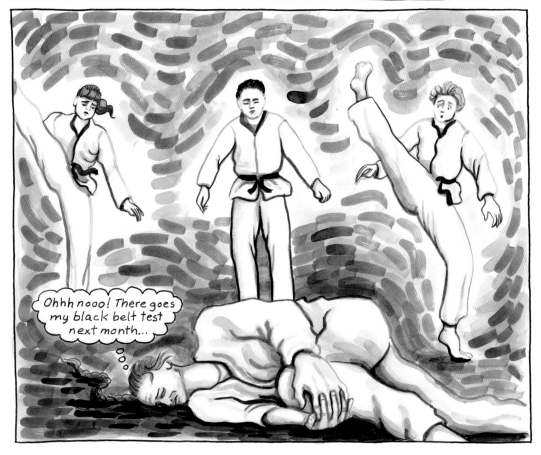

I flew back to Illinois to have knee surgery. During the next three months in a plaster cast up to my hip and nine months on crutches, I couldn't move the way I had, but I could still move pens and brushes.

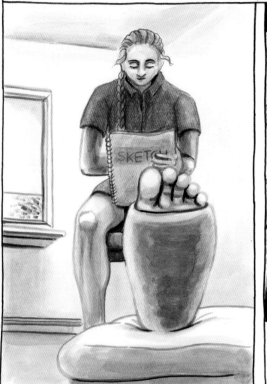

A self-portrait from that time shows me using my crutches to navigate rapids in a canoe laden with essentials: art supplies, food, and cats as companions.

As soon as my cast was off, I was back on trails.

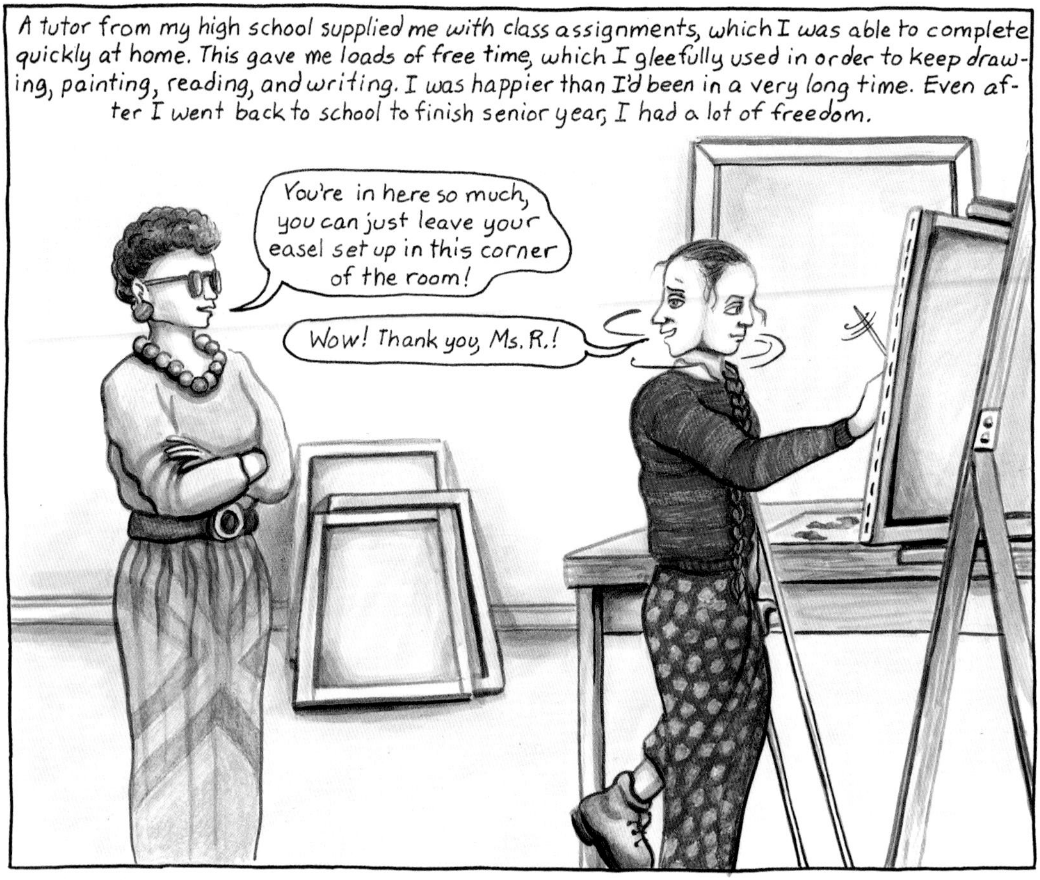
A tutor from my high school supplied me with class assignments, which I was able to complete quickly at home. This gave me loads of free time, which I gleefully used in order to keep drawing, painting, reading, and writing. I was happier than I'd been in a very long time. Even after I went back to school to finish senior year, I had a lot of freedom.
You're in here so much, you can just leave your easel set up in this corner of the room!
Wow! Thank you, Ms. R.!

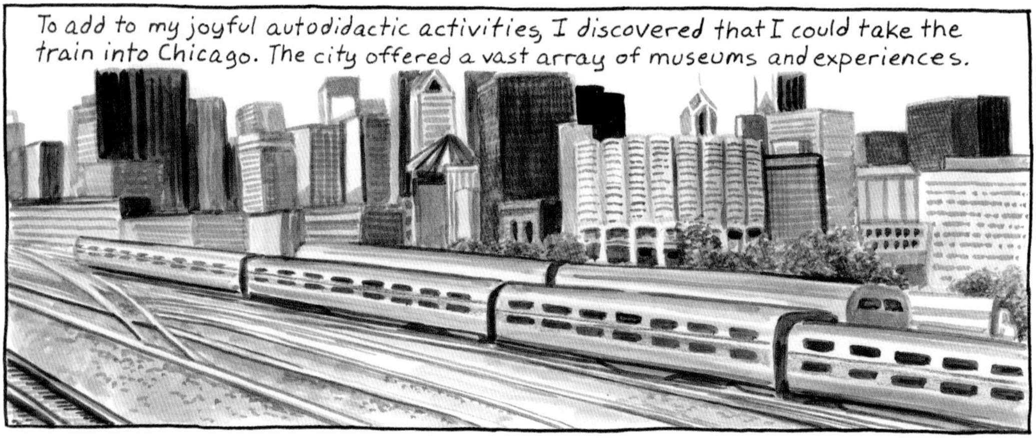
To add to my joyful autodidactic activities, I discovered that I could take the train into Chicago. The city offered a vast array of museums and experiences.

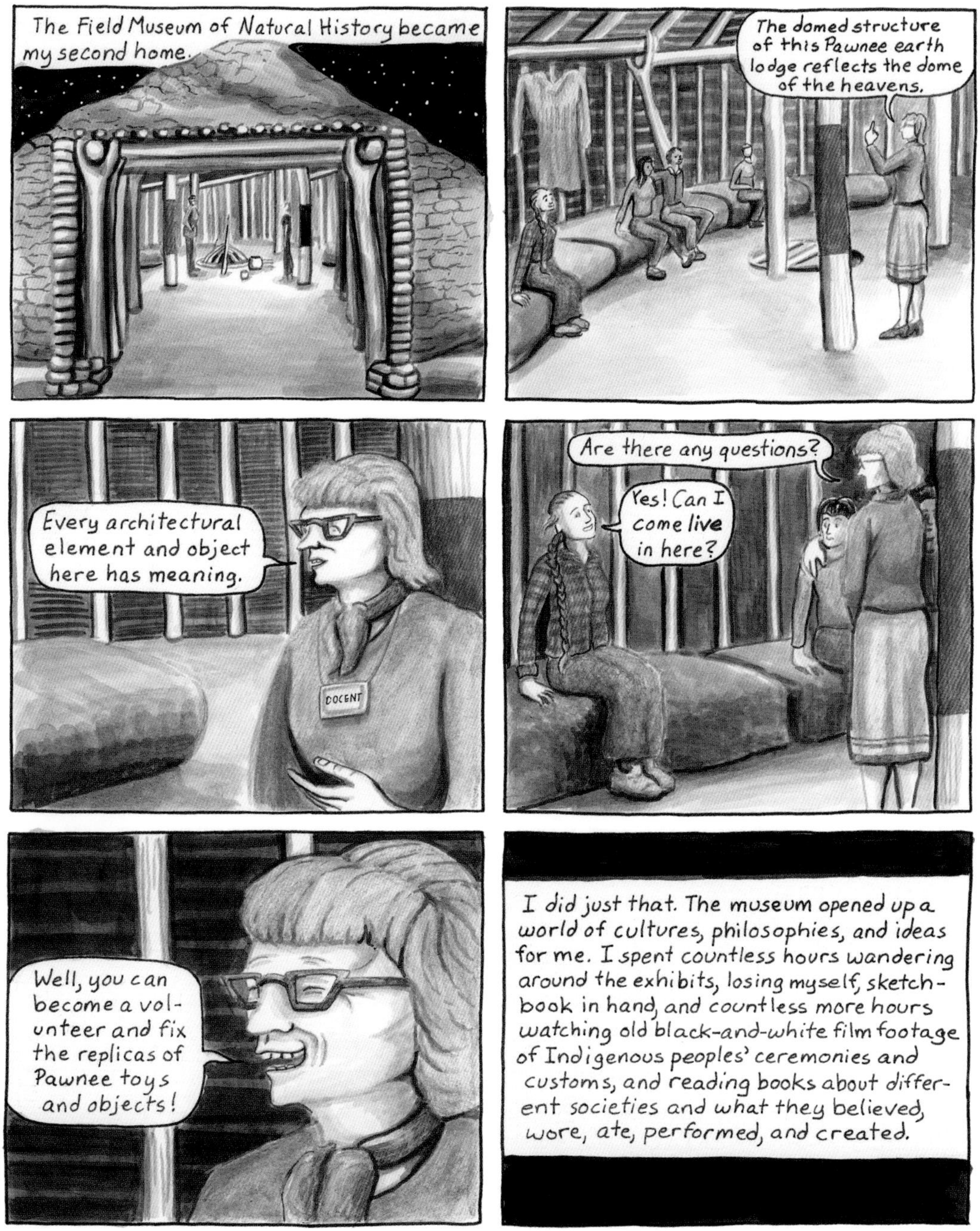

The Field Museum of Natural History became my second home.
The domed structure of this Pawnee earth lodge reflects the dome of the heavens.
Every architectural element and object here has meaning.
DOCENT
Are there any questions?
Yes! Can I come live in here?
Well, you can become a volunteer and fix the replicas of Pawnee toys and objects!
I did just that. The museum opened up a world of cultures, philosophies, and ideas for me. I spent countless hours wandering around the exhibits, losing myself, sketchbook in hand, and countless more hours watching old black-and-white film footage of Indigenous peoples' ceremonies and customs, and reading books about different societies and what they believed, wore, ate, performed, and created.

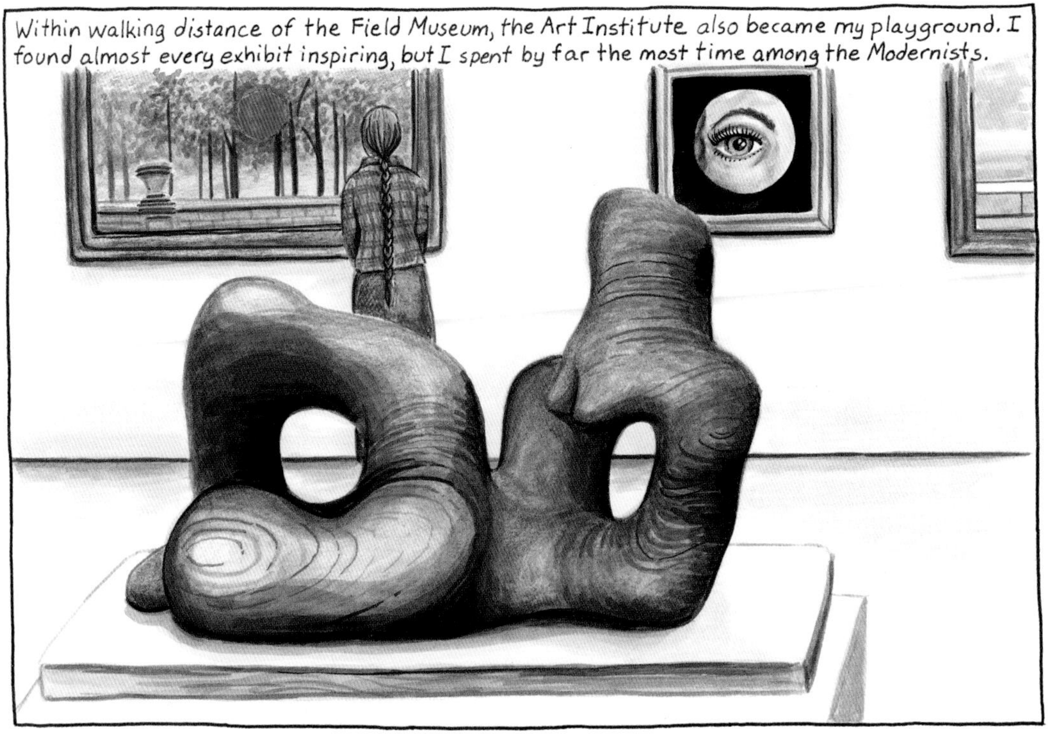
Within walking distance of the Field Museum, the Art Institute also became my playground. I found almost every exhibit inspiring, but I spent by far the most time among the Modernists.

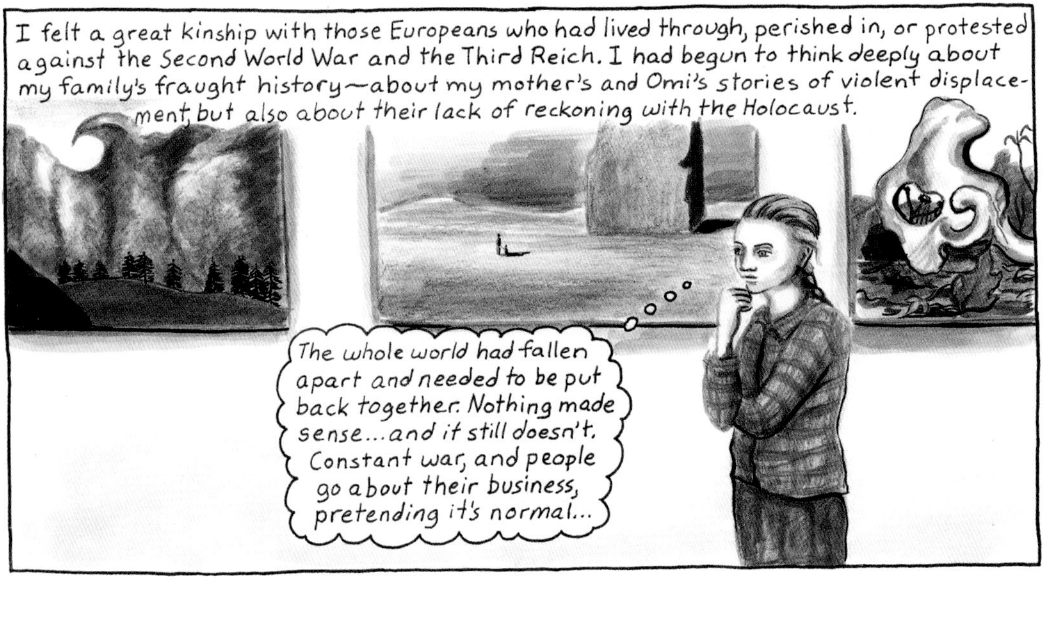
I felt a great kinship with those Europeans who had lived through, perished in, or protested against the Second World War and the Third Reich. I had begun to think deeply about my family's fraught history—about my mother's and Omi's stories of violent displacement, but also about their lack of reckoning with the Holocaust.
The whole world had fallen apart and needed to be put back together. Nothing made sense...and it still doesn't. Constant war, and people go about their business, pretending it's normal...

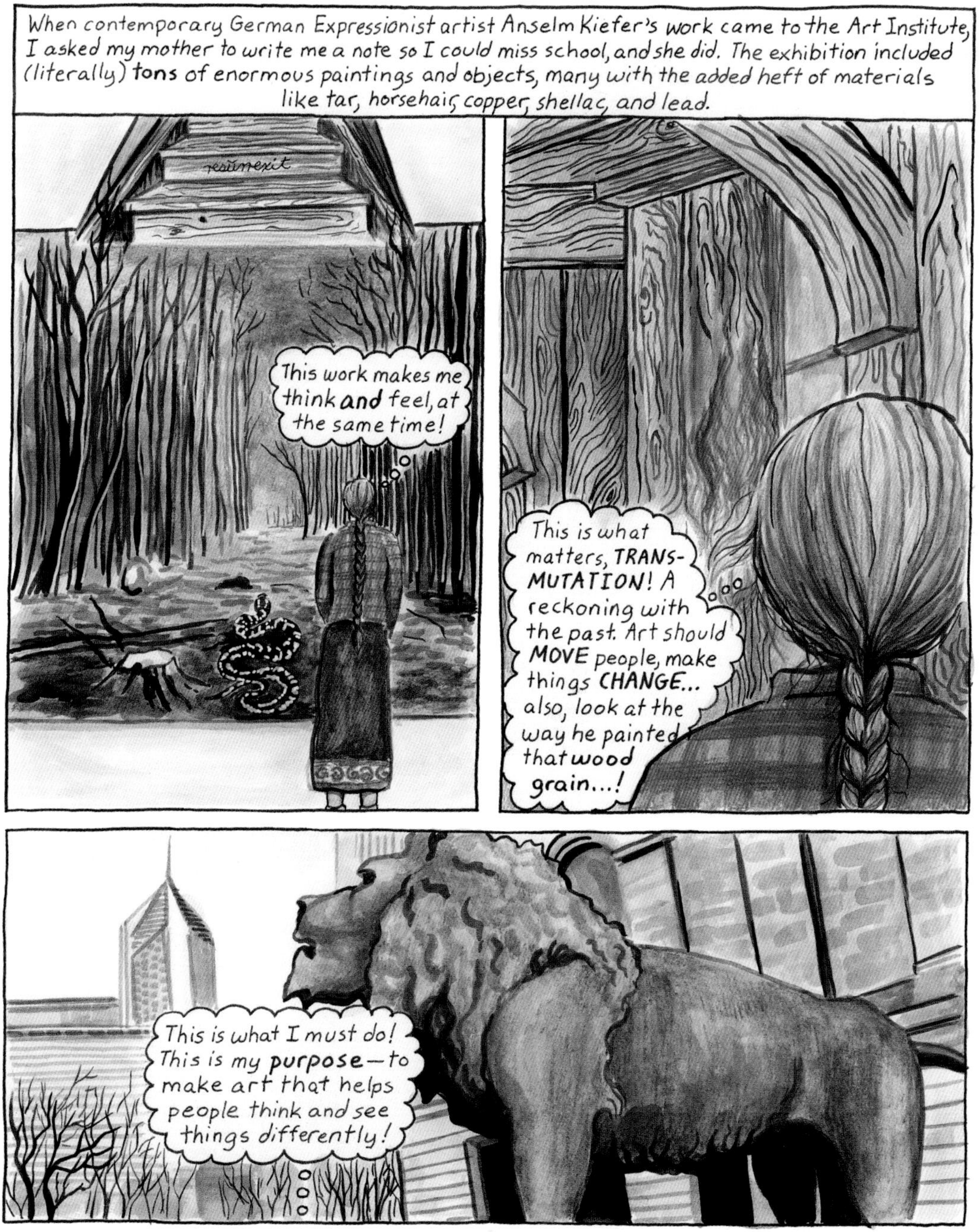
When contemporary German Expressionist artist Anselm Kiefer's work came to the Art Institute, I asked my mother to write me a note so I could miss school, and she did. The exhibition included (literally) **tons** of enormous paintings and objects, many with the added heft of materials like tar, horsehair, copper, shellac, and lead.
This work makes me think **and** feel, at the same time!
This is what matters, **TRANSMUTATION**! A reckoning with the past. Art should **MOVE** people, make things **CHANGE**... also, look at the way he painted that **wood grain**...!
This is what I must do! This is my **purpose**—to make art that helps people think and see things differently!

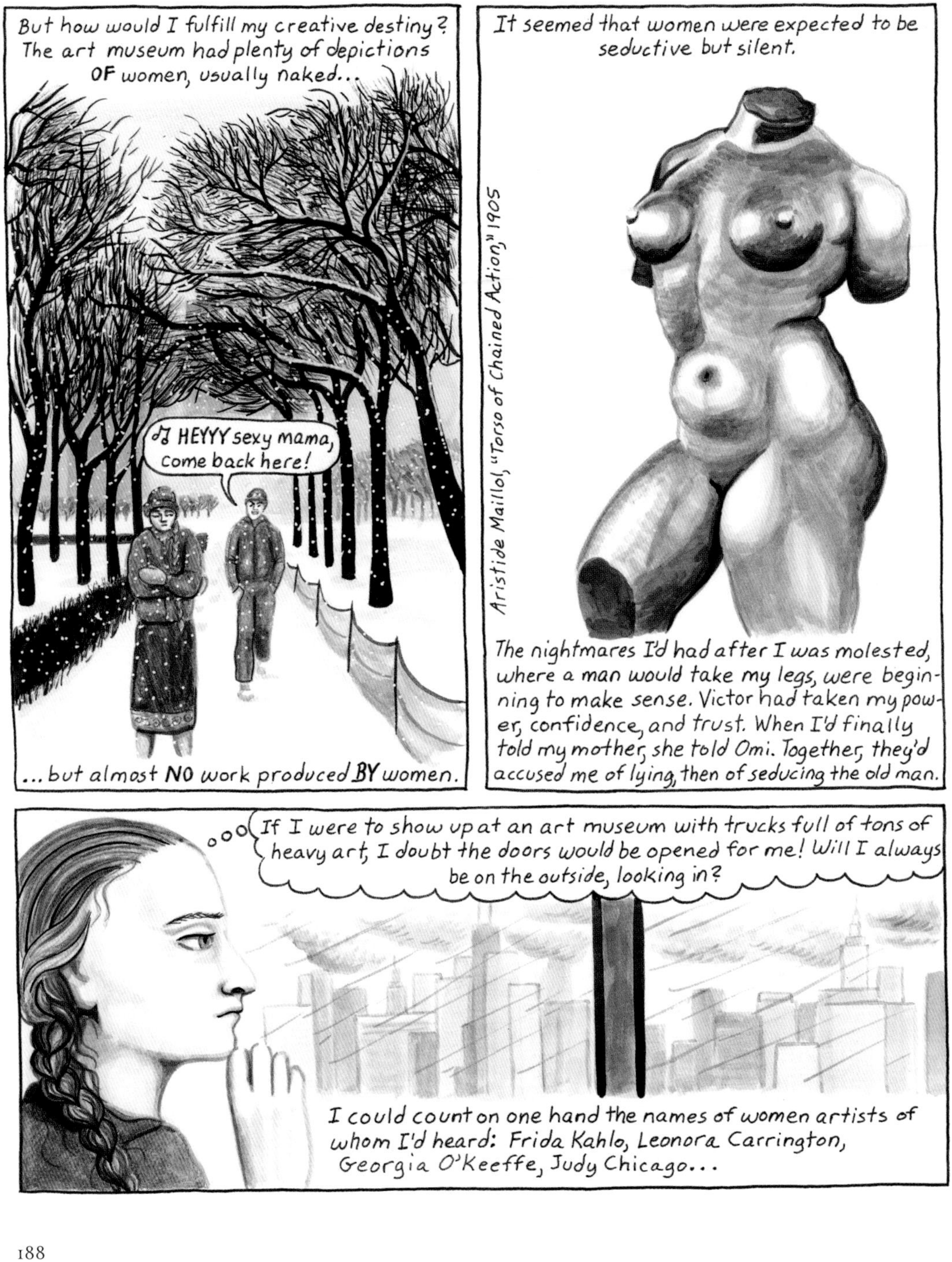

But how would I fulfill my creative destiny? The art museum had plenty of depictions OF women, usually naked...
HEYYY sexy mama, come back here!
...but almost NO work produced BY women.
It seemed that women were expected to be seductive but silent.
Aristide Maillol, "Torso of Chained Action," 1905
The nightmares I'd had after I was molested, where a man would take my legs, were beginning to make sense. Victor had taken my power, confidence, and trust. When I'd finally told my mother, she told Omi. Together, they'd accused me of lying, then of seducing the old man.
If I were to show up at an art museum with trucks full of tons of heavy art, I doubt the doors would be opened for me! Will I always be on the outside, looking in?
I could count on one hand the names of women artists of whom I'd heard: Frida Kahlo, Leonora Carrington, Georgia O'Keeffe, Judy Chicago...

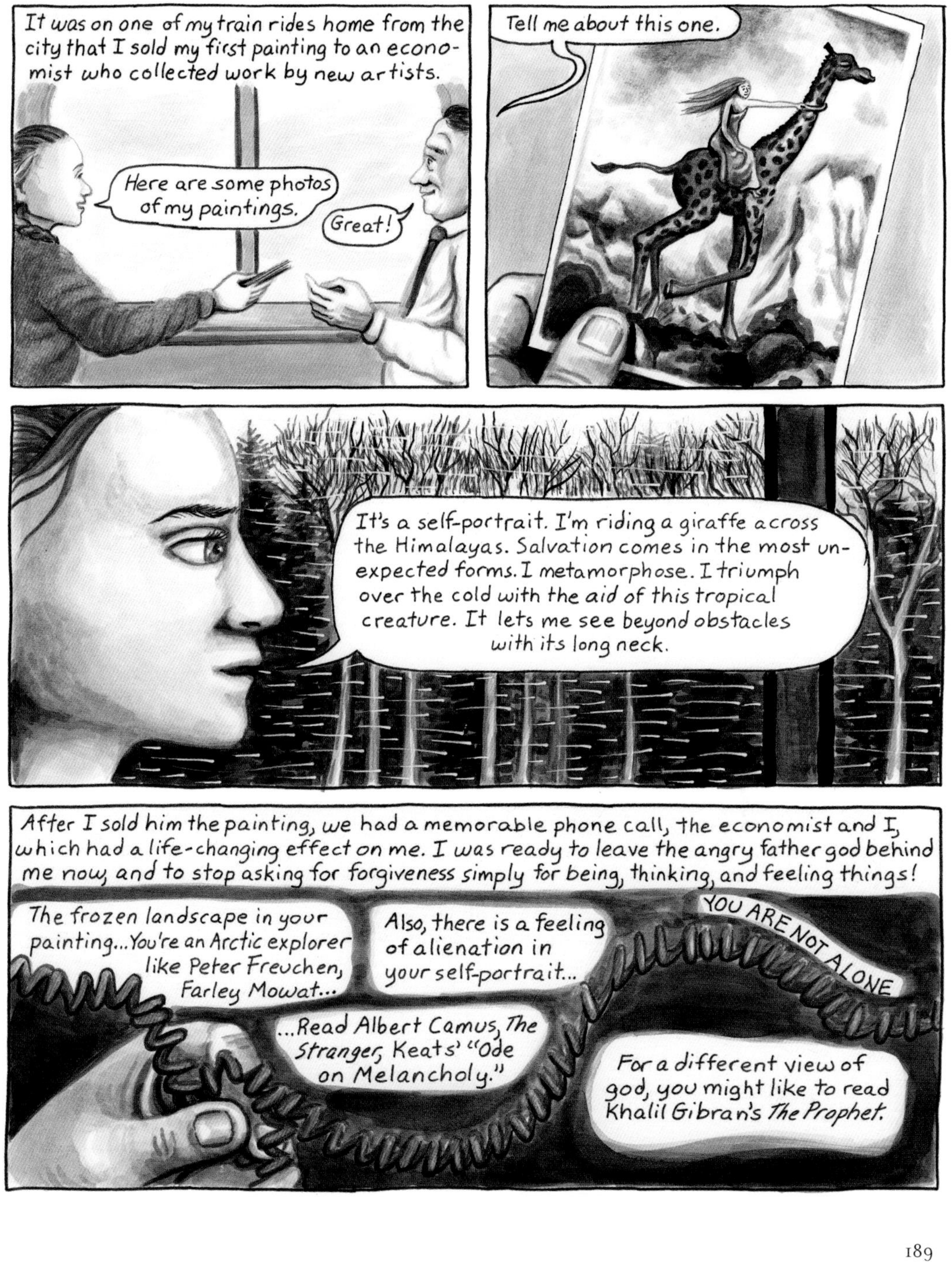
It was on one of my train rides home from the city that I sold my first painting to an economist who collected work by new artists.
Here are some photos of my paintings.
Great!
Tell me about this one.
It's a self-portrait. I'm riding a giraffe across the Himalayas. Salvation comes in the most unexpected forms. I metamorphose. I triumph over the cold with the aid of this tropical creature. It lets me see beyond obstacles with its long neck.
After I sold him the painting, we had a memorable phone call, the economist and I, which had a life-changing effect on me. I was ready to leave the angry father god behind me now, and to stop asking for forgiveness simply for being, thinking, and feeling things!
The frozen landscape in your painting... You're an Arctic explorer like Peter Freuchen, Farley Mowat...
Also, there is a feeling of alienation in your self-portrait...
YOU ARE NOT ALONE
...Read Albert Camus, *The Stranger*, Keats' "Ode on Melancholy."
For a different view of god, you might like to read Khalil Gibran's *The Prophet*.

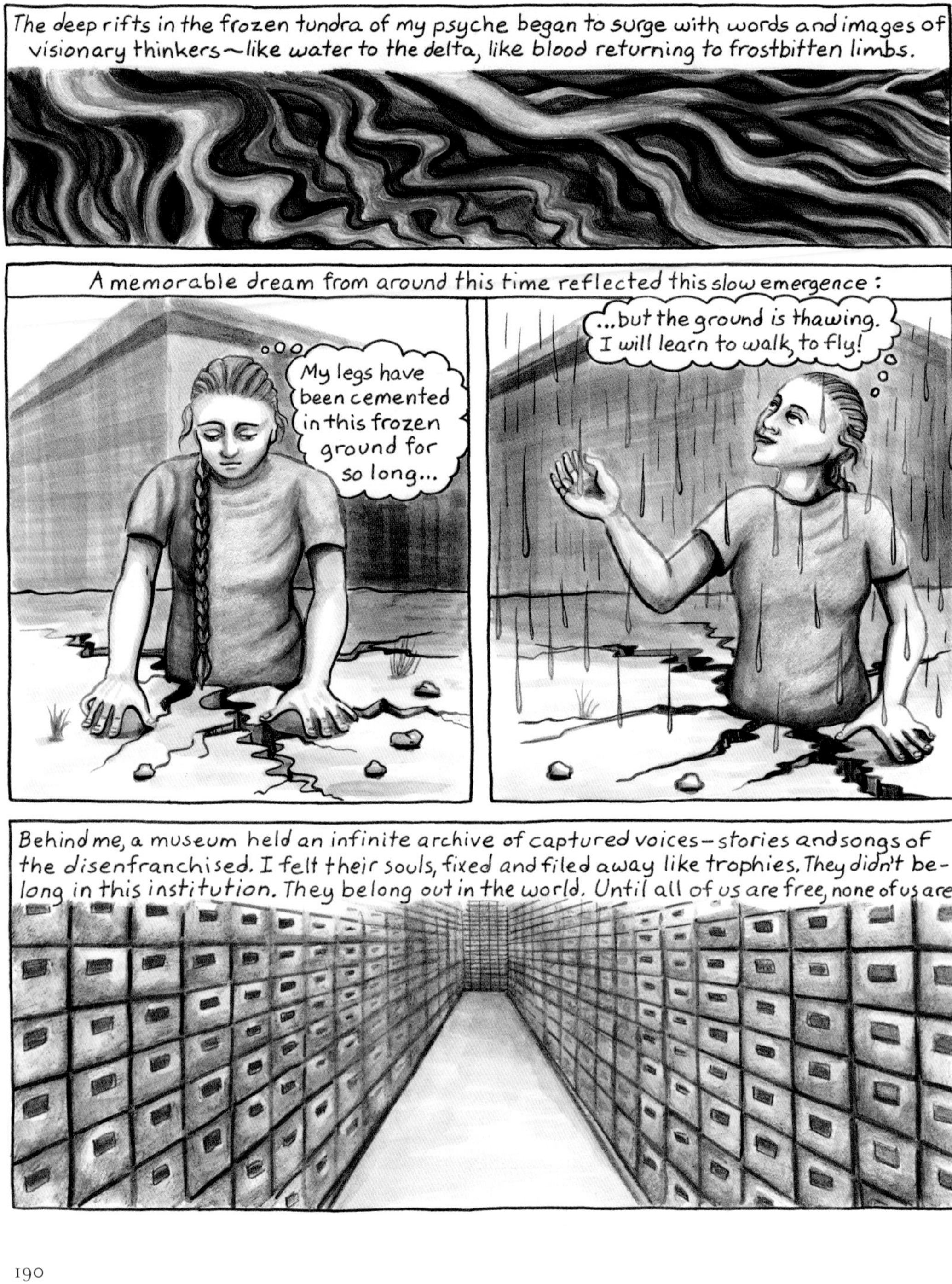

The deep rifts in the frozen tundra of my psyche began to surge with words and images of visionary thinkers—like water to the delta, like blood returning to frostbitten limbs.
A memorable dream from around this time reflected this slow emergence:
My legs have been cemented in this frozen ground for so long...
...but the ground is thawing. I will learn to walk, to fly!
Behind me, a museum held an infinite archive of captured voices—stories and songs of the disenfranchised. I felt their souls, fixed and filed away like trophies. They didn't belong in this institution. They belong out in the world. Until all of us are free, none of us are.

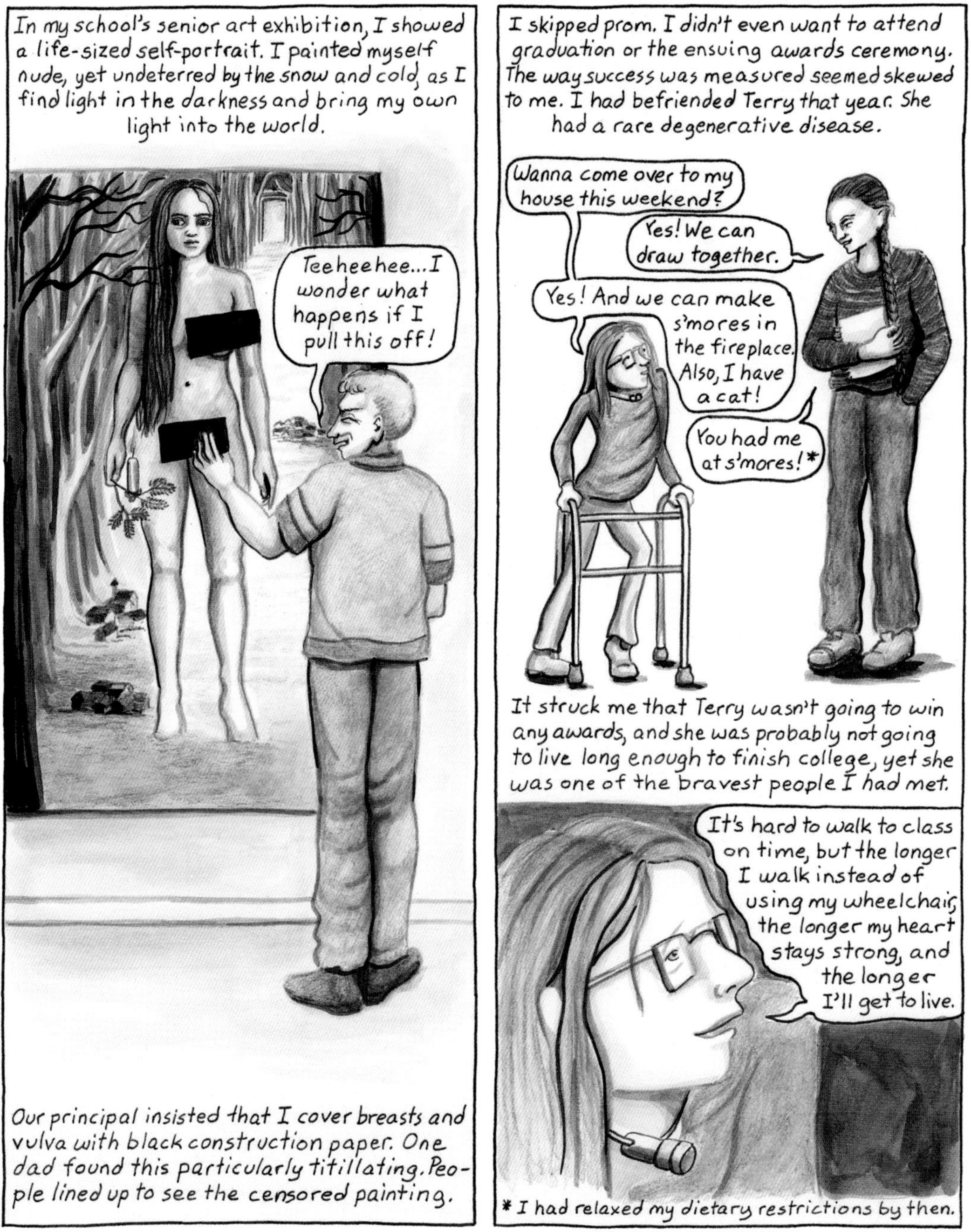
In my school's senior art exhibition, I showed a life-sized self-portrait. I painted myself nude, yet undeterred by the snow and cold, as I find light in the darkness and bring my own light into the world.
Teeheehee... I wonder what happens if I pull this off!
Our principal insisted that I cover breasts and vulva with black construction paper. One dad found this particularly titillating. People lined up to see the censored painting.
I skipped prom. I didn't even want to attend graduation or the ensuing awards ceremony. The way success was measured seemed skewed to me. I had befriended Terry that year. She had a rare degenerative disease.
Wanna come over to my house this weekend?
Yes! We can draw together.
Yes! And we can make s'mores in the fireplace. Also, I have a cat!
You had me at s'mores!*
It struck me that Terry wasn't going to win any awards, and she was probably not going to live long enough to finish college, yet she was one of the bravest people I had met.
It's hard to walk to class on time, but the longer I walk instead of using my wheelchair, the longer my heart stays strong, and the longer I'll get to live.
* I had relaxed my dietary restrictions by then.

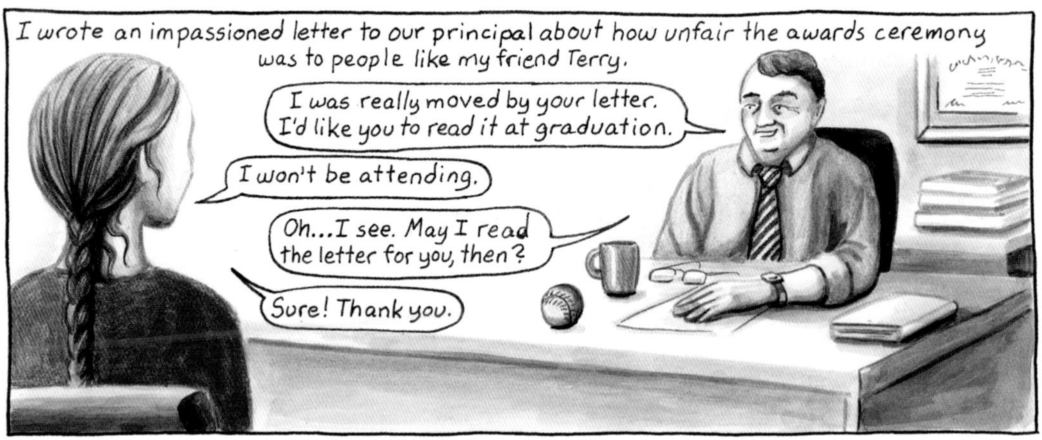
I wrote an impassioned letter to our principal about how unfair the awards ceremony was to people like my friend Terry.
I was really moved by your letter. I'd like you to read it at graduation.
I won't be attending.
Oh...I see. May I read the letter for you, then?
Sure! Thank you.

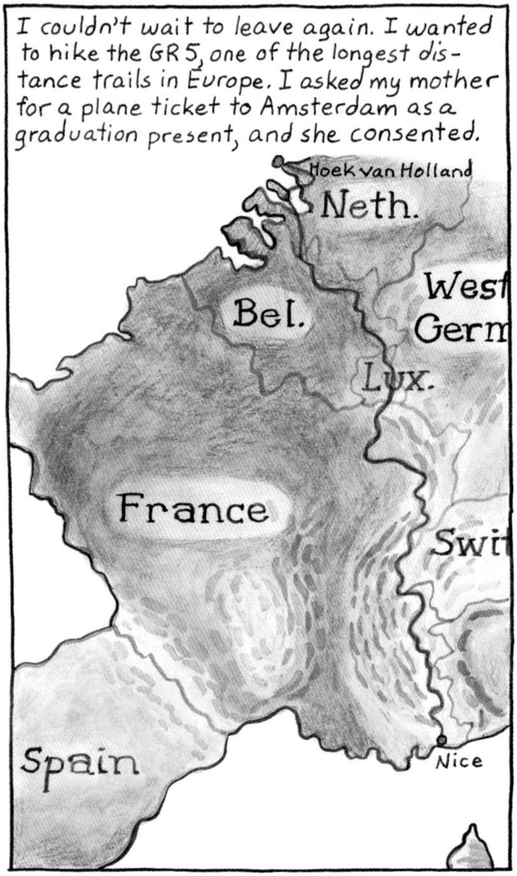
I couldn't wait to leave again. I wanted to hike the GR 5, one of the longest distance trails in Europe. I asked my mother for a plane ticket to Amsterdam as a graduation present, and she consented.
Hoek van Holland
Neth.
West Germ
Bel.
Lux.
France
Swit
Spain
Nice

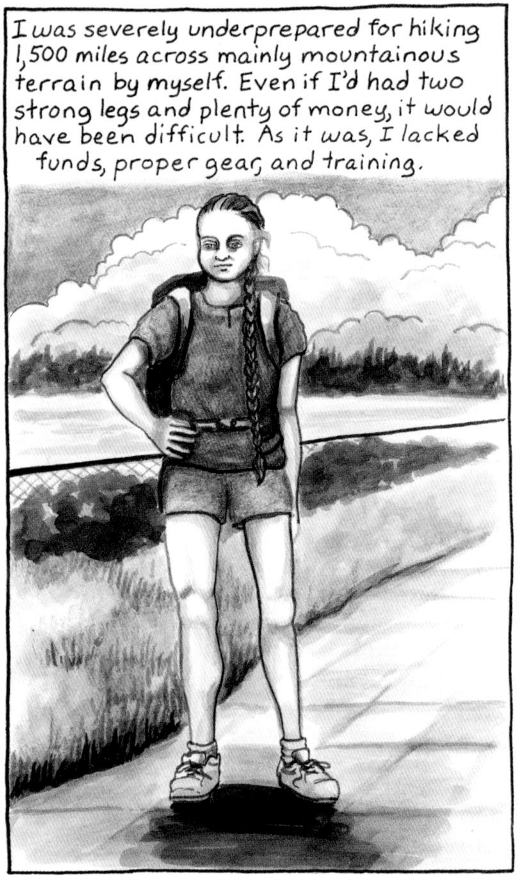
I was severely underprepared for hiking 1,500 miles across mainly mountainous terrain by myself. Even if I'd had two strong legs and plenty of money, it would have been difficult. As it was, I lacked funds, proper gear, and training.

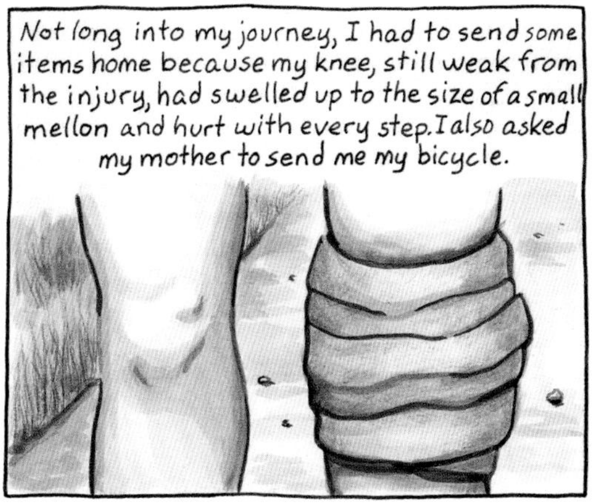
Not long into my journey, I had to send some items home because my knee, still weak from the injury, had swelled up to the size of a small mellon and hurt with every step. I also asked my mother to send me my bicycle.

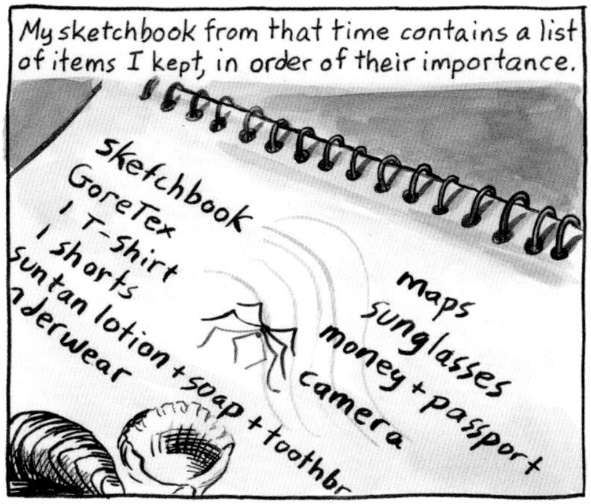
My sketchbook from that time contains a list of items I kept, in order of their importance.
Sketchbook
GoreTex
1 T-Shirt
1 shorts
suntan lotion + soap + toothbr
nderwear
maps
sunglasses
money + passport
camera

My belongings now fit into a daypack. I abandoned roads whenever possible and slept in fields, in orchards, and on beaches. I loved walking as close to the North Sea as possible.

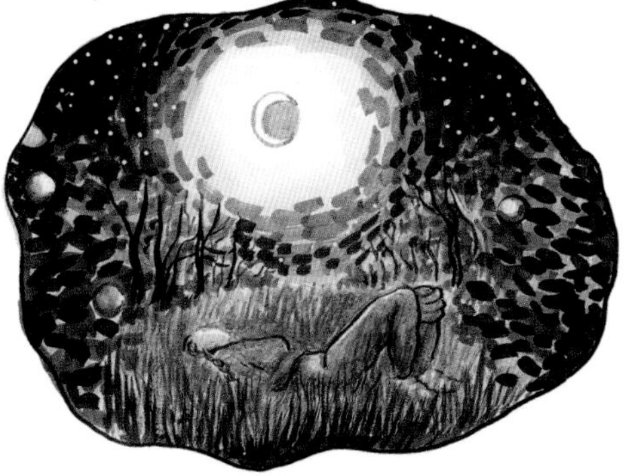

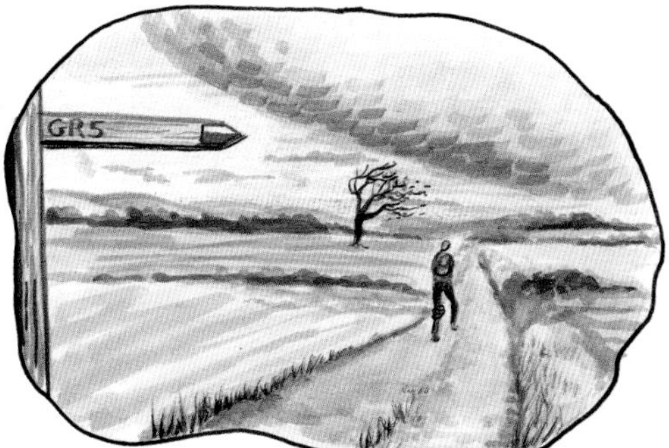
GR5

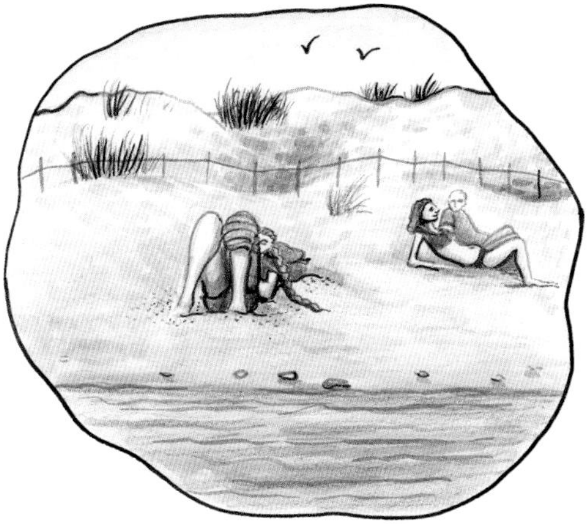

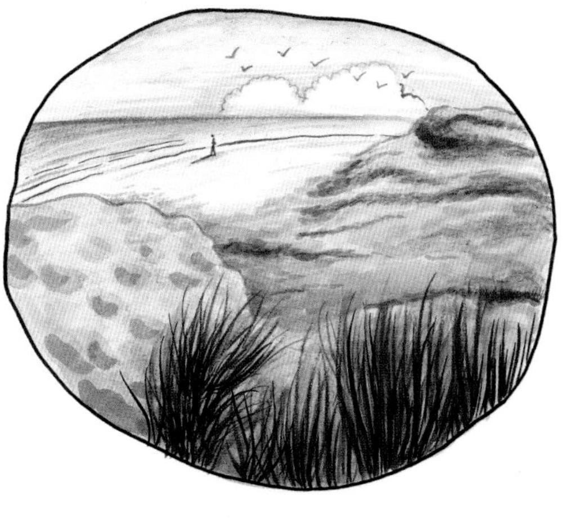

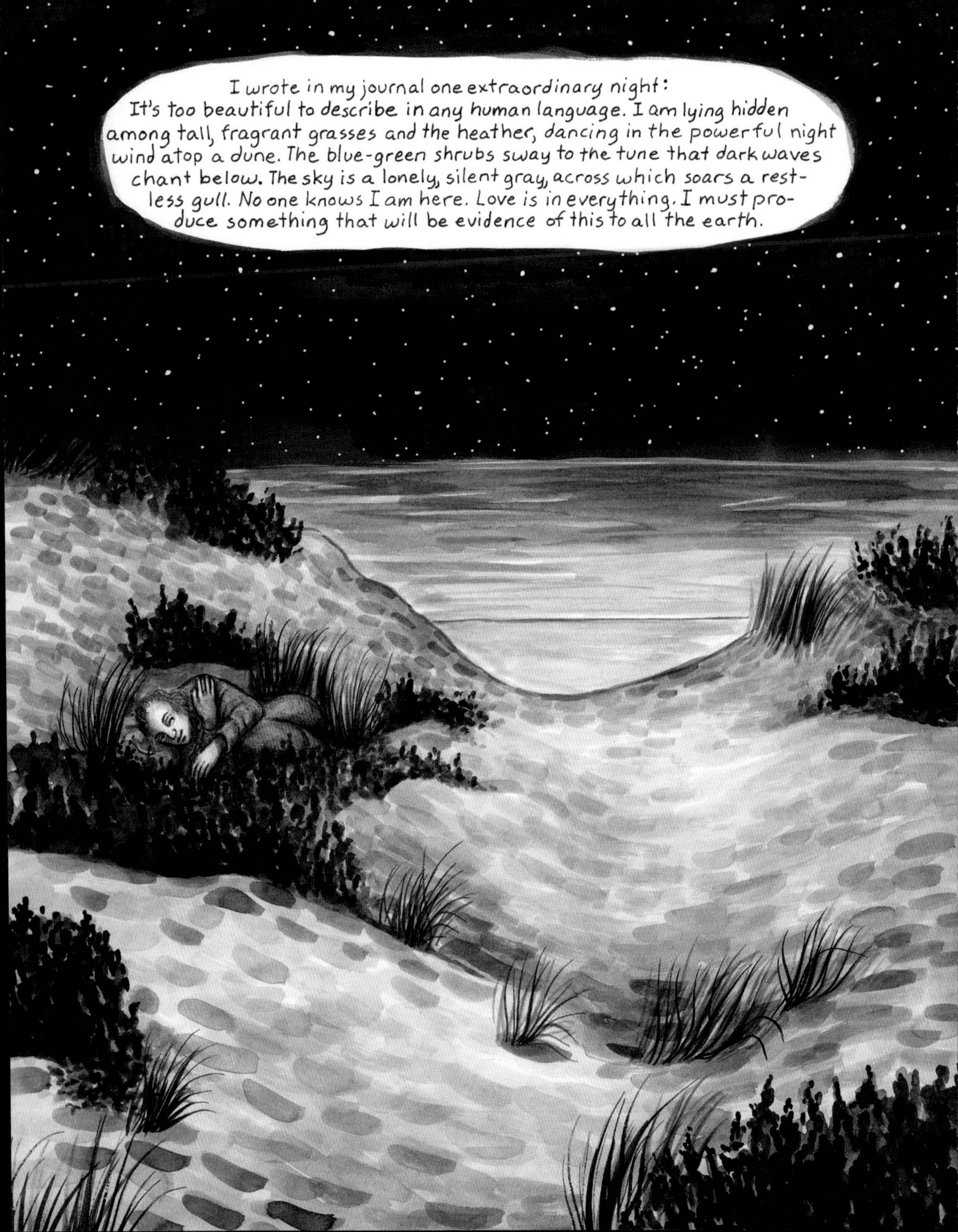
I wrote in my journal one extraordinary night:
It's too beautiful to describe in any human language. I am lying hidden among tall, fragrant grasses and the heather, dancing in the powerful night wind atop a dune. The blue-green shrubs sway to the tune that dark waves chant below. The sky is a lonely, silent gray, across which soars a restless gull. No one knows I am here. Love is in everything. I must produce something that will be evidence of this to all the earth.

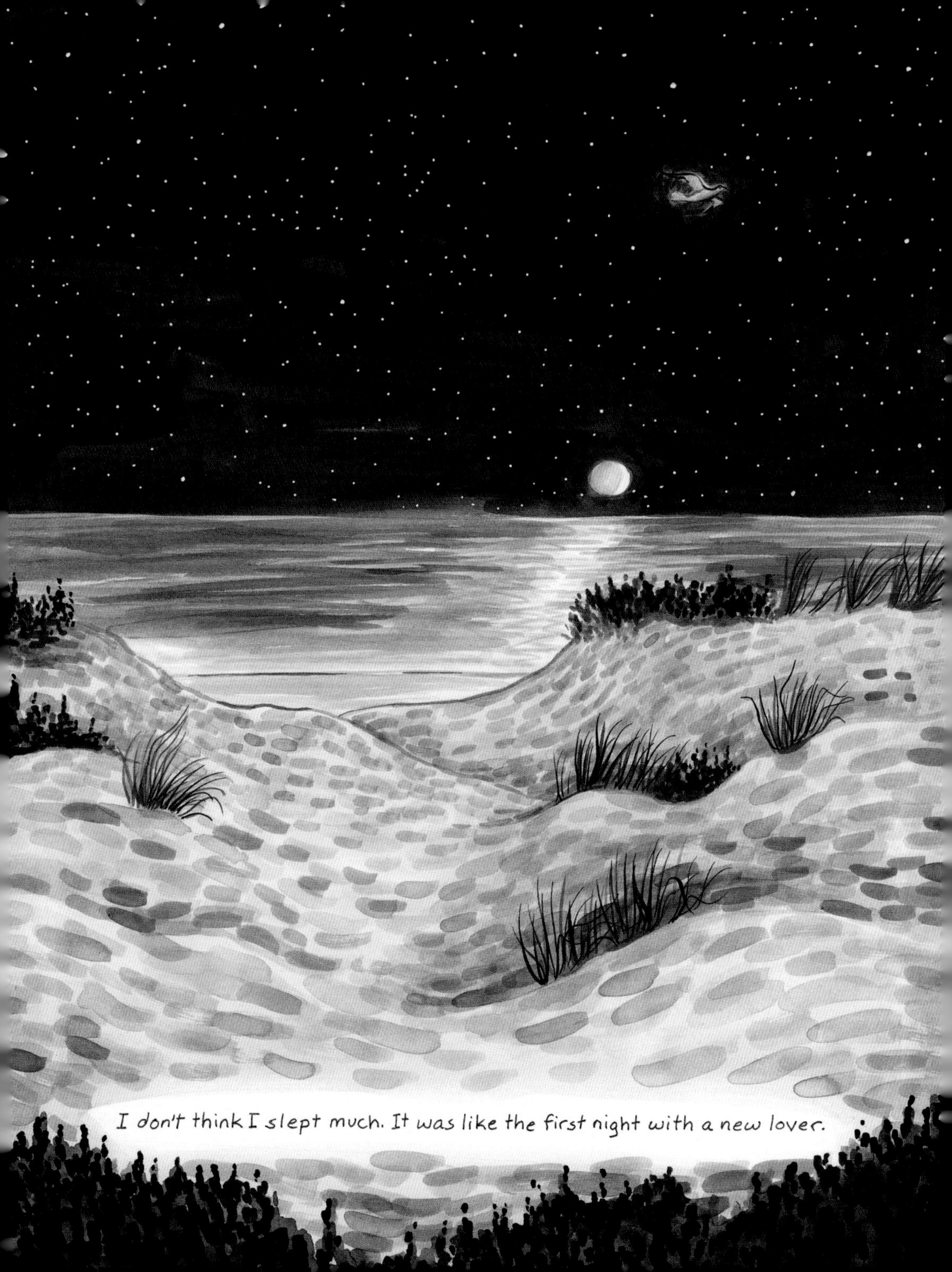
I don't think I slept much. It was like the first night with a new lover.

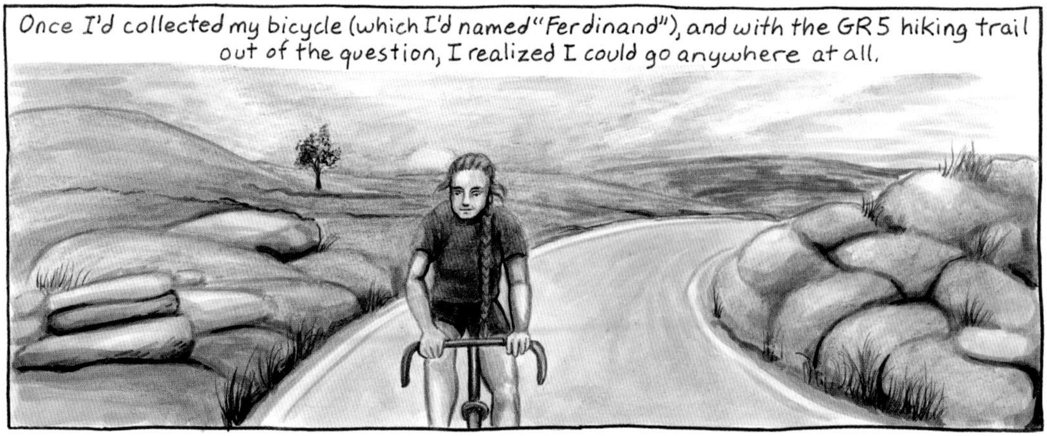
Once I'd collected my bicycle (which I'd named "Ferdinand"), and with the GR5 hiking trail out of the question, I realized I could go anywhere at all.

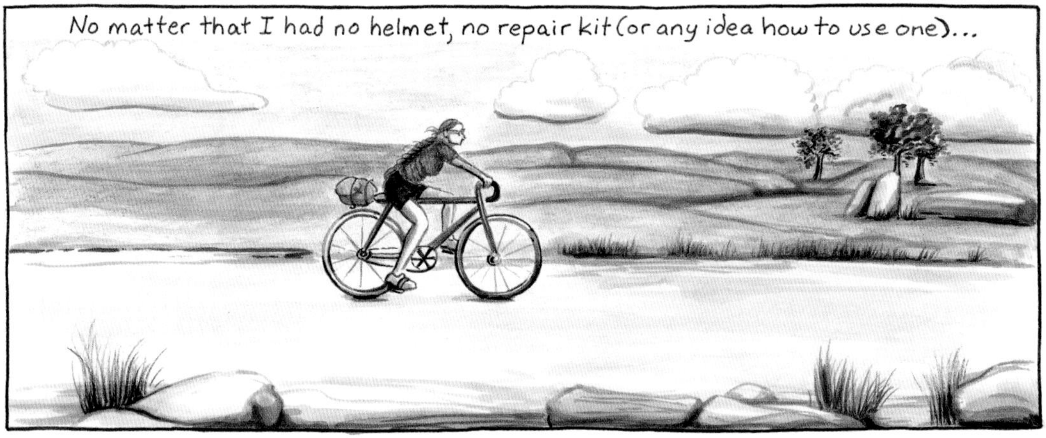
No matter that I had no helmet, no repair kit (or any idea how to use one)...

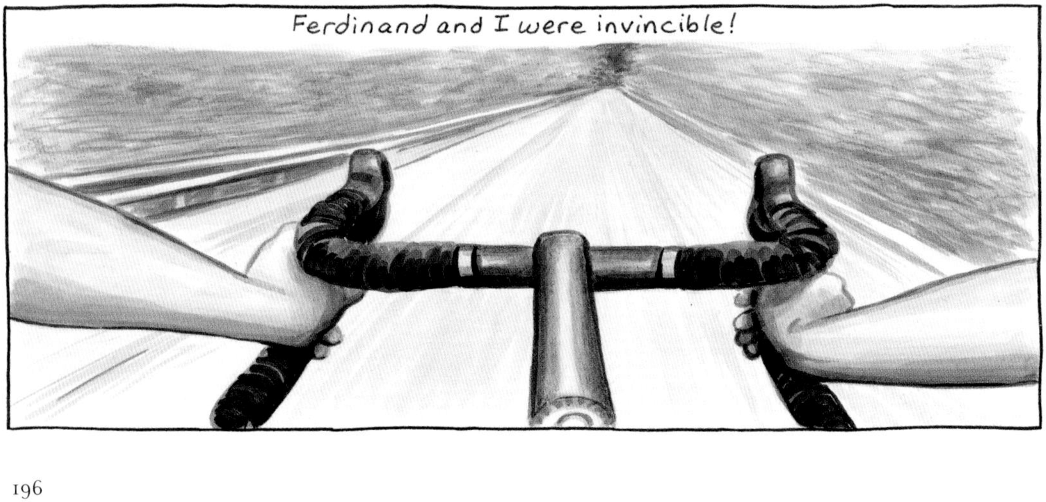
Ferdinand and I were invincible!

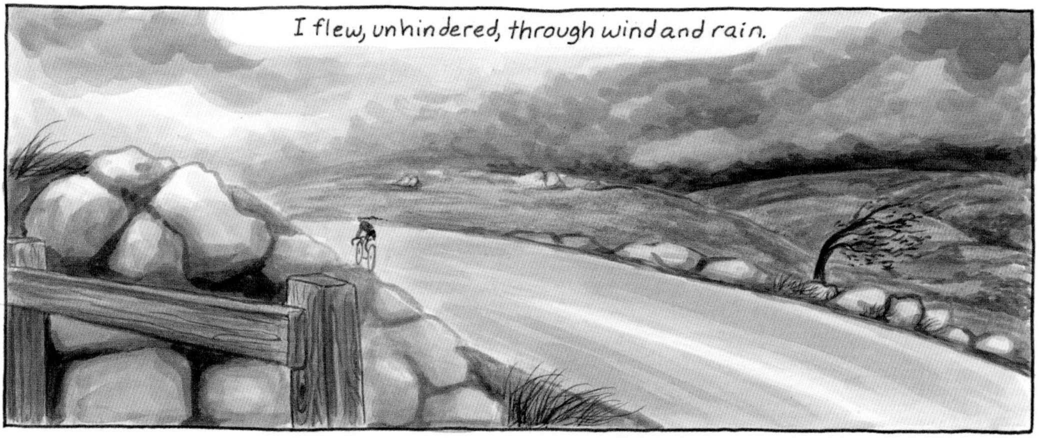
I flew, unhindered, through wind and rain.

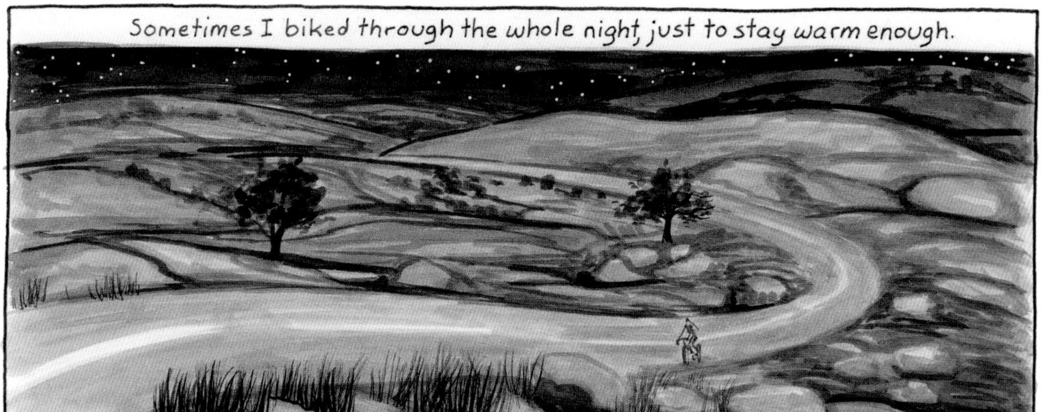
Sometimes I biked through the whole night, just to stay warm enough.

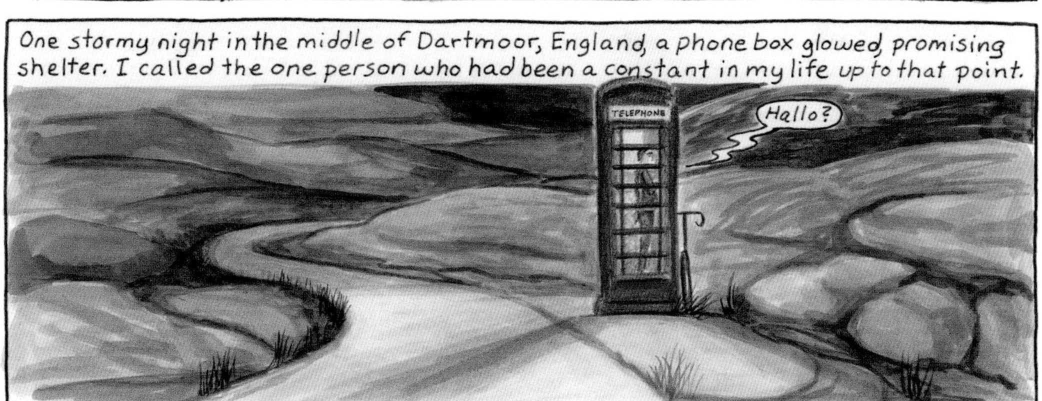
One stormy night in the middle of Dartmoor, England, a phone box glowed, promising shelter. I called the one person who had been a constant in my life up to that point.
TELEPHONE
Hallo?
I felt pleased when my mother's voice sounded glad to hear from me.

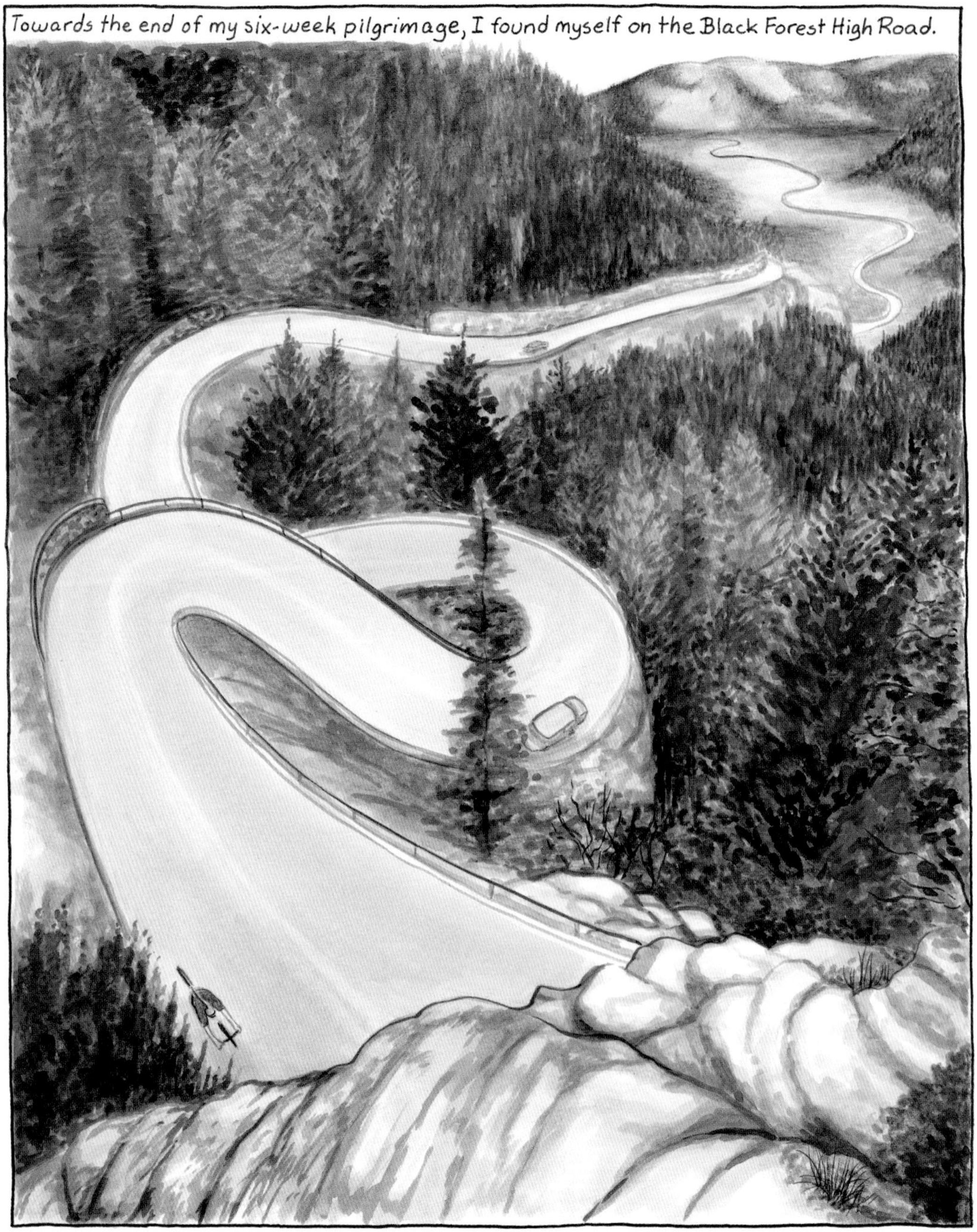
Towards the end of my six-week pilgrimage, I found myself on the Black Forest High Road.

I was headed towards Lahr, the city of my birth and the home of my father.

Maybe I'd always known I'd end up there. I, the snail with the cracked shell...

...seeking my home garden.

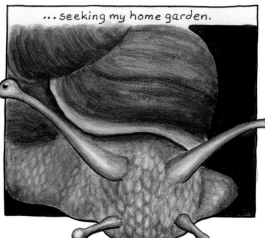

199

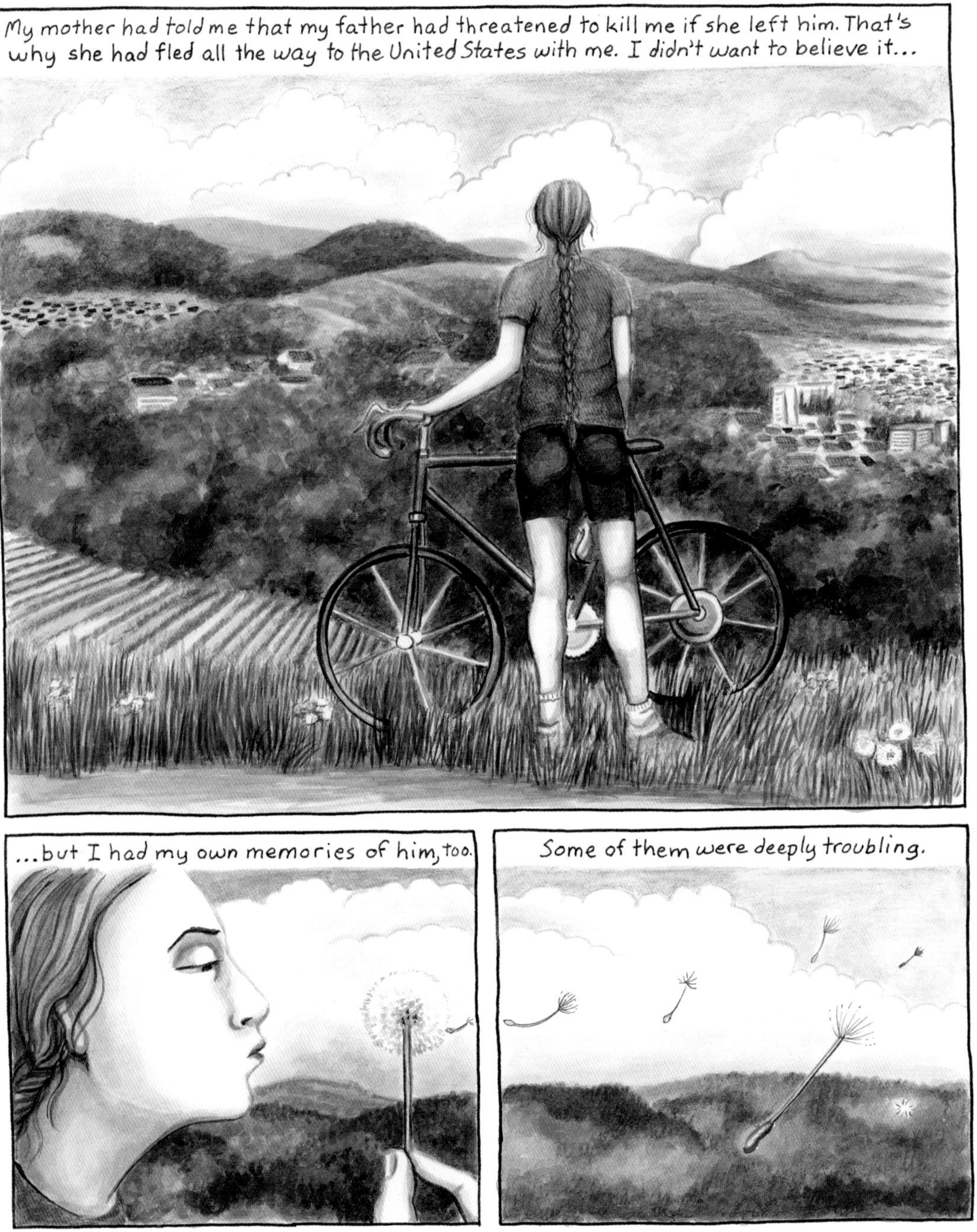
My mother had told me that my father had threatened to kill me if she left him. That's why she had fled all the way to the United States with me. I didn't want to believe it...
...but I had my own memories of him, too.
Some of them were deeply troubling.

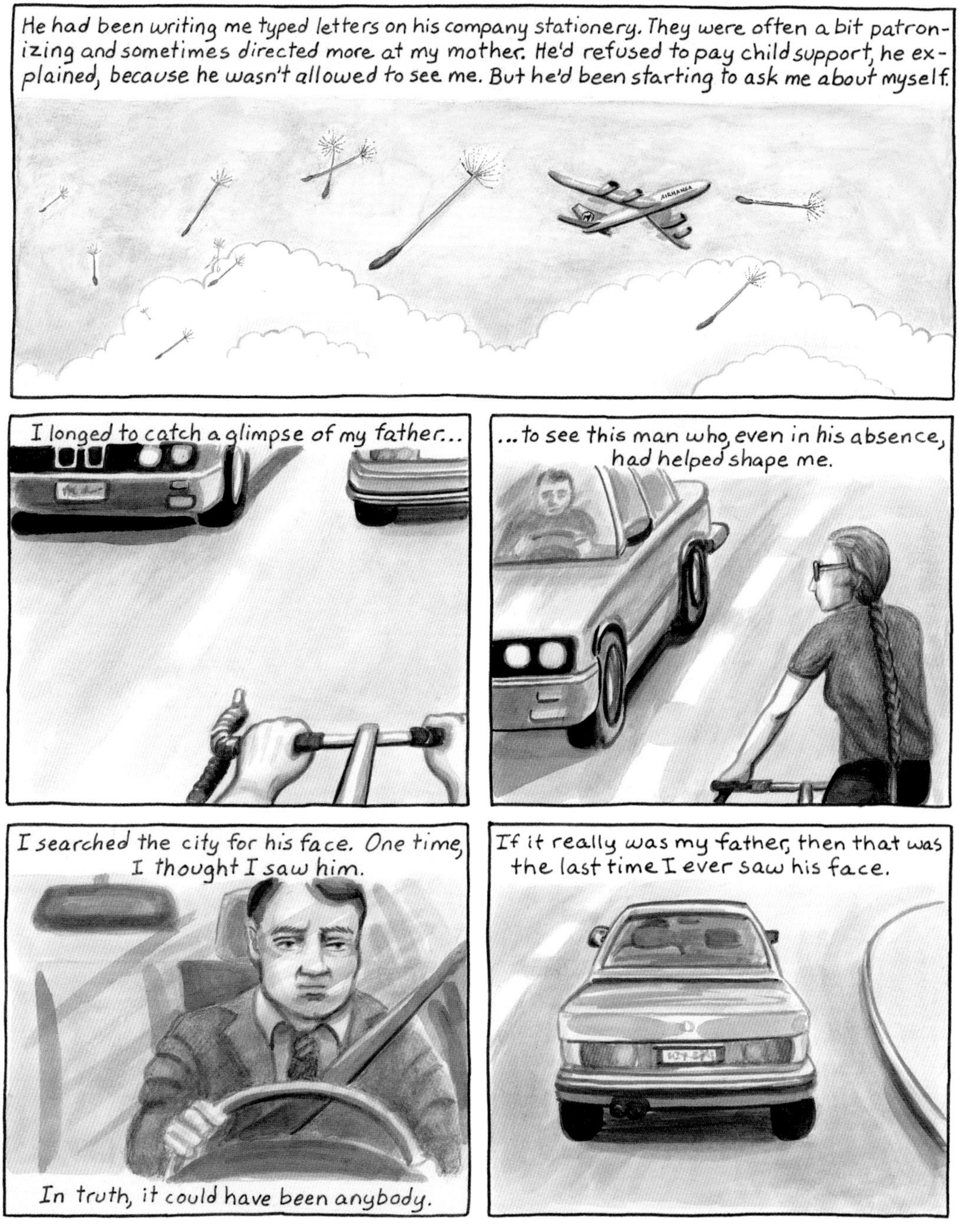
He had been writing me typed letters on his company stationery. They were often a bit patronizing and sometimes directed more at my mother. He'd refused to pay child support, he explained, because he wasn't allowed to see me. But he'd been starting to ask me about myself.
I longed to catch a glimpse of my father...
...to see this man who, even in his absence, had helped shape me.
I searched the city for his face. One time, I thought I saw him.
In truth, it could have been anybody.
If it really was my father, then that was the last time I ever saw his face.

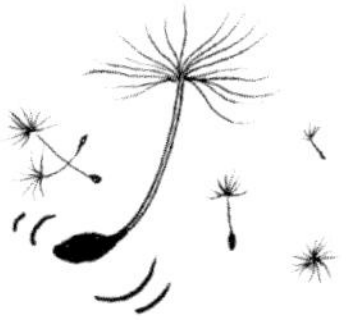

Let borders become sunlight
so we traverse this Earth as one nation
and drive the darkness out.

~ Kamand Kojouri

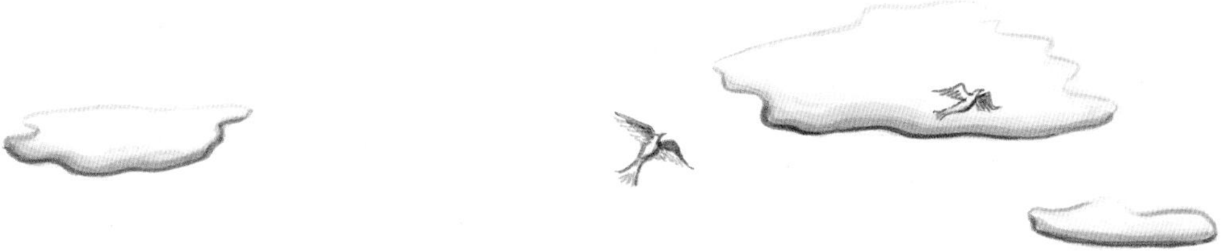

Epilogue

REUNIFICATION

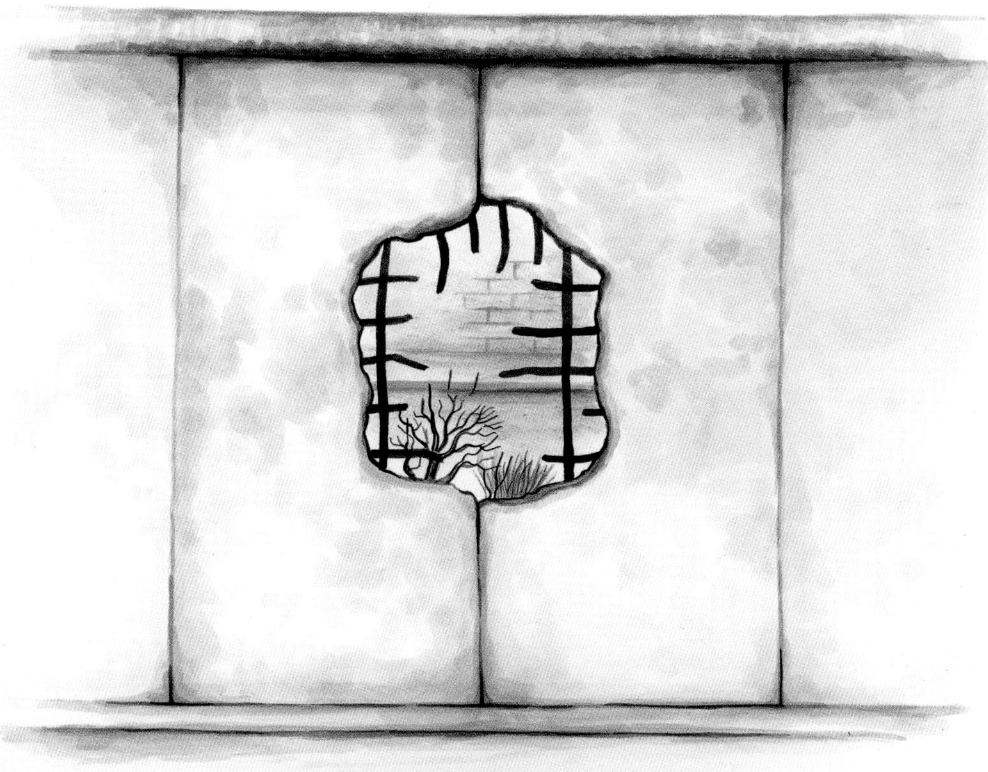

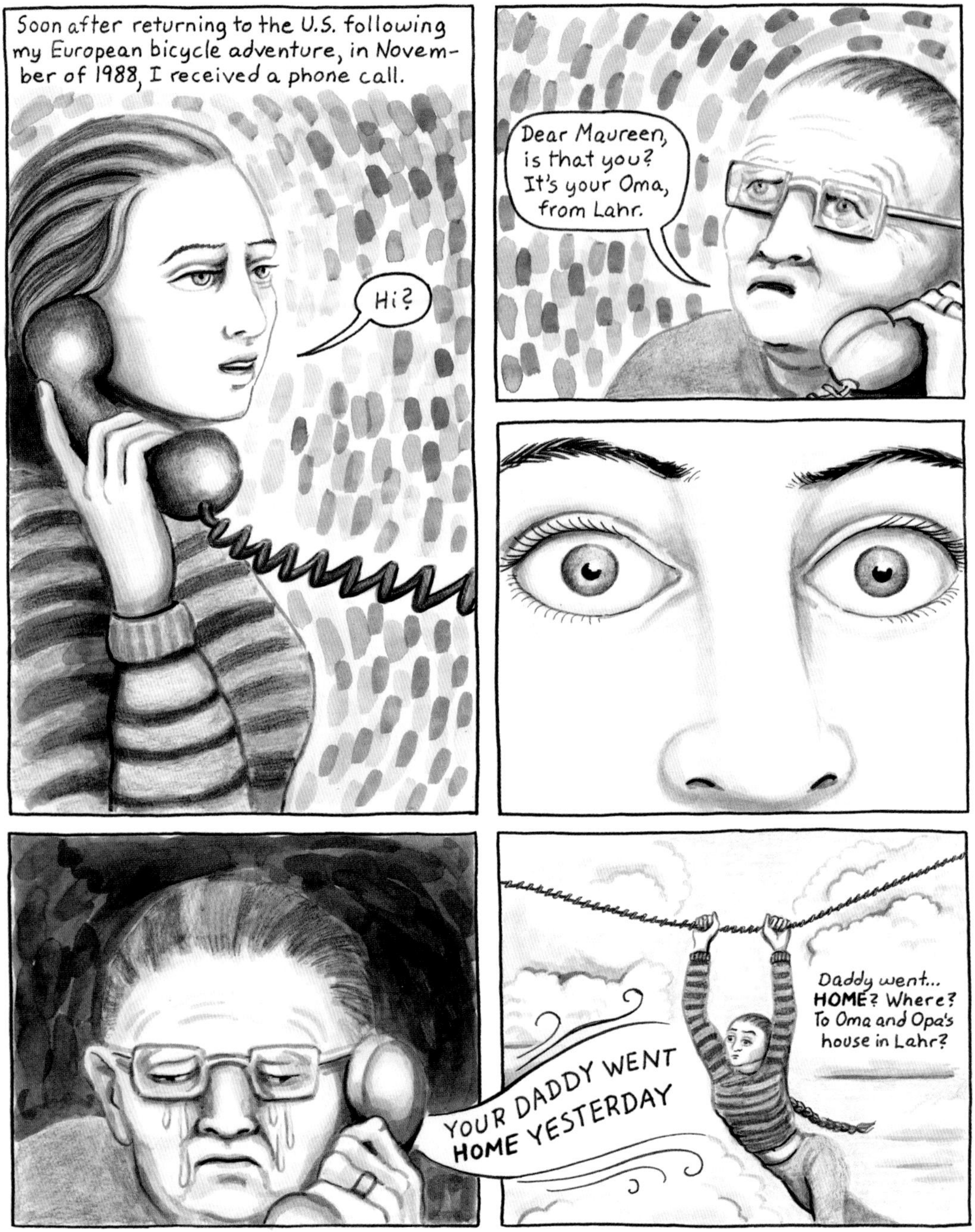
Soon after returning to the U.S. following my European bicycle adventure, in November of 1988, I received a phone call.
Hi?
Dear Maureen, is that you? It's your Oma, from Lahr.
YOUR DADDY WENT HOME YESTERDAY
Daddy went... HOME? Where? To Oma and Opa's house in Lahr?

It was his 48th birthday. He'd had pain in his leg and went to the hospital.

It was deep vein thrombosis. Right after his wife, who is a nurse, brought him his birthday cake, he had a lung embolism. He couldn't get any air. He was choking...

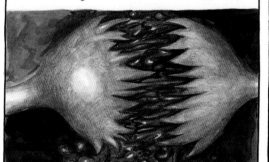
They couldn't save him. Did he manage to write you one more nice letter?

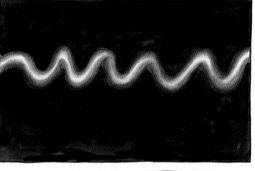
One good thing about this... Now it's safe for you to come and visit us! We will send you a plane ticket to come this spring.

I had recently met someone. I became pregnant soon after my father's death. I believed that perhaps my father had chosen to be reincarnated as my son, so that we would be reunited and could heal our ruptured bond.

When I miscarried in the third month, I grieved for two abruptly aborted relationships.

My loss was made palpable by the painful cramping and bleeding of my womb, emptying itself of life. My visual journals from that time show my body, broken and distorted, tenuously navigating barren landscapes. In some of these drawings, my connection with Earth is completely severed.

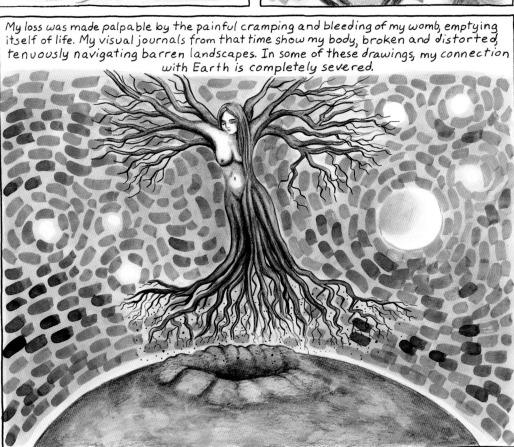

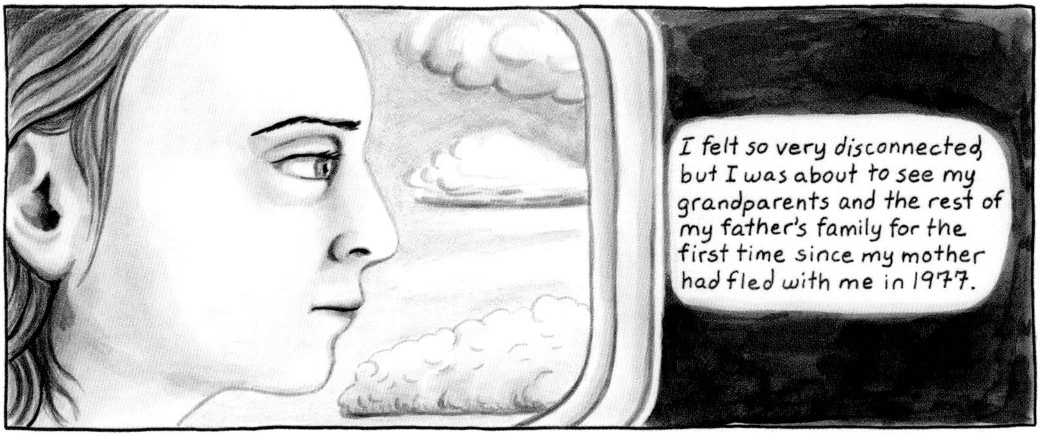
I felt so very disconnected, but I was about to see my grandparents and the rest of my father's family for the first time since my mother had fled with me in 1977.

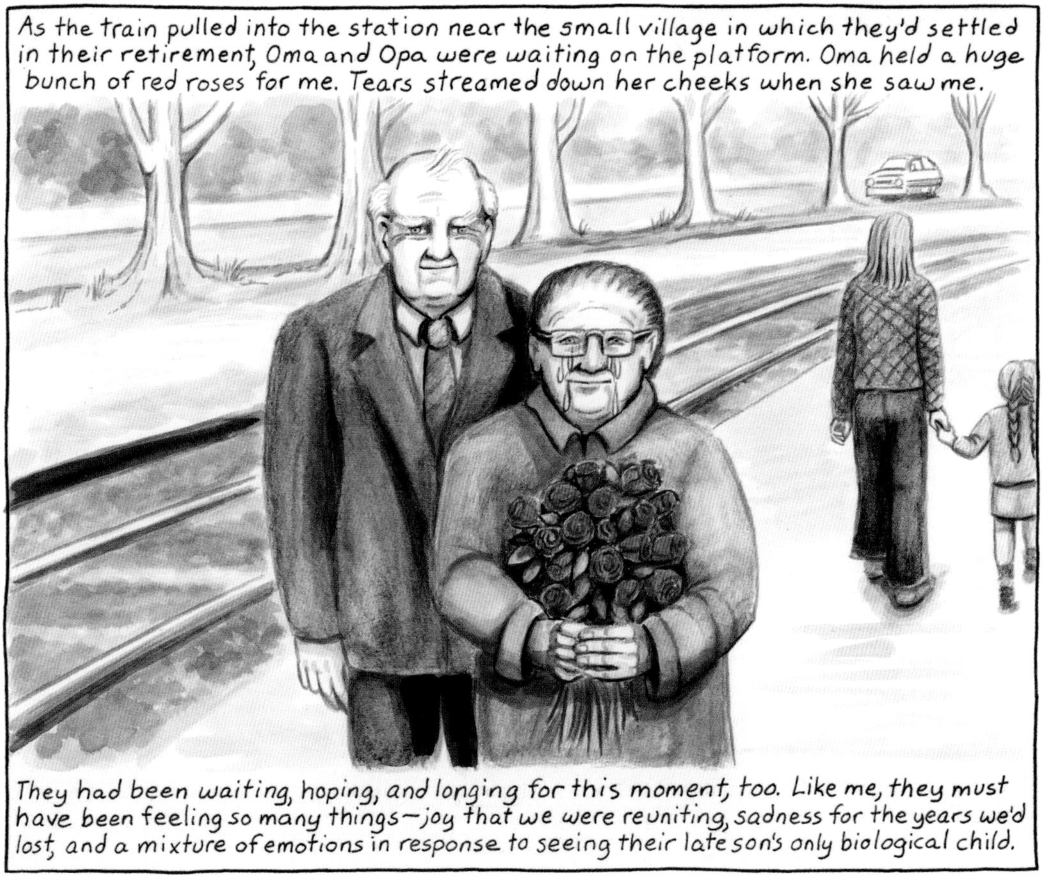
As the train pulled into the station near the small village in which they'd settled in their retirement, Oma and Opa were waiting on the platform. Oma held a huge bunch of red roses for me. Tears streamed down her cheeks when she saw me.
They had been waiting, hoping, and longing for this moment, too. Like me, they must have been feeling so many things—joy that we were reuniting, sadness for the years we'd lost, and a mixture of emotions in response to seeing their late son's only biological child.

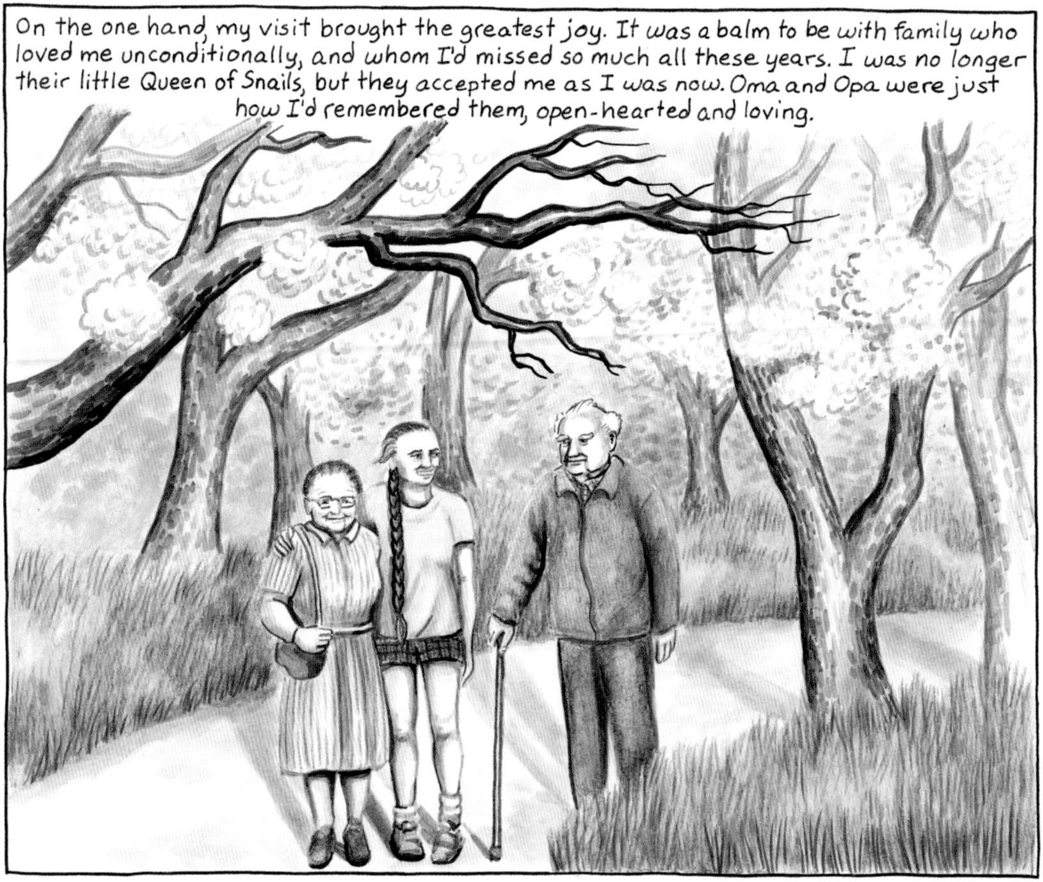
On the one hand, my visit brought the greatest joy. It was a balm to be with family who loved me unconditionally, and whom I'd missed so much all these years. I was no longer their little Queen of Snails, but they accepted me as I was now. Oma and Opa were just how I'd remembered them, open-hearted and loving.

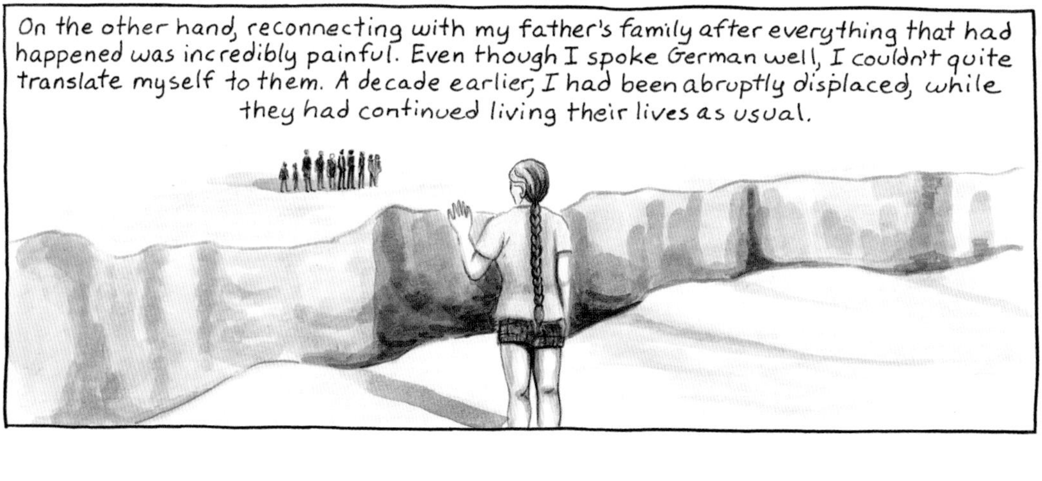
On the other hand, reconnecting with my father's family after everything that had happened was incredibly painful. Even though I spoke German well, I couldn't quite translate myself to them. A decade earlier, I had been abruptly displaced, while they had continued living their lives as usual.

I was learning that reconnecting could be a fraught process. My personal experience of reunification mirrored political events of the day. In November of 1989, one year after my father's death, the Berlin Wall fell.

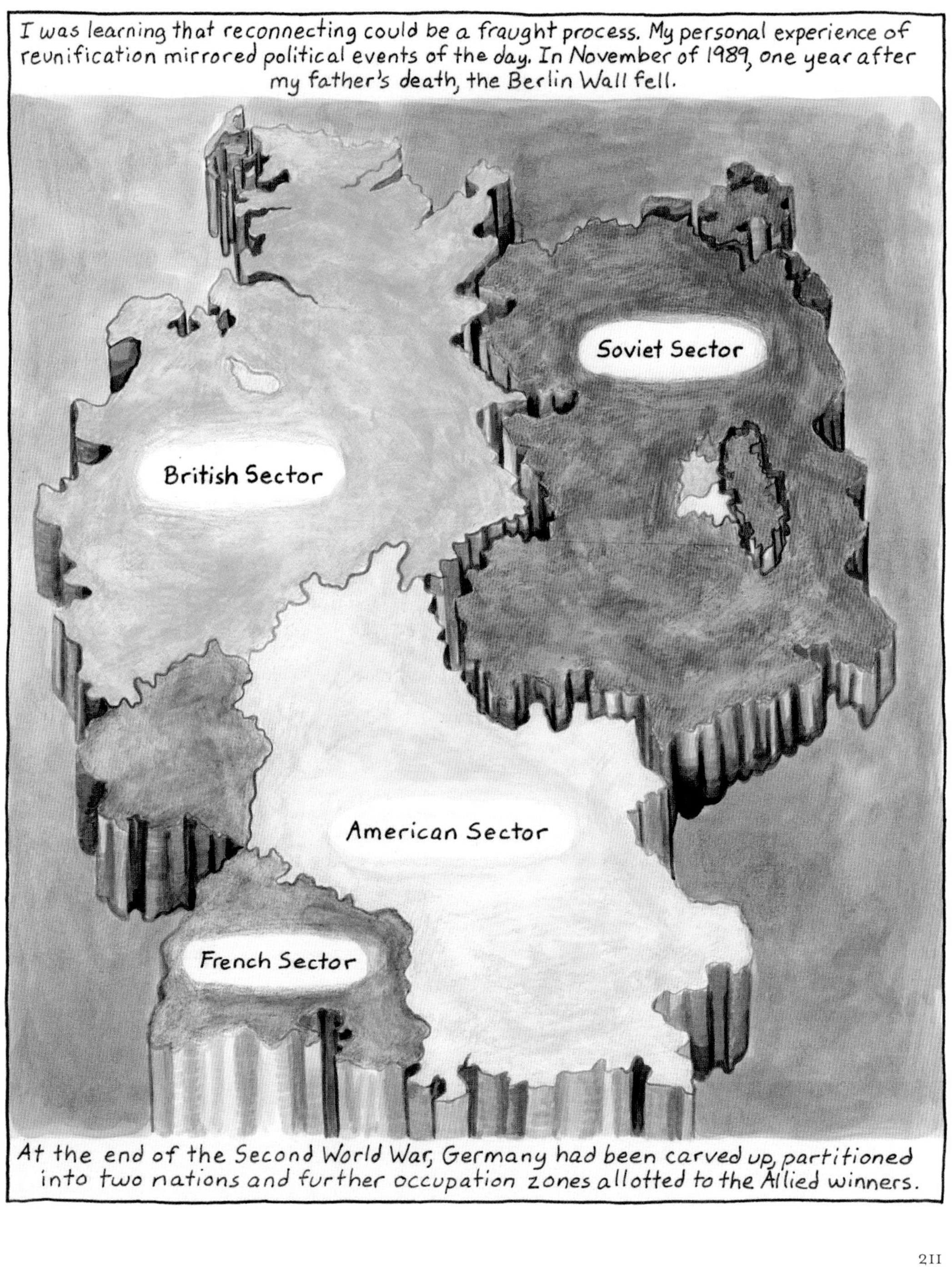
Soviet Sector
British Sector
American Sector
French Sector

At the end of the Second World War, Germany had been carved up, partitioned into two nations and further occupation zones allotted to the Allied winners.

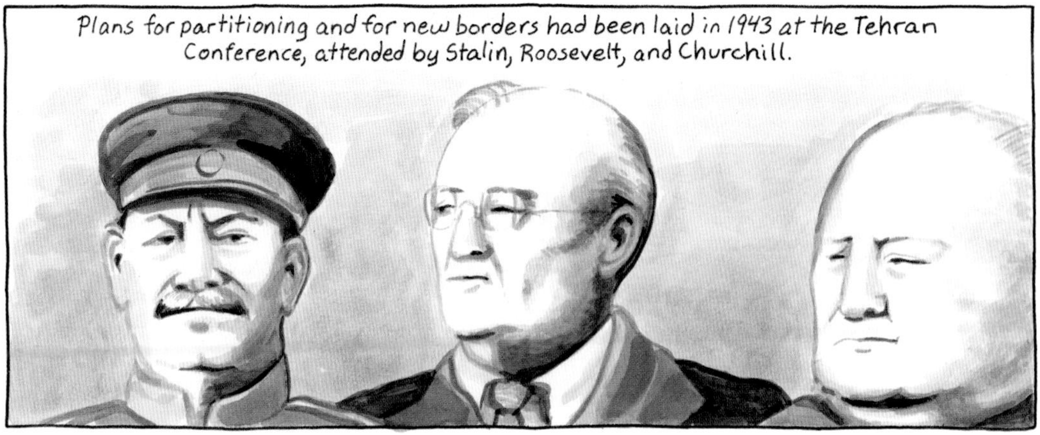
Plans for partitioning and for new borders had been laid in 1943 at the Tehran Conference, attended by Stalin, Roosevelt, and Churchill.

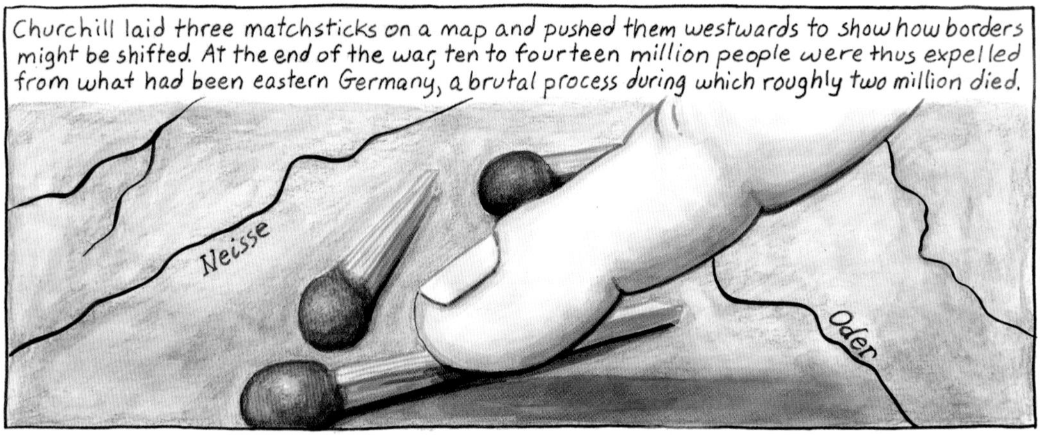
Churchill laid three matchsticks on a map and pushed them westwards to show how borders might be shifted. At the end of the war, ten to fourteen million people were thus expelled from what had been eastern Germany, a brutal process during which roughly two million died.
Neisse
Oder

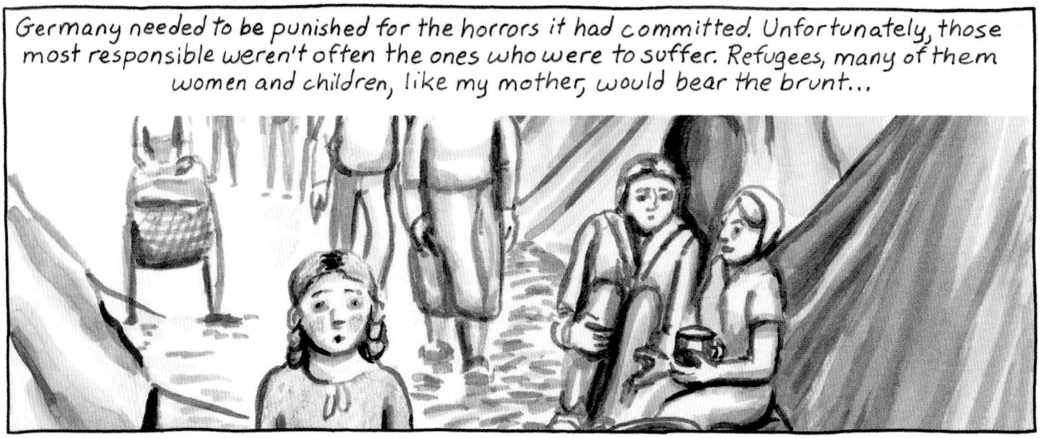
Germany needed to be punished for the horrors it had committed. Unfortunately, those most responsible weren't often the ones who were to suffer. Refugees, many of them women and children, like my mother, would bear the brunt...

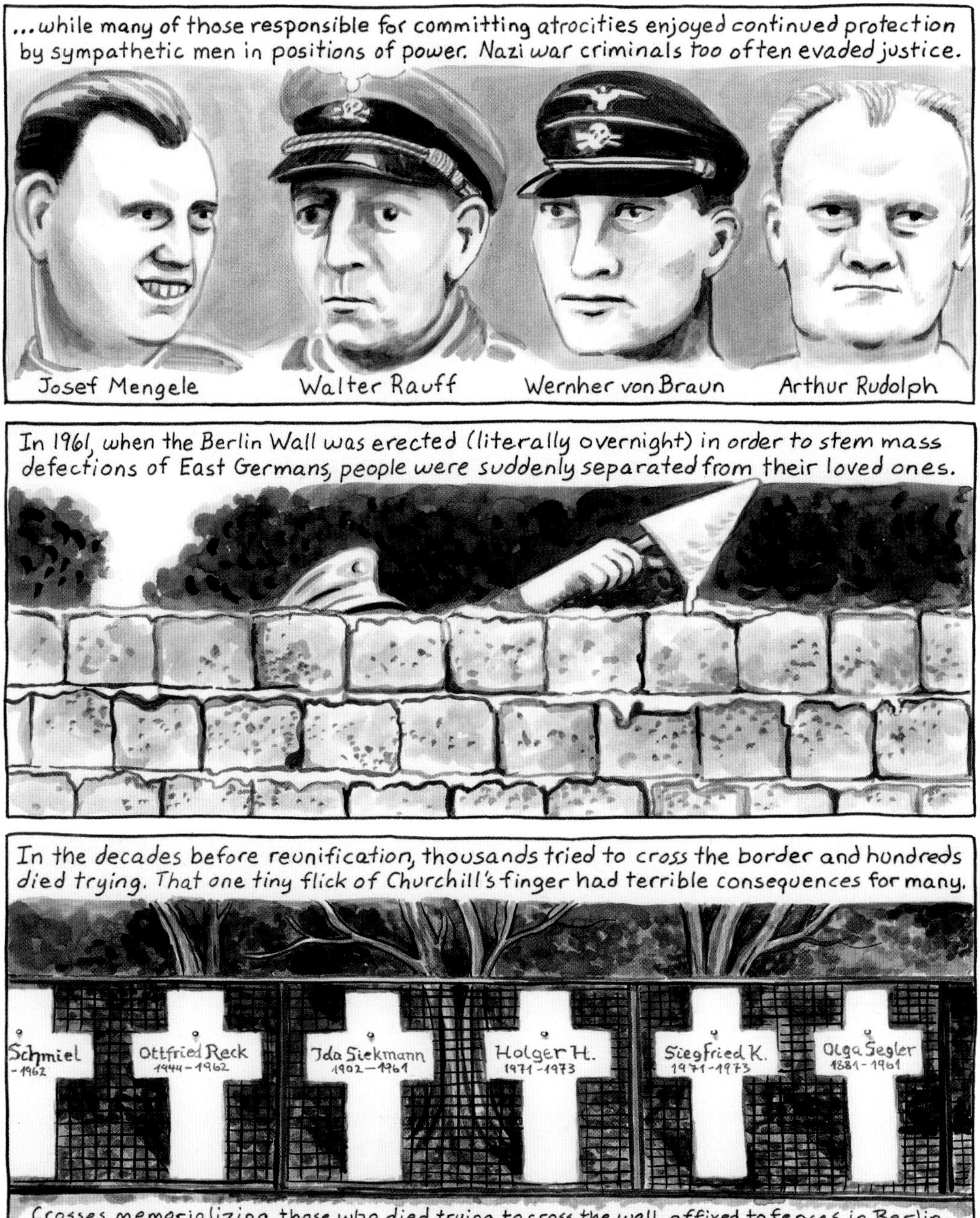
...while many of those responsible for committing atrocities enjoyed continued protection by sympathetic men in positions of power. Nazi war criminals too often evaded justice.
Josef Mengele
Walter Rauff
Wernher von Braun
Arthur Rudolph
In 1961, when the Berlin Wall was erected (literally overnight) in order to stem mass defections of East Germans, people were suddenly separated from their loved ones.
In the decades before reunification, thousands tried to cross the border and hundreds died trying. That one tiny flick of Churchill's finger had terrible consequences for many.
Schmiel -1962
Ottfried Reck 1944–1962
Ida Siekmann 1902–1961
Holger H. 1971–1973
Siegfried K. 1971–1973
Olga Segler 1881–1961
Crosses memorializing those who died trying to cross the wall, affixed to fences in Berlin.

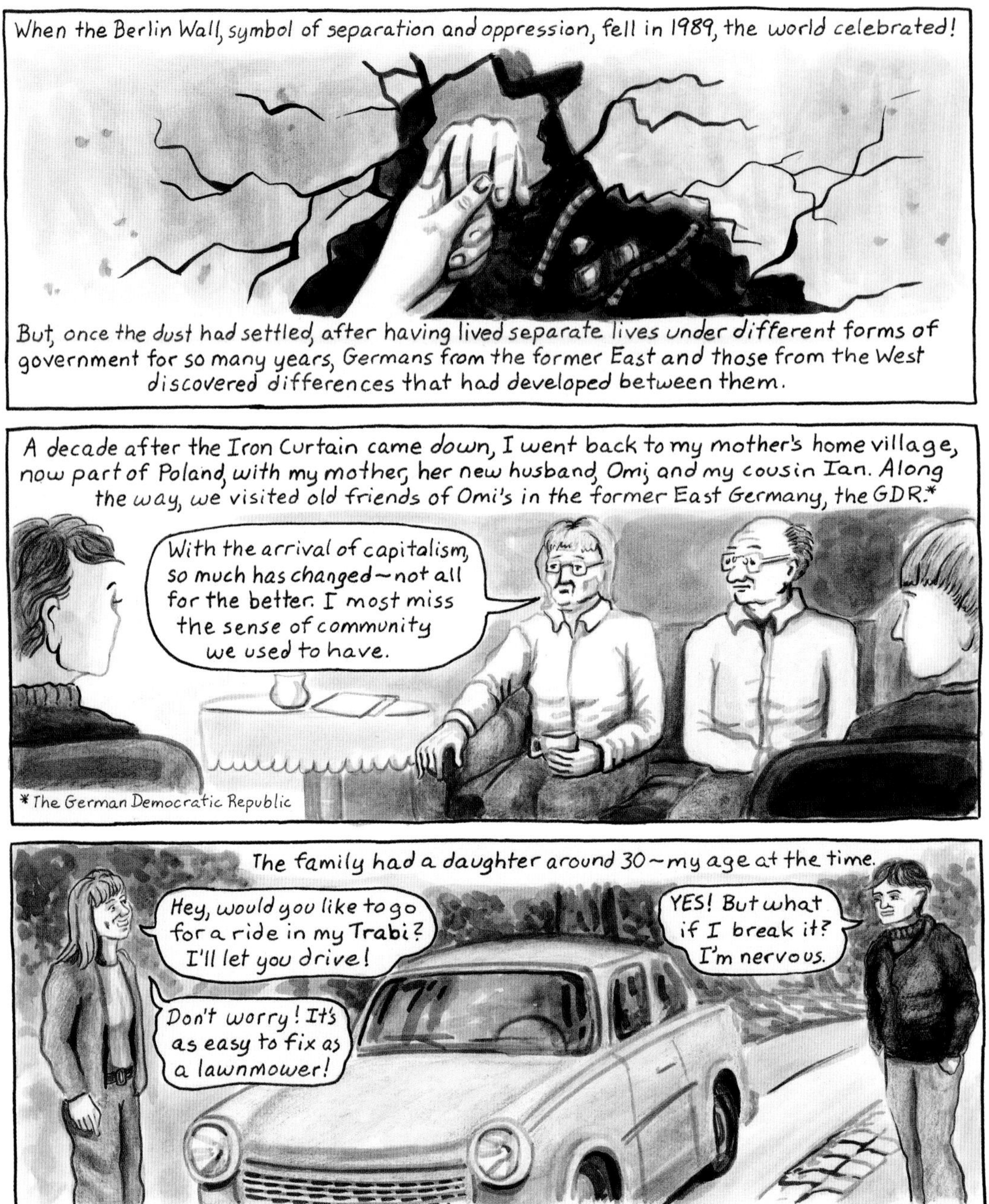
When the Berlin Wall, symbol of separation and oppression, fell in 1989, the world celebrated!
But, once the dust had settled, after having lived separate lives under different forms of government for so many years, Germans from the former East and those from the West discovered differences that had developed between them.
A decade after the Iron Curtain came down, I went back to my mother's home village, now part of Poland, with my mother, her new husband, Omi, and my cousin Ian. Along the way, we visited old friends of Omi's in the former East Germany, the GDR.*
With the arrival of capitalism, so much has changed—not all for the better. I most miss the sense of community we used to have.
* The German Democratic Republic
The family had a daughter around 30—my age at the time.
Hey, would you like to go for a ride in my Trabi? I'll let you drive!
YES! But what if I break it? I'm nervous.
Don't worry! It's as easy to fix as a lawnmower!
* The Trabant 601, or "Trabi," was the most common car, and it became a cherished emblem of the GDR.

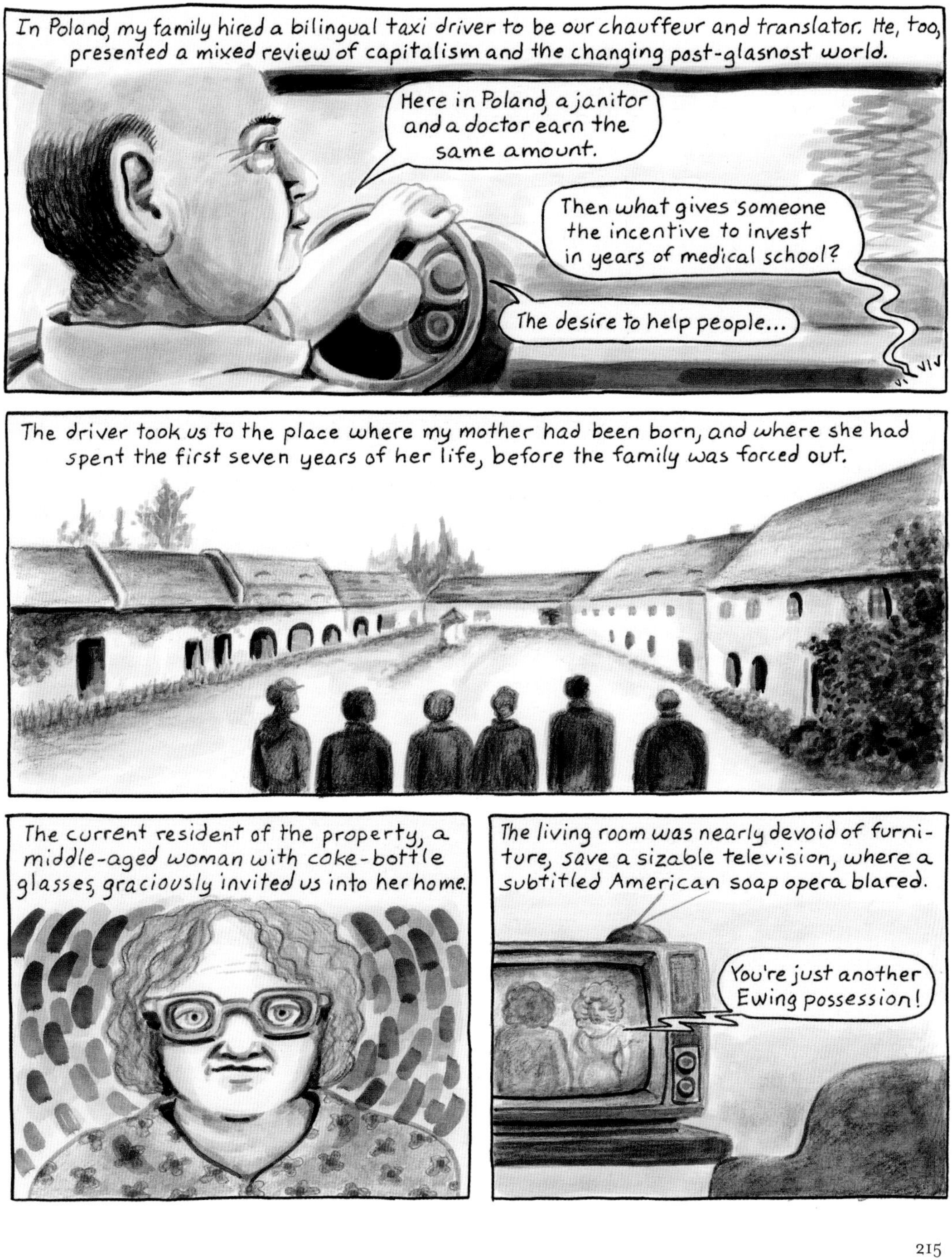
In Poland, my family hired a bilingual taxi driver to be our chauffeur and translator. He, too, presented a mixed review of capitalism and the changing post-glasnost world.
Here in Poland, a janitor and a doctor earn the same amount.
Then what gives someone the incentive to invest in years of medical school?
The desire to help people...
The driver took us to the place where my mother had been born, and where she had spent the first seven years of her life, before the family was forced out.
The current resident of the property, a middle-aged woman with coke-bottle glasses, graciously invited us into her home.
The living room was nearly devoid of furniture, save a sizable television, where a subtitled American soap opera blared.
You're just another Ewing possession!

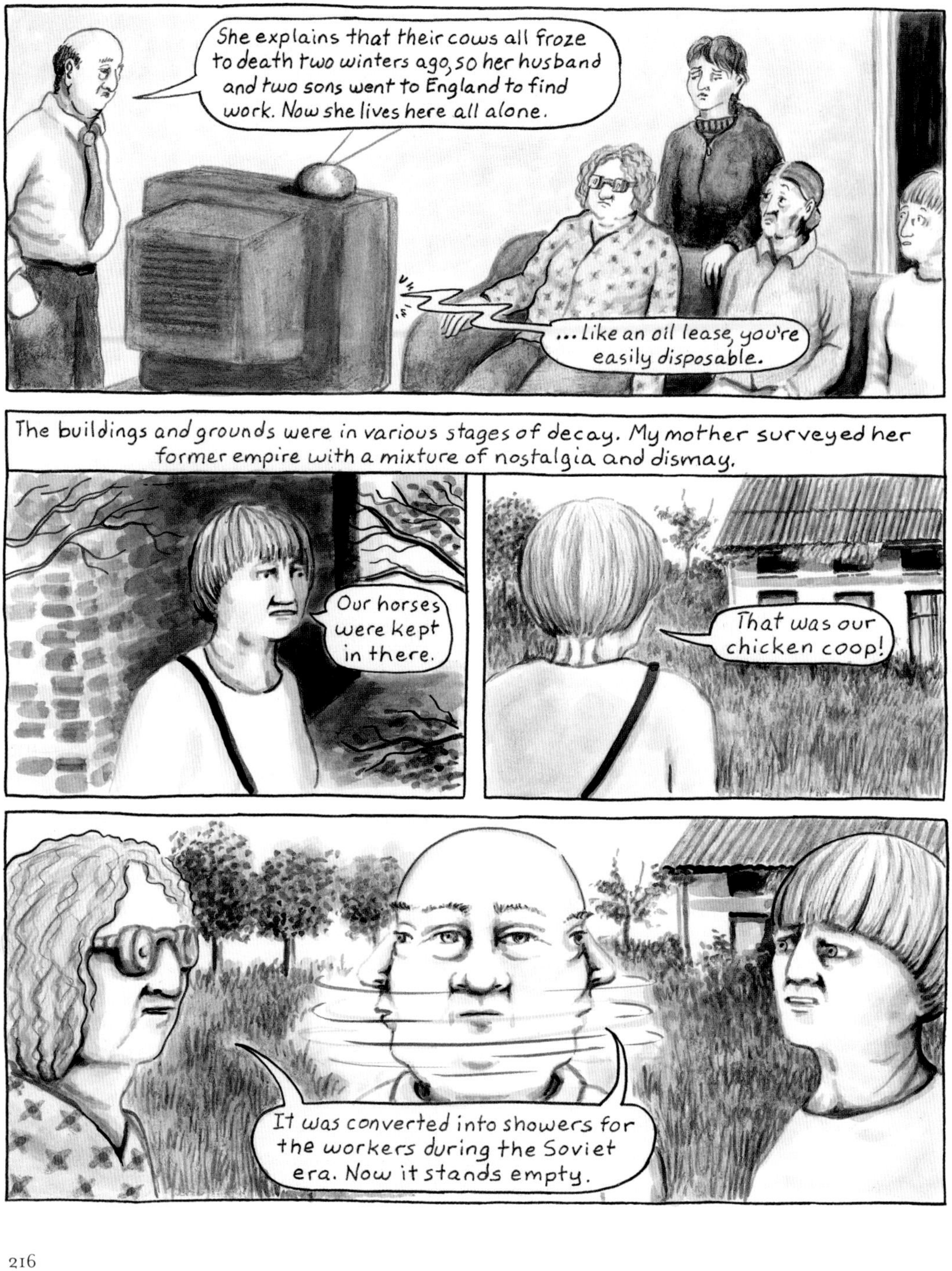
She explains that their cows all froze to death two winters ago, so her husband and two sons went to England to find work. Now she lives here all alone.
...like an oil lease, you're easily disposable.
The buildings and grounds were in various stages of decay. My mother surveyed her former empire with a mixture of nostalgia and dismay.
Our horses were kept in there.
That was our chicken coop!
It was converted into showers for the workers during the Soviet era. Now it stands empty.

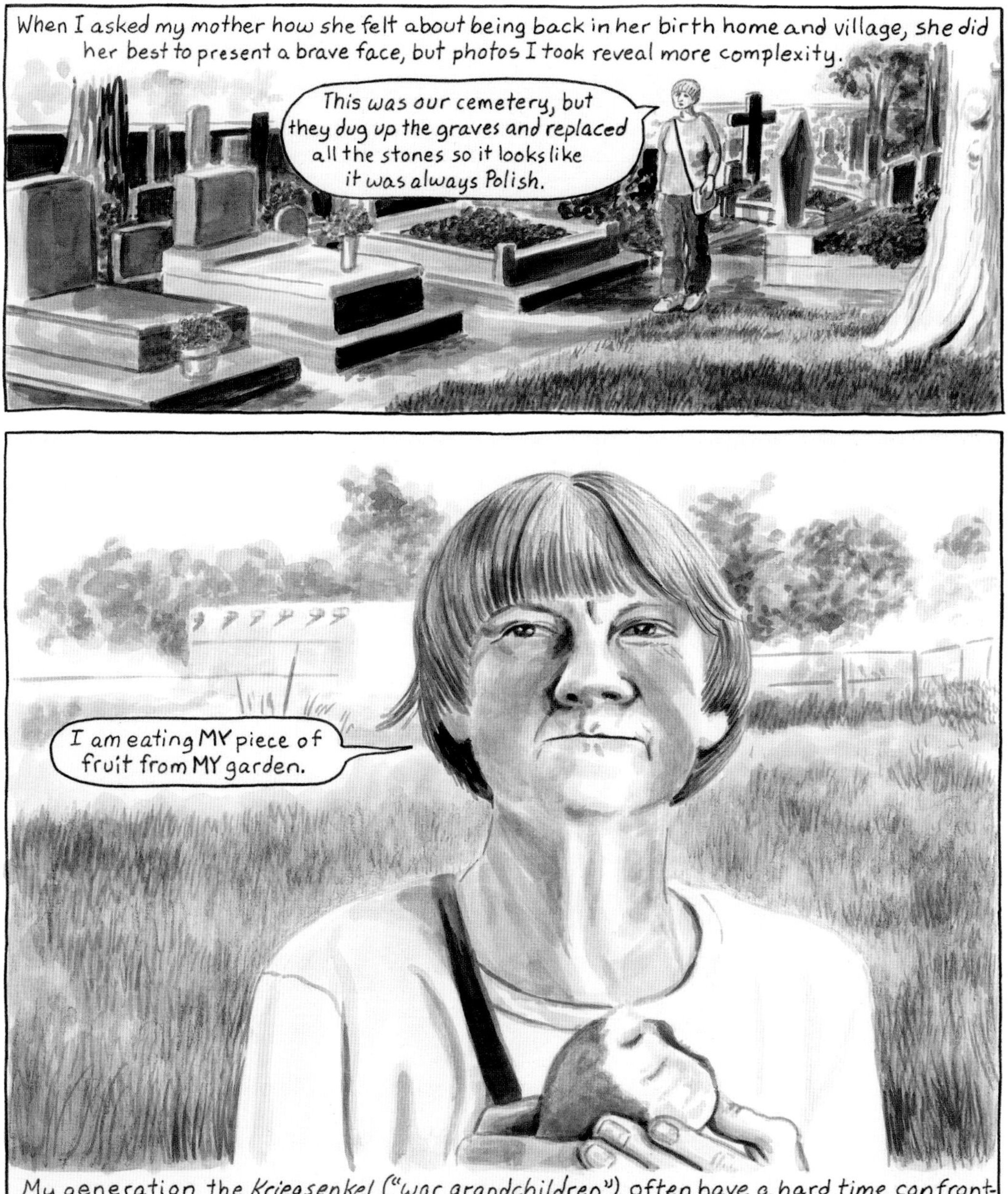
When I asked my mother how she felt about being back in her birth home and village, she did her best to present a brave face, but photos I took reveal more complexity.
This was our cemetery, but they dug up the graves and replaced all the stones so it looks like it was always Polish.
I am eating MY piece of fruit from MY garden.
My generation, the *Kriegsenkel* ("war grandchildren"), often have a hard time confronting our parents. For me, being direct with my mother about difficulties—her own or mine—was like punching a shadow. I became an expert at inference.

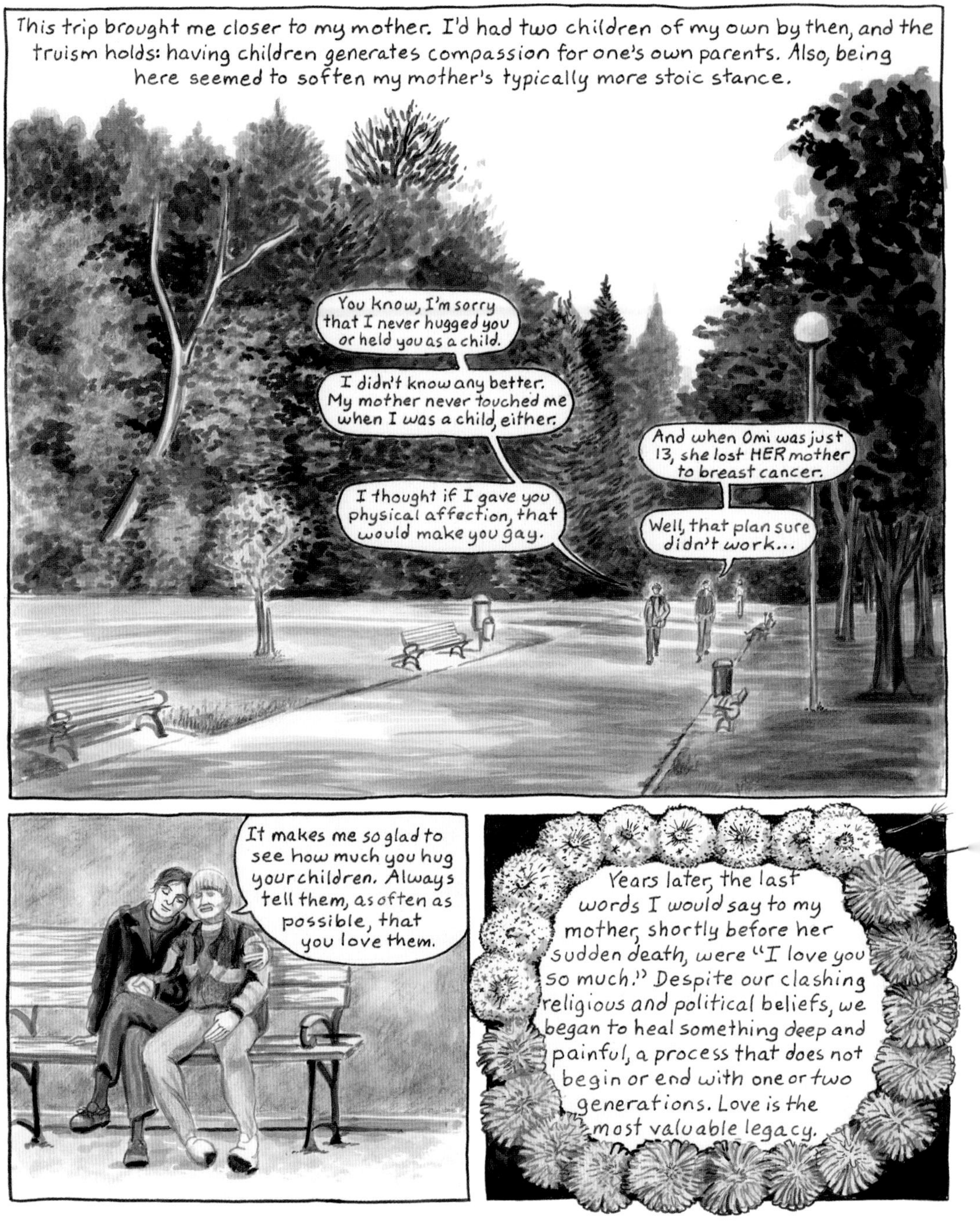
This trip brought me closer to my mother. I'd had two children of my own by then, and the truism holds: having children generates compassion for one's own parents. Also, being here seemed to soften my mother's typically more stoic stance.
You know, I'm sorry that I never hugged you or held you as a child.
I didn't know any better. My mother never touched me when I was a child, either.
I thought if I gave you physical affection, that would make you gay.
And when Omi was just 13, she lost HER mother to breast cancer.
Well, that plan sure didn't work...
It makes me so glad to see how much you hug your children. Always tell them, as often as possible, that you love them.
Years later, the last words I would say to my mother, shortly before her sudden death, were "I love you so much." Despite our clashing religious and political beliefs, we began to heal something deep and painful, a process that does not begin or end with one or two generations. Love is the most valuable legacy.

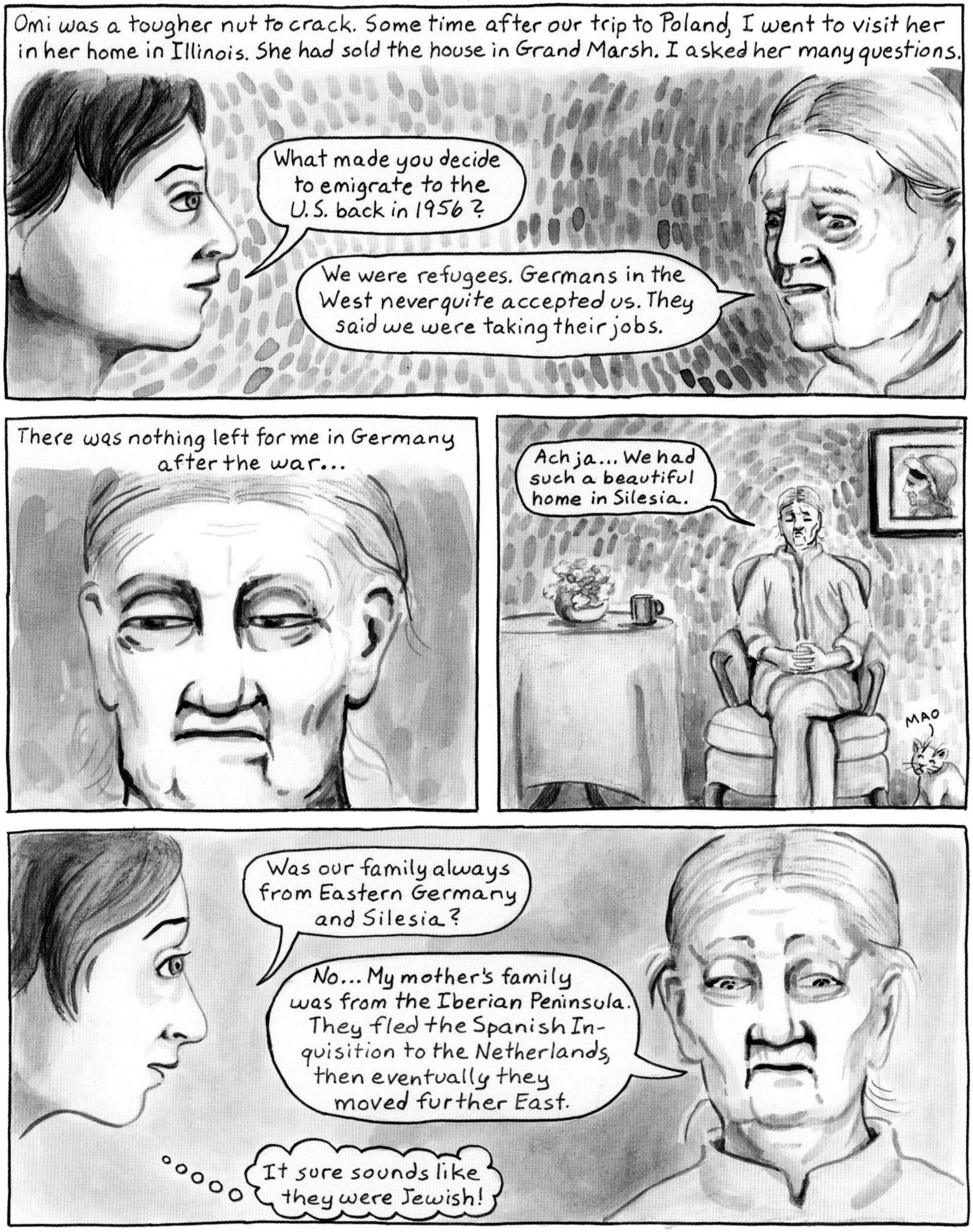
Omi was a tougher nut to crack. Some time after our trip to Poland, I went to visit her in her home in Illinois. She had sold the house in Grand Marsh. I asked her many questions.
What made you decide to emigrate to the U.S. back in 1956?
We were refugees. Germans in the West neverquite accepted us. They said we were taking their jobs.
There was nothing left for me in Germany after the war...
Ach ja... We had such a beautiful home in Silesia.
MAO
Was our family always from Eastern Germany and Silesia?
No... My mother's family was from the Iberian Peninsula. They fled the Spanish Inquisition to the Netherlands, then eventually they moved further East.
It sure sounds like they were Jewish!

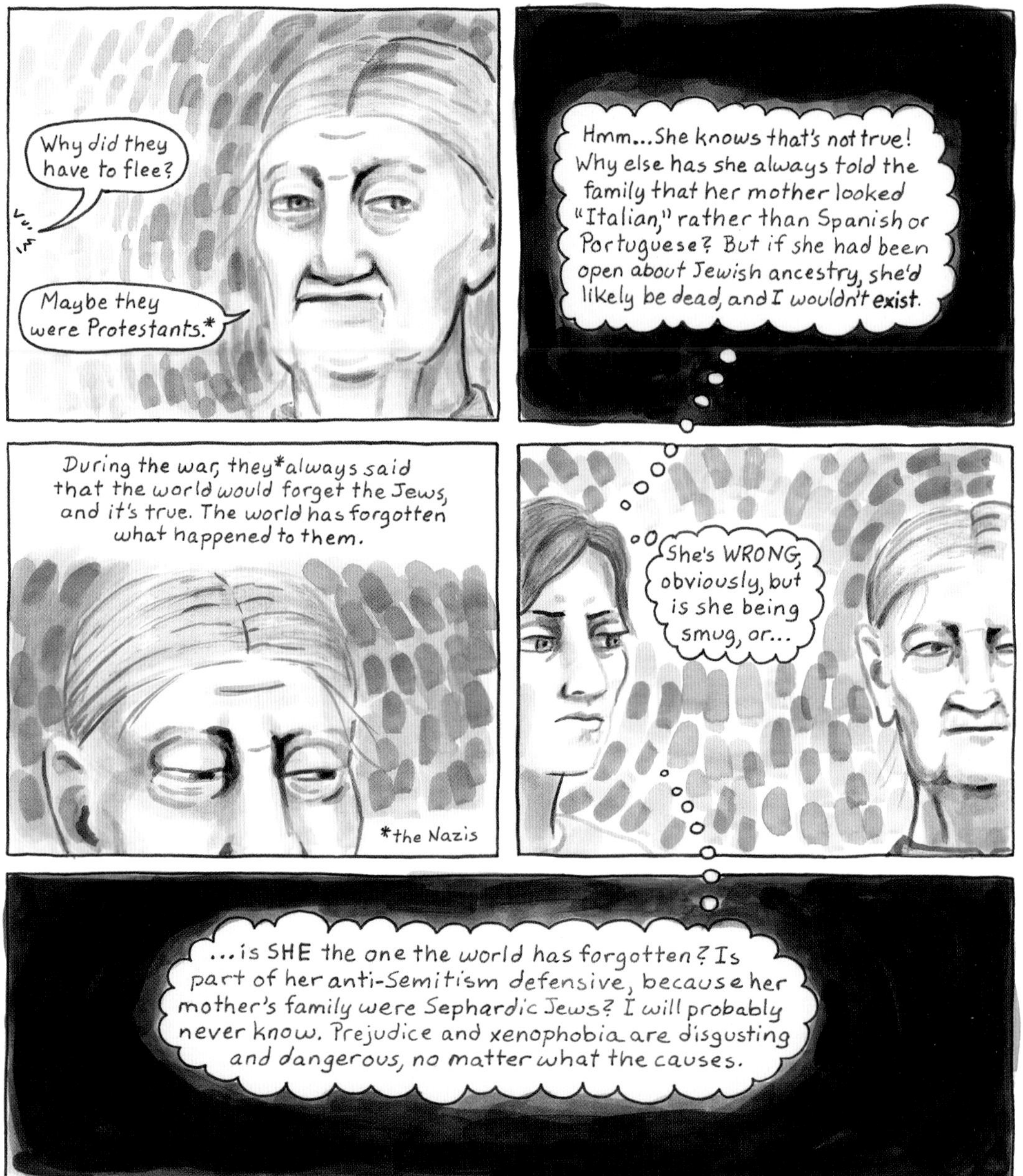
Why did they have to flee?
Maybe they were Protestants.*
Hmm...She knows that's not true! Why else has she always told the family that her mother looked "Italian," rather than Spanish or Portuguese? But if she had been open about Jewish ancestry, she'd likely be dead, and I wouldn't exist.
During the war, they* always said that the world would forget the Jews, and it's true. The world has forgotten what happened to them.
*the Nazis
She's WRONG, obviously, but is she being smug, or...
...is SHE the one the world has forgotten? Is part of her anti-Semitism defensive, because her mother's family were Sephardic Jews? I will probably never know. Prejudice and xenophobia are disgusting and dangerous, no matter what the causes.

*I later learned that, starting in the late 15th century, there was a mass migration of Jews who had been forcibly expelled from the Iberian Peninsula. Some regions in Europe were more tolerant than others. Newly independent Dutch provinces provided sanctuary for many of these refugees. Protestantism was uncommon in Spain and Portugal, and did not result in any kind of mass exodus.

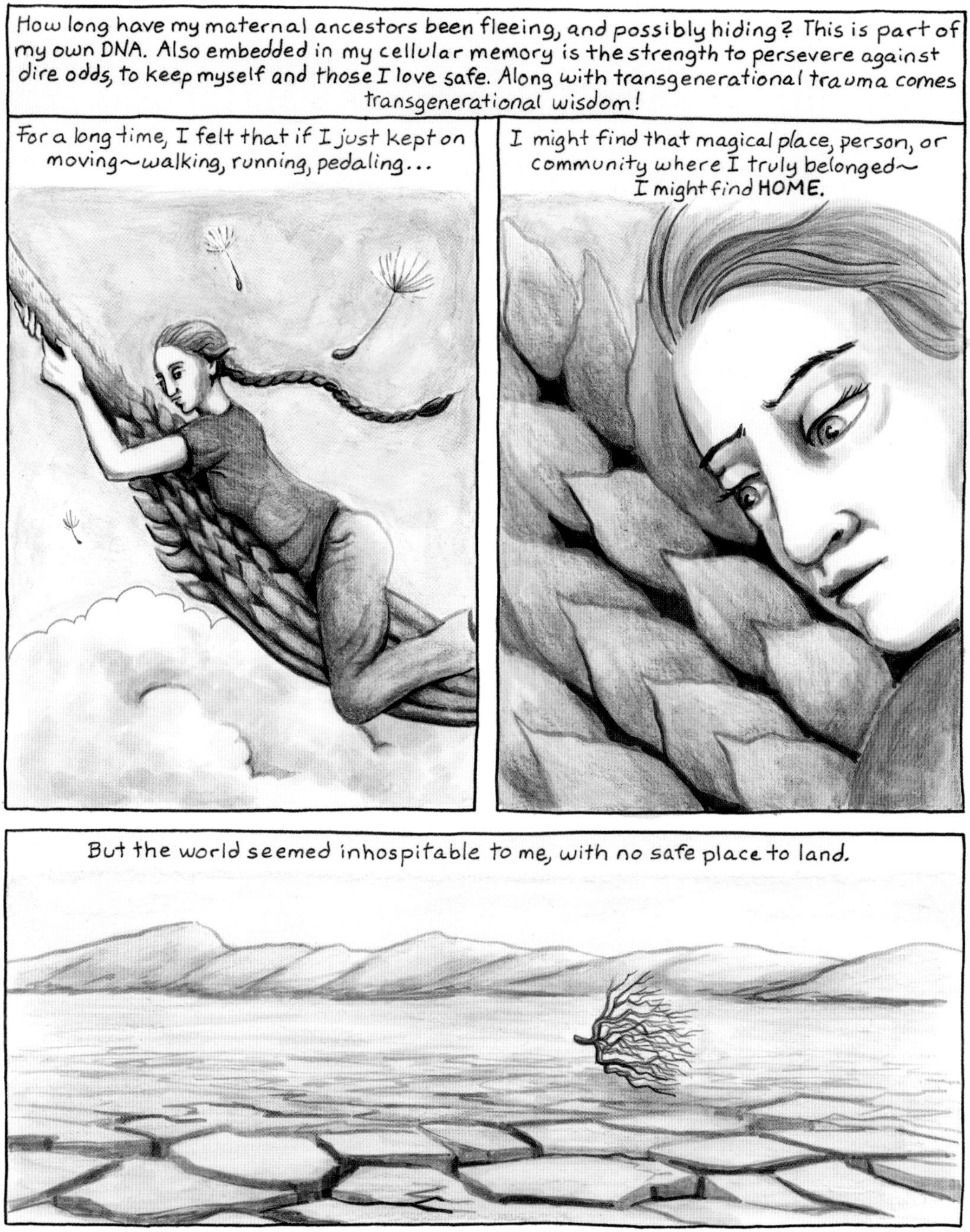
How long have my maternal ancestors been fleeing, and possibly hiding? This is part of my own DNA. Also embedded in my cellular memory is the strength to persevere against dire odds, to keep myself and those I love safe. Along with transgenerational trauma comes transgenerational wisdom!
For a long time, I felt that if I just kept on moving~walking, running, pedaling...
I might find that magical place, person, or community where I truly belonged~ I might find HOME.
But the world seemed inhospitable to me, with no safe place to land.

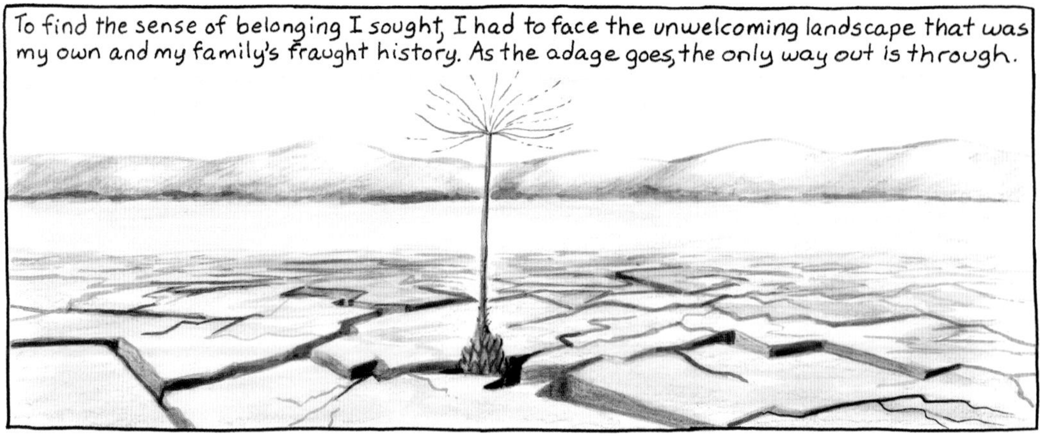
To find the sense of belonging I sought, I had to face the unwelcoming landscape that was my own and my family's fraught history. As the adage goes, the only way out is through.

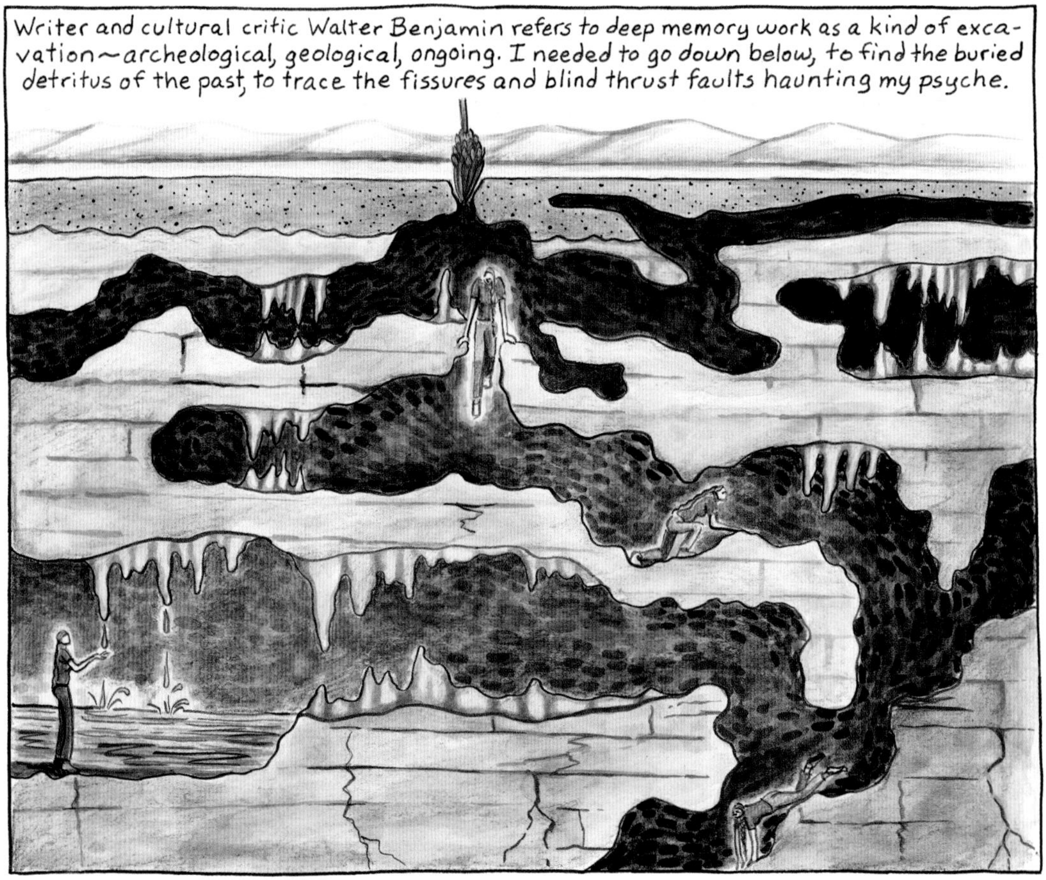
Writer and cultural critic Walter Benjamin refers to deep memory work as a kind of excavation~archeological, geological, ongoing. I needed to go down below, to find the buried detritus of the past, to trace the fissures and blind thrust faults haunting my psyche.

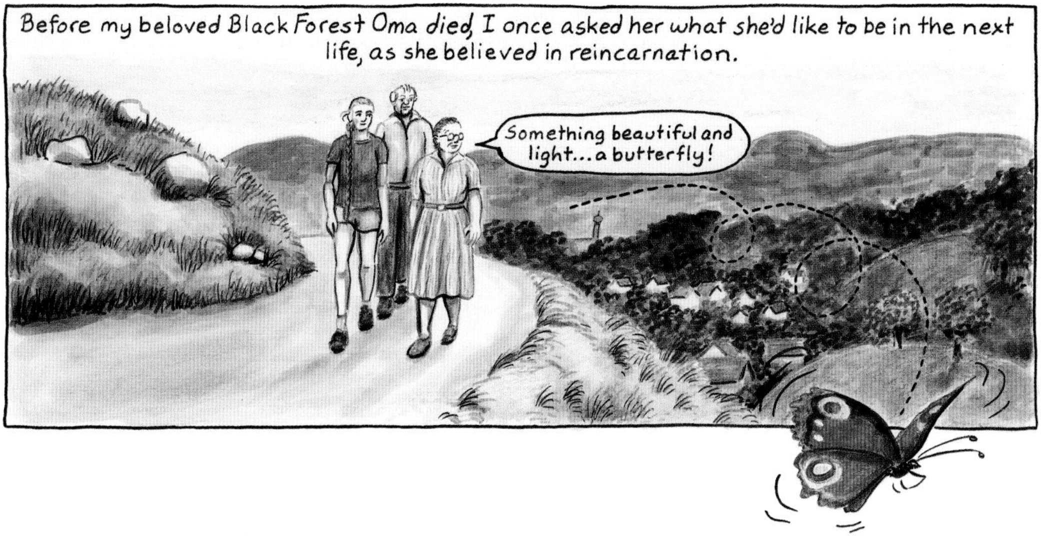
Before my beloved Black Forest Oma died, I once asked her what she'd like to be in the next life, as she believed in reincarnation.
Something beautiful and light... a butterfly!

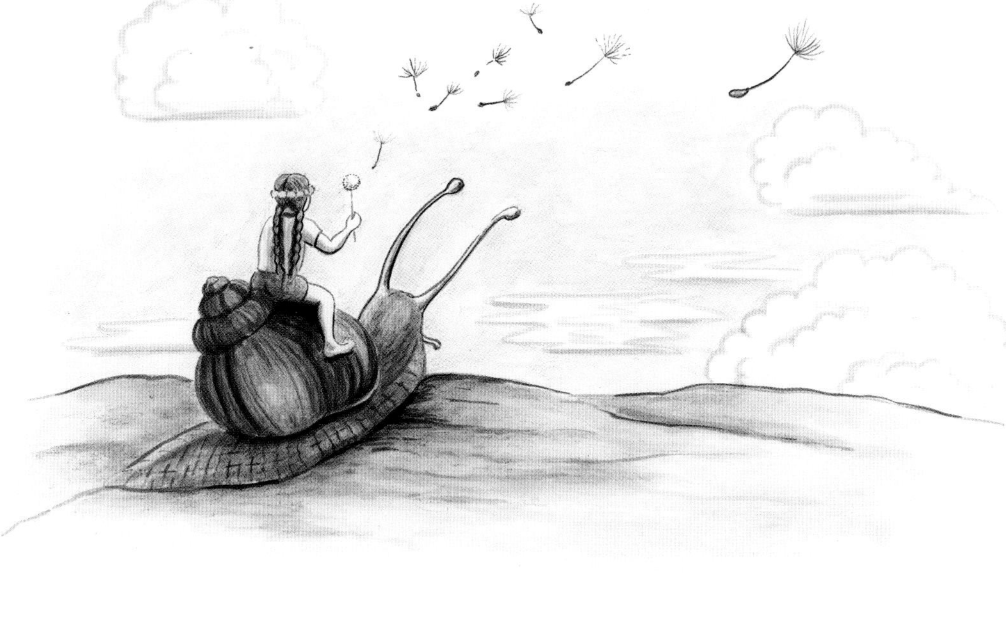

Somewhere between the embodied past and the future worlds of which we dream lies **home**~a process of continual reckoning and reinvention. I don't need to belong to a particular religion, group, or nation in order to find purpose and contentment. I just need to keep being and unfolding, with an open heart and mind.

Acknowledgments

Very special thanks to my friend and mentor, Elisabeth Krimmer, for the countless hours she committed to reading my work and to giving me thoughtful feedback when this project was still a dissertation. I will always remember those lovely lunches and dinners in Berkeley spent talking with her! Thanks also to Maceo Montoya and Michael Lazarra for all of the generous and generative conversations we had about this work as I was developing it. I couldn't have dreamed of a more brilliant and supportive dissertation committee! I also owe a note of gratitude to Robert Irwin, Gail Finney, Caren Kaplan, and the rest of my incredible community at the University of California, Davis.

Thanks to all at Pennsylvania State University Press, and especially to Kendra Boileau for her excellent and sensitive editorial feedback and for regular doses of genuine warmth and caring, which made the process of completing this book a real pleasure. Thanks also to Susan Squier for her enthusiasm and support when I was just starting the work and throughout the process of creating Queen of Snails!

A giant shout-out to the wonderful international graphic medicine network, and to my community of scholar-artist peers for much encouragement and for reading sections of my book in progress: Sarah Lightman, Ariela Freedman, Dana Walrath, Michael Green, Monalesia Earle, Justin Hall, Stef Lenk, Miriam Katin, Marianne Rodriguez Petit, Roger Sabin, and Nick Sousanis.

I am thankful to my mother, Ingrid, for the many phone calls and emails where she answered my questions about our family history. She died just before I finished the book. I think she would have liked it. I am grateful that the project helped us forge a deeper connection. A nod of appreciation also goes to my Aunt Rickie (Ulrike Rachuy) for her compilation and translation of "Omi's Diaries," which I consulted in order to accurately portray events and dates.

Thank you to my boxer puppy, Gracie, for forcing me to take breaks from my drawing table for snuggles, walks, and tug games!

Thank you to my family and adopted kin: Karen Glazier, Kris Glazier, Leslie Nathanson, and Ellen Kleiner for your kindness and encouragement!

Last but definitely not least, so much love and thanks to my wife, KimAlix, for unfalteringly believing in me and in this work, for nurturing me so generously, and for supplying me with sushi along the way! I am endlessly grateful to my children, Onawa and Seth. You are two of the most exceptional people I have ever met. I hope this work helps you to understand, even more than you already do, yourselves and our family as strands of a much broader helix.

Notes

Part I: Queen of Snails

Page

27   In an experiment she started in 2009, amateur scientist Ruth Brooks showed that her garden snails have a homing instinct for distances up to 90 feet. For her innovative work, Brooks won the Britain Amateur Scientist of the Year Award in 2010.

29   Elderflower fritters are made from the flowers of the elder shrub before they bear fruit.

       Oma spoke a Swabian dialect that I couldn't understand. She enjoyed teasing me about my High German pronunciation.

48   The Heiner und Hanni series of books—written by Dutch author Annie M. G. Schmidt and illustrated by her longtime collaborator, Dutch illustrator Sophia Maria "Fiep" Westendorp—were common reading primers in Bavaria in the 1970s.

Part II: Whippoorwill's Requiem

79   Several Native American tribes, including the Algonquin, believed that the whippoorwill's song was an omen of death, or that dangerous enemies were close by. See http://temagami.nativeweb.org/tale-folklore-7.html. The whippoorwill's call as dark omen was also a theme in early American folk literature.

84   The cultural climate in the US during the Cold War era was definitely anti-German. Children were exposed to various films featuring barking Nazi officers and to animations and comics vilifying Germans. See B. C. Etheridge, *Enemies to Allies: Cold War Germany and American Memory* (Lexington: University Press of Kentucky, 2016).

86   The messages I was getting from my mother and grandmother (about Germans as victims at the end of and after the war) were completely at odds with what I was learning from my classmates and teachers. My mother and grandmother portrayed Gildisch as a victim of the postwar courts, not as a perpetrator. Recent research by historian Bernhard Sauer is useful in understanding the nature and extent of Gildisch's crime against Erich Klausener, as well as Gildisch's career trajectory and documented issues with alcoholism and antisocial outbursts. Gildisch was prosecuted, and later convicted, for the murder of Klausener. See B. Sauer, *In Heydrichs Auftrag: Kurt Gildisch und der Mord an Erich Klausener während des "Röhm-Putsches"* (Berlin: Metropol, 2017).

89   The poster referenced in this drawing was published in Germany around 1939. It was meant to emphasize the obligation of every young girl to join the Bund Deutscher Mädel (BDM) in service to Hitler and the Nazi cause. German History Museum, Berlin, https://www.dhm.de/lemo/bestand/objekt/jugend-dient-dem-fuehrer-um-1939.html.

91   The book my grandmother is holding in

the top left panel of this page, *Wir Mädel singen* (*We Girls Sing*), was the official songbook for the BDM. It contained songs about building the Third Reich and about a bright future for Germany, as well as drawings of swastikas and quotes from Hitler's speeches. Reichsjugendführung, *Wir Mädel singen: Liederbuch des Bundes Deutscher Mädel* (Wolfenbüttel: Georg Kallmeyer, 1939).

93   The top panel on this page refers to the snow-covered Treblinka site in Poland, where archaeological work continues to this day to uncover evidence of mass killings, as in the case of the Treblinka extermination camp. There, Nazis had planted trees to conceal the mass graves containing the bodies of between 700,000 to 900,000 Jews and around 2,000 Romani people. The anti-Soviet poster I draw from in the bottom right panel is one of many of its type published during the Nazi era to stoke anti-Communist and anti-Semitic hostilities. See https://research.calvin.edu/german-propaganda-archive/anti-bolshevism.htm.

94   Some Ukrainians collaborated with Nazi Germany against the Red Army for various reasons; it is possible, though not at all certain, that Andreas was also fleeing from the Russians because he had previously fought against them.

96   The cousin my grandmother refers to, Franek Klausenitzer, once explained to me that he had been a high-ranking officer. He told a story of being ordered to annihilate an entire village on the Eastern Front, a command he had allegedly refused. He said that instead of carrying out the genocide, he commanded his troops to turn around. I was always

curious about this. Would Klausenitzer have gotten away with this act of treason? After the war, he became an active member of the Green Party. He and his wife lived in a renovated old one-room schoolhouse in rural Hessen. They ate whole grains and produce from their large garden and were some of the kindest, most peace-loving relatives I knew on my mother's side.

98   In retelling my grandmother's—Magdalene von Reitzenstein's—stories here, I rely on my own conversations with her in various locations and time periods, some noted in journals, others audio-recorded or videotaped. For specific dates and for some of her unique phrasing, I refer to Omi's diaries, organized and translated by my aunt, Ulrike Rachuy, in 2012. I have pieced together a more or less chronological narrative, filling in some of the blank spaces my grandmother left in her diaries with information gleaned from conversations with my mother.

    Victims of trauma, as well as perpetrators, tend to recall stories fragmentarily and not linearly. German literary scholar Elisabeth Krimmer notes that many devoted Nazi party members, unable to come to terms with their complicity with that regime, produce a "grammar of complicity: a web of ruptured narratives, conceptual and visual blind spots, and silences." E. Krimmer, *German Women's Life Writing and the Holocaust: Complicity and Gender in the Second World War* (Cambridge: Cambridge University Press, 2018), 3.

112   The panels on pages 112 and 113 are my translations of a selection of the postcards my mother wrote to my

grandmother during her time in the orphanage.

114   For more on the topic of displaced children at the end of the war, see Michelle Mouton, "Missing, Lost, and Displaced Children in Postwar Germany: The Great Struggle to Provide for the War's Youngest Victims," *Central European History* 48, no. 1 (2015): 53–78, doi:10.1017/S0008938915000035.

115   Alice Bailey, *The Problems of the Children in the World Today: Essentials of Post War Education* (New York, 1946), 9–10.

120   N. Lee, "Un/Forgettable Histories of US Camptown Prostitution in South Korea: Women's Experiences of Sexual Labor and Government Policies," *Sexualities* 21, nos. 5–6 (2017): 751–75, doi:10.1177/1363460716688683.

130   H. Quest, dir., *Wenn der Vater mit dem Sohne*, prod. K. Ulrich (Munich: Constantin Film, 1955).

134   The Soviet–Afghan war started when Afghan insurgent groups, or guerrilla fighters, known collectively as the *mujahideen*, fought back against communist reforms by Afghanistan's communist party, which had taken over by staging a coup in 1978. Soviets arrived in 1979 to aid the Afghan communists. The United States trained the *mujahideen* and sold them weapons.

Part III: Tumbleweed

156   The U.S. government forced tribal chiefs of the United Nations of Ojibwe, Ottawa, and Potawatomi peoples to sell five million acres of their land in 1833 as part of the Treaty of Chicago. Part of that land included the area that is now Wauconda.

186   Artworks referenced on this page (top panel, left to right): René Magritte, *The Banquet*, 1958; Henry Moore, *Reclining Figure*, 1936; René Magritte, *L'Oeil*, 1968; (bottom panel): René Magritte, *The Forerunner (Le Précurseur)*, 1936; Salvador Dalí, *The Hour of the Cracked Face*, 1934; Leonor Fini, *Hip Bone*, no date.

187   Artworks referenced (top left panel): Anselm Kiefer, *Resurrexit*, 1973; (top right panel): Anselm Kiefer, *Germany's Spiritual Heroes*, 1973.

188   Sculpture referenced (top right panel): Aristide Maillol, *Torso of Chained Action*, 1905.

Epilogue: Reunification

212   Statistics pertaining to the displacement of Germans at the end of the Second World War are derived from Maja Zehfuss, *Wounds of Memory* (Cambridge: Cambridge University Press, 2007).

212   Daniel Todman, *Britain's War: A New World, 1942–1947* (Oxford: Oxford University Press, 2020), 491.

213   In the middle panel, the image of the wall going up is based on a photo in a special edition of the *Berliner Illustrirte Zeitung*, December 1989, 52–53.